GCSE Edexcel B
Geography

There's been a seismic shift in GCSE Edexcel B Geography, and the latest Grade 9-1 course is tougher than ever. Luckily, this CGP book has it all covered...

It's packed with brilliant study notes, clear diagrams and cracking case studies — plus plenty of exam-style practice to test how much you've *really* learned.

We've also included top advice for the exams, so there won't be any earth-shattering shocks on the day.

Complete
Revision & Practice
Everything you need to pass the exams!

Contents

Component 3:
People and Environment Issues —
Making Geographical Decisions

Published by CGP

Contributors:
Barbara Melbourne, Paddy Gannon.

Editors:
Alex Billings, Charlotte Burrows, Ellen Burton, Charles Kitts.

Proofreading:
Glenn Rogers, Karen Wells.

ISBN: 978 1 78908 091 9

With thanks to Emily Smith for the copyright research.

Printed by Elanders Ltd, Newcastle upon Tyne
Clipart from Corel®

Based on the classic CGP style created by Richard Parsons.

Structure of the Course

'Know thy enemy', 'forewarned is forearmed'... There are many boring quotes that just mean <u>being prepared is a good thing</u>. <u>Don't</u> stumble <u>blindly</u> into a GCSE course — find out what you're facing.

You'll have to do **Three Exams**

GCSE Edexcel Geography B is divided into <u>three components</u>: <u>Global Geographical Issues</u>, <u>UK Geographical Issues</u> and <u>People and Environment Issues — Making Geographical Decisions</u>.

You'll have to do <u>three</u> exams — <u>one</u> on each of the three components. <u>Geographical skills</u> will be assessed in <u>all three</u> exams, but <u>fieldwork</u> (see p. 115) will only be assessed in <u>Paper 2</u>. <u>All</u> your <u>exams</u> will take place at the <u>end of the course</u>.

Paper 1: Global Geographical Issues

Paper 1 is divided into <u>three sections</u>.

- <u>Section A</u> covers <u>Hazardous Earth</u>.
- <u>Section B</u> covers <u>Development Dynamics</u>.
- <u>Section C</u> covers <u>Challenges of an Urbanising World</u>.

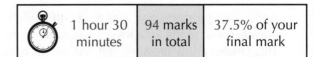

| 1 hour 30 minutes | 94 marks in total | 37.5% of your final mark |

Paper 2: UK Geographical Issues

Paper 2 is divided into <u>three sections</u>.

- <u>Section A</u> covers <u>The UK's Evolving Physical Landscape</u>.
- <u>Section B</u> covers <u>The UK's Evolving Human Landscape</u>.

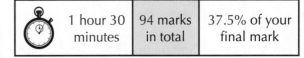

| 1 hour 30 minutes | 94 marks in total | 37.5% of your final mark |

- <u>Section C</u> is split into two parts (C1 and C2). Both parts cover <u>Geographical Investigations</u>:
  — C1 covers <u>physical geography fieldwork</u> (<u>Coastal Change and Conflict</u> and <u>River Processes and Pressures</u>).
  — C2 covers <u>human geography fieldwork</u> (<u>Dynamic Urban Areas</u> and <u>Changing Rural Areas</u>).

You need to <u>answer all the questions</u> in Sections A and B.
In Section C, make sure you <u>only</u> answer questions on the fieldwork <u>you carried out</u>.

Paper 3: People and Environment Issues — Making Geographical Decisions

In the exam, you'll get a <u>Resource Booklet</u> with lots of information about a geographical <u>issue</u>. All the questions on Paper 3 will be based on <u>these resources</u>.

Paper 3 is split into <u>four sections</u>.

- <u>Section A</u> covers <u>People and the Biosphere</u>.
- <u>Section B</u> covers <u>Forests Under Threat</u>.
- <u>Section C</u> covers <u>Consuming Energy Resources</u>.
- <u>Section D</u> is a <u>decision-making exercise</u>, where you will have to use the sources you have been given and your own knowledge to come to a <u>justified decision</u> about the <u>issue</u>.

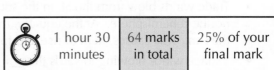

| 1 hour 30 minutes | 64 marks in total | 25% of your final mark |

There's more about how to answer the question in Section D on <u>page 161</u>.

In <u>each exam</u>, there will be one question which has <u>4 extra marks</u> available for <u>spelling</u>, <u>punctuation</u> and <u>grammar</u> as well as the use of <u>specialist terminology</u> (see p.162). These marks are <u>included</u> in the <u>total marks</u> given for each paper.

Be clear on what you've got to do in your exams

It's worthwhile knowing this stuff so nothing comes as a shock to you. It also stops you from being the person who doesn't realise there's a third exam — there's a fine line between being relaxed and sabotaging yourself...

Global Atmospheric Circulation

There's an overall <u>movement</u> of air between the <u>equator</u> and the <u>poles</u> that affects the Earth's <u>climate</u>.

Winds Transfer Heat from the Equator to the Poles

1) The <u>Sun</u> heats the Earth's surface <u>unevenly</u> — <u>insolation</u> (the <u>solar radiation</u> that reaches the Earth's surface) is <u>greater</u> at the equator than the poles.

2) The differences in <u>temperature</u> cause differences in <u>air pressure</u> (see below).

3) Winds blow <u>FROM</u> the areas of <u>high</u> pressure <u>TO</u> the areas of <u>low pressure</u>, transferring heat <u>away</u> from the equator.

4) Winds are part of <u>global atmospheric circulation</u> loops (called <u>cells</u>). These loops have <u>warm rising air</u> which creates a <u>low pressure belt</u>, and <u>cool falling air</u> which creates a <u>high pressure belt</u>.

5) There are <u>three cells</u> in each hemisphere — the <u>Hadley</u>, <u>Ferrel</u> and <u>Polar</u> cells.

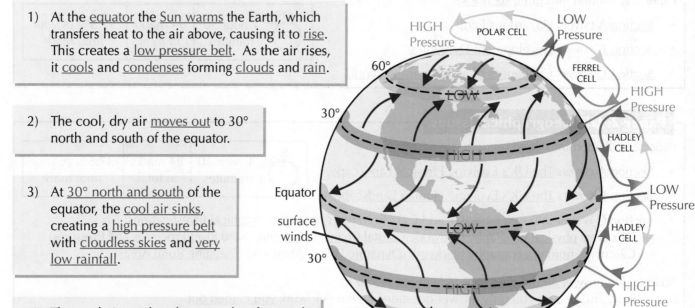

1) At the <u>equator</u> the <u>Sun warms</u> the Earth, which transfers heat to the air above, causing it to <u>rise</u>. This creates a <u>low pressure belt</u>. As the air rises, it <u>cools</u> and <u>condenses</u> forming <u>clouds</u> and <u>rain</u>.

2) The cool, dry air <u>moves out</u> to 30° north and south of the equator.

3) At <u>30° north and south</u> of the equator, the <u>cool air sinks</u>, creating a <u>high pressure belt</u> with <u>cloudless skies</u> and <u>very low rainfall</u>.

4) The cool air reaches the ground surface and moves as surface winds either <u>back to the equator</u> or <u>towards the poles</u>:
   - Surface winds blowing towards the <u>equator</u> are called <u>trade winds</u>.
   - Trade winds blow from the SE in the southern hemisphere and from the NE in the northern hemisphere. At the equator, these <u>trade winds meet</u> and are heated by the sun. This causes them to rise and form <u>clouds</u>.
   - Surface winds blowing towards the <u>poles</u> are called <u>westerlies</u>. They blow from the NW in the southern hemisphere and from the SW in the northern hemisphere.

5) At <u>60° north and south of the equator</u>, the warmer surface winds meet colder air from the poles. The warmer air is less dense than the cold air so it is forced to <u>rise</u>, creating <u>low pressure</u> and <u>frontal rain</u> (rain that forms where the <u>warm</u> and <u>cold</u> air masses <u>meet</u>).

6) Some of the air <u>moves back</u> towards the equator, and the rest moves towards the <u>poles</u>.

7) At the <u>poles</u> the <u>cool air sinks</u>, creating <u>high pressure</u>. The high pressure air is drawn back towards the equator as <u>surface winds</u>.

Global Atmospheric Circulation

Heat is also Transferred by Ocean Currents

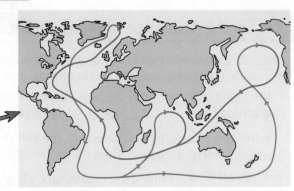

1) Ocean currents are large scale movements of water that <u>transfer</u> heat energy from <u>warmer</u> to <u>cooler</u> regions.

2) <u>Surface currents</u> are caused by <u>winds</u> and help transfer heat <u>away</u> from the Equator, e.g. the <u>Gulf Stream</u> brings warm water from the <u>Caribbean</u> and keeps <u>Western Europe</u> warmer than it would otherwise be.

3) There are also <u>deep ocean currents</u> driven by differences in <u>water density</u>.

4) When water <u>freezes</u> at the poles, the surrounding water gets <u>saltier</u>, increasing its <u>density</u>.

5) As it gets denser, it <u>sinks</u>, causing <u>warmer</u> water to flow in at the surface — creating a current.

6) This <u>warmer</u> water is <u>cooled</u> and <u>sinks</u>, continuing the <u>cycle</u>.

7) This cycle of cooling and sinking moves water in a big <u>loop</u> round the Earth — this is known as the <u>thermohaline circulation</u>.

~ deep cold currents   ~ shallow warm currents

There are Different Climate Zones Around the World

The <u>pressure belts</u> caused by <u>global atmospheric circulation</u> (see previous page) cause <u>variations</u> in <u>climate</u>.

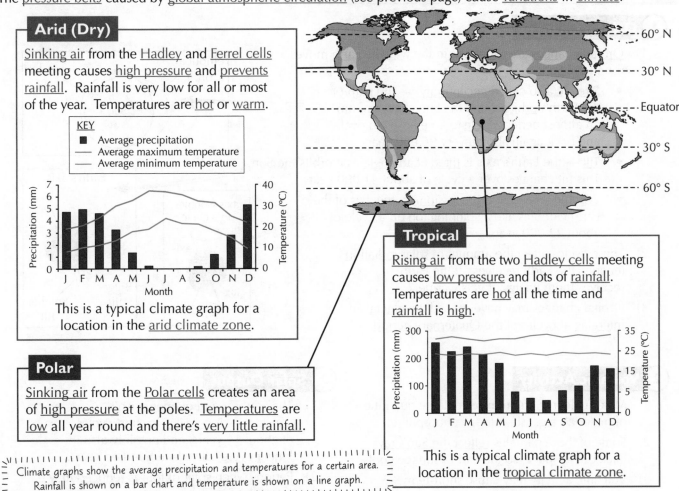

Arid (Dry)

<u>Sinking air</u> from the <u>Hadley</u> and <u>Ferrel cells</u> meeting causes <u>high pressure</u> and <u>prevents rainfall</u>. Rainfall is very low for all or most of the year. Temperatures are <u>hot</u> or <u>warm</u>.

KEY
■ Average precipitation
— Average maximum temperature
— Average minimum temperature

This is a typical climate graph for a location in the <u>arid climate zone</u>.

Polar

<u>Sinking air</u> from the <u>Polar cells</u> creates an area of <u>high pressure</u> at the poles. <u>Temperatures</u> are <u>low</u> all year round and there's <u>very little rainfall</u>.

Tropical

<u>Rising air</u> from the two <u>Hadley cells</u> meeting causes <u>low pressure</u> and lots of <u>rainfall</u>. Temperatures are <u>hot</u> all the time and <u>rainfall</u> is <u>high</u>.

This is a typical climate graph for a location in the <u>tropical climate zone</u>.

Climate graphs show the average precipitation and temperatures for a certain area. Rainfall is shown on a bar chart and temperature is shown on a line graph.

Pressure belts and surface winds are determined by global circulation

Air moves in loops (called cells) from the equator to the poles and back. This gives us surface winds and creates belts of high and low pressure that affect the climate — they're why deserts are so dry and rainforests are so wet.

Natural Climate Change

Climate change <u>isn't</u> a new phenomenon — it's been happening for <u>millions of years</u>. Believe it or not, there are quite a few <u>natural causes</u> of climate change and there's also plenty of <u>evidence</u> we can use to <u>study</u> past climate.

The Earth's **Climate** is **Always Changing**

<u>Climate change</u> is any significant <u>change</u> in the <u>Earth's climate</u> over a <u>long period</u>. The climate <u>constantly changes</u>, it always has, and it always will.

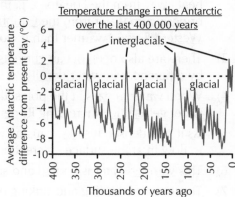

Temperature change in the Antarctic over the last 400 000 years

1) The <u>Quaternary period</u> is the most recent geological time period, spanning from about <u>2.6 million years ago</u> to the present day.

2) In the period <u>before</u> the Quaternary, the Earth's climate was <u>warmer</u> and quite <u>stable</u>. Then things <u>changed</u> a lot.

The Quaternary period includes the whole of human history.

3) During the Quaternary, <u>global temperature</u> has shifted between cold <u>glacial periods</u> that last for around 100 000 years, and warmer <u>interglacial periods</u> that usually last for around 10 000 years.

4) The <u>last</u> glacial period <u>ended</u> around 15 000 years ago. Since then the climate has been <u>warming</u>.

There are **Natural Causes** of **Climate Change**

① Orbital Changes

1) <u>Orbital changes</u> are <u>variations</u> in the <u>way</u> the <u>Earth</u> moves round the <u>Sun</u>.

- <u>Stretch</u> (also called <u>eccentricity</u>) — the path of the Earth's <u>orbit</u> around the Sun changes from an almost perfect <u>circle</u> to an <u>ellipse</u> (an oval) and back again about every 96 000 years.

- <u>Tilt</u> — the Earth's axis is <u>tilted</u> at an <u>angle</u> as it orbits the Sun. This tilt changes over a cycle of about 41 000 years.

- <u>Wobble</u> (also called <u>precession</u>) — the <u>axis</u> of the Earth wobbles like a <u>spinning top</u> on a cycle of about 22 000 years.

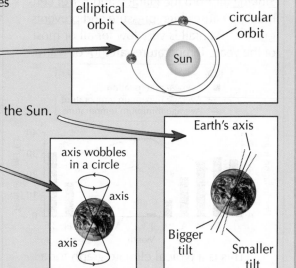

2) These cycles affect the amount of <u>solar radiation</u> (energy) the Earth receives. If the Earth receives <u>more energy</u>, it gets <u>warmer</u>.

3) Orbital changes may have caused the <u>glacial</u> and <u>interglacial cycles</u> of the <u>Quaternary period</u>.

② Volcanic Activity

1) Major <u>volcanic eruptions</u> eject large quantities of material, e.g. ash, into the atmosphere.

2) Some of these particles <u>reflect</u> the <u>Sun's rays</u> back out to space, so the Earth's surface <u>cools</u>.

3) Volcanic activity may cause <u>short-term changes</u> in climate, e.g. the eruption of <u>Mount Tambora</u> in Indonesia in 1815 led to the '<u>Year Without a Summer</u>' in 1816.

③ Solar Output

1) The Sun's <u>output</u> of <u>energy</u> isn't constant — it <u>changes</u> in short cycles of about 11 years, and possibly also in <u>longer cycles</u> of several hundred years.

2) Periods when solar output is <u>reduced</u> may cause the Earth's climate to become <u>cooler</u>.

3) The <u>Maunder Minimum</u> was a period of reduced solar activity between <u>1645</u> and <u>1715</u> which coincided with the <u>Little Ice Age</u> (see p.5).

Natural Climate Change

(4) Asteroid Collisions

1) <u>Asteroids</u> hitting the Earth's <u>surface</u> can throw up huge amounts of <u>dust</u> into the <u>atmosphere</u>.

2) These particles <u>prevent</u> the Sun's energy from reaching the Earth's surface so global temperatures <u>fall</u> (possibly for <u>several years</u>).

3) Some scientists believe that an asteroid collision caused a period of <u>global cooling</u> (the <u>Younger Dryas</u>) around <u>12 000 years ago</u>.

Evidence for **Natural Climate Change** Comes from **Many Sources**

Scientists can <u>work out</u> how the climate has <u>changed over time</u> using a range of <u>methods</u>. For example:

Tree Rings

1) Most trees produce one <u>ring</u> within their trunks <u>every year</u>.

2) The <u>thickness</u> of the ring depends on the <u>climate</u> when the ring was formed — when it's <u>warmer</u> the rings are <u>thicker</u>.

3) Scientists take <u>cores</u> through tree trunks then <u>date</u> each ring by <u>counting</u> them back from when the core was taken. By looking at the <u>thickness</u> of the rings, they can see what the <u>climate</u> was like <u>each year</u>.

Ice Cores

1) Ice sheets are made up of <u>layers</u> of ice — <u>one</u> layer is formed each <u>year</u>.

2) Scientists drill into ice sheets to get <u>long cores</u> of ice.

3) By analysing the <u>gases</u> (e.g. <u>carbon dioxide</u>) trapped in the layers of ice, they can tell what the <u>temperature</u> was each year.

4) One ice core (the <u>Vostok Ice Core</u>) from <u>Antarctica</u> shows the temperature changes over the last <u>400 000 years</u> (see graph on p.4).

Historical Records

1) Since the <u>1850s</u> global temperatures have been measured accurately using <u>thermometers</u>. This gives a <u>reliable</u> but <u>short-term record</u> of temperature change.

2) <u>Historical records</u> (e.g. <u>diaries</u> and <u>paintings</u>) can extend the <u>record</u> of climate change a bit <u>further back</u>.

3) For example, <u>historical diaries</u> can show what the <u>climate</u> was like in the past, e.g. by giving the number of days of <u>rain</u> or <u>snow</u> and the dates of <u>harvests</u> (an <u>early</u> harvest suggests <u>warm</u> weather).

4) Paintings of <u>fairs</u> and <u>markets</u> on <u>frozen rivers</u> show that <u>winters</u> in Europe were regularly much <u>colder</u> 500 years ago than they are now.

These **Sources** have been used to **Reconstruct** the **UK's Past Climate**

<u>MEDIEVAL WARM PERIOD</u>

- The Medieval Warm Period was a period of <u>warming</u> between <u>900</u> and <u>1300</u>.

- <u>Harvest records</u> show that England was warm enough to grow <u>large amounts</u> of <u>grapes</u>.

- <u>Tree ring data</u> suggests this was also the case during <u>Roman times</u>, when temperatures were almost <u>1.0 °C</u> warmer than today.

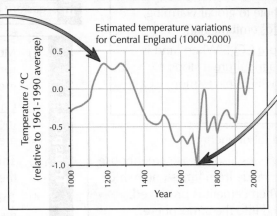

Estimated temperature variations for Central England (1000-2000)

The Inuit are an indigenous people from parts of Canada, Greenland and Alaska.

<u>LITTLE ICE AGE</u>

- The Little Ice Age was a period of <u>cooling</u> that <u>followed</u> the Medieval Warm Period.

- Paintings from the <u>17th century</u> show the <u>London Frost Fairs</u>, which took place on a <u>frozen</u> River Thames.

- <u>Historical records</u> talk about <u>arctic ice</u> reaching as far south as <u>Scotland</u> and sightings of <u>Inuits</u>.

Many natural factors have contributed to historical climate change

There were no thermometers 2.6 million years ago, but scientists can reconstruct climates using the clever methods shown on this page. Climate change is a hot topic, so make sure you learn this stuff inside out before the exam.

Climate Change — Human Activity

In the last 150 years or so, human activities have begun to have an impact on the Earth's climate.

The **Natural Greenhouse Effect** is **Essential** for Keeping Our Planet **Warm**

1) The temperature of the Earth is a balance between the heat it gets from the Sun and the heat it loses to space.

2) The incoming energy from the Sun is short-wave radiation. The outgoing energy from the Earth is long-wave radiation.

3) Gases in the atmosphere naturally act like an insulating layer — they let short-wave radiation in, but trap long-wave radiation, helping to keep the Earth at the right temperature.

4) This is called the greenhouse effect ('cos it's a bit like a greenhouse trapping heat).

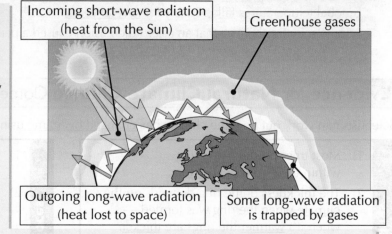

Incoming short-wave radiation (heat from the Sun)

Greenhouse gases

Outgoing long-wave radiation (heat lost to space)

Some long-wave radiation is trapped by gases

5) Gases that trap heat are called greenhouse gases — they include carbon dioxide (CO_2) and methane (CH_4).

6) Some greenhouse gases are stronger than others, e.g. methane absorbs more heat than carbon dioxide.

7) Different greenhouse gases stay in the atmosphere for different lengths of time. For example, methane usually stays in the atmosphere for around 10 years after it has been emitted.

8) The longer the gases stay in the atmosphere, the more they'll contribute to warming.

Human Activities are Making the Greenhouse Effect **Stronger**

1) The rate of the recent rise in global temperature (global warming) is unheard of.

2) There's a scientific consensus (general agreement) that human activities are causing global warming by making the greenhouse effect stronger. This is called the enhanced greenhouse effect.

3) Too much greenhouse gas in the atmosphere means too much energy is trapped and the planet warms up.

4) Humans are increasing the concentration of greenhouse gases:

Farming

1) Farming of livestock produces a lot of methane — cows love to fart...

2) Rice paddies contribute to global warming, because flooded fields emit methane.

3) Trees absorb and store CO_2. When land is cleared of trees for agriculture it stops the absorption of CO_2, which leaves more CO_2 in the atmosphere.

Industry

1) Most industry uses a lot of energy.

2) Some industrial processes also release greenhouse gases, e.g. cement is made from limestone, which contains carbon. When cement is produced, lots of CO_2 is released into the atmosphere.

3) Industrial waste may end up in landfill sites where it decays, releasing methane.

Energy

CO_2 is released into the atmosphere when fossil fuels like coal, oil and natural gas are burnt, e.g. in power stations.

Transport

1) Most cars, lorries, ships and planes run on fossil fuels, which release greenhouse gases when burnt.

2) Car ownership is rapidly increasing in countries which are developing, e.g. China.

3) This means there are more cars on the roads (especially in urban areas).

4) This increases congestion. As a result, car engines are running for longer, so the amount of greenhouse gases released increases.

Global warming is caused by an enhanced greenhouse effect

You may have to explain the causes of climate change in your exam — try writing an explanation in your own words of how human activities can cause the greenhouse effect to become stronger.

Climate Change — Human Activity

There is Some **Evidence** that **Human Activity** is causing **Climate Change**

Scientists have identified several factors which support the idea that humans are causing global warming.

Declining Arctic Ice

1) Sea ice forms around the poles in winter when ocean temperatures fall below -1.8 °C and melts during the summer when it's warmer.

2) The extent of arctic sea ice in winter has decreased by more than 3% each decade over the past 35 years.

Global Temperature Rise

Temperatures have increased by nearly 1 °C since 1880 and are expected to rise by 0.3-4.8 °C between 2005 and 2100. The top ten warmest years since records began have all been since the year 2000.

Sea Level Rise and Warming Oceans

Since 1901 sea levels have risen by almost 0.2 m. Scientists have highlighted two factors behind this rise:

- **Eustatic Sea Level Rise**

  Warmer temperatures are causing glaciers to shrink and ice sheets to melt. The melting of ice on land, especially from the Greenland and Antarctic ice sheets, means that water stored on land as ice returns to the oceans. This causes sea levels to rise.

- **Thermal Expansion**

  Water in the oceans expands as it gets warmer — this is called thermal expansion. Scientists think this accounts for about half of the measured rise in sea levels.

Extreme Weather Events

1) Since 1950 there has been a higher frequency of heat waves in many areas and fewer cold weather extremes.

2) In the UK, more rainfall records were broken in 2010-2014 than in any decade on record, even after only half a decade. 2013 was one of the wettest years on record and December 2015 was the wettest month ever recorded in the UK.

Climate Change Could have **Serious Impacts** on **People**

Changes in climate are already having an impact on people, but there could be more serious consequences in the future:

1) In some places deaths due to heat have increased — but deaths due to cold have decreased.

2) Some areas could become so hot and dry that they're difficult or impossible to inhabit. Low-lying coastal areas could be lost to the sea or flood so often that they also become impossible to inhabit. This could lead to migration and overcrowding in other areas.

3) Climate change is affecting farming in different ways around the world:
   - Globally, some crops have suffered from climate change (e.g. maize crops have got smaller due to warming in recent years).
   - But some farmers in high-latitude countries (countries further from the equator) are finding that crops benefit from warmer conditions.

4) Lower crop yields could increase malnutrition, ill health and death from starvation, particularly in lower latitudes (nearer the equator).

5) Climate change means the weather is getting more extreme. This means more money has to be spent on predicting extreme weather events, reducing their impacts and rebuilding after them.

Flooding is becoming more common in the UK

Learn the evidence that human activity is changing the climate

Scientists still don't know what the exact impacts of climate change will be, but some effects are already being seen. Make sure you know how climate change could impact human populations around the world.

Climate Change Projections

You should now be an <u>expert</u> in the <u>causes</u> and <u>evidence</u> for climate change — so it's time to find out all about how our <u>current understanding</u> of climate change can be used to try and <u>predict future changes</u> to the climate.

Data about Climate Change can be used to Make Predictions

1) <u>Physical processes</u>, e.g. <u>atmospheric circulation</u> and the effect of <u>volcanic eruptions</u> on the climate, can be <u>modelled</u> on computers.

2) <u>Human activity</u>, e.g. growth of <u>industry</u> or development of <u>clean energy</u>, can also be modelled using data that's been collected about <u>greenhouse gas emissions</u>.

3) <u>Scientists</u> can use these models to work out how the <u>climate</u> would be <u>affected</u> under certain <u>scenarios</u>, e.g. what would happen if there was a volcanic eruption in 20 years' time and there were still <u>high levels</u> of greenhouse gas emissions.

4) The <u>Intergovernmental Panel on Climate Change</u> (<u>IPCC</u>) is an international group of scientists that uses models to <u>predict</u> how the climate might <u>change</u> and the <u>consequences</u> of any changes.

5) The IPCC have chosen four "<u>Representative Concentration Pathways</u>" (RCPs) — <u>possible scenarios</u> covering the <u>best</u> to the <u>worst</u> possible outcomes.

6) The IPCC uses <u>projection graphs</u> to show the predicted changes in <u>temperature</u> and <u>sea level</u> by <u>2100</u>.

7) Lines for the <u>best</u> and <u>worst</u> scenarios are plotted on the graphs. All <u>other</u> outcomes fall <u>between</u> these lines.

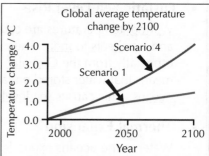

SCENARIO 1 — Minimum Emissions

This is the best outcome, in which levels of greenhouse gases peak, then reduce (i.e. greenhouse gas emissions are significantly reduced).

SCENARIOS 2 & 3 — Stabilising Scenarios

These are scenarios in which greenhouse gas levels continue to increase, but eventually level off (after steps are taken to reduce emissions).

SCENARIO 4 — Maximum Emissions

This is the worst outcome, in which the rate of production of emissions continues to increase and greenhouse gas levels end up very high.

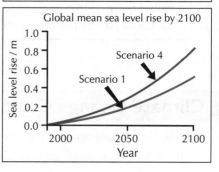

You need to be able to use and interpret projection graphs for your exam.

There is Lots of Uncertainty about Future Climate Change

It's <u>difficult to predict</u> the impacts of changes in climate because there's so much <u>uncertainty</u>.

1) <u>EMISSIONS</u> — we don't actually know <u>how</u> emissions will change, i.e. which scenario is <u>most accurate</u>.
   - Predictions have to take into account things like <u>population increase</u> and <u>economic development</u>.
   - It's hard to know how <u>global population</u> will change in the future (i.e. whether it'll keep <u>growing</u> at the rate it is today) or how much <u>development</u> will take place in the future.

2) <u>COMPLEXITY</u> — we don't know what <u>exact climate changes</u> each scenario will cause.
   - There are lots of <u>natural processes</u> that we don't fully understand, which makes it difficult to predict what will change. We don't know how these natural factors could have an <u>impact</u> on climate change.

3) <u>MANAGEMENT</u> — we don't know what <u>attempts</u> there will be to <u>manage</u> the amount of greenhouse gases in the atmosphere, or how <u>successful</u> they'll be.

No-one can accurately predict the future of climate change

Some people think the rate of greenhouse gas emissions will continue to rise, leading to further climate change and sea level rises. Others think emissions will lessen in the future, reducing the impacts of long-term global warming.

Worked Exam Questions

Exam questions are the best way to practise what you've learnt. After all, they're exactly what you'll have to do on the big day — so work through these worked examples very carefully.

1 Study **Figure 1**, a map of climatic zones.

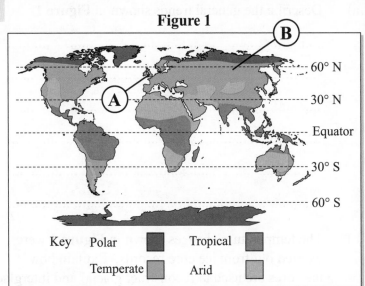

Figure 1

Key Polar Tropical
Temperate Arid

a) The average annual temperature at A is 11 °C, but is less than 1 °C at B. Suggest **one** reason for the difference in temperature between A and B.

Places near the ocean can be warmer

than other places at the same latitude

because ocean currents bring warm

water from the equator.

[2]

b) Explain why arid areas are often found around 30° from the equator.

There is sinking air where two cells meet around 30° from the equator. This causes high pressure,

which limits rainfall, making the area arid.

[2]

[Total 4 marks]

2 Study **Figure 2**, which shows data on sea level rise between 1900 and 2100.

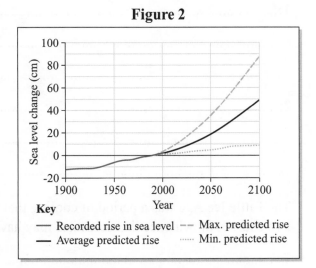

Figure 2

Key
— Recorded rise in sea level -- Max. predicted rise
— Average predicted rise ⋯ Min. predicted rise

a) Explain how sea level rise provides evidence for global warming.

Warmer temperatures lead to sea level rise

because water in the ocean expands as it

gets warmer.

[2]

b) Suggest **two** reasons for the range in the predictions for sea level rise shown in **Figure 2**.

The natural processes causing sea level rise are very complex so it's hard to predict what effect they

will have. There could be different attempts to manage climate change and its effect on sea level rise.

Scientists don't know how successful these attempts may be.

[4]

[Total 6 marks]

Exam Questions

1   Study **Figure 1**, a graph showing temperature changes during the Quaternary period.

a)   Describe the general trends shown in **Figure 1**.

Figure 1

....

....

....

....

....

....
                                                                            [2]

Temperature change in the Antarctic over the last 400 000 years

b)   The temperature changes shown in **Figure 1** were
      worked out from ice core records. Explain how
      ice cores are used to reconstruct glacial and interglacial climates during the Quaternary period.

....

....

....
                                                                                                                            [2]

c)   Explain **two** possible causes of the changes in temperature between
      400 000 and 100 000 years ago shown in **Figure 1**.

      1:...

      ....

      ....

      2:...

      ....

      ....
                                                                                                                            [4]

d)   The Little Ice Age was a period of cooling that began about 700 years ago in the UK. Suggest
      two sources of evidence that scientists may have used to reconstruct the climate of this period.

....

....

....

....

....
                                                                                                                            [4]

                                                                                            [Total 12 marks]

Tropical Cyclones

Tropical cyclones are <u>intense low pressure</u> weather systems with <u>heavy rain</u> and <u>strong winds</u> that spiral around the <u>centre</u>. They have a couple of other names (<u>hurricanes</u> and <u>typhoons</u>), but they're all the <u>same thing</u>.

Tropical Cyclones **Develop** over **Warm Water**

1) Tropical cyclones develop when the <u>sea temperature</u> is <u>26.5 °C</u> or higher and when the <u>wind shear</u> (the difference in windspeed) between <u>higher</u> and <u>lower</u> parts of the atmosphere is <u>low</u>.

2) The source area of most tropical cyclones is between <u>5°</u> and <u>30°</u> north and south of the equator — any further from the equator and the water <u>isn't warm enough</u>.

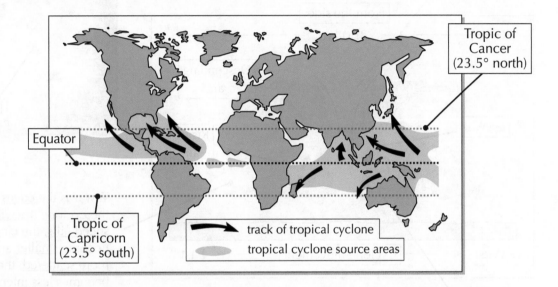

3) The majority of cyclones occur when sea temperatures are <u>highest</u> — in the <u>northern</u> hemisphere this is <u>June</u> to <u>November</u>. In the <u>southern</u> hemisphere, <u>November</u> to <u>April</u>.

4) <u>Warm</u>, <u>moist</u> air <u>rises</u> and <u>condensation</u> occurs. This releases huge amounts of <u>energy</u>, which makes the storms <u>powerful</u>. The <u>rising air</u> creates an area of <u>low pressure</u>, which increases <u>surface winds</u>.

5) The Earth's <u>rotation</u> deflects the paths of the winds, which causes the cyclone to <u>spin</u>.

6) Tropical cyclones <u>move towards the west</u> because of the <u>easterly winds</u> near the equator (see p.2).

7) When cyclones travel further away from the equator, their path may start to <u>curve</u> to the <u>east</u> as they get caught in the <u>mid-latitude westerlies</u>.

8) Cyclones <u>intensify</u> (<u>get stronger</u>) due to <u>energy</u> from the warm <u>water</u>.

9) They <u>dissipate</u> (<u>lose strength</u>) when they move over <u>land</u> or <u>cooler water</u> because the energy supply from the warm water is <u>cut off</u>. Changes in <u>windspeed</u>, e.g. from meeting other <u>weather systems</u>, can also cause a cyclone to dissipate.

10) <u>Climate change</u> may cause tropical cyclone source areas to <u>change</u>. If sea temperatures <u>rise</u>, more of the world's oceans could be <u>above 26.5 °C</u>. This means <u>more</u> places in the world may <u>experience</u> tropical cyclones.

Tropical cyclones form at low latitudes — between 5° and 30° N & S

You don't need to know exactly how tropical cyclones form, but you might be asked to outline how global atmospheric circulation leads to them forming in source areas, or why they intensify or dissipate.

Tropical Cyclones

Tropical cyclones have a <u>distinctive shape</u> and <u>structure</u>. This makes them quite easy to spot on <u>satellite images</u>...

Learn the **Features** and **Structure** of A Tropical Cyclone

Tropical cyclones are <u>circular</u> in shape, <u>hundreds of kilometres wide</u> and usually last <u>7-14 days</u>.

The <u>centre</u> of the cyclone is called the <u>eye</u> — it's up to <u>50 km across</u> and is caused by <u>descending air</u>. There's very <u>low pressure</u>, <u>light</u> <u>winds</u>, <u>no clouds</u>, <u>no rain</u> and a <u>high temperature</u> in the eye.

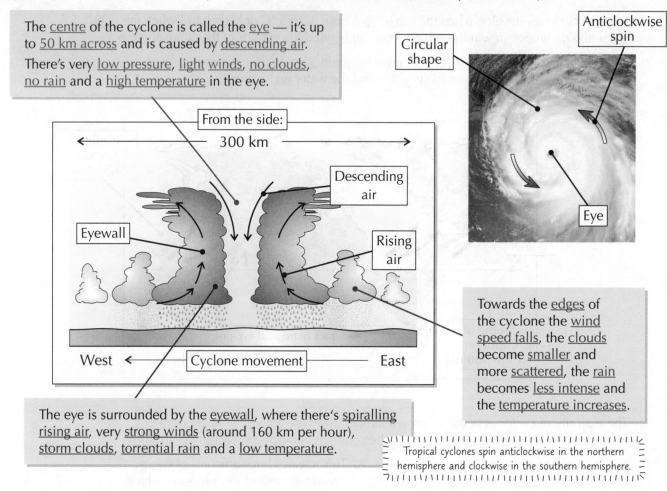

From the side:

300 km

Descending air

Eyewall

Rising air

West ← | Cyclone movement | East

The eye is surrounded by the <u>eyewall</u>, where there's <u>spiralling rising air</u>, very <u>strong winds</u> (around 160 km per hour), <u>storm clouds</u>, <u>torrential rain</u> and a <u>low temperature</u>.

Circular shape

Anticlockwise spin

Eye

Towards the <u>edges</u> of the cyclone the <u>wind speed falls</u>, the <u>clouds</u> become <u>smaller</u> and more <u>scattered</u>, the <u>rain</u> becomes <u>less intense</u> and the <u>temperature increases</u>.

Tropical cyclones spin anticlockwise in the northern hemisphere and clockwise in the southern hemisphere.

Tropical Cyclones cause **Physical Hazards**

When a tropical cyclone hits <u>land</u>, it causes <u>physical hazards</u>:

- **HIGH WINDS** — <u>windspeeds</u> in a tropical cyclone can reach <u>250 km/h</u>.
- **INTENSE RAINFALL** — tropical cyclones can release <u>trillions</u> of <u>litres</u> of water per day as rain. The rain gets <u>heavier</u> as you get <u>closer</u> to the <u>eye</u> of the cyclone.
- **STORM SURGES** — a <u>storm surge</u> is a large rise in <u>sea level</u> caused by <u>low pressure</u> and <u>high winds</u>.

- **COASTAL FLOODING** — <u>flooding</u> happens as a result of <u>storm surges</u> and <u>strong winds</u> driving <u>large waves</u> onto the shore.
- **LANDSLIDES** — <u>heavy rain</u> makes hills <u>unstable</u>, causing <u>landslides</u>.

REVISION TIP

Air is descending at the eye of a cyclone, and rising in the eyewall

You should learn the structure and other features of a tropical cyclone, so you won't be fazed by anything the examiners throw at you. Try testing yourself by sketching the diagram above — remember the labels.

Tropical Cyclones — Impacts

Tropical cyclones can have <u>serious effects</u> on <u>people</u> and the <u>environment</u>.

The **Physical Hazards** Caused by Tropical Cyclones have an **Impact** on **People**...

- People may <u>drown</u> in the <u>strong currents</u> created by <u>floodwater</u> and <u>storm surges</u>.

- <u>Windspeeds</u> in tropical cyclones can be strong enough to completely <u>destroy</u> buildings, which means people are left <u>homeless</u>.

- <u>High winds</u> and <u>floodwater</u> can carry large amounts of <u>debris</u>, which can <u>kill</u> or <u>injure people</u>.

- <u>Electricity supplies</u> are cut off because cables are damaged or swept away by floodwater.

- Flooding causes <u>sewage</u> overflows which <u>contaminate water supplies</u>.

- The <u>shortage</u> of <u>clean water</u> and <u>lack</u> of proper <u>sanitation</u> makes it easier for <u>diseases</u> to spread.

- In <u>poorer countries</u> there's often a <u>shortage</u> of <u>food</u> because <u>crops</u> are damaged and <u>livestock</u> killed.

- <u>Unemployment</u> increases because <u>businesses</u> are damaged or destroyed.

- <u>Damaged roads</u> make it very difficult for <u>aid</u> and <u>emergency vehicles</u> to get through.

...and the Environment

1) Trees are <u>uprooted</u> by high winds which can <u>damage</u> or completely <u>destroy</u> wooded habitats.

2) Storm surges can <u>erode</u> beaches and damage <u>coastal habitats</u> (e.g. coral reefs).

3) Flooding caused by storm surges can <u>pollute</u> freshwater environments with <u>saltwater</u>.

4) Landslides deposit <u>sediment</u> in rivers and lakes, which can <u>kill</u> fish and other <u>wildlife</u>.

5) Flooding can damage <u>industrial buildings</u> on the coast, e.g. <u>oil</u> or <u>chemical factories</u>. This causes harmful chemicals to leak into the environment and cause pollution.

Tropical cyclones can release trillions of litres of rain, which causes flooding

Flooding can have devastating effects on human settlements and on the natural environment. A lot of the impacts from tropical cyclones, including those that result from flooding, can last for a long time after the storm has passed.

Tropical Cyclones — Preparation and Responses

Preparation is important in reducing the impacts of tropical cyclones.

Some Countries are More Vulnerable than Others

Countries can be vulnerable to the impacts of tropical cyclones for different reasons.

1 Physical Vulnerability

1) Low-lying coastlines are vulnerable to storm surge flooding as well as large waves caused by the high winds.

2) Areas in the path of tropical cyclones are hit more frequently.

3) Steep hillsides may increase the risk of landslides.

2 Economic Vulnerability

Poorer countries are economically vulnerable because:

1) Many people depend on agriculture which is often badly affected — this leads to a loss of livelihoods.

2) People may not have insurance to cover the costs of repairing damage caused by cyclones.

However, the economic impact is often greater in richer countries as the buildings and infrastructure (roads, rail, bridges etc.) damaged are worth a lot of money.

3 Social Vulnerability

Poorer countries are often more socially vulnerable because:

1) Buildings are poorer quality so more easily damaged.

2) Health care isn't as good so they struggle to treat all the casualties.

3) There is little money for flood defences or training emergency teams.

4) It's harder to rescue people because of poor infrastructure.

There are Many Strategies to Prepare for and Respond to Tropical Cyclones

Forecasting

1) When and where tropical cyclones will hit land can be predicted.

2) Scientists can use weather forecasting and satellite technology to monitor cyclones. Computer models are then used to calculate a predicted path for the cyclone.

3) The cyclone's magnitude can be monitored by measuring its windspeeds.

4) Predicting where and when a tropical cyclone is going to happen gives people time to evacuate and protect their homes and businesses, e.g. by boarding up windows.

Tropical cyclones are classified using the Saffir-Simpson Scale, which is based on windspeed. Category 5 is the strongest (winds over 250 km/h) and 1 is the weakest (winds of 120-150 km/h).

Evacuation

1) Warning strategies are used to alert people to a tropical cyclone. An alert will give people enough time to leave their homes and get to a safe place.

2) Governments can plan evacuation routes to get people away from storms quickly. In Florida, evacuation routes are signposted all along the coast.

3) Successful evacuations can reduce the number of deaths and injuries.

4) Emergency services can train and prepare for disasters, e.g. by practising rescuing people from flooded areas with helicopters. This reduces the number of people killed.

Defences

1) Defences (e.g. sea walls) can be built along the coast to prevent damage from storm surges. Buildings can also be designed to withstand a storm surge, e.g. they can be put on stilts so they're safe from floodwater.

2) This will reduce the number of buildings destroyed, so fewer people will be killed, injured, made homeless and made unemployed.

Richer countries are often more prepared for cyclones than poorer countries

Some countries are more vulnerable to tropical cyclones because of their location and the physical characteristics of the land. The amount of money the country has is also a major factor in how bad the impacts are likely to be.

Tropical Cyclones — Hurricane Katrina

It's time to put all that theory into practice with a couple of examples. First up, Hurricane Katrina.

A Cyclone's Impact is Linked to Preparation and Responses

The impacts of tropical cyclones depend on how a country prepares for and responds to the event. Wealthier, more developed countries, e.g. the USA, tend to be better prepared, so they can respond quickly.

Hurricane Katrina is an Example of a Tropical Cyclone in a Developed Country

Name: Hurricane Katrina
Magnitude: Category 3 at landfall
Place: South east USA
Date: 29th August, 2005

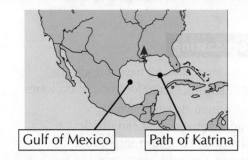

Gulf of Mexico | Path of Katrina

1 Forecasting

- The USA has a sophisticated monitoring system to predict if (and where) a hurricane will hit.
- The National Hurricane Centre (NHC) in Florida tracks and predicts hurricanes using satellite images and planes that collect weather data on approaching storms.

2 Warning & Evacuation

- The NHC issued a hurricane warning on 26th August for Louisiana, Mississippi and Alabama. It continued to track the hurricane, updating the government on where and when it would hit.
- Mississippi and Louisiana declared states of emergency and 70-80% of New Orleans residents were evacuated before the hurricane reached land. This reduced the number of people killed because lots of people had left the areas where the hurricane hit.

3 Defences

- The city of New Orleans was very badly damaged — flood defences (e.g. embankments) that were supposed to protect the city failed.
- This caused widespread flooding (over 80% of the city was underwater).

4 Impacts on the Environment

- Coastal habitats such as sea turtle breeding beaches were damaged.
- Some coastal conservation areas were destroyed, e.g. around half of Breton National Wildlife Refuge in Louisiana was washed away.
- Flooding damaged oil refineries in Louisiana, causing massive oil spills.

5 Impacts on People

- More than 1800 people were killed.
- 300 000 houses were destroyed and hundreds of thousands of people were made homeless.
- 3 million people were left without electricity.
- Roads were damaged and some bridges collapsed.
- 230 000 jobs were lost from damaged businesses.

The facts on Katrina make for grim reading

You don't have to learn about Katrina if you've studied another tropical cyclone in a developed country — try copying out the titles of the boxes above and jotting points under each for your chosen cyclone.

Tropical Cyclones — Cyclone Nargis

Cyclone Nargis caused a lot of damage, and led to a lot of deaths.

Cyclone Nargis is an Example of a Tropical Cyclone in a Developing Country

Name: Cyclone Nargis
Magnitude: Category 4 at landfall
Place: Irrawaddy delta, Myanmar
Date: 2nd May, 2008

1 Forecasting

- Myanmar doesn't have a dedicated monitoring centre for tropical cyclones.
- Myanmar doesn't have a radar network that can predict the height of storm surges and waves caused by cyclones.

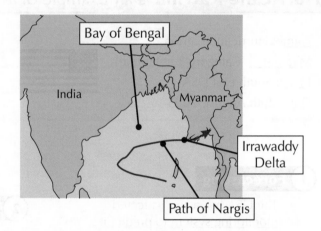

Bay of Bengal
India
Myanmar
Irrawaddy Delta
Path of Nargis

2 Warning & Evacuation

- Indian weather agencies warned the government of Myanmar that Cyclone Nargis was likely to hit the country 48 hours before it did.
- Warnings were issued on the TV and radio, but they didn't reach people in poor rural communities. This meant more people were killed because they didn't know what to do or where to evacuate to.
- There were no emergency preparation plans, no evacuation plans and the country didn't have an early warning system.

3 Defences

Mangrove forests protect the coast from flooding, but loads had been chopped down in the decade before Nargis hit, reducing the natural protection.

4 Impacts on the Environment

- The Irrawaddy delta in Myanmar was the hardest hit area — a large proportion of it is only just above sea level and 14 000 km² of land was flooded.
- 38 000 hectares of mangrove forests were destroyed.
- The flooding caused erosion and salination (increased salt content) of the land.

5 Impacts on People

- More than 140 000 people were killed.
- 450 000 houses were destroyed and 350 000 were damaged.
- Around 65% of rice paddies in the Irrawaddy delta were damaged, which led to a loss of livelihoods.
- A lot of people suffered from diseases caused by poor sanitary conditions and contaminated water.

The slow response to Cycle Nargis made the consequences worse

Be prepared for some sort of comparison question on examples of tropical cyclones in your exam — you could be asked to compare any of the five things above. If you've studied different examples in class, revise them — just make sure one is from a developed country and one from a developing country.

Worked Exam Questions

These exam questions are just like the type you'll get in the exam — except they've got the answers written in for you already. Have a look to see the sorts of things you should be writing.

1   Study **Figure 1**, a map showing the areas affected by tropical cyclones.

Figure 1

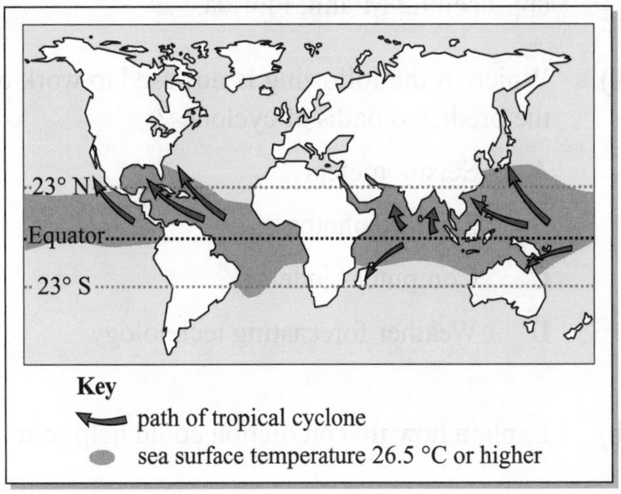

Key
- path of tropical cyclone
- sea surface temperature 26.5 °C or higher

a)   Using **Figure 1**, explain the global distribution of tropical cyclones.

Tropical cyclones form near the equator,

because they only form over water that is

26.5 °C or higher.

[2]

b)   Explain the seasonal distribution of tropical cyclones in the northern hemisphere.

In the northern hemisphere, the majority of cyclones occur from June to November, because this is

when sea temperatures are highest.

[2]

c)   State **two** features of tropical cyclones.

1: Tropical cyclones have a circular shape.

2: Tropical cyclones have an eye at their centre, which is up to 50 km across.

[2]

d)   Which of the following would cause a tropical cyclone to intensify?

A   The cyclone moving over land.   ⬭

B   The cyclone meeting another weather system.   ⬭

C   The cyclone moving over warmer water.   ⬛

D   The cyclone changing direction.   ⬭

[1]

e)   Explain how the global circulation of the atmosphere affects the track of tropical cyclones.

The easterly winds near the equator cause tropical cyclones to move west. When they travel

further away from the equator, their path may start to curve east as they get caught in the

mid-latitude westerlies.

[4]

[Total 11 marks]

Exam Questions

1   Study **Figure 1**, a forecast map showing the predicted path of a hurricane over Cuba, approaching Miami, Florida.

Figure 1

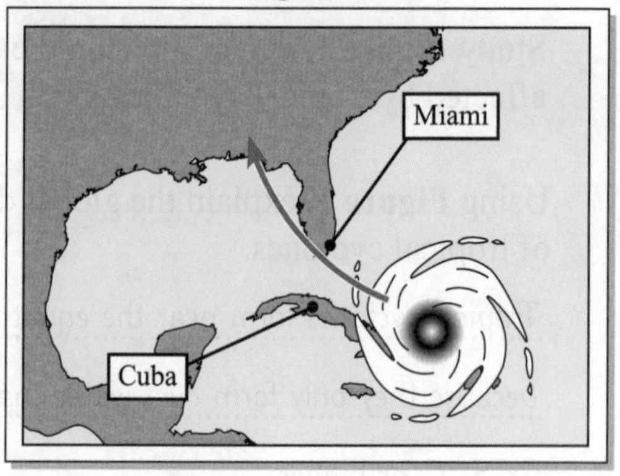

a)   Which of the following is **not** used to work out the predicted paths of cyclones?

   A   Seismometers ◯

   B   Satellite photos ◯

   C   Computer models ◯

   D   Weather forecasting technology ◯

[1]

b)   Explain how this prediction could help to reduce the effects of the cyclone in Miami.

....

....

....
[2]

c)   Explain how cities such as Miami could defend themselves to reduce the impacts of tropical cyclones.

....

....

....

....

....
[4]

d)   Compare the vulnerability of developed and developing countries to the impacts of tropical cyclones.

....

....

....

....
[3]

e)   Referring to **two** countries with contrasting levels of development, assess the effectiveness of the preparation methods used in reducing the impacts of tropical cyclones.
[8]

[Total 18 marks]

Structure of the Earth

The <u>Earth's surface</u> is made of <u>huge floating plates</u> that are constantly moving...

The **Earth** has a **Layered Structure**

1) At the <u>centre</u> of the Earth is the <u>core</u>:

- The core is a ball of <u>solid</u> (inner) and <u>liquid</u> (outer) <u>iron</u> and <u>nickel</u>.
- At the <u>centre</u>, it's <u>very dense</u>. It becomes <u>less dense</u> further out.
- The <u>temperature</u> inside the core ranges from <u>4400-6000 °C</u>.

2) Around the core is the <u>mantle</u>:

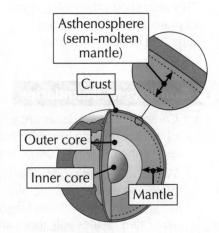

- The mantle is made up of <u>silicon-based rocks</u>.
- The part of the mantle <u>nearest the core</u> is <u>quite rigid</u>.
- The <u>layer above</u> this, called the <u>asthenosphere</u>, is <u>semi-molten</u> (it can flow).
- And the <u>very</u>, <u>very top bit</u> of the mantle is <u>rigid</u>.
- The temperature of the mantle is between <u>1000</u> and <u>3700 °C</u>. It's <u>hotter</u> towards the core and <u>cooler</u> towards the Earth's surface.

3) The solid <u>outer layer</u> of the Earth is called the <u>crust</u>:

- The crust is also made up of <u>silicon-based rocks</u>.
- There are <u>two</u> types of crust — <u>continental</u> and <u>oceanic</u>.
  - Continental crust is <u>thicker</u> and <u>less dense</u>.
  - Oceanic crust is <u>thinner</u> and <u>more dense</u>.

4) The crust is <u>divided</u> into <u>slabs</u> called <u>tectonic plates</u>.

Tectonic Plates **Move** due to **Convection Currents** in the **Mantle**

1) The tectonic plates <u>float</u> on the mantle.

2) <u>Radioactive decay</u> of some elements in the <u>mantle</u> and <u>core</u>, e.g. uranium, generates <u>a lot of heat</u>.

3) When <u>lower parts</u> of the <u>asthenosphere heat up</u> they become <u>less dense</u> and slowly <u>rise</u>.

4) As they move towards the <u>top</u> of the asthenosphere they <u>cool down</u>, become <u>more dense</u>, then slowly <u>sink</u>.

5) These <u>circular movements</u> of semi-molten rock are called <u>CONVECTION CURRENTS</u>.

6) Convection currents in the asthenosphere <u>create drag</u> on the <u>base</u> of the <u>tectonic plates</u> (which are solid and rigid) — and this causes them to <u>move</u>.

Earth's structure = core, then mantle, then crust on the outside

Make sure you understand the Earth's structure and what tectonic plates are. Spend some time getting convection clear in your head as well. Once that's sorted, you'll be ready to move onto plate boundaries...

Plate Boundaries

Plate boundaries are where plates meet. The direction the plates are moving in determines the type of boundary.

There are **Three Types** of **Plate Boundary**

1) Convection currents in the mantle move tectonic plates in different directions.

2) Plate boundaries are where the plates meet.

3) The movement of the plates creates three types of boundary (see below).

4) This map shows the global distribution of plate boundaries and the direction of plate movement.

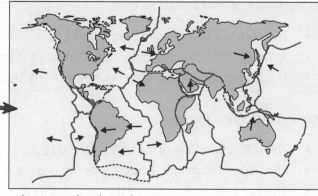

—— divergent plate boundary ⋯⋯ conservative plate boundary
—— convergent plate boundary → direction of plate movement

1 Convergent Boundaries
con destructive

- Convergent boundaries are where two plates are moving towards each other, e.g. along the west coast of South America.

- Where an oceanic plate meets a continental plate, the denser oceanic plate is forced down into the mantle and destroyed. This often creates volcanoes and ocean trenches (very deep sections of the ocean floor where the oceanic plate goes down).

- Where two continental plates meet, the plates collide, and the ground is folded and forced upwards to create mountain ranges.

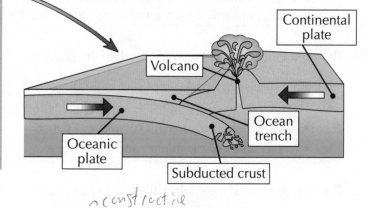

2 Divergent Boundaries
constructive

Divergent boundaries are where two plates are moving away from each other, e.g. at the mid-Atlantic ridge. Magma (molten rock) rises from the mantle to fill the gap and cools, creating new crust.

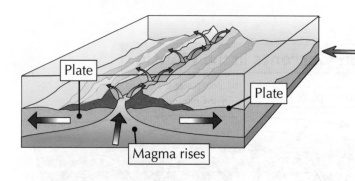

3 Conservative Boundaries

Conservative boundaries are where two plates are moving sideways past each other, or are moving in the same direction but at different speeds, e.g. along the west coast of the USA. Crust isn't created or destroyed.

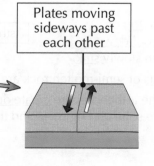

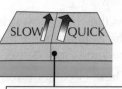

+ collision.

 Make sure you understand the differences between each boundary
Each boundary has different characteristics — the direction the plates move in affects what happens there. Practise sketching and labelling the diagrams on this page to learn how tectonic plates move.

Volcanic Hazards

Volcanoes usually look like mountains... until they <u>explode</u> and throw <u>molten rock</u> everywhere.

Volcanoes are Found at **Convergent** and **Divergent Plate Boundaries**

1) At <u>convergent plate boundaries</u> the <u>oceanic plate</u> goes <u>under</u> the <u>continental plate</u> because it's <u>more dense</u>.

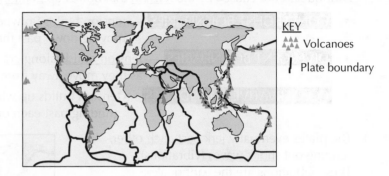

- The <u>oceanic plate</u> moves down into the <u>mantle</u>, where it's <u>melted</u> and <u>destroyed</u>.
- A <u>pool</u> of <u>magma</u> forms.
- The <u>magma rises</u> through <u>cracks</u> in the crust called <u>vents</u>.
- The magma <u>erupts</u> onto the surface (where it's called <u>lava</u>) forming a <u>volcano</u>.

KEY
▲▲▲ Volcanoes
Ɩ Plate boundary

2) At <u>divergent boundaries</u> the magma <u>rises up</u> into the <u>gap</u> created by the plates moving apart, forming a <u>volcano</u>.

3) When a volcano erupts, it emits <u>lava</u> and <u>gases</u>. Some volcanoes emit <u>lots</u> of <u>ash</u>, which can <u>cover land</u>, <u>block out</u> the <u>sun</u> and form <u>pyroclastic flows</u> (<u>super-heated</u> currents of <u>gas</u>, <u>ash</u> and <u>rock</u>).

Hotspots are Found **Away From Plate Boundaries**

Some volcanoes form in the <u>middle</u> of tectonic plates over <u>hotspots</u>:

1) They occur where a <u>plume</u> of <u>hot magma</u> from the <u>mantle</u> moves towards the <u>surface</u>, causing an unusually large <u>flow of heat</u> from the mantle to the crust.

2) Sometimes the magma can <u>break through</u> the crust and reach the <u>surface</u>. When this happens, there is an <u>eruption</u> and a <u>volcano</u> forms.

3) Hotspots remain <u>stationary</u> over time, but the <u>crust moves above them</u>. This can create <u>chains</u> of <u>volcanic islands</u>, e.g. <u>Hawaii</u> is a chain of volcanic islands in the middle of the <u>Pacific plate</u>.

There are **Different Types** of **Volcano**

1) <u>Composite volcanoes</u> (E.g. Mount Fuji in Japan)

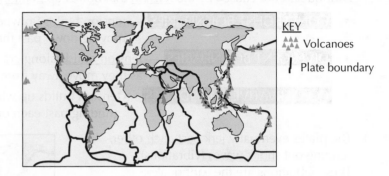

- Occur at <u>convergent plate boundaries</u> (see p.20).
- Subducted <u>oceanic crust</u> contains lots of <u>water</u>. The water <u>reacts</u> with <u>magma</u> and creates <u>gases</u>, which cause the subducted crust to <u>erupt</u>.
- They have <u>explosive eruptions</u> that start with <u>ashy explosions</u> that deposit a <u>layer of ash</u>.
- They erupt <u>andesitic lava</u> that has a <u>high silica content</u> which makes it <u>thick</u> and <u>sticky</u>. The lava <u>can't flow far</u> so forms a <u>steep-sided cone</u>.

Steep-sided volcano

Layer of lava   Layer of ash

2) <u>Shield volcanoes</u> (E.g. Mauna Loa on the Hawaiian islands)

- Occur at <u>hotspots</u> or <u>divergent plate boundaries</u> (see p.20).
- They are <u>not very explosive</u> and are made up of <u>only lava</u>.
- They erupt <u>basaltic lava</u>, which has <u>low silica content</u> and is <u>runny</u>. It flows <u>quickly</u> and spreads over a <u>wide area</u>, forming a <u>low, gentle-sided</u> volcano.

Low, flat volcano   Runny lava   Layers of lava

Volcanoes only occur in some parts of the world

Most volcanoes are found at plate boundaries, but don't forget that some of them aren't. Make sure you know what hotspots are, and that you can explain why there are different types of volcanoes in different places.

Earthquake Hazards

Earthquakes happen more often than you think. Obviously there are the big ones that cause loads of damage and make the headlines on the news, but there are also lots of small earthquakes every year that hardly anyone notices.

Earthquakes Occur at All Three Types of Plate Boundary

1) Earthquakes are caused by the tension that builds up at all three types of plate boundary:

   • CONVERGENT BOUNDARIES — tension builds up when one plate gets stuck as it's moving down past the other into the mantle.

   • DIVERGENT BOUNDARIES — tension builds along cracks within the plates as they move away from each other.

   • CONSERVATIVE BOUNDARIES — tension builds up when plates that are grinding past each other get stuck.

2) The plates eventually jerk past each other, sending out shock waves (vibrations). These vibrations are the earthquake.

3) Earthquakes are measured using the moment magnitude scale, which measures the energy released by an earthquake. You may still see some references to the Richter scale (which also measures the energy released) but it's no longer used by scientists.

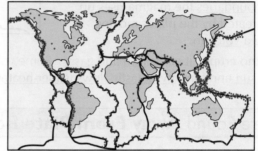

KEY
* Earthquakes
/ Plate margin

Earthquakes Occur at Various Depths

1) The focus of an earthquake is the point in the Earth where the earthquake starts. This can be at the Earth's surface, or anywhere up to 700 km below the surface.

2) Shallow-focus earthquakes are caused by tectonic plates moving at or near the surface. They have a focus between 0 km and 70 km below the Earth's surface.

3) Deep-focus earthquakes are caused by crust that has previously been subducted into the mantle (e.g. at convergent plate boundaries) moving towards the centre of the Earth, heating up or decomposing. They have a focus between 70 km and 700 km below the Earth's surface.

4) In general, deeper earthquakes do less damage at the surface than shallower earthquakes. Shock waves from deeper earthquakes have to travel through more rock to reach the surface, which reduces their power (and the amount of shaking) when they reach the surface.

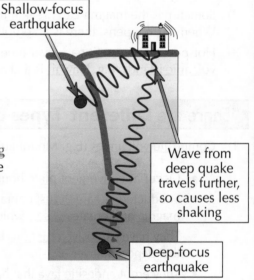

Shallow-focus earthquake

Wave from deep quake travels further, so causes less shaking

Deep-focus earthquake

Earthquakes can Cause Tsunamis

1) Tsunamis are a series of enormous waves caused when huge amounts of water get displaced.

2) Underwater earthquakes cause the seabed to move, which displaces water. Waves spread out from the epicentre of the earthquake (the point on the Earth's surface that's straight above the focus).

3) The depth of an earthquake affects the size of a tsunami — shallow-focus earthquakes displace more water because they're closer to the Earth's surface. This increases the size of a tsunami.

4) The waves travel very fast in deep water so they can hit the shore without much warning. This means they can cause a high death toll.

Shallow-focus earthquakes usually do the most damage

I'd better say this now... don't be put off by maps like the one at the top of the page — you won't ever have to draw them in your exam. But you should know where earthquakes happen and why, so have another read of this page.

Management of Tectonic Hazards

Plenty of people live in areas affected by tectonic hazards, so they need ways to manage them.

There are Methods for Predicting Tectonic Hazards

Earthquakes

1) Earthquakes cannot be reliably predicted, but scientists can still monitor certain signs that could indicate that an earthquake is likely.

2) Lasers can be used to detect the movement of tectonic plates before an earthquake.

3) Vibrations in the Earth's crust can be monitored using seismometers. If vibrations increase, it could mean there's going to be an earthquake.

4) Scientists can measure gases (e.g. radon) that escape from cracks in the crust just before an earthquake.

5) Rocks will crack and expand because of the increased pressure just before an earthquake.

Volcanoes

1) Volcanic eruptions can be predicted if the volcano is well-monitored to look for the tell-tale signs that come before a volcanic eruption.

2) Things such as tiny earthquakes and changes in the shape of the volcano (e.g. bulges in the land where magma has built up under it) all mean an eruption is likely.

3) Thermal imaging cameras can be used to detect changes in temperature around the volcano. Temperatures increase before an eruption.

4) Scientists can analyse the gases escaping from a volcano. Volcanoes emit lots of sulfurous gases before an eruption.

Long-Term Planning helps to Prepare a Country for Tectonic Hazards

Wealthier, more developed countries can plan for tectonic hazards to help reduce the impacts:

1) Emergency services can train and prepare for disasters, e.g. by practising rescuing people from collapsed buildings or setting up shelters. This will reduce the number of people killed.

2) Buildings can be designed to withstand earthquakes, e.g. by using strong materials like reinforced concrete or building special foundations that absorb an earthquake's energy.

3) People can be educated so that they know what to do if an earthquake or eruption happens.

4) Governments can plan evacuation routes to get people out of dangerous areas quickly and safely in case of an earthquake or volcanic eruption. This reduces the number of people killed or injured by things like fires, pyroclastic flows or mudflows.

5) Emergency supplies like blankets, clean water and food can be stockpiled. If a natural hazard is predicted the stockpiles can be moved close to areas likely to be affected.

Short-Term Relief is Needed After a Disaster

Short-term relief deals with the immediate impacts of a tectonic hazard.
Well-prepared countries are better able to:

1) Provide food, drink and shelter to help the evacuated people.

2) Treat people who have been injured (e.g. from falling debris) to prevent more deaths.

3) Recover dead bodies to prevent the spread of disease.

4) Rescue people who have been trapped (e.g. in collapsed buildings) or cut off by damage to roads or bridges.

5) Provide temporary supplies of gas, electricity and communications systems if regular supplies have been damaged.

Predicting a volcanic eruption gives people time to evacuate

Being able to predict and plan for tectonic hazards can save lives. As a general rule of thumb, the more wealthy and developed a country is, the better its long-term planning and ability to provide short-term relief will be.

Tectonic Hazards

And you thought I'd forgotten all about the real-world examples.

Some Countries are **More Prepared** than Others

1) Preparedness for tectonic hazards is different in countries of contrasting wealth and development.
2) Japan (a developed country) and Pakistan (a developing country) have a long history of earthquakes, and both countries have different levels of preparedness.

	Japan	Pakistan
Prediction	• The Japan Meteorological Agency (JMA) and local governments monitor seismic activity all over the country. • If an earthquake is detected, people are warned immediately.	• Up until recently, there wasn't extensive monitoring of seismic activity in Pakistan. • This means earthquakes could strike without warning.
Preparation	• Strict building laws help prevent major damage during an earthquake. • Buildings are reinforced with steel frames to prevent them from collapsing. • High-rise buildings have deep foundations with shock absorbers to reduce vibrations and shaking in the building. • Japan has early warning systems to alert residents to earthquakes and tsunamis. • High-speed 'bullet' trains automatically brake in the event of an earthquake to stop them derailing. • Automatic alarms stop mechanical equipment to alert workers and prevent injuries.	• As a developing country, Pakistan doesn't have access to the same building materials or technologies as Japan. • Many buildings are constructed using wood and cement, which are easily destroyed during earthquakes. • Up until recently, building laws didn't include measures of protection against earthquake damage. Even now, they're often ignored when constructing new buildings. • Poor communication networks make it difficult to alert the population.
Long-Term Planning	• Japan's population is educated on being prepared for earthquakes, e.g. Disaster Prevention Day is an annual nationwide drill to practise evacuations in the event of an earthquake. • Schools carry out drills to teach children what to do if there's an earthquake. • People living in coastal communities practise getting to higher ground or emergency bunkers in the event of a tsunami.	• There are lots of poor, remote settlements in Pakistan that have no education programme for teaching people what to do if there's an earthquake. • Planning evacuations is difficult because there are very few roads and poor communications.

Recent Earthquakes have tested their **Preparedness**

Japan

1) On 11th March 2011, a powerful earthquake struck north-east Japan.
2) It measured 9.0 on the moment magnitude scale and triggered a tsunami that overwhelmed the coast and inland areas.
3) Japanese scientists had predicted a smaller earthquake to hit the north of the country, but an earthquake of this magnitude was unexpected.

Pakistan

1) On 8th October 2005, Kashmir, Pakistan was struck by a major earthquake.
2) It measured 7.6 on the moment magnitude scale, causing landslides, rockfalls and huge amounts of destruction.
3) Although scientists monitor seismic activity in the area, the earthquake was unpredicted.

Tectonic Hazards

Both Earthquakes had Major Impacts

The primary impacts of an earthquake are the immediate impacts of the ground shaking.

Primary Impacts

Japan

- Thousands of buildings were damaged.
- The earthquake caused severe liquefaction (where waterlogged soil behaves like a liquid). This caused many buildings to tilt and sink into the ground.

Pakistan

- The Pakistan earthquake caused around 80 000 deaths, mostly from collapsed buildings.
- Tens of thousands of people were injured.
- Hundreds of thousands of buildings were damaged or destroyed, including whole villages.
- Around 3 million people were made homeless.
- Water pipelines and electricity lines were broken, cutting off supply.

The secondary impacts happen later on, often as a result of the primary impacts, e.g. landslides and tsunamis.

Secondary Impacts

- The earthquake triggered a tsunami which killed thousands of people.
- Hundreds of thousands of buildings were completely destroyed. Over 230 000 people were made homeless.
- The tsunami cut off the power supplies to the Fukushima nuclear power plant, causing a meltdown.
- Road and rail networks suffered severe damage, e.g. 325 km of railway tracks were washed away.

- Landslides buried buildings and people. They also blocked access roads and cut off telephone lines.
- Diarrhoea and other diseases spread due to lack of clean water.
- Freezing winter conditions shortly after the earthquake caused more casualties and meant rescue and rebuilding operations were difficult.

Short-Term Relief was Slow to Reach People in Pakistan

Short-Term Relief

- International aid and search and rescue teams were brought in.
- Rescue workers and soldiers were sent to help deal with the aftermath.
- Transport and communications were restored a couple of weeks after the earthquake.
- Power supplies were restored in the weeks following the earthquake.

- The Pakistani army was initially slow to respond to the disaster.
- Help from India was refused because of political tensions between Pakistan and India.
- Help didn't reach many areas for days or weeks, and many people had to be rescued by hand without any equipment or help from emergency services.
- Tents, blankets and medical supplies were distributed, although it took up to a month for them to reach most areas.

Long-Term Planning in Japan was Very Effective

Effects of Long-Term Planning

- The Japanese authorities gave an advance warning of the earthquake and the tsunami, which gave people time to evacuate and get to higher ground.
- Despite very strong shaking in Tokyo, not a single building collapsed thanks to buildings designed to prevent earthquake damage.
- Nobody died on the bullet train network because of the automatic braking systems.

- Fault lines in the Himalayas were poorly monitored, which meant the Pakistan earthquake was unpredicted.
- The absence of building laws meant buildings weren't reinforced and were extremely vulnerable to damage from earthquake shaking.
- Most buildings had been constructed using poor quality materials, e.g. cement made from sand which crumbled during the earthquake.

EXAM TIP

Responses to tectonic hazards are more effective in wealthy areas

Whether you use these examples or the ones you were taught in class, learn this stuff so you're prepared for an exam question asking you to contrast the responses to tectonic hazards in different countries.

Worked Exam Questions

Working through exam questions is a great way of testing what you've learned and practising for the exam.
This worked example will give you an idea of the kind of answers examiners are looking for.

1   Study **Figure 1**, a diagram showing the Earth's structure.

Figure 1

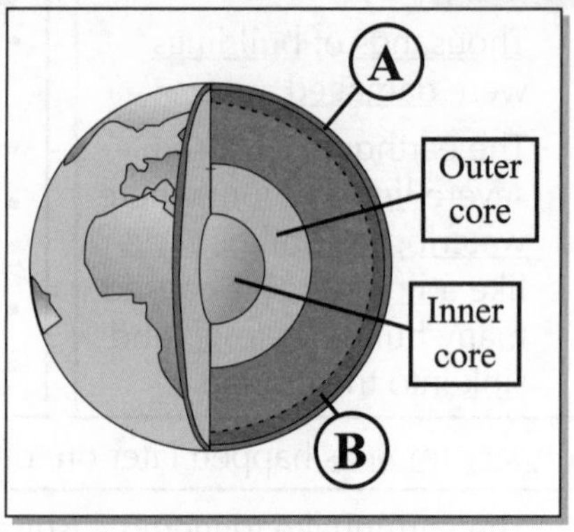

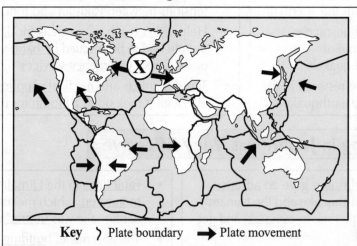

a)   What feature is labelled A in **Figure 1**?

    A   Crust ●

    B   Plate boundary ○

    C   Mantle ○

    D   Magma ○

    [1]

b)   Name and describe the feature labelled B in **Figure 1**.

    B is the asthenosphere. It is semi-molten rock that can flow.

    [2]

c)   Which statement below best describes the difference between the inner core and the outer core?

    A   The inner core is liquid; the outer core is solid. ○

    B   The inner core is solid; the outer core is liquid. ●

    C   The outer core is divided into tectonic plates; the inner core is not. ○

    D   The inner core is divided into tectonic plates; the outer core is not. ○

    [1]

d)   Study **Figure 2**, which shows the Earth's tectonic plates.

Figure 2

Name the type of plate boundary labelled X in **Figure 2** and explain why new crust forms there.

    Plate boundary X is a divergent plate boundary. As the two plates move away from each other,

    magma rises from the mantle to fill the gap. The magma then cools, creating new crust.

    [3]

    [Total 7 marks]

Exam Questions

1 Earthquakes occur at tectonic plate boundaries.

a) Explain how earthquakes are caused at convergent plate boundaries.

....

....

....

....

[3]

b) Which of the following best describes deep-focus earthquakes?

    A   They do more damage than shallow-focus earthquakes.   ◯

    B   Their focus is on or near the Earth's surface.   ◯

    C   They have a lower magnitude than shallow-focus earthquakes.   ◯

    D   They are caused by subducted crust moving towards the centre of the Earth.   ◯

[1]

c) Explain how shallow-focus earthquakes cause tsunamis.

....

....

....

[2]

[Total 6 marks]

2 Study **Figure 1**, which shows a cross-section through a shield volcano.

a) Explain how the volcano gets its characteristic shape.

....

....

....

....

[2]

Figure 1

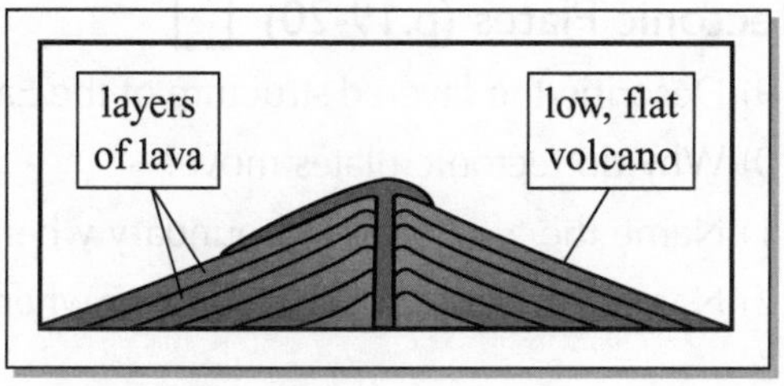

layers of lava

low, flat volcano

b) Compare the characteristics of shield volcanoes and composite volcanoes.

....

....

....

....

[3]

[Total 5 marks]

Revision Summary

That wraps up <u>Topic 1</u> — time to put yourself to the test and find out <u>how much you really know</u>.
- Try these questions and <u>tick off each one</u> when you <u>get it right</u>.
- When you've done <u>all the questions</u> under a heading and are <u>completely happy</u> with it, tick it off.

Global Atmospheric Circulation (p.2-3) ☑
1) How does global atmospheric circulation lead to high and low pressure belts? ☑
2) Describe how ocean currents transfer heat around the Earth. ☑
3) How do high and low pressure belts create climatic zones? ☑

Climate Change (p.4-8) ☑
4) Describe how climate has changed from the beginning of the Quaternary period to the present day. ☑
5) Describe how asteroid collisions might cause climate change. ☑
6) List three other natural causes of climate change. ☑
7) List two useful sources of information about past climate. ☑
8) What is the greenhouse effect? ☑
9) Name two greenhouse gases. ☑
10) Give four ways that human activities increase the concentration of greenhouse gases in the atmosphere. ☑
11) Give three pieces of evidence for human activity causing climate change. ☑
12) Give two possible future impacts of climate change on people. ☑
13) Explain why it is difficult to predict the impacts of climate change. ☑

Tropical Cyclones (p.11-16) ☑
14) What conditions are required for a tropical cyclone to develop? ☑
15) What can cause a tropical cyclone to dissipate? ☑
16) Describe two impacts of tropical cyclones on people. ☑
17) What can make a country physically vulnerable to the impacts of tropical cyclones? ☑
18) Give three strategies that are used to prepare for and respond to tropical cyclones. ☑

Tectonic Plates (p.19-20) ☑
19) Describe the layered structure of the Earth. ☑
20) Why do tectonic plates move? ☑
21) Name the type of plate boundary where two plates of continental crust are moving towards each other. ☑
22) Name the type of plate boundary where two plates are moving sideways against each other. ☑

Tectonic Hazards (p.21-25) ☑
23) How do volcanoes form at convergent plate boundaries? ☑
24) What is a hotspot? ☑
25) What causes earthquakes? ☑
26) Describe how scientists can try to predict earthquakes. ☑
27) For one developed and one developing country that you have studied:
    a) Compare the secondary impacts of tectonic hazards sthat occurred in each of the countries. ☑
    b) Compare the effectiveness of the long-term planning for tectonic hazards in each of the countries. ☑

Measuring Development

This topic is a little <u>tricky</u> — but this <u>page</u> will set you up well, so make sure you take a <u>good look</u> at it.

Development is when a **Country is Improving**

When a country <u>develops</u> it basically gets <u>better</u> for the people living there.
There are <u>different aspects</u> to development:

- <u>Economic</u> — progress in <u>economic growth</u>, e.g. how <u>wealthy</u> a country is, its level of <u>industrialisation</u> and use of <u>technology</u>.
- <u>Social</u> — improvement in people's <u>standard of living</u>, e.g. <u>better health care</u> and access to <u>clean water</u>.
- <u>Political</u> — having a <u>stable</u> political system with <u>institutions</u> that can <u>meet the needs</u> of society.

There Are Loads of **Measures of Development**

Development is <u>pretty hard to measure</u> because it <u>includes so many things</u>. But you can <u>compare</u> the development of different countries using 'measures of development'.

Name	What it is	A measure of...	As a country develops, it gets...
<u>Gross Domestic Product (GDP)</u>	The <u>total value</u> of <u>goods</u> and <u>services</u> a <u>country produces</u> in a <u>year</u>. It's often given in US$.	Wealth	Higher
<u>GDP per capita</u>	The GDP <u>divided</u> by the <u>population</u> of a <u>country</u>. It's often given in <u>US$</u> and is sometimes called <u>GDP per head</u>.	Wealth	Higher
<u>Gross National Income (GNI)</u> and <u>GNI per capita</u>	The <u>total value</u> of <u>goods</u> and <u>services</u> produced by a <u>country</u> in a <u>year</u>, including income from <u>overseas</u>. It's often given in <u>US$</u>. <u>GNI per capita</u> is the GNI <u>divided</u> by the <u>population</u> of a <u>country</u>.	Wealth	Higher
<u>Birth rate</u>	The number of <u>live babies born per thousand</u> of the population <u>per year</u>.	Women's rights	Lower
<u>Death rate</u>	The number of <u>deaths per thousand</u> of the population <u>per year</u>.	Health	Lower
<u>Fertility rate</u>	The average number of <u>births per woman</u>.	Women's rights	Lower
<u>Infant mortality rate</u>	The number of <u>babies</u> who <u>die under 1 year old</u>, <u>per thousand babies born</u>.	Health care	Lower
<u>Maternal mortality rate</u>	The number of <u>women</u> who <u>die</u> due to <u>pregnancy</u> related problems <u>per hundred thousand</u> live births.	Health care	Lower
<u>Doctors per 1000 of population</u>	The number of <u>working doctors per thousand</u> of the population.	Access to health care	Higher
<u>Gini coefficient</u>	A measure of <u>economic inequality</u>. Countries are given a score between <u>0</u> (<u>equal</u>) and <u>1</u> (total <u>inequality</u>).	Inequality	Lower
<u>Gender Inequality Index</u>	A number that's calculated using data on e.g. <u>women's education</u>, access to <u>jobs</u>, <u>political rights</u> and <u>health</u> during <u>pregnancy</u>. The <u>higher</u> the score, the <u>more inequality</u>.	Women's rights	Lower
<u>Human Development Index (HDI)</u>	This is a number that's calculated using <u>life expectancy</u>, <u>education level</u> (e.g. average number of years of schooling) and <u>income per head</u>. Every country has an HDI value between <u>0</u> (<u>least developed</u>) and <u>1</u> (<u>most developed</u>).	Lots of things	Higher
<u>Corruption Perceptions Index (CPI)</u>	A measure of the level of <u>corruption</u> that is believed to exist in the public sector on a scale of <u>1-100</u>. The <u>lower</u> the score, the <u>more corruption</u>.	Corruption	Higher

There are lots of ways of measuring development

These measures of development could well come up in the exam, so make sure you know what each of them means and whether it gets higher or lower as a country develops. In fact, shut the book and test yourself now.

Measuring Development

Single measures of development (e.g. GDP) can be useful, but sometimes it makes sense to look at more than one.

Composite Indicators use Multiple Measures of Development

1) Single indicators can be misleading if they are used on their own because, as a country develops, some aspects develop before others. So it might seem that a country's more developed than it actually is.

2) Using a composite indicator of development, where more than one measure is used (i.e. wealth and something else) avoids these problems. The Human Development Index is a composite indicator.

Development affects Fertility and Mortality Rates

1) Countries can be classified based on their level of development.

2) Developed countries, e.g. the UK, have very high human development.
Emerging countries, e.g. India, have medium to high human development.
Developing countries, e.g. Chad, have low human development.

3) A country's level of development (particularly its birth and death rates) affects the growth and age structure of its population.

	Chad	India	UK
Human Development Index (2014)	0.392	0.609	0.907
Fertility rate (per woman)	4.45	2.5	1.9
Birth rate (per 1000)	36.1	19.3	12.1
Death rate (per 1000)	14	7.3	9.4
Maternal mortality rate (per 100 000 live births)	856	174	9
Infant mortality rate (per 1000 babies born)	87	40.5	4.3

Developing Countries have High Birth and Death Rates

1) Developing countries have higher fertility and birth rates because there's no use of contraception. People also have lots of children because poor health care means that many infants die.

2) The death rate is also high due to poor health care, and life expectancy is low (few people reach old age).

3) This means that there are lots more children than older people — population pyramids for developing countries have a very wide base, which rapidly narrows.

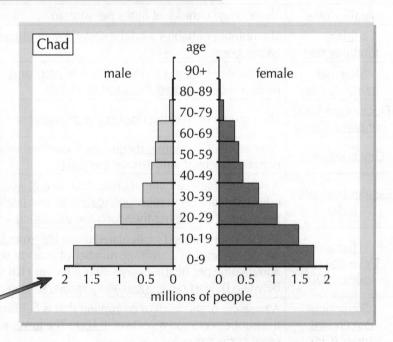

A country's demographic data is related to its level of development

'Demographic data' just means all the measures to do with a country's population size and structure — so it includes birth, death and fertility rates, and the infant and maternal mortality rates. As a country becomes more developed, its population structure changes significantly due to changes in these factors, as you'll see over the page.

Measuring Development

Now that you've learned about what the <u>population structure</u> looks like in a <u>developing</u> country, it's time to see what it looks like for an <u>emerging</u> or <u>developed</u> country.

Emerging Countries Have **Falling Fertility Rates**

1) Emerging countries see their <u>fertility rates fall</u> rapidly as women have a more <u>equal</u> place in society and a <u>better education</u>.

2) The use of <u>contraception increases</u> and more women <u>work</u> instead of having children.

3) <u>Health care improves</u> so <u>life expectancy increases</u>.

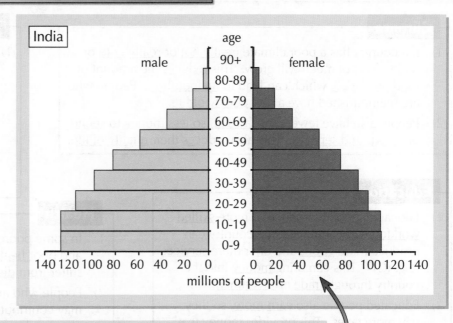

4) This means that there are more people of <u>working age</u> and there is a <u>lower proportion</u> of <u>children</u> — the <u>base</u> of the pyramid starts to <u>narrow</u> and the <u>top</u> starts to <u>widen</u>.

Developed Countries Have **More Older People**

1) In developed countries <u>fertility rates</u> are <u>low</u> because people want <u>possessions</u> and a <u>high quality of life</u>, and may have <u>dependent elderly relatives</u>, so there is <u>less money available</u> for having children.

2) <u>Health care</u> is <u>good</u>, so the <u>death rate</u> is <u>low</u> and <u>life expectancy</u> is <u>high</u>.

3) This means there are lots <u>more older people</u> and the proportion of <u>children decreases</u> — the top of the pyramid <u>widens</u> further and the <u>base</u> gets <u>narrower</u>, so the <u>middle bulges</u> out.

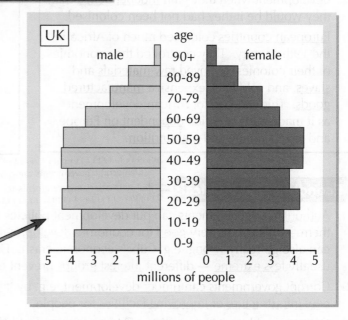

You need to be able to interpret population pyramids

In your exam, you might be given a country's population pyramid and have to explain what it tells you about the level of development. Think carefully about its shape. The bottom part of the graph represents how many young people there are — if this is narrower than the middle, it shows that the birth rate has been falling, resulting in fewer children. This suggests the country is at a high level of development.

Causes of Global Inequalities

You need to know the <u>reasons why</u> there are <u>global inequalities</u> — i.e. why <u>countries differ</u> in how <u>developed</u> they are. There are a fair few to get through, but take it steady and you'll be okay...

Lots of **Factors** can Affect **How Developed** a Country is

Climate

1) If a country has a poor climate (<u>really hot</u> or <u>really cold</u> or <u>really dry</u>) not much will grow. This <u>reduces</u> the amount of <u>food produced</u>, which can lead to <u>malnutrition</u>. People who are malnourished have a <u>low quality of life</u>.

2) People also have <u>fewer crops to sell</u>, so <u>less money</u> to <u>spend</u> on <u>goods and services</u>. This also <u>reduces</u> their <u>quality of life</u>.

Topography (shape of land)

1) If the land in a country is <u>steep</u>, then it <u>won't</u> produce a lot of <u>food</u>. This has the same effect as a <u>poor climate</u> (see left).

2) <u>Steep land</u> can also make it difficult to develop <u>infrastructure</u>, e.g. roads, power lines etc. This can <u>limit trade</u> and make it hard to provide <u>basic services</u>.

Education

1) Educating people produces a more <u>skilled workforce</u>, meaning that the country can produce more <u>goods</u> and offer more <u>services</u> (e.g. ICT). This can bring <u>money</u> into the country through <u>trade</u> or <u>investment</u>.

2) Educated people also <u>earn more</u>, so they pay more <u>taxes</u>. This provides <u>money</u> that the country can spend on <u>development</u>.

Health

1) In some poorer countries, <u>lack of clean water</u> and <u>poor health care</u> mean that many people suffer from <u>diseases</u> such as <u>malaria</u> and <u>cholera</u>.

2) People who are ill are <u>less able</u> to <u>work</u> and so may contribute less to the <u>economy</u>. They may also need <u>expensive medicine</u> or <u>health care</u>.

3) Lower economic <u>contribution</u> and higher <u>spending</u> on health care means that there's <u>less money</u> available to spend on <u>development</u>.

Colonialism

1) Countries that were <u>colonised</u> (<u>ruled</u> by a <u>foreign country</u>) are often at a <u>lower</u> level of development when they gain <u>independence</u> than they <u>would be</u> if they had <u>not been colonised</u>.

2) <u>European countries</u> colonised much of Africa in the 19th century. They controlled the economies of their colonies, <u>removed raw materials</u> and <u>slaves</u>, and sold back expensive <u>manufactured goods</u>. This was <u>bad</u> for African development as it made parts of Africa <u>dependent</u> on Europe, and led to <u>famine</u> and <u>malnutrition</u>.

Neo-colonialism

1) After colonies gained their <u>independence</u>, <u>richer</u> countries <u>continued</u> to <u>control</u> them <u>indirectly</u>.

2) For example, some transnational corporations (TNCs) <u>exploit</u> the <u>cheap labour</u> and <u>raw materials</u> of <u>poorer</u> countries (see p. 37).

3) <u>International organisations</u> sometimes offer <u>conditional loans</u>, which mean <u>poorer</u> countries have to <u>develop</u> in the way their <u>donors want</u> them to.

Democratic governments are chosen by the people but authoritarian governments tell people what to do.

Economic and Political

1) <u>Authoritarian</u> governments can put development policies in place <u>without worrying</u> about anyone <u>stopping</u> them — this can be very <u>good</u> for economic <u>development</u>, e.g. the rapid growth of China, but things can also go really <u>wrong</u>, e.g. Cuba's economic crash. Development under <u>democratic</u> governments is usually <u>less extreme</u> — different <u>interest groups</u> prevent either <u>huge growth</u> or <u>economic collapse</u>.

2) <u>Corrupt</u> governments can <u>hinder</u> development, e.g. by <u>taking money</u> that's intended for building <u>new infrastructure</u> or <u>improving facilities</u> for people.

3) Countries with good <u>international relations</u> are more likely to get good <u>trade agreements</u>. They can also get <u>loans</u> from international organisations to invest in <u>development projects</u>.

EXAM TIP

Learn these causes of global inequalities

If you get a long answer question about the factors that affect development, scribble down a quick plan with the key points before starting your answer — examiners are looking for a logical structure.

Consequences of Global Inequalities

Countries have a tough time trying to develop. And things don't look great if you can't make it off the bottom of the pile either. Inequalities affect all of us though — just some more than others...

Uneven Development Leads to Inequalities Between Countries

Wealth is not spread evenly across all countries in the world. People in the richest 20% of the world's countries (the 5th quintile) have 70.1% of the world's wealth (GDP per capita), whereas people in the poorest 20% (the 1st quintile) have just 1.0% of the world's wealth.

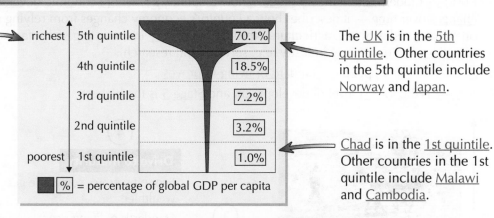

The UK is in the 5th quintile. Other countries in the 5th quintile include Norway and Japan.

Chad is in the 1st quintile. Other countries in the 1st quintile include Malawi and Cambodia.

richest   5th quintile   70.1%
           4th quintile   18.5%
           3rd quintile   7.2%
           2nd quintile   3.2%
poorest   1st quintile   1.0%

% = percentage of global GDP per capita

Global Inequalities have Social and Political Consequences

Differences in wealth can make things difficult for poorer people and developing countries:

Education

1) Poorer countries can't afford to invest as much in education as richer countries.

2) Poorer people may not be able to afford school fees or children may have to work to support their families instead of attending school.

3) Lack of education means people can't get better-paid, skilled jobs in the future, so the cycle of poverty continues.

Health

1) People in developing countries are at higher risk for many diseases than people in developed countries leading to lower life expectancies.

2) Infant mortality is also much higher in developing countries.

3) Poorer people find it harder to get quality health care and healthy food.

Politics

1) Inequalities can increase political instability, crime and discontent in poorer countries.

2) This means civil wars are more likely in developing countries. Conflict can increase inequality — poverty increases as money is spent on fighting rather than development.

3) Developing countries are often dependent on richer countries. This means they have less influence over regional and global decisions.

Global Inequalities also Cause Environmental Problems

1) Economic development leads to more consumption of food, water and energy as people get wealthier. This puts pressure on scarce resources and can threaten ecosystems, e.g. as more land is built on.

2) Industrialisation leads to increased air, water and land pollution. The release of greenhouse gases enhances the greenhouse effect, contributing to climate change. Waste is dumped in landfill sites and untreated sewage, chemical waste and runoff from farmland ends up in rivers and lakes.

3) Many developed countries have factories in developing countries or buy goods that are produced there. This means that local pollution levels are often much higher in developing countries.

4) Poorer people can also be trapped in a cycle of environmental damage, e.g. if they can't afford fuel they have to collect firewood from their local environment which can lead to deforestation.

Global inequalities have major consequences for people and the environment

There are huge differences between the world's poorest and richest countries. Make sure you can list some examples of social, political and environmental problems that have come about as a result of uneven development.

Theories of Development

Rostow and Frank came up with theories about how countries develop (or don't develop, in Frank's case).

Rostow's Theory shows Five Stages of Economic Development

1) Rostow's modernisation theory predicts how a country's level of economic development changes over time — it describes how a country's economy changes from relying mostly on primary industry (e.g. agriculture), through secondary industry (e.g. manufacturing goods) to tertiary and quaternary industry (e.g. services and research).

2) At the same time, people's standard of living improves.

3) Stage 1 is the lowest level of development and Stage 5 is the highest.

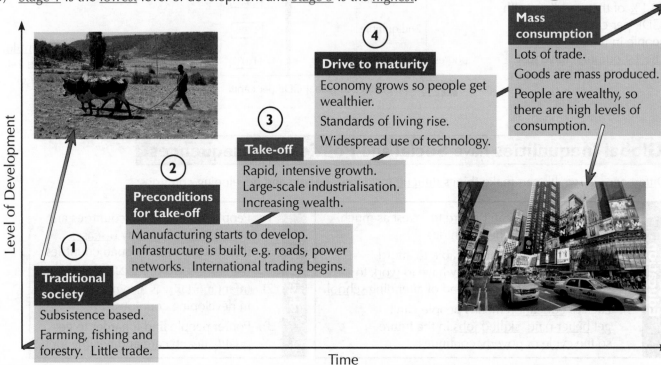

Level of Development (vertical axis) / **Time** (horizontal axis)

1 — Traditional society
Subsistence based. Farming, fishing and forestry. Little trade.

2 — Preconditions for take-off
Manufacturing starts to develop. Infrastructure is built, e.g. roads, power networks. International trading begins.

3 — Take-off
Rapid, intensive growth. Large-scale industrialisation. Increasing wealth.

4 — Drive to maturity
Economy grows so people get wealthier. Standards of living rise. Widespread use of technology.

5 — Mass consumption
Lots of trade. Goods are mass produced. People are wealthy, so there are high levels of consumption.

Frank's Dependency Theory says Poor Countries Rely On Rich Countries

1) Frank's dependency theory was developed as an alternative to Rostow's model to explain why some countries are more developed than others.

2) The theory suggests that some poorer, weaker countries (the periphery) remain poor because they are dependent on the core countries (those that are richer and more powerful).

3) It argues that the exploitation that started during the colonial period has continued — this is neo-colonialism (see p. 32). The richer, former colonial countries continue to dominate the trading system even though the colonised countries have gained independence — richer countries continue to take advantage of the cheap raw materials and labour available in poorer countries.

4) For example, poorer countries have been encouraged to plant crops for export and produce primary products to sell cheaply to richer countries. This means they need to import manufactured goods at higher cost from richer countries to provide for their own population. This traps them in poverty and makes them dependent on the economy of the core countries.

5) Richer countries may also exploit poor countries by interfering in local politics in poorer countries or loaning them money with high rates of interest, leading to large debts.

6) This means that poor countries remain dependent on richer countries. Some people think that as long as they remain part of the capitalist (free trade, profit-seeking) system, these countries can't develop.

REVISION TIP

Neither of these theories is perfect

See if you can come up with a way to summarise Frank's dependency theory in five phrases or sentences. Then make sure you spend plenty of time revising the differences between the two theories on this page.

Worked Exam Questions

Here are some handy worked exam questions to get you in the exam mood. Use them wisely.

---

1 Study **Figure 1**, an article about Libya written in 2016.

Figure 1

Libya is the fourth largest country in Africa. It's located on the northern edge of the Sahara desert. More than 90% of the country is a desert or semi-desert environment.

Libya was an Italian colony for much of the early 20th century until it was captured and occupied by Allied forces during the Second World War. Libya declared independence in December 1951.

Since gaining independence, Libya has suffered from periods of poor international relations and conflict. It currently has a medium level of development.

a) Which of the following statements about political influences on development is true?

    A   Authoritarian governments often have better international relations, increasing development. ◯

    B   Democratic governments usually have poor trade links, so there will be less money to spend on development. ◯

    C   Countries with good international relations can get loans from international organisations to invest in development projects. ⬤

    D   Corrupt governments take money that isn't theirs to spend on development. ◯

[1]

b) Explain how being a former colony may affect a country's economic development.

Countries that were colonised often have a lower level of development when they gain independence than they would if they had not been colonised. This is because colonisers control the economies of their colonies, e.g. by exploiting raw materials.

[2]

c) Using **Figure 1**, explain how climate may have affected the level of development of Libya.

Libya has a very dry climate — more than 90% of the country is desert or semi-desert. This probably means that it can't grow much food. This can lead to malnutrition, which reduces people's quality of life. With fewer crops to sell, people have less money to spend on goods and services, which also reduces their quality of life.

[4]

d) State **one** other physical factor that can affect how developed a country is.

Topography

[1]

[Total 8 marks]

Exam Questions

1 Study **Figure 1**, which shows measures of development for Canada, Malaysia and Angola.

a) Explain how the differences in birth rates shown in **Figure 1** could be a consequence of differences in the level of development.

Figure 1

	Canada	Malaysia	Angola
GNI per capita	$51 770	$11 120	$4800
Birth rate	10.28	19.71	38.78
Death rate	8.42	5.03	11.49
Infant mortality rate	4.65	13.27	78.26
Life expectancy	81.76	74.75	55.63
Literacy rate	97.1%	94.6%	71.1%
HDI value	0.913	0.779	0.532

....

....

....

....

....

[2]

b) Explain why the Human Development Index (HDI) values given in **Figure 1** may be a better measure of development than any of the other measures.

....

....

....

[2]

c) Explain **one** political indicator that can be used to determine the level of development in a country.

....

....

....

....

....

[3]

d) Explain which of the countries shown in **Figure 1** is the most developed.

....

....

....

....

....

[3]

[Total 10 marks]

Globalisation

Reducing global inequalities is a massive task. Let's start at the very beginning with some globalisation...

Globalisation is the Process of Countries Becoming More Integrated

1) Every country has its own political and economic systems as well as its own culture.

2) Globalisation is the process of all the world's systems and cultures becoming more integrated — it's the whole world coming together like a single community.

3) It happens because of the movement of money and people between countries, as well as businesses locating their operations and selling their products in more countries. Here are a few reasons why globalisation is increasing:

   - Improvements in ICT include e-mail, the internet, mobile phones and phone lines that can carry more information and faster. This has made it quicker and easier for businesses all over the world to communicate with each other.

   - Improvements in transport include more airports, high-speed trains and larger ships. This has made it quicker and easier for people all over the world to communicate with each other face to face. It's also made it easier for companies to get supplies and to distribute their products all over the world.

TNCs and Governments are Increasing Globalisation

TNCs

1) Transnational corporations (TNCs) are companies that produce products, sell products or are located in more than one country. For example, Sony is a TNC — it manufactures electronic products in China and Japan, and sells many of them in Europe and the USA.

2) TNCs increase globalisation by linking together countries through the production and sale of goods.

3) They also bring the culture from their country of origin to many different countries, e.g. McDonald's brings Western-style fast food to other countries.

4) TNCs also promote a culture of consumerism — people in developing and emerging countries see all the products that people in developed countries have, e.g. mobile phones and TVs, and want to have them too. This makes people's lifestyles more similar.

Governments

1) Free trade — governments increase globalisation by promoting free trade, e.g. reducing tariffs on goods. This means it's much easier to move goods, money and services between countries.

2) Investment — governments compete with each other to attract investment by TNCs. They think that TNCs will bring jobs, increase income from taxes and promote economic growth in their country.

3) Privatisation — governments hand over services and industries to private companies, e.g. in the UK, some rail services are now run by companies from the Netherlands, Germany and France.

Globalisation Benefits Some Countries More than Others

1) Some countries have benefited from globalisation, e.g. China, India, Brazil. This is because they have, e.g:

   - large, cheap workforces
   - governments open to foreign investment
   - less strict environmental, labour and planning laws
   - lots of cheap raw materials
   - reasonable infrastructure
   - available land

2) However, some people think that globalisation is increasing global inequality.

   - Free trade benefits richer countries — TNC profits normally return to their headquarters, which are often in developed countries, and poor countries can struggle to compete, i.e. produce cheaper goods.

   - Richer countries benefit from freer movement of labour — skilled workers are attracted by higher wages and better living conditions in richer countries, leading to a 'brain drain' in poorer countries.

Globalisation is increasing the amount of links between countries

Draw a rough outline of the UK, then take another look at this page and add a labelled arrow to your outline for everything that is increasing links between the UK and other countries across the world.

Reducing Global Inequalities

Strategies to help countries to develop can be divided into two categories, depending on who makes the decisions.

Development Strategies can be Top-Down or Bottom-Up

1) Some people are trying to decrease global inequalities by helping poor countries develop.

2) Development projects can include building schools to improve literacy rates, making dams to provide clean water or providing farming education and equipment to improve agriculture.

3) There are two different approaches to development strategies:

	Top-down approaches	Bottom-up approaches
Type of strategy	A government or large organisation, e.g. an inter-governmental organisation (IGO) (see p. 39) or transnational corporation (TNC) makes decisions about how to increase development and direct the project.	Local people and communities decide on ways to improve things for their own community. Non-governmental organisations (NGOs) are often involved (see p. 39).
Scale and aims	• Often used for large projects, e.g. dams for hydroelectric power (HEP) or irrigation schemes. • These aim to solve large scale problems and improve the lives of lots of people.	• Usually small-scale, e.g. building or maintaining a well in a village. • They often aim to improve the quality of life for the poorest and most vulnerable people in society.
Funding	• The projects are usually very expensive. • Some projects are funded by TNCs or governments from developed countries who will profit from the development, e.g. by selling the HEP produced. • Other projects may be funded by loans from international organisations, e.g. the World Bank or the International Monetary Fund (IMF). The money may have to be paid back later or the organisation may have conditions for lending the money, e.g. removing trade barriers.	• Projects are usually much cheaper. • Most money comes from charities, which often rely on donations from people in richer countries.
Technology	• The projects are often high-tech and energy intensive. The construction usually involves machinery and technology, which is often operated by skilled workers from developed countries rather than local people. • The recipient country becomes dependent on technology and workers from the donor country for operation and maintenance.	• Projects involve intermediate technology. • Local materials are used and local people are employed. This means people have the materials and skills to maintain the project.

For more on intermediate technology see next page.

Top-down schemes are often large-scale and expensive

Bottom-up approaches tend to be cheaper, but they might not make as big a difference as top-down strategies. Development's a complex matter with no easy solutions. There's more on the pros and cons of different approaches on the next page but, for now, focus on learning the differences between top-down and bottom-up strategies.

Reducing Global Inequalities

There are <u>lots</u> of different ways to help a country to <u>develop</u>, but none of them are <u>trouble-free</u>...

Approaches to **Development** Include **NGO-Led Intermediate Technology**...

1) <u>Non-governmental organisations</u> (<u>NGOs</u>) are not-for-profit groups which are <u>independent</u> from governments. They're often charities, e.g. the <u>British Red Cross</u> or <u>Oxfam</u>.

2) <u>NGO-led development projects</u> often involve the use of <u>intermediate technology</u>. This includes tools, machines and systems that are <u>simple to use</u>, <u>affordable</u> to buy or build and cheap to <u>maintain</u>.

Advantages

1) Projects are designed to <u>address</u> the <u>needs</u> of people <u>local</u> to where the projects are carried out.

2) <u>Locally available</u>, <u>cheap</u> materials are used so the community <u>isn't</u> dependent on <u>expensive imports</u>.

3) Projects are <u>labour intensive</u> — they create <u>jobs</u> for <u>local people</u>.

Disadvantages

1) Projects are often <u>small-scale</u>, so they may <u>not</u> benefit <u>everyone</u>.

2) Different organisations may <u>not work together</u>, so projects may be <u>inefficient</u>.

...IGO-Funded Large **Infrastructure**...

<u>Inter-governmental organisations</u> (<u>IGOs</u>), e.g. the World Bank, the International Monetary Fund (IMF) and the United Nations (UN), are made up of the <u>governments</u> of <u>several countries</u>.

Advantages

1) <u>IGOs</u> can afford to fund <u>large infrastructure</u> projects in <u>developing</u> and <u>emerging</u> countries.

2) Projects can improve the country's <u>economy</u>, helping with <u>long-term development</u>, e.g. HEP stations may <u>promote industry</u>, which <u>provides jobs</u> and <u>boosts</u> the <u>economy</u>.

3) Projects can also <u>improve</u> people's <u>quality of life</u>, as people have better access to <u>reliable power</u>, <u>clean water</u> etc.

Disadvantages

1) Large projects are often <u>expensive</u> and the country may have to <u>pay back the money</u> (if it's a loan). This can lead to lots of <u>debt</u>.

2) They <u>may not benefit everyone</u> — e.g. HEP may not supply power to remote areas.

3) If governments are <u>corrupt</u>, they may use the <u>money</u> for their <u>own purposes</u>.

4) Projects tend to be <u>energy intensive</u> — they use <u>scarce resources</u>, <u>release greenhouse gases</u> and lead to <u>loss</u> of <u>ecosystems</u>.

...and **Investment** by **TNCs**

<u>TNCs</u> are also involved in <u>development</u> through <u>investment</u> in the <u>countries</u> they operate in.

Advantages

1) TNCs provide <u>employment</u> for <u>local</u> people.

2) More <u>companies</u> mean a <u>greater income</u> from <u>taxes</u> for the <u>host</u> country.

3) Some TNCs run programmes to <u>help development</u>.

4) TNCs may also <u>invest</u> in <u>infrastructure</u>, <u>improving roads</u>, <u>basic services</u> and <u>communication links</u> in the area. This may improve the <u>quality of life</u> of local people.

Disadvantages

1) Some <u>profits leave</u> the <u>host</u> country.

2) TNCs can cause <u>environmental problems</u> — <u>developing</u> countries may have <u>less strict environmental regulations</u>, leading to e.g. the dumping of <u>toxic waste</u>.

3) TNCs may <u>move around</u> the country to take advantage of <u>local tax breaks</u>, leaving people <u>jobless</u> as the company moves on.

All approaches to development have both advantages and disadvantages

Different projects might benefit different people, and some might cause financial problems. Try covering each section of this page and drawing a table of the pros and cons for each type of approach.

CASE STUDY

Development in India

India is an emerging country with a huge population and lots of potential.

India is an Emerging Country in Southern Asia

1) India is a rapidly developing emerging country. It has the second largest population in the world (approx. 1.3 billion) and is still growing.

2) India was a British colony until 1947, but now has its own democratically elected government.

3) India has a rich and diverse cultural background. It's renowned for its production of 'Bollywood' films, which are exported worldwide.

4) India has a beautiful and varied landscape, including areas of mountains, desert, great plains and a large coastline, making it an attractive tourist destination.

5) The large coastline also allows the development of ports, such as Mumbai, increasing trade.

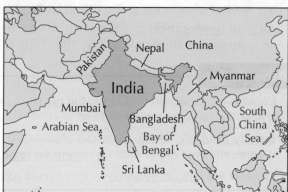

India's Economy has Changed a lot Since 1990

1) India is getting rapidly wealthier.

2) India has a medium level of development (HDI = 0.61). There are large inequalities — some people are very wealthy, but the majority are poor.

	1990	2015
GDP ($ trillion)	0.3	2.1
GNI per capita ($)	390	1600

3) Economic development has changed the importance of the different economic sectors. Primary and secondary industry (see page 49) employ 77% of the workforce, but contribute less than half of India's GDP. India's tertiary service and high-tech quaternary industries have grown hugely in recent years, now accounting for 45% of GDP.

4) These changes have affected what India imports and exports.

	1990	2015
Exports	Low-value manufactured goods, e.g. clothing, and primary products, e.g. tea	High-value manufactured goods, e.g. machinery
Imports	Manufactured goods, e.g. machinery, chemicals	Crude oil (for transport and industry)

Globalisation has Increased Development

1) More than 50% of all Indian people now own a mobile phone. This has enabled lots of people to start their own small businesses, giving them a larger income.

2) India has 12 major ports and more than 20 international airports. It also has an extensive rail network, carrying 8 billion passengers a year and almost 3 million tonnes of freight per day. This makes it easier to transport goods, so trade can increase, and TNCs are more likely to invest.

3) Some large TNCs, e.g. Microsoft®, Nokia, Unilever and Coca-Cola®, outsource some manufacturing and IT to India. These bring jobs, greater income from taxes and the latest technology and business practices.

India has attracted many large transnational corporations

Over the last few decades, India has experienced a lot of changes to its economy — it wasn't long ago that its main imports and exports were completely different. The tertiary and quaternary industries are growing more and more.

Development in India

Government Policies have also Helped to Increase Development

1) In 1991, India received US $2.2 billion in <u>aid</u> from the <u>IMF</u> in exchange for the government <u>changing</u> its <u>economic policies</u>, e.g. by <u>reducing tariffs</u> (extra taxes) on imported goods.

2) In 2009 India made primary education <u>free</u> and <u>compulsory</u> — 96% of children now <u>enrol</u> for school. Having a <u>more educated</u> workforce helps to <u>fuel development</u> — see page 32.

3) The <u>rail network</u> is being upgraded and <u>new roads</u> and <u>airports</u> are being built. These <u>reduce travel time</u> — e.g. the Delhi metro enables thousands of <u>commuters</u> to get to <u>work</u>.

4) India is one of the <u>top locations</u> in the world for FDI (foreign direct investment — <u>foreign</u> companies buy <u>land</u>, <u>buildings</u> or parts of <u>companies</u> in a country). <u>Most investment</u> comes from Singapore, Mauritius, Japan and the USA. India is trying to attract <u>more FDI</u> by <u>relaxing</u> the <u>rules</u> on <u>how much</u> land, property etc. <u>foreign companies</u> can <u>own</u>.

Development is Causing Population Change in India

1) <u>Birth rates</u> in India are <u>high</u>. <u>Death rates</u> and <u>infant mortality</u> have <u>fallen</u>, partly due to <u>better health care</u> and <u>health education</u>, e.g. encouraging people to wash their hands. This means that:

- India's population is <u>rapidly increasing</u> — it grew from about <u>870 million</u> in 1990, to <u>1.3 billion</u> in 2015.
- The majority of the population are <u>young</u> — about 28% are <u>under 14</u>.
- <u>Life expectancy</u> has <u>increased</u> from <u>58</u> in 1990 to <u>68</u> in 2014.

2) The <u>fertility rate</u> is starting to <u>fall</u> — it <u>decreased</u> from <u>4.0</u> in 1990 to <u>2.4</u> in 2014, partly due to growing <u>wealth</u> and better <u>education</u> (see p. 31). So <u>population growth rates</u> are gradually <u>slowing down</u>.

3) As the country gets <u>wealthier</u>, <u>urban</u> areas are growing because of <u>migration</u> and <u>natural increase</u>:

- In 1990, only <u>26%</u> of the population lived in <u>urban</u> areas. By 2015 this had risen to <u>33%</u>.
- India already has <u>4 megacities</u> (see p. 47) — New Delhi, Mumbai, Kolkata and Bengaluru, and is expected to have <u>3 more</u> by <u>2030</u>.

Some Regions of India are Developing Faster than Others

1) <u>Rapid economic growth</u> has increased <u>inequality</u> within India — the <u>gap</u> between the <u>richest</u> and <u>poorest</u> states has been <u>widening</u>.

2) The growth of <u>manufacturing</u> and <u>services</u> has benefited <u>urban</u> areas more than <u>rural</u> areas. <u>GDP</u> per capita is <u>highest</u> in the <u>south</u> and <u>west states</u>, e.g. Maharashtra, which have the <u>highest</u> urban population.

3) <u>More money</u> gets spent on these areas in order to <u>attract</u> more <u>FDI</u> and <u>TNCs</u>. The wealth generated can then be spent on development projects improving <u>literacy rates</u> and <u>quality of life</u>.

4) More <u>rural states</u>, e.g. Bihar, have higher rates of <u>poverty</u>. This has led to undernourishment and <u>health problems</u> because people <u>can't afford</u> to buy enough <u>food</u>. Many children have to <u>work</u> rather than <u>attend school</u> leading to <u>low literacy rates</u>. Poor health and education leads to a <u>low HDI score</u>. <u>Older</u> people are <u>less likely</u> to <u>migrate</u> to urban areas, instead remaining in rural areas.

	Maharashtra	Bihar
Urban population (%)	45	11
GDP per capita ($)	2561	682
HDI	0.572	0.367
Literacy rate (%)	83	64

There is still a lot of poverty in India

Different countries have different levels of development, but it's important to understand there's also inequality within countries — when there's economic change, some areas end up more developed than others.

Development in India

Economic development in India has had a range of <u>impacts</u> on <u>people</u> and the <u>environment</u>.

Economic Development has **Pros** and **Cons** for **Different Groups** of People

Economic development is <u>good</u> news for <u>some people</u>, but can cause <u>problems</u> for <u>others</u>:

Positive Impacts

1) All age groups have <u>better health</u>:
   - <u>Elderly</u> people are living <u>longer</u>.
   - There is a <u>lower</u> infant mortality rate.
   - There is a <u>lower</u> maternal mortality rate.
2) Some age groups have <u>better education</u>:
   - <u>Higher education</u> has given <u>young graduates</u> access to better-paid <u>jobs</u>, e.g. in technical firms and ICT.
   - Many adults have better <u>literacy</u>.
3) There can be better <u>gender equality</u>:
   - Women have better <u>access</u> to <u>education</u> — <u>literacy rates</u> for Indian women have <u>increased</u> from 34% in 1991 to 59% in 2011.
   - Women have better access to <u>contraception</u> and <u>family planning</u> advice.

Negative Impacts

1) Rapid <u>industrialisation</u> means some people may have to do <u>dangerous jobs</u>. Working <u>conditions</u> may also be <u>poor</u> due to a lack of <u>regulations</u> put in place by Indian <u>authorities</u>.
2) As <u>young</u> people move to urban areas to find work, there are <u>fewer workers</u> in <u>rural villages</u>. This means:
   - <u>Children</u> in rural areas may get a <u>poor education</u> due to a <u>lack</u> of <u>skilled teachers</u> — nearly 50% of teachers have only completed <u>secondary</u> education.
   - Children may have to work as <u>agricultural labourers</u> to support their families.
3) There is still a lot of <u>gender inequality</u>:
   - It is <u>unsafe</u> for <u>women</u> in many <u>urban</u> areas. E.g. in Delhi, <u>crimes against women</u> increased by 20% from 2014-15.
   - If men leave to find work in cities, women may be left to <u>care for</u> and <u>provide for</u> the entire household — balancing a <u>job</u> with <u>housework</u>.

Economic Development has **Impacts** on the **Environment**

1) <u>Industrialisation</u> leads to higher <u>energy consumption</u>. Increased <u>demand</u> for <u>fossil fuels</u> in industry, homes and vehicles means <u>more greenhouse gases</u> are released, contributing to <u>climate change</u>. India releases almost <u>7%</u> of all global greenhouse gas emissions.

2) More <u>factories</u> and <u>cars</u> mean more <u>air pollution</u>. The pollution is so <u>bad</u> in some cities, e.g. New Delhi, that a thick, toxic <u>smog</u> often forms. <u>Gases</u> such as sulfur dioxide and <u>smoke particles</u> damage people's health and cause <u>breathing problems</u> and <u>lung diseases</u>. More than <u>0.5 million</u> people in India <u>die</u> from diseases related to air pollution each year.

3) <u>Urban sprawl</u> leads to <u>land</u> and <u>water pollution</u> — lack of <u>infrastructure</u> means that about <u>70%</u> of India's sewage flows <u>untreated</u> into <u>rivers</u>. Waste may not be <u>correctly sorted</u> and <u>disposed of</u>, e.g. <u>dangerous contaminated waste</u> from a factory in Kodaikanal was initially <u>dumped</u> instead of being <u>disposed</u> of <u>safely</u>.

Economic development has both positive and negative impacts

Even if you learned about a different country for your case study in class, it's likely that some of these impacts will be very similar — economic development usually comes at a cost to the environment, because it means an increase in pollution and demand for energy. The impacts on people can be good or bad — it may depend on who you ask.

Development in India

CASE STUDY

Economic development has changed India's international role.

India's **Global Influence** is **Increasing**

1) India is playing a larger role in regional and global politics as it develops. In recent years the Indian government has improved relations with its immediate neighbours (e.g. joining ASEAN, a political and economic organisation made up of countries in southeast Asia).

2) India is a member of several international organisations — India was one of the founding members of the United Nations (UN), which works towards sustainable development. It is also part of the World Trade Organisation (WTO) and a member of G20, a group of 20 of the world's largest economies.

3) Economic growth has also changed India's relationship with the USA and EU:

India and the USA

1) India used to have a poor relationship with the USA but this has been improving.

2) The USA expects the economic development of India to increase trade, employment and economic growth in both countries.

3) The USA also sees India as a huge market for renewable and nuclear energy because of the number of increasingly wealthy people and the growth of industry.

India and the EU

1) India has had a good relationship with the EU and they became strategic partners in 2004, agreeing to cooperate on certain issues.

2) Negotiations for a free trade agreement began in 2007. The EU is one of India's biggest markets and trading partners.

3) The EU supports health and education programmes in India to promote continued development.

There are **Costs** and **Benefits** to **Foreign Influences** on India

India is increasingly open to the influence of the rest of the world — but not everyone is happy about this.

1) Changing international relations have costs and benefits:

- Costs — there is increasing tension between India and China — both have rapidly growing economies. Developed nations are also concerned about losing economic power as India grows.

- Benefits — improved relations mean India can cooperate with other countries on global issues, e.g. climate change, FDI brings economic benefits to both India and the country of origin, and global trade agreements mean that political actions, e.g. sanctions, are more effective.

2) Foreign investment (TNCs) is bringing wealth and jobs to India but there are problems too:

- TNCs can cause environmental problems — e.g. the concern of local communities about the amount of water being extracted by Coca-Cola® bottling plants led to plants in Kerala and Varanasi being closed.

- Large global retail chains can offer cheap prices on goods — Indian street traders are concerned that this will destroy their livelihoods as people choose to shop in supermarkets instead.

- TNCs could withdraw their business from India at any time, e.g if the economic climate changes.

India is experiencing rapid change

You might have studied a different emerging country in class — it's fine to learn that one instead. Just make sure you know about the economic changes caused by globalisation, the impacts the economic changes have had on people and the environment, and how the country's role in the world has been changing.

Worked Exam Questions

Another set of worked exam questions to look at here. It's tempting to skip over them without thinking, but it's worth taking time to look carefully — similar questions might just come up in your own exams...

1 Study **Figure 1**, which shows the contributions of primary industry, secondary industry and services to the total GDP of an emerging country.

Figure 1

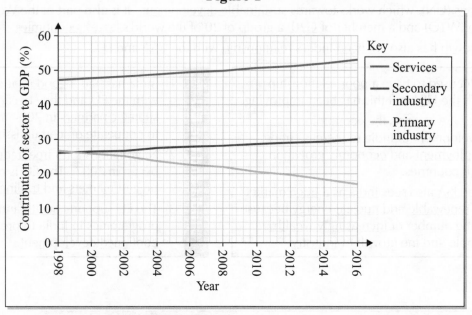

a) The country's total GDP in 2016 was US$ 1.9 trillion.
Calculate the amount of GDP contributed by primary industry in 2016 in US$.

$$\frac{\% \text{ of total GDP}}{100} \times \text{total GDP} = \frac{17}{100} \times 1.9 \text{ trillion} = \text{US\$ 0.32 trillion (2 d.p.)}$$

....
[2]

b) Using **Figure 1**, give **one** piece of evidence that suggests that the data is from an emerging country.

Primary and secondary industry together account for about half of all GDP.
....
[1]

c) For an emerging country you have studied, explain the changes to imports and exports since 1990.

In India, there has been a shift in major imports from manufactured goods such as machinery and

chemicals to crude oil. As the country has industrialised it requires more oil to fuel the new industries.

Industrialisation has meant that India now manufactures lots more of the goods that it previously

imported. As a result, major exports have shifted from low-value goods such as tea to high-value

goods like machinery.
[4]

[Total 7 marks]

Exam Questions

1 Study **Figure 1**, which shows development data for four different regions of an emerging country. Two of the regions are urban and two are rural.

Figure 1

Region	A	B	C	D
Infant mortality rate (per 1000 live births)	34	15	11	31
Literacy rate (%)	63	87	91	69
GDP per capita (US$)	686	2201	2507	798

a) Which two of the regions are most likely to be rural?

A A and D ◯

B A and B ◯

C B and C ◯

D B and D ◯

[1]

b) Suggest **one** reason for the regional variation in GDP per capita.

....

....

....

[2]

c) Suggest why literacy rate varies between the regions in **Figure 1**.

....

....

....

[2]

d) Economic development can cause changes to population structure. For an emerging country that you have studied, explain how the population structure has changed as the country has developed.

....

....

....

....

....

[4]

e) Evaluate the positive and negative impacts of economic development on different groups of people in an emerging country that you have studied.

[8 + 4 SPaG]

[Total 21 marks]

Revision Summary

Hurrah, you've reached the end of Topic 2 — time to see how good your understanding of this topic is.
- Try these questions and tick off each one when you get it right.
- When you've done all the questions under a heading and are completely happy with it, tick it off.

Measuring Development (p.29-31) ☑

1) Other than economic, give two other types of development.
2) What's the difference between GDP and GDP per capita?
3) What is HDI?
4) True or false: developing countries have high fertility and birth rates.
5) Why do fertility rates fall rapidly in emerging countries?

Causes and Consequences of Global Inequalities (p.32-33) ☑

6) Explain how climate can affect how developed a country is.
7) How can topography affect how developed a country is?
8) What is meant by neo-colonialism?
9) Give two possible social consequences of global inequality.
10) Give one possible political consequence of global inequality.

Theories of Development (p.34) ☑

11) List the five stages of economic development according to Rostow's theory.
12) Briefly summarise Frank's dependency theory.

Globalisation (p.37) ☑

13) What is globalisation?
14) Give one reason why globalisation is increasing.
15) What does TNC stand for?
16) Give one reason why some people think that globalisation increases global inequality.

Reducing Global Inequalities (p.38-39) ☑

17) Explain what is meant by a top-down approach to development.
18) Give one advantage of the top-down approach.
19) Give one benefit of using bottom-up development.
20) What is intermediate technology? What are its advantages?
21) Give one advantage and one disadvantage of IGO-funded large infrastructure.

Development — Case Study (p.40-43) ☑

Answer these questions for an emerging country you have studied:
22) Give one example of the cultural importance of the country.
23) How has the economy of the country changed since 1990?
24) How has globalisation helped increase development in the country?
25) Give an example of how development has had an impact on the country's environment.
26) Give one advantage and one disadvantage of foreign investment in the country.

Urbanisation

Urban areas (towns and cities) are popular places to be and getting ever more so — some faster than others...

Urbanisation is Happening **Fastest** in **Poorer Countries**

1) Urbanisation is the growth in the proportion of a country's population living in urban areas.

2) It's happening in countries all over the world — more than 50% of the world's population currently live in urban areas (3.9 billion people) and this is increasing every day.

3) Urbanisation happened earlier in developed countries (see p. 31), e.g. during the Industrial Revolution (in the 18th and 19th centuries), and most (79%) of the population now already live in urban areas. Developed countries have very slow rates of urban growth.

4) A smaller proportion (35%) of the population in developing countries currently live in urban areas. In general, the fastest rates of urbanisation in the world are in developing countries.

5) The percentage of the population living in urban areas varies in emerging countries. Some, such as Thailand and China, are experiencing rapid urban growth.

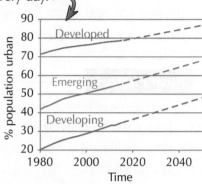

6) Urbanisation is predicted to continue at a fast rate in regions that still have large rural populations. By 2050, the majority of people in every global region are predicted to live in urban areas.

The Number of **Megacities** is **Increasing**

1) High rates of urbanisation are leading to the growth of megacities. A megacity is an urban area with over 10 million people living there, e.g. Mumbai in India.

2) In 1950 the biggest and most influential cities were largely in developed countries. There were only 2 megacities — Tokyo and New York.

3) By 2014 there were 28 megacities and this number is still growing — it's predicted to rise to 41 by 2030.

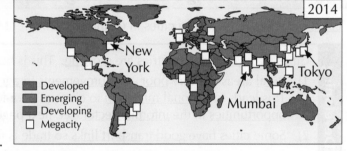

4) More than two-thirds of current megacities are in developing and emerging countries, mostly in Asia, e.g. Jakarta in Indonesia, Karachi in Pakistan and Dhaka in Bangladesh.

A **Primate City Dominates** a **Country**

1) Urban primacy is when one city dominates the country it is in. These 'primate cities' have a much larger population than other cities in the country — usually more than twice as many people as the next biggest city.

2) They influence the country economically:

- Investment — businesses often locate there, attracting investment in infrastructure and services.
- Migration — there are lots of jobs so people move there to find work. Highly-skilled workers are attracted by better opportunities, e.g. higher-paid, more prestigious jobs.
- Transport — international ports and airports are often located there, encouraging further investment and migration.

3) They also have political influences:

Governments and the headquarters of large, powerful businesses are often located there. This can mean that decisions about development favour the city rather than the rest of the country.

Urbanisation happened in developed countries first

Most countries are urbanising, but rates of urbanisation are usually fastest in developing and emerging countries. As a result, most new megacities are found in poorer countries. They can be found in developed countries too though.

Cities — Growth and Decline

The lure of the <u>city lights</u> can be strong, but there are things that can drive people and businesses <u>out</u> of a city, too.

Migration is a Result of Push and Pull Factors

1) Migration to <u>cities</u> can be <u>national</u> or <u>international</u>:
   - <u>NATIONAL MIGRATION</u> — when people move to a city <u>in</u> the <u>same</u> country, e.g. <u>rural-urban migration</u> is the <u>movement</u> of people from the <u>countryside</u> to the <u>cities</u>.
   - <u>INTERNATIONAL MIGRATION</u> — when people move from one country to a <u>city</u> in <u>another country</u>.
2) Migration <u>to</u> a city is affected by <u>push factors</u> (things that <u>encourage</u> people to <u>leave</u> an area) and <u>pull factors</u> (things that <u>encourage</u> people to <u>move to</u> the city).

Push Factors	**Pull Factors**
• A <u>shortage</u> of jobs or <u>low</u> wages.	• <u>More</u> employment opportunities and <u>higher</u> wages.
• <u>Poor</u> standard of living.	• <u>Better</u> standard of living.
• <u>Poor</u> healthcare and education.	• <u>Better</u> health care and education.
• <u>War</u> or conflict.	• A <u>safe</u> place with little crime or risk of natural disasters.
• <u>Natural disasters</u> like earthquakes or floods.	• A <u>cleaner</u> environment.
• A <u>poor environment</u> due to pollution or crime.	

Economic Change Leads to Migration

<u>Economic change</u> is causing cities in countries of different levels of development to <u>grow</u> or to <u>decline</u>.

Developing

Cities in <u>developing</u> countries are <u>growing</u>. This is because:
1) <u>Rural</u> areas are very <u>poor</u> — <u>improvements</u> in <u>agriculture</u> mean <u>fewer</u> farm workers are needed. This leads to <u>national migration</u> to cities as people seek <u>better jobs</u>. There are lots of <u>opportunities</u> in the <u>informal sector</u> (see next page) for low-skilled migrants from rural areas.
2) Some cities have <u>good transport links</u> so <u>trade</u> is focused there — providing <u>lots</u> of <u>jobs</u>.
3) Some cities are attracting <u>foreign companies</u> and <u>manufacturing industry</u> is <u>expanding</u>.

Emerging

Some cities in <u>emerging</u> countries are <u>growing</u> and some have <u>stabilising</u> populations.
1) Some cities have become <u>industrial centres</u> — there are lots of <u>manufacturing jobs</u>. Other cities have a <u>rapidly expanding service sector</u>, e.g. the IT industry in India. People <u>move to</u> the cities to work in the <u>new industries</u> and in <u>services</u> supporting them.
2) As countries get <u>wealthier</u> they are <u>investing</u> in flagship projects, e.g. sports stadiums for international events, to attract <u>foreign investment</u>. This creates <u>more jobs</u>, attracting <u>workers</u>.

Developed

Some cities in <u>developed</u> countries have <u>stable</u> populations and others are <u>declining</u>.
1) <u>De-industrialisation</u> has led to the <u>decline</u> of industrial areas (see p. 101) — people moved <u>away</u> to find work elsewhere. Some cities are <u>still declining</u>, e.g. Sunderland, however many cities have been <u>regenerated</u> and are <u>attracting</u> people again, e.g. Bristol.
2) A lot of <u>low-paid workers</u>, e.g. cleaners and factory-line workers, are <u>attracted</u> to more <u>successful cities</u> in the region. This leads to the <u>decline</u> of the <u>cities</u> they are <u>leaving</u>.

People usually move to cities to look for better jobs and services

Urbanisation isn't a random process — it's mainly the result of people moving to where there are jobs and away from where there aren't many. The tricky bit is working out why it's different in different places — see the next page.

Urban Economies

Cities in <u>richer</u> and <u>poorer</u> countries are quite <u>different</u>. This is partly because they have different <u>economic structures</u> — people work in <u>different</u> kinds of <u>jobs</u>. First up, you're going to need some <u>definitions</u>...

There are **Different Kinds** of **Work**

1) There are <u>two</u> different types of <u>employment</u> — <u>formal</u> and <u>informal</u>.

- <u>Formal</u> employment is <u>officially</u> recognised — workers are <u>protected</u> by the <u>laws</u> of country. There are rules about how many <u>hours</u> people can work, the <u>age</u> of workers and <u>health</u> and <u>safety</u>. Workers pay <u>tax</u> to the <u>government</u> out of the <u>wages</u> they earn.
- <u>Informal</u> employment is <u>unofficial</u> — jobs <u>aren't taxed</u> or <u>regulated</u> by the government. People often work <u>long hours</u> in <u>dangerous</u> conditions for <u>little pay</u>.

2) There are also <u>four</u> different <u>economic sectors</u> — <u>primary</u>, <u>secondary</u>, <u>tertiary</u> and <u>quaternary</u>.

- The <u>primary</u> sector involves collecting <u>raw materials</u>, e.g. <u>farming</u>, <u>fishing</u>, <u>mining</u> and <u>forestry</u>.
- The <u>secondary</u> sector involves turning a <u>product</u> into <u>another product</u> (<u>manufacturing</u>), e.g. making <u>textiles</u>, <u>furniture</u>, <u>chemicals</u>, <u>steel</u> and <u>cars</u>.
- The <u>tertiary</u> sector involves providing a <u>service</u> — anything from <u>financial</u> services, <u>nursing</u> and <u>retail</u> to the <u>police force</u> and <u>transport</u>.
- The <u>quaternary</u> sector is the <u>information economy</u> — e.g. <u>research and development</u>, where scientists and researchers investigate and develop new products (e.g. in the <u>electronics</u> and <u>IT industry</u>), and <u>consultancy</u> (e.g. advising businesses).

Urban Economies **Vary** By **Level of Development**

	Developing countries	Emerging countries	Developed countries
Formal and informal employment	<u>Many</u> workers are employed in the informal sector.	Number of workers in the informal sector <u>decreases</u> as the country develops.	<u>Few</u> workers in the informal sector.
Economic sectors	Lots of people work in <u>low-skilled tertiary sector</u> jobs, e.g. on market stalls. <u>Few people</u> work in the <u>secondary</u> sector because there's <u>not enough money</u> to <u>invest</u> in the <u>technology needed</u> for this type of industry, e.g. to build large factories. A <u>small percentage</u> of people work in high-skilled <u>tertiary</u> jobs, e.g. in government offices or IT.	<u>Employment</u> in the <u>secondary sector</u> is <u>high</u>. There are established <u>industrial zones</u> and <u>good infrastructure</u>. There are also lots of <u>low-skilled</u> <u>tertiary</u> jobs, e.g. in retail or tourism. As the <u>industrial economy grows</u> people have <u>more money</u> to spend on services — jobs are created in <u>higher-skilled jobs</u> in the <u>tertiary sector</u>, e.g. in medicine or law. Some cities <u>specialise</u> in certain <u>services</u>, e.g. Hyderabad, India specialises in <u>IT development</u>.	<u>Fewer people</u> work in the <u>secondary sector</u> than in <u>emerging</u> countries. <u>Most people</u> work in the <u>tertiary sector</u> because there's a <u>skilled</u> and <u>educated</u> workforce, and there's a <u>high demand</u> for services like banks and shops. There's some employment in the <u>quaternary sector</u> because the country has lots of <u>highly skilled labour</u> and has <u>money</u> to <u>invest</u> in the <u>technology needed</u>.
Working conditions	Conditions are <u>poor</u>. Pay is <u>low</u>, hours are <u>long</u> and conditions can <u>be dangerous</u>.	Conditions <u>improve</u> and workers' rights <u>increase</u>.	Conditions are <u>good</u>. Pay is <u>high</u>, workers have many <u>rights</u> protected by <u>law</u>.

Urban economies differ in different parts of the world

A country's level of development affects urban economies — developing countries have large informal and primary sectors, but the number of people employed in these sectors decreases as the countries develop.

Urban Change

Urban areas go through a <u>lot</u> of changes as they <u>develop</u>. Changes in the <u>economy</u> mean people <u>move in</u>, then they <u>move out</u>, and then they <u>move in</u> again. There's a lot of new words on this page, but soon it'll all make sense.

Cities Go Through Different Stages as they Develop

Urbanisation

Urbanisation is the <u>increase</u> in the <u>proportion</u> of the population living in built-up <u>urban areas</u>. Urban areas <u>spread</u> into the <u>surrounding countryside</u> as the population increases.

- Cities in <u>developed</u> countries grew during the <u>Industrial Revolution</u> (1760-1850). Workers lived in <u>small terraced houses</u> around the <u>factories</u> in the <u>city centres</u>.
- When factories <u>relocated</u> to <u>emerging</u> countries in the <u>1970s</u> and <u>80s</u>, <u>slums</u> and <u>apartment blocks</u> sprang up around them to house the <u>workers</u>.

Suburbanisation

Suburbanisation is the movement of people from the <u>middle</u> of the city to the <u>edges</u> — urban areas <u>expand rapidly</u> (sprawl) as <u>housing</u> is <u>built</u> in the <u>outskirts</u>. It began occurring in the <u>early 20th century</u> in many <u>developed</u> counties.

- Urbanisation caused urban areas to become <u>overcrowded</u> and <u>polluted</u>, with <u>little</u> 'natural' space. Suburban areas offered more open <u>green spaces</u> and seemed more <u>family-friendly</u>.
- Improvements in <u>transport networks</u> meant that people could live in the suburbs and <u>commute</u> in to the city to work.

De-industrialisation

1) As countries <u>develop</u>, they experience <u>de-industrialisation</u> (<u>manufacturing</u> moving <u>out</u> of an area). Urban areas are affected by industry moving:
   - out of <u>city centres</u> into <u>rural areas</u> where <u>rents</u> are <u>cheaper</u>.
   - <u>overseas</u> to countries where <u>costs are lower</u> — this is known as <u>global shift</u>.
2) De-industrialisation can lead to <u>de-population</u> as people <u>leave</u> the old industrial areas.
3) The <u>city centre</u> and <u>industrial zones</u> on the <u>edges of cities</u> decline — <u>unemployment increases</u> leading to <u>lower living standards</u> and <u>poverty</u>. Shops, restaurants and other amenities <u>close</u>.

Counter-urbanisation

<u>Counter-urbanisation</u> is the movement of people <u>away</u> from large <u>urban areas</u> to smaller settlements and <u>rural areas</u>. In many <u>developed</u> countries this process began in the <u>1970s</u> and <u>80s</u>.

- People think they'll have a <u>higher quality of life</u> in <u>rural</u> areas and house prices are often <u>lower</u>.
- Increased <u>car ownership</u> and improved <u>public transport</u> mean that people can live <u>further</u> from the city and <u>commute</u> to work.
- Improved <u>communication services</u> (e.g. high-speed internet connections) make it easier for people to live in rural areas and <u>work from home</u>. This also means that some companies <u>no longer</u> need to be in a city centre and can move to <u>rural areas</u> where land is <u>cheaper</u>.

Regeneration

Since the <u>1990s</u> some <u>city centres</u> in <u>developed countries</u> have undergone <u>regeneration</u> to <u>reverse</u> the <u>decline</u> of urban areas because of suburbanisation, de-industrialisation and counter-urbanisation.

- To <u>attract</u> people and businesses <u>back</u> to the <u>city centre</u>, governments and private companies <u>invest</u> in <u>new developments</u>, e.g. <u>high quality flats</u> and <u>office blocks</u>, and <u>upgrade infrastructure</u>.
- Once re-urbanisation has <u>started</u> it tends to <u>continue</u> — as soon as a few businesses invest and people start to return, it encourages <u>other businesses</u> to invest.
- <u>Young</u>, <u>single people</u> often want to live <u>close to their work</u> in areas with <u>good entertainment services</u> (e.g. bars and nightclubs).

The movement of people back into urban areas is known as re-urbanisation.

As a developed country, some UK cities have been through all five stages

This stuff will be coming up again in Topic 5, so it's worth getting a solid grasp of it now.
Try making a revision card about each of the five processes, with the key points for each one.

Urban Land Use

In general, cities have a similar layout — there are four distinct zones with different land uses.

Land Use in Cities can be Commercial, Industrial or Residential

Land in cities can be used for different purposes:

*   Commercial — e.g. office buildings, shopping centres and hotels
*   Industrial — e.g. factories, warehouses
*   Residential — e.g. houses, flats and apartments (anything that people live in)

Different types of land use are found in particular areas of the city because they have similar requirements.
This creates distinct zones within a city, which can be identified on maps and satellite images:

*   The central business district (CBD) has commercial and public buildings.
    Look for high density buildings and the meeting of major roads.

*   The inner city is mainly residential (low-class housing) and older industry.
    Look for short, parallel roads of terraced housing and larger factory buildings.

*   The suburbs are mainly residential (medium-class housing).
    Look for lots of short, curved streets and cul-de sacs.

*   The rural-urban fringe has a mix of commercial business parks and residential
    (high-class housing). Look for more green space between built-up areas and
    clusters of larger office buildings or shopping centres with car parks.

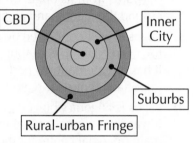

The zones of a 'model' city form concentric rings:

CBD · Inner City · Suburbs · Rural-urban Fringe

Land Use is Influenced by Accessibility, Availability, Cost and Regulations

Accessibility

1) City centres are usually very accessible —
    they are the location of the main train and bus
    stations and the centre of the road network.

2) Shops and offices locate in city centres because
    they need to be accessible to lots of people.

3) Some businesses now locate on the edges
    of cities — these are near major motorway
    junctions and out-of-town airports, so avoid
    traffic congestion in the city centre.

Planning Regulations

1) City planners try to control how cities develop
    by deciding what types of buildings can be built
    in different parts of the city.

2) There are often strict planning regulations in city
    centres — polluting industries may be banned.

3) Some cities have strict limits on development in
    the rural-urban fringe, e.g. designated greenbelt
    land that can't be built on. This stops the city
    sprawling into the countryside.

Availability

1) In the city centre almost all land is in use and demand is
    high. Businesses may extend upwards as ground space is
    limited — the tallest buildings are often in the centre.

2) Brownfield land in city centres, such as old industrial sites,
    may be redeveloped as shops or offices. Some of the old
    terraced housing and apartment blocks in inner cities are
    redeveloped as luxury homes for young professionals.

3) There is lots of space on the edges of cities where
    larger buildings, e.g. shopping centres, science parks,
    industrial estates and houses, can be built (if allowed).

Cost

1) The city centre has the highest
    land prices — the cost of land
    falls towards the edge of the city.

2) Some businesses and shops can
    afford to locate offices and shops
    in the city centre but there are
    few houses.

3) Houses tend to increase in size
    from the inner city to the suburbs
    as the price of land decreases.

Land use changes as you move through the different zones of a city

It's a good idea to learn the four main parts of a city and the land use in each bit, but remember that land use is
affected by many different things. In reality, the layout of a city isn't usually as simple as the diagram above.

Urban Change in Lagos

Lagos is a great example of the <u>attraction</u> of cities and the <u>problems</u> caused by <u>rapid urban growth</u>.

Lagos is the **Biggest** City in **Africa**

<u>Lagos</u> is a megacity in <u>Nigeria</u> — a <u>developing</u> country, but the <u>richest</u> country in <u>Africa</u>. The city's population is over <u>21 million</u>, and it's one of the <u>fastest-growing</u> urban areas in the world.

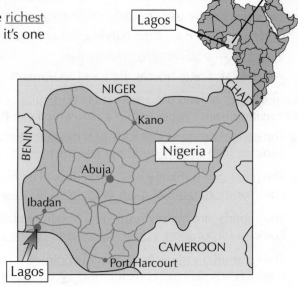

1) Lagos is located at the outlet of the massive <u>Lagos Lagoon</u> (see map on the next page) on the <u>Atlantic western coast</u> of <u>Nigeria</u>.

2) This location is ideal for its <u>port</u>, which is one of the <u>biggest</u> in <u>Africa</u>. The city has spread <u>outwards</u> from its origin on Lagos Island around the <u>lagoon</u> and <u>along the coast</u>.

3) Lagos is well <u>connected</u> by <u>road</u> to the other <u>major towns</u> in <u>Nigeria</u>, e.g. <u>Abuja</u> (the national capital). It has an <u>international port</u> and <u>airport</u>, making it an important centre for <u>regional</u> and <u>global trade</u>.

4) Lagos is Nigeria's <u>biggest city</u> for <u>population</u> and <u>business</u>. It was the <u>national capital</u> until 1991 and remains the <u>main financial centre</u> for the whole of <u>West Africa</u>. The city contains <u>80%</u> of Nigeria's <u>industry</u> and lots of <u>global companies</u> are located there.

5) It is the centre of the <u>Nigerian film industry</u> '<u>Nollywood</u>' and has a <u>thriving music scene</u>, which has introduced music styles such as Afrobeat and Afro hip-hop — this gives it <u>cultural importance</u> in Nigeria.

Different **Areas** of Lagos have Different **Functions**

1) The development of Lagos means that land use and <u>building age varies</u> across the city.

2) The <u>oldest parts</u> of the city are on <u>Lagos Island</u>, which is now the CBD. Many of the old buildings have been <u>redeveloped</u> as <u>high rise office blocks</u> and <u>luxury shops</u>. Land is very <u>expensive</u>.

3) By <u>1960</u> the <u>city</u> had <u>spread north</u> and <u>east</u> along the <u>main road</u> and <u>rail links</u>, e.g. creating <u>Mushin</u>. <u>Industries</u> developed <u>near major transport links</u>, e.g. <u>Ikeja industrial estate</u> near the airport.

4) Rapid expansion meant that <u>by 1990</u> Lagos had <u>merged</u> with the <u>smaller surrounding towns</u> to form a <u>continuous urban area</u>. The city has continued to <u>sprawl</u> into the <u>surrounding countryside</u>.

5) It has mainly spread <u>north</u> as it is hemmed in by the <u>lagoon</u> to the <u>east</u> and <u>major rivers</u> to the <u>west</u>. It has also <u>expanded west</u> along the <u>Lagos-Badagry express-way</u>, e.g. in <u>Ojo</u>.

6) <u>Slums</u> have developed on less desirable land on the <u>outskirts</u> of Lagos throughout its history. However, over time, the city has <u>sprawled</u> outwards, <u>beyond</u> many of the slums and they now form part of the <u>main urban area</u> of Lagos.

You need to know about a megacity in a developing or emerging country

You might want to stick with the megacity you studied in class, but make sure you know enough about it — you need to know the same sorts of information on your chosen city as what's covered on these six pages about Lagos.

Urban Change in Lagos

You need to learn more about the <u>structure</u> of a megacity, like Lagos, and its <u>population growth</u>.

Lagos has **Different Zones** That Were Built at **Different Times**

The different <u>areas</u> of Lagos that you learnt about on the previous page can be classed as different <u>zones</u> of a <u>model city</u>, as shown in the <u>table</u> below. These zones are also shown on the <u>map</u> opposite.

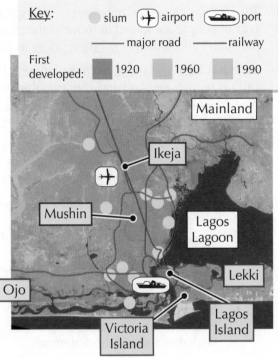

	Area	Age and function
CBD	<u>Lagos Island</u>	<u>Modern high-rise office buildings</u>, local government <u>headquarters</u> and <u>banks</u>.
Inner city	<u>Mushin</u>	<u>Older</u>, <u>high-density</u>, <u>low-quality</u> houses.
	<u>Ikeja</u>	Large <u>industrial estate</u> built in the <u>1960s</u>, with <u>factories</u> making e.g. plastics and textiles.
Suburbs	<u>Victoria Island</u>	<u>Modern</u>, <u>high-class residential</u> and <u>commercial</u> — lots of businesses and shops.
Rural-urban fringe	<u>Ojo</u>	<u>Sprawling</u>, <u>low-density new housing</u> on the <u>outskirts</u> of the city.
	<u>Lekki</u>	<u>New industrial zone</u> and <u>port</u> being built.

Lagos's Population is **Growing Rapidly**

Lagos's population has <u>grown</u> for <u>different reasons</u> at different <u>times</u>:

Historic

1) The city was under <u>British rule</u> during <u>colonial</u> times and was a centre of <u>trade</u>. This attracted <u>traders</u> and <u>merchants</u> to the city.

2) Many <u>ex-slaves</u> also came to Lagos, e.g. from <u>Sierra Leone</u>, <u>Brazil</u> and the <u>West Indies</u>.

1960s-1990s

1) After Lagos gained <u>independence</u> there was <u>rapid economic development</u> — the <u>export</u> of <u>oil</u> made some people very <u>wealthy</u>.

2) The government financed lots of <u>construction projects</u>, e.g. building <u>sea ports</u>, <u>oil refineries</u> and <u>factories</u>. The <u>jobs</u> created led to <u>rapid urbanisation</u> — lots of people moved <u>to</u> Lagos from <u>rural Nigeria</u>.

3) <u>Birth rates</u> were <u>high</u> and <u>death rates</u> were <u>lower</u> leading to <u>high rates</u> of <u>natural increase</u> — a rapidly <u>growing</u> population.

Recent

1) <u>Most</u> of the population growth in Lagos is due to <u>rural-urban migration</u>.

2) The countries <u>bordering</u> Nigeria, e.g. Chad and Niger, are <u>poor</u> and <u>involved</u> in conflict — many people leave these countries for a <u>better life</u> in Lagos.

3) There are also lots of <u>national migrants</u> from the <u>northern states</u> of Nigeria where there is lots of <u>ethnic</u> and <u>religious conflict</u> and high levels of <u>poverty</u>.

4) There is some international migration from the <u>USA</u>, the <u>UK</u> and <u>China</u>. This is mainly people who are employed by <u>foreign businesses</u> operating in <u>Lagos</u>.

5) The rate of <u>natural increase</u> is still high — <u>birth</u> rates are still higher than <u>death</u> rates though <u>both</u> are slowly falling.

Lagos has grown incredibly quickly

You're expected not just to know about why your chosen city's population is growing now, but also the reasons behind its past changes in population too. So, make sure you know a bit about the history of the place.

Urban Change in Lagos

A lot more of the land in and around Lagos has been built on over the last few decades, to keep up with the rapidly growing population of the city. This growth has provided some opportunities for people living in Lagos.

Lagos's Growth has Caused **Changes** in **Land Use**

1) The city has expanded outwards — a larger area is now built on. Lots of people are forced to move to the rural-urban fringe as they can't afford the rising house prices in the inner city.

2) Land has been reclaimed from the lagoon. Land around the CBD is in high demand and very valuable, so artificial islands have been built, e.g. Banana Island and Eko Atlantic are built on reclaimed land and contain huge houses in gated communities.

3) Previously empty areas are now built on, e.g. slums are built on areas of wasteland. In other undesirable locations (like Makoko), people have built wooden huts on stilts in the lagoon.

4) The land use in some areas has also changed, for example:

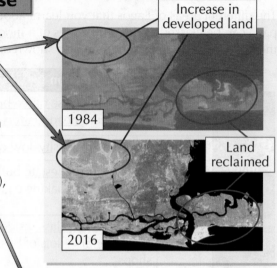

Increase in developed land

1984

Land reclaimed

2016

- Some slums have been upgraded and made more permanent. The huts have been removed and new 3-4 storey apartments have been built in their place, e.g. in Badia East.

- Some parts of the Makoko slum have been cleared by the government to allow development of desirable areas of the waterfront.

- Some of the old middle-class residential areas have become high-class luxury housing, e.g. the old middle-class area of Ikoyi is now one of the richest neighbourhoods in Lagos with lots of luxury shops and hotels alongside the redeveloped apartments.

People in Lagos have **More Opportunities**

There is better access to employment in Lagos than in rural Nigeria and the surrounding countries:

1) Incomes are about 4 times higher in Lagos than those in rural areas and informal sector jobs mean most people can find a way of making money — the huge population means there is a large market for services.

2) Lagos is home to many of the country's banks, government departments and manufacturing industries (e.g. making food and drink). There are two major ports and a fishing industry, all of which provide employment. Rapid growth of the city means there are lots of construction jobs.

3) There are more health care centres and hospitals and a better range of medicines in Lagos and there is better access to higher education — Lagos has six universities.

Even though there are major problems with the provision of services in Lagos (see next page), people still have better access to resources than in rural Nigeria.

4) It is possible to access electricity and water networks as well as TV and the internet.

Life in Lagos is different to life in rural Nigeria

It's easier for people in Lagos to find employment, and they are more likely to have access to things like health care and safe drinking water. However, there are a lot of problems in Lagos too, as you'll see on the next page...

Urban Change in Lagos

You've read about some of the <u>positive</u> impacts of the rapid population <u>growth</u> in Lagos but, as you might expect, the city is also experiencing a lot of <u>negative</u> impacts too. Some of the main ones are listed below.

Lagos faces **Challenges** in **Housing**, **Traffic**, **Waste**, **Jobs** and **Services**

1) Squatter Settlements

Over <u>60%</u> of the city's population live in <u>slums</u>.

1) Houses are often <u>flimsy</u>, <u>wooden huts</u>. These are <u>illegally</u> built — people face <u>eviction</u> if slums are <u>demolished</u> to <u>clean up</u> the city.

2) The only <u>electricity</u> comes from <u>illegal connections</u> that often <u>cut out</u>.

3) There are high levels of <u>crime</u> — many slums are <u>patrolled</u> by gangs called '<u>area boys</u>' who both <u>commit crimes</u> and act as <u>informal</u> '<u>police</u>' in the slum.

2) Traffic Congestion

Lagos has some of the <u>worst traffic congestion</u> in the <u>world</u> because:

1) There has been very little <u>investment</u> in transport <u>infrastructure</u>, despite the city growing enormously.

2) <u>Public transport</u> is <u>limited</u>, although there are plans to improve it, e.g. a light rail train.

3) The <u>CBD</u> is on an <u>island</u>, with only <u>three bridges</u> linking it to the rest of the city.

3) Limited Service Provision

1) There aren't enough schools for the population (e.g. there is only <u>one primary school</u> in Makoko) and many families <u>can't afford</u> to send their children to school.

2) There aren't enough <u>health care facilities</u> and many people can't <u>afford</u> to pay for treatment.

4) Poor Employment Conditions

1) There aren't enough <u>formal jobs</u> for the <u>growing population</u> — people have to make money <u>any way they can</u>, e.g. by <u>scavenging</u> in the Olusosun rubbish dump for items to sell.

2) About <u>60%</u> of the population work in <u>informal</u> jobs (see p. 49), e.g. street sellers, barbers.

3) There's <u>no protection</u> for informal workers. <u>Street-sellers</u>' stalls are <u>bulldozed</u> to make way for <u>new developments</u> and <u>road widening</u>.

4) Lots of people live on less than <u>$1.25 per day</u>.

5) Waste Disposal

1) Most of the city doesn't have access to proper <u>sewers</u>, e.g. in Makoko <u>communal toilets</u> are shared by <u>15 households</u> and most of the waste goes <u>straight</u> into the <u>lagoon</u> below — it's always full of <u>rubbish</u> and <u>raw sewage</u>. This <u>causes health problems</u>, e.g. cholera.

2) The <u>huge</u> population produces <u>lots</u> of waste — approximately <u>9000 tonnes per day</u>.

3) Only about <u>40% of rubbish</u> is officially collected and there are <u>large rubbish dumps</u>, e.g. Olusosun, which contain <u>toxic waste</u>. <u>Waste disposal</u> and <u>emissions</u> from factories are <u>not controlled</u>, leading to <u>air</u> and <u>water pollution</u>.

6) Water Supply

1) Only about <u>40%</u> of the city is <u>connected</u> to the <u>state water supply</u>. The pipes are <u>old</u> and <u>rusty</u> — the water often gets <u>contaminated</u> with <u>sewage</u>.

2) The state water company <u>supplies less than half</u> of what is <u>needed</u>. Water is in such short supply that people pay <u>hugely inflated prices</u> to get water from <u>informal sellers</u>.

Rapid growth brings a lot of difficulties for megacities

Try drawing a table with two columns, one for the opportunities (from page 54) and one for the challenges created by rapid population growth in Lagos. See how many points you can remember to jot down in each, then come back to these pages to remind yourself of any you might have missed.

CASE STUDY

Urban Change in Lagos

There are **Big Inequalities** in Lagos

There are <u>big differences</u> between the <u>rich</u> and the <u>poor</u> in Lagos, which leads to differences in <u>quality of life</u>.

Rich

1) Wealthy people can afford <u>better housing</u> — the very rich live in luxurious and very expensive <u>gated communities</u>, e.g. on <u>Banana Island</u>.

2) They can also <u>afford</u> to <u>live closer</u> to <u>work</u>, so don't have to <u>face</u> traffic jams every day.

3) Lagos does not have enough electricity-generating <u>capacity</u> to satisfy the <u>whole</u> city, so neighbourhoods have to <u>take it in turns</u> to have electricity. The very wealthy improve their quality of life by running their own <u>powerful generators</u>.

Poor

The poor can't afford <u>high quality housing</u> — they end up living in <u>slums</u> on land that regularly <u>floods</u> or is close to <u>polluting factories</u>. Electricity is not available to the <u>poorest</u> people in slums, meaning they are reliant on <u>polluting cooking stoves</u> or small petrol <u>generators</u>, which cause <u>pollution</u> and <u>reduce quality of life</u>. Lack of <u>waste disposal</u> leads to <u>high health risks</u>.

The <u>inequalities</u> above make <u>political</u> and <u>economic management</u> of Lagos <u>challenging</u>:

1) There are <u>different development priorities</u>, e.g. the <u>wealthy</u> want <u>investment</u> in more high-class, modern <u>office space</u> (e.g. <u>Eko Atlantic</u>) to relieve pressure on the existing CBD, but the poor who live in slums need investment in <u>housing improvement</u> and in <u>more services</u>.

2) <u>Corruption</u> is very common in Nigeria. The government can introduce laws, e.g. to regulate traffic, but the wealthy know they can <u>ignore them</u> and <u>bribe</u> the police if they get caught.

3) The wealthy elite are <u>very powerful</u> — e.g. proposals to improve railways in and around Lagos for people and freight have been <u>stopped</u> by people who have a business interest in the lorries that currently supply the city.

The **Government** is Trying to make Lagos **More Sustainable**

1) <u>Sustainability</u> means <u>improving</u> things for people <u>today</u> without <u>negatively affecting</u> future generations. Basically, it means behaving in a way that doesn't <u>irreversibly</u> <u>damage the environment</u> or <u>use up resources</u> faster than they can be <u>replaced</u>.

2) Some strategies to improve sustainability are <u>top-down</u> (<u>large-scale</u>, <u>expensive</u> infrastructure projects run by <u>governments</u> and IGOs — see p. 39). In Lagos, <u>top-down</u> strategies include:

> Sustainability should consider the economy and people as well as the environment.

Improving Water Supply

The government has begun work on a <u>US $2.5 billion plan</u> which includes <u>new water treatment plants</u> and <u>distribution networks</u>. In the meantime <u>water kiosks</u> are being introduced, where people can <u>buy water</u> at a <u>lower price</u> than from informal water sellers, until they are connected.

Improving Waste Disposal

The <u>Lagos Waste Management Authority</u> (LAWMA) is working to improve <u>rubbish collection</u> by making sure collection <u>vans</u> can get to each area of the city, e.g. by doing collections at <u>night</u> when there's <u>less traffic</u>. <u>Recycling banks</u> are being put in <u>every estate</u> and people are <u>encouraged</u> to <u>sort</u> and <u>recycle</u> their <u>waste</u>.

Reducing Traffic Congestion

Two <u>light rail lines</u> are under construction to relieve <u>road congestion</u>. The lines will connect the <u>CBD</u> on <u>Lagos Island</u> with the <u>north</u> and <u>west</u> of the city (including the <u>airport</u>) along major <u>commuter routes</u>. The trains will be <u>emission free</u> to <u>limit air pollution</u> and the route will take <u>35 minutes</u> instead of up to <u>4 hours</u> by car.

Improving Air Quality

<u>Small electricity generators</u> (used by households when the power goes out) are a big source of <u>air pollution</u>. To <u>improve air quality</u> the government <u>banned</u> the <u>import</u> of small generators — instead communities are encouraged get <u>together</u> to run <u>one larger generator</u>, which will produce <u>less emissions</u> overall.

Urban Change in Lagos

CASE STUDY

There's been a lot of information on Lagos to get through, but there's just one page left...

Communities and NGOs are Also Trying to Improve Lagos's Sustainability

Other strategies to improve sustainability in Lagos are bottom-up (smaller-scale projects run by communities and non-governmental organisations — see p. 39). In Lagos, bottom-up strategies include:

Improving Health

CHIEF is an NGO that aims to develop sustainable health care in deprived areas of Lagos by opening community health centres, particularly for disadvantaged women and children. They also run education projects in local communities, to make people more aware of health issues.

Improving City Housing

SEAP is a Nigerian NGO that promotes sustainable livelihoods for the poorest people in society. For example, it offers small loans (microfinance) to poor communities at affordable rates, so that people can afford to get a mortgage on a house. This means that people can move out of slum housing into small affordable apartments with better access to services.

Improving Education

The Oando Foundation is a charity that is aiming to create a sustainable education system in Nigeria by improving school attendance and the quality of education on offer. The foundation involves local communities in each project so they support the school. It has 'adopted' and renovated schools in Lagos — this is reducing the number of primary children out of school. It is also working to improve teachers' skills through training programmes.

There are Pros and Cons to Top-Down and Bottom-Up Strategies

	Advantages	Disadvantages
Top-down	• Can achieve large improvements that affect the whole city, e.g. the improved water supply should provide enough water for everyone at a low cost by 2020. • Can carry out higher-cost projects that communities or NGOs would struggle to fund. • Can address economic, social and environmental sustainability.	• Often very expensive, e.g. Nigeria had to borrow almost US $1 billion from the World Bank to fund construction of its light rail line. • Top-down approaches don't always have the support of communities, who may decide to ignore or undermine the strategy. For example the bus rapid transit is often delayed due to cars and stalls blocking the bus lane. • May not help those most in need, e.g. the ban on small generators affects the poor more than the rich as they are less able to afford cleaner alternatives.
Bottom-up	• Planned with the local community, so it has their support and can target issues that most concern local people. • Often funded by donations from more developed countries or wealthy people, so there's low cost to the people they help or the Nigerian government.	• Smaller scale so projects reach fewer people. • Funds may be limited — especially during economic recessions (periods of economic decline) when the need may be greatest. Schemes often rely on donations from people in more developed countries but people can't afford to give as much during a recession. • Can lack coordination — there may be several NGOs with the same aims working separately.

EXAM TIP

Include lots of specific facts when you write about a case study

If you've studied a different example of urban growth in class and you'd rather write about that instead, then no problem — just make sure you have enough information to cover the key points on this page.

Worked Exam Questions

Here are some worked exam questions for this section — for an extra bit of practice, try covering the answers and thinking about how you would answer each question before you read the suggested answer.

1   Study **Figure 1**, which shows the global distribution of megacities in 1975 and 2014.

Figure 1

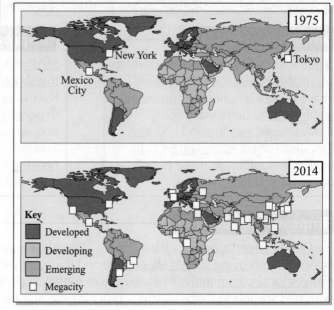

a)   Describe the changes in the number and distribution of megacities between 1975 and 2014 shown in **Figure 1**.

The number of megacities increased from

three in 1975 to twenty-eight in 2014.

By 2014 there were a few more megacities in

developing and developed countries.

However, most of the new megacities that had

developed by 2014 are in emerging countries.

[3]

b)   What is meant by the term 'primate city'?

A city that has a much larger population than other cities in the country.

[1]

[Total 4 marks]

2   Study **Figure 2**, which shows the employment structure of an urban area in 2016.

a)   What is meant by the term 'tertiary industry'?

Figure 2

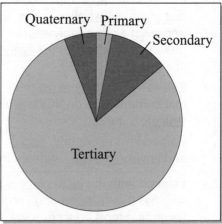

Tertiary industry involves providing a service.

[1]

b)   Suggest whether the urban area in **Figure 2** is in a developed or developing country. Give a reason for your answer.

The urban area is in a developed country. There is a

high proportion of people working in the tertiary and

quaternary sectors.

[2]

c)   Describe how the proportion of people working in the informal sector changes as a country develops.

There is often a high proportion of people working in the informal sector in developing countries.

As a country develops, the number of people working in the informal sector generally decreases until

there are very few people working in it.

[2]

[Total 5 marks]

Exam Questions

1 Study **Figure 1**, a photograph of some students in a city in Indonesia, an emerging country.

a) Using **Figure 1** and your own knowledge, state **two** opportunities for people living in a megacity in a developing or emerging country compared to living in rural areas.

Figure 1

1:..

....

....

....

....

2:..

....

....

[2]

b) Suggest why there are big differences in quality of life within megacities in emerging countries.

....

....

....

....

....

[4]

c) Explain how inequalities create challenges for the management of a named megacity.

....

....

....

....

....

[4]

d) For a named megacity in an emerging or developing country, assess the effectiveness of top-down and bottom-up strategies that have been used to make it more sustainable.

[8 + 4 SPaG]

[Total 22 marks]

Revision Summary

Now you've finished <u>Topic 3</u>, go ahead and see what you can remember.
- Try these questions and <u>tick off each one</u> when you <u>get it right</u>.
- When you've done <u>all the questions</u> under a heading and are <u>completely happy</u> with it, tick it off.

Urban Growth (p.47-48) ☐

1) What is urbanisation?
2) Where is urbanisation taking place most rapidly?
3) Describe the trend in urbanisation in developed countries.
4) What is a megacity?
5) Give two influences of a primate city on the country that it is in.
6) Give three push factors that lead to rural-urban migration.
7) Outline why many cities in developing countries are growing.
8) Give an example of an economic change that is leading to migration in developed countries.

Urban Characteristics and Trends (p.49-51) ☐

9) What is formal employment?
10) In which type of country does most informal employment take place?
11) What are the working conditions like in cities in developing countries?
12) Describe the urban economic structure of emerging countries.
13) What is suburbanisation?
14) Give two reasons why de-industrialisation occurs.
15) Define counter-urbanisation.
16) Give two pull factors that lead to counter-urbanisation.
17) a) What is urban regeneration?
    b) Why might it lead to re-urbanisation?
18) Describe where you might find commercial land use in a city.
19) How does accessibility affect urban land use?
20) How do planning regulations affect urban land use?

Urban Change — Case Study (p.52-57) ☐

For a megacity in a developing or emerging country that you have studied:
21) Where are the oldest buildings found?
22) Describe where most new growth is taking place in the city.
23) Give one reason why the population has grown rapidly in recent years.
24) Outline one way that population growth has led to a change in land use in the city.
25) Give three opportunities that the megacity offers to the people who live there.
26) Give two reasons for the differences in the quality of life within the megacity.

The UK Physical Landscape

Ah, the UK landscape. Majestic <u>mountains</u>, cracking <u>coasts</u> and raging <u>rivers</u>.

The UK has large **Upland** and **Lowland** Areas, and Important **Rivers**

The UK's main <u>upland</u> areas (orange and red on the map below) tend to be in the <u>north</u> and <u>west</u> of the country, and <u>lowland</u> areas (green on the map) to the <u>south</u> and <u>east</u>. You need to be able to <u>identify</u> them on a map.

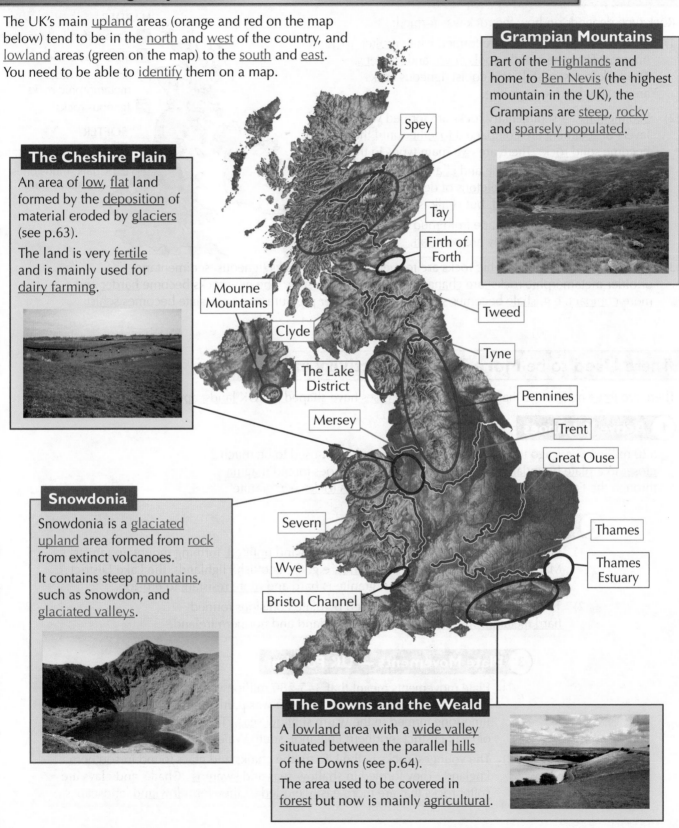

Grampian Mountains

Part of the <u>Highlands</u> and home to <u>Ben Nevis</u> (the highest mountain in the UK), the Grampians are <u>steep</u>, <u>rocky</u> and <u>sparsely populated</u>.

The Cheshire Plain

An area of <u>low</u>, <u>flat</u> land formed by the <u>deposition</u> of material eroded by <u>glaciers</u> (see p.63).

The land is very <u>fertile</u> and is mainly used for <u>dairy farming</u>.

Snowdonia

Snowdonia is a <u>glaciated</u> <u>upland</u> area formed from <u>rock</u> from extinct volcanoes.

It contains steep <u>mountains</u>, such as Snowdon, and <u>glaciated valleys</u>.

The Downs and the Weald

A <u>lowland</u> area with a <u>wide valley</u> situated between the parallel <u>hills</u> of the Downs (see p.64).

The area used to be covered in <u>forest</u> but now is mainly <u>agricultural</u>.

Map labels: Spey, Tay, Firth of Forth, Tweed, Tyne, Pennines, Trent, Great Ouse, Thames, Thames Estuary, Mourne Mountains, Clyde, The Lake District, Mersey, Severn, Wye, Bristol Channel

Most uplands are found in the north and west of the UK

This is a lovely introduction to the rest of the UK physical landscapes topic. Make sure you've got a grasp of the distribution of the UK's geographical features before you turn over. It'll help you understand the rest of the topic.

Rocks and the UK Physical Landscape

There are three types of rock — igneous, sedimentary and metamorphic. They're formed in different ways.

There are Three Types of Rocks

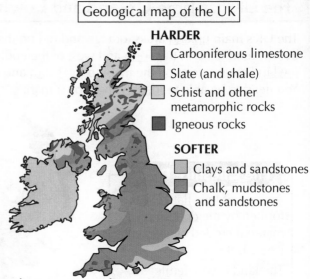

Geological map of the UK

HARDER
- Carboniferous limestone
- Slate (and shale)
- Schist and other metamorphic rocks
- Igneous rocks

SOFTER
- Clays and sandstones
- Chalk, mudstones and sandstones

Rock type depends on how the rock was formed:

1) Igneous — igneous rocks are formed when molten rock (magma) from the mantle cools down and hardens. The rock forms crystals as it cools. Igneous rocks are usually hard, e.g. granite.

2) Sedimentary — sedimentary rocks are formed when layers of sediment are compacted together until they become solid rock. There are two main types in the UK:
   - Carboniferous limestone and chalk are formed from tiny shells and skeletons of dead sea creatures. Limestone is quite hard, but chalk is a much softer rock.
   - Clays and shales are made from mud and clay minerals. They are very soft.

3) Metamorphic — metamorphic rocks are formed when other rocks (igneous, sedimentary or older metamorphic rocks) are changed by heat and pressure. The new rocks become harder and more compact, e.g. shale becomes slate and, with further pressure and heat, slate becomes schist.

There Used to be More Tectonic Activity in the UK

There are three main ways that past tectonic processes have shaped the UK landscape:

1 Active Volcanoes

520 million years ago the land that now makes up the UK used to be much closer to a plate boundary than it is now. Active volcanoes forced magma through the Earth's crust which cooled to form igneous rocks, e.g. granite.

2 Plate Collisions

1) Plate collisions caused the rocks to be folded and uplifted, forming mountain ranges. Many of these areas remain as uplands, e.g. the Scottish Highlands, the Lake District and north Wales — the igneous granite is hard and more resistant to erosion.

2) The intense heat and pressure caused by plate collisions formed hard metamorphic rocks in northern Scotland and northern Ireland.

3 Plate Movements — UK Position

1) Plate movements meant that 345-280 million years ago Britain was in the tropics and higher sea levels meant it was partly underwater — carboniferous limestone formed in the warm shallow seas. This can be seen in the uplands of Peak District (northern England), south Wales and south west England.

2) The youngest rocks in the UK are the chalks and clays found in southern England. They formed in shallow seas and swamps. Chalks and clays are softer rocks that are more easily eroded — they form lowland landscapes.

Different areas of the UK are made up of different types of rock

Igneous and metamorphic rocks are mostly found in the north and west of the UK. Sedimentary rocks are mostly found in the south and east. Thinking of them as 'SEdimentary' might help you remember this.

Rocks and the UK Physical Landscape

Each <u>rock type</u> has <u>different characteristics</u>. The characteristics of each rock type influence the type of <u>landscape</u> that forms. Much of the UK landscape has also been affected by <u>erosion</u> and <u>deposition</u> caused by <u>glaciers</u>.

The **Characteristics** of Different **Rock Types** Create Different **Landscapes**

Granite

1) Granite is very <u>resistant</u> and forms <u>upland landscapes</u>.
2) It has lots of <u>joints</u> (cracks) which <u>aren't evenly spread</u>. The parts of the rock where there are more joints wear down faster. Areas that have <u>fewer joints</u> are weathered <u>more slowly</u> than the surrounding rock and <u>stick out</u> at the surface forming <u>tors</u>.
3) Granite is <u>impermeable</u> — it <u>doesn't</u> let water through. This creates <u>moorlands</u> — large areas of <u>waterlogged land</u> and <u>acidic</u> soil, with <u>low-growing vegetation</u>.

Slate and Schist

1) <u>Slate</u> forms in <u>layers</u> creating <u>weak planes</u> in the rock. It is generally very <u>hard</u> and <u>resistant</u> to weathering but it is <u>easily split</u> into <u>thin slabs</u>.
2) <u>Schist</u> has <u>bigger crystals</u> than slate and also <u>splits easily</u> into small <u>flakes</u>.
3) Slate and schist often form <u>rugged</u>, upland landscapes. They are <u>impermeable</u>, which can lead to <u>waterlogged</u> and <u>acidic soils</u>.

Carboniferous Limestone

1) Rainwater slowly <u>eats away</u> at limestone through <u>carbonation weathering</u> (see p.68). Most weathering happens along <u>joints</u> in the rock, creating some spectacular <u>features</u>, e.g. <u>limestone pavements</u> (flat areas with deep weathered cracks), <u>caverns</u> and <u>gorges</u>.
2) Limestone is <u>permeable</u>, so limestone areas also have <u>dry valleys</u> and <u>resurgent rivers</u> (rivers that pop out at the surface when limestone is on top of impermeable rock).

Chalk and Clay

1) <u>Chalk</u> is <u>harder</u> than clay. It forms <u>escarpments</u> (hills) in <u>UK lowlands</u> and <u>cliffs</u> at the coast. One side of the hill is usually <u>steep</u> and the other side is more <u>gentle</u>.
2) Chalk is <u>permeable</u> — water <u>flows through</u> it and emerges as a <u>spring</u> where it meets impermeable rock.
3) <u>Clay</u> is very soft and <u>easily eroded</u>. It forms <u>wide flat valleys</u> in UK lowlands. It is <u>impermeable</u> so water flows over the surface — there are <u>lots</u> of <u>streams</u>, <u>rivers</u> and <u>lakes</u>.

Much of the **UK** Used to be **Covered** in **Ice**

1) There have been lots of <u>glacial</u> (cold) <u>periods</u> during the last <u>2.6 million years</u> (see p.4).
2) During some glacial periods, parts of the <u>UK</u> were covered in a <u>massive ice sheet</u>.
3) At its maximum, ice covered most of <u>Scotland</u>, <u>Ireland</u> and <u>Wales</u> and came as far south as the <u>Bristol Channel</u> in England.
4) Ice is very <u>powerful</u>, so it was able to <u>erode</u> the landscape, carving out large U-shaped <u>valleys</u> in upland areas such as the Lake District.
5) Glaciers also <u>deposited</u> lots of material as they <u>melted</u>. Landscapes formed by <u>glacial meltwater</u> and <u>deposits</u> extend <u>south</u> of the ice sheets. E.g. large parts of <u>eastern England</u> are covered in <u>till</u> (an unsorted mixture of clay, sand and rocks) <u>deposited</u> by melting glaciers.

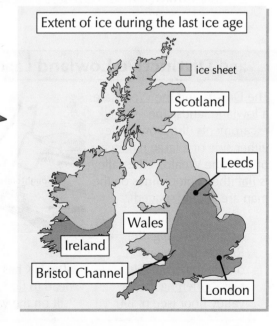

Extent of ice during the last ice age

☐ ice sheet

Scotland

Leeds

Wales

Ireland

Bristol Channel

London

The UK landscape is influenced by rock type and the action of ice

Make sure you're clued up on how rock types and glaciers have affected the UK's landscape before turning over.

Landscape Processes — Physical

It might look like nothing's changing, but <u>rocks</u> are constantly being <u>broken down</u>, <u>moved around</u> and <u>dumped</u>.

Physical Processes Alter the Landscape

1) <u>Physical processes</u> are constantly <u>changing</u> the <u>landscape</u> of the UK. They include:
   - <u>Weathering</u> — weathering is the <u>breakdown</u> of rock into smaller pieces. It can be <u>mechanical</u>, <u>chemical</u> or <u>biological</u> (see pages 68 and 82).
   - <u>Erosion</u> — erosion <u>wears away</u> rock. During the last glacial period, <u>ice</u> eroded the landscape. <u>Rivers</u> and the <u>sea</u> now <u>constantly</u> erode the landscape.
   - <u>Post-glacial river processes</u> — <u>melting ice</u> at the <u>end</u> of <u>glacial periods</u> made rivers <u>much bigger</u> than normal with more <u>power</u> to <u>erode</u> the <u>landscape</u>. The ice also left <u>distinctive landforms</u> when it <u>melted</u>, e.g. hanging valleys (little valleys that are left at a higher level than the main valley).
   - <u>Slope processes</u> — including <u>mass movements</u>, e.g. rockfalls, slides, slumps and <u>soil creep</u> (see pages 68 and 89).

2) Physical process are affected by <u>climate</u>. For example, a <u>cold</u> climate increases the likelihood of <u>freeze-thaw weathering</u> (see p.82) and a <u>wet climate</u> increases the <u>number</u> of <u>streams</u> and <u>rivers</u>.

Physical Processes Interact to Create Distinctive Upland Landscapes...

<u>Snowdonia</u> is an <u>upland</u> landscape — the map shows <u>tightly packed contours</u> and there are lots of <u>rocky crags</u>.

<u>Llyn Idwal</u> is a <u>tarn</u>. It sits in a corrie (basin) that was <u>hollowed out</u> by ice during glacial times.

<u>Freeze-thaw weathering</u> occurs on the <u>steep back wall</u> of the corrie. As the rocks are <u>broken up</u> there are <u>rock falls</u>, which form <u>scree slopes</u>.

This <u>large U-shaped valley</u> was eroded by ice — it has a <u>flat floor</u> and <u>steep sides</u>. The valley contains a <u>misfit river</u> that looks <u>too small</u> to have created it.

There is lots of <u>rain</u> in <u>Snowdonia</u> and the rocks are mostly <u>impermeable</u>. This means there are lots of <u>streams</u> that are eroding the steep sides of the corrie and forming <u>gullies</u>.

... and Distinctive Lowland Landscapes

<u>The Downs and the Weald</u> are a <u>lowland</u> landscape — <u>chalk escarpments</u> (the Downs) lie either side of a <u>large flat area</u> of <u>clay</u> (the Weald). The valley is <u>flat</u> (the contour lines on the map are <u>widely spaced</u>).

Large rivers, e.g. the River Arun, <u>meander</u> on the <u>impermeable</u> clay, <u>widening</u> the valley floor (see p. 84).

The UK has a <u>wet climate</u> — heavy rain can lead to <u>flooding</u>. The overflowing river <u>deposits</u> <u>silt</u> on the valley floor forming a <u>flood plain</u>.

<u>Dry valleys</u> are found in UK lowland landscapes. These are valleys with <u>no streams</u> visible (they flow <u>underground</u> in the <u>permeable chalk</u>). They formed during <u>glacial periods</u> when the <u>colder</u> climate led to more <u>freeze-thaw weathering</u> and <u>glacial snow melt</u> meant that <u>streams</u> had much <u>more water</u> in them than they do today.

Physical processes combine to create the different landscapes of the UK

Make sure you can explain a few ways that physical processes interact to shape upland and lowland landscapes.

Landscape Processes — Human

The UK is <u>small</u> and there are <u>a lot</u> of <u>people</u> — wherever you go, the <u>actions</u> of people have <u>changed</u> the <u>landscape</u>.

Humans have **Changed** the **Landscape** Through **Agriculture**...

1) People have <u>cleared</u> the land of <u>forest</u> to make space for <u>farming</u>.

2) Over time <u>hedgerows</u> and <u>walls</u> have been put in to mark out <u>fields</u>.

3) Different landscapes are best for <u>different types</u> of farming:

- <u>Arable</u> — <u>flat land</u> with good <u>soil</u>, e.g. east England, is used for arable farming (growing <u>crops</u>).

- <u>Dairy</u> — warm and wet areas, e.g. south west England, are good for <u>dairy farming</u>. There are lots of <u>large</u>, <u>grassy fields</u>.

- <u>Sheep</u> — sheep farming takes place in the <u>harsher</u> conditions in the <u>uplands</u>. Sheep are well suited to upland landscapes because they can cope with the <u>steep slopes</u> and <u>cold weather</u>. Sheep farming has led to a <u>lack of trees</u> on the hills (<u>young trees</u> are <u>eaten</u> or <u>trampled</u> before they get a chance to mature).

4) <u>OS®</u> <u>maps</u> show the influence of agriculture, including <u>field boundaries</u> and <u>drainage ditches</u> (dug to make the land dry enough for farming).

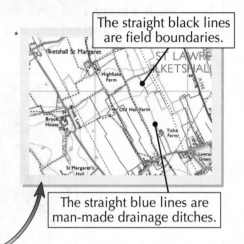

The straight black lines are field boundaries.

The straight blue lines are man-made drainage ditches.

... **Forestry**...

1) <u>Forestry</u> is the management of areas of <u>woodland</u> — they can be used for <u>timber</u>, <u>recreation</u> or <u>conservation</u>.

2) The UK used to be covered in <u>deciduous woodland</u>, but there is very <u>little</u> natural woodland <u>left</u>.

3) <u>Coniferous</u> (evergreen) forests have been planted for <u>timber</u>. The trees are often planted in <u>straight lines</u> — the forests don't look natural. When areas are <u>felled</u>, the landscape is left <u>bare</u>.

4) In some places, <u>deciduous</u> woodland is being <u>replanted</u> to try to <u>return</u> the area to a more <u>natural state</u>.

5) OS® maps show <u>forestry plantations</u> and areas that are being <u>managed</u>.

Coniferous forest is shown by this tree symbol.

Tracks are often used by forestry vehicles.

... and **Settlement**

1) Lots of factors influence <u>where settlements</u> have developed. For example, early settlers needed a <u>water supply</u>, somewhere that could easily be <u>defended</u> or that was <u>sheltered</u> from wind and rain.

2) Other factors such as <u>bridging points</u> over rivers and the <u>availability</u> of <u>resources</u>, e.g. wood for building, also played a part.

3) As settlements grew they further influenced the landscape. For example:

- land was <u>concreted</u> over for <u>roads</u> and <u>buildings</u>, which affected <u>drainage patterns</u>.

- some <u>rivers</u> were diverted through <u>underground channels</u>.

- some river channels were <u>straightened</u> or had <u>embankments</u> built to prevent flooding.

4) Most of the biggest cities are <u>ports</u> and <u>industrial areas</u>, e.g. London, West Midlands, Manchester and Portsmouth. These landscapes are <u>more urban</u> than natural.

5) Look for <u>buildings</u>, <u>railways</u>, <u>canals</u> and <u>embankments</u> to identify settlements on OS® maps.

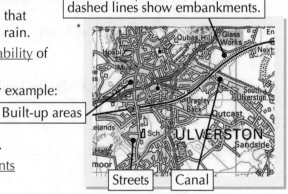

The land has been raised so the railway line is level — the dashed lines show embankments.

Built-up areas

Streets   Canal

REVISION TIP

Farming, forestry and construction have changed the UK landscape

If you're struggling to remember the different landscape processes, cover the pages and try drawing some mind maps showing both the human and physical processes and how they affect the landscape. When you've written everything you can remember, have a peek at the pages and fill in any gaps you've left.

Worked Exam Questions

Practice questions are useful for finding any areas that you need to look at again. Work through the questions on the next two pages — the first one has been done for you to help show what the examiners are after.

1   Study **Figure 1**, an Ordnance Survey® map of Thetford, Norfolk, a lowland area in the east of England.

Figure 1

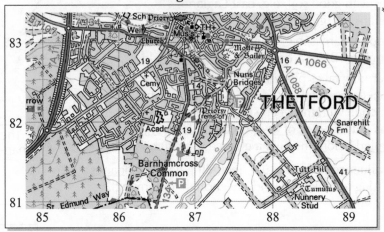

a)   Using **Figure 1**, give **one** piece of evidence that agriculture is taking place in this area.

A farm building is labelled on the map (Snarehill Farm).

[1]

b)   Using **Figure 1**, identify **two** ways that human settlement has altered the landscape in grid square 8582.

1: People have built roads.

2: Embankments have been built to make the road level.

[2]

c)   Using **Figure 1**, describe **one** way that forestry may be influencing the landscape.

Areas of coniferous forest have been planted. These areas are often planted in straight rows,

resulting in an unnatural landscape.

[2]

d)   Give **two** possible reasons why the land surrounding Thetford is suitable for arable farming.

1: The land is flat.

2: The land has good soils.

[2]

e)   Explain how farming in upland areas is different to farming in lowland areas.

Conditions in upland areas are harsher than in lowland areas. Farming there tends to be

sheep farming because they can cope with the steep slopes and colder weather.

[2]

[Total 9 marks]

Exam Questions

1   Study **Figure 1**, a map of the UK's upland and lowland areas.

a)   Identify area A in **Figure 1**.

Figure 1

    A   The Grampian Mountains in Scotland   ◯

    B   The Pennines in England   ◯

    C   The Lake District in England   ◯

    D   The Cairngorms in Scotland   ◯

[1]

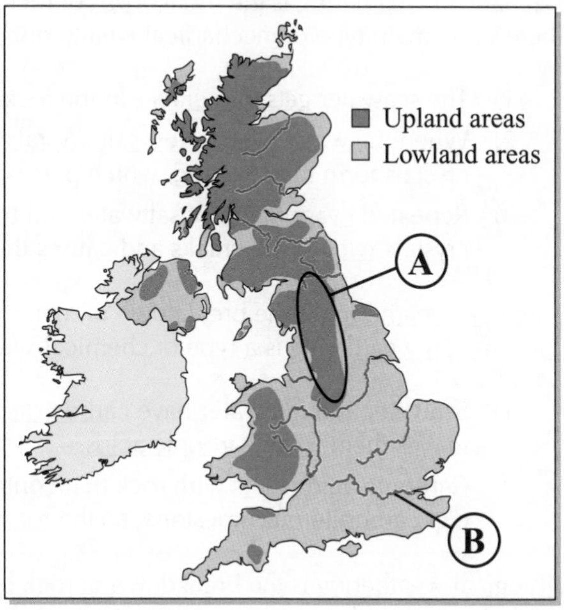

b)   Identify the feature marked B in **Figure 1**.

    A   The River Severn   ◯

    B   The Firth of Forth   ◯

    C   The Bristol Channel   ◯

    D   The River Thames   ◯

[1]

c)   State **two** ways in which past glacial processes have shaped upland areas in the UK.

1:...

2:...

[2]

[Total 4 marks]

2   Study **Figure 2**, a photo of a lowland area in the UK.

Explain how the interaction of physical processes may lead to the formation of lowland landscapes such as the one shown in **Figure 2**.

Figure 2

....

....

....

....

....

....

....

[Total 3 marks]

Coastal Change and Conflict

Coastal Weathering and Erosion

Weathering is the <u>breakdown</u> of rocks <u>where they are</u> and <u>erosion</u> is when the rocks are broken down and <u>carried away</u> by something, e.g. by seawater.

Rock is **Broken Down** by Mechanical, Chemical and **Biological Weathering**

1) <u>Mechanical weathering</u> is the <u>breakdown</u> of rock <u>without changing</u> its <u>chemical composition</u>. There's <u>one</u> main type of mechanical weathering that affects coasts — <u>salt weathering</u>:

> 1) The seawater <u>gets into cracks</u> in the rock.
> 2) When the water <u>evaporates</u>, <u>salt crystals</u> form. As the salt crystals form they <u>expand</u>, which puts <u>pressure</u> on the rock.
> 3) Repeated <u>evaporation</u> of saltwater and the <u>forming</u> of salt crystals <u>widens</u> the cracks and causes the rock to <u>break up</u>.

2) <u>Chemical weathering</u> is the breakdown of rock by <u>changing</u> its <u>chemical composition</u>. <u>Carbonation weathering</u> is a type of chemical weathering that happens in <u>warm</u> and <u>wet</u> conditions:

> 1) Seawater and rainwater have <u>carbon dioxide</u> dissolved in them, which makes them <u>weak carbonic acids</u>.
> 2) Carbonic acid <u>reacts</u> with rock that contains <u>calcium carbonate</u>, e.g. carboniferous limestone, so the <u>rocks</u> are <u>dissolved</u> by the rainwater.

3) <u>Biological weathering</u> is the breakdown of rock by <u>living things</u>, e.g. <u>plant roots</u> break down rocks by <u>growing into cracks</u> on their surface and <u>pushing them apart</u>.

Mass Movement is when **Material Falls Down** a **Slope**

Weathering and mass movement are called 'sub-aerial processes'.

1) Mass movement is the <u>shifting</u> of <u>rocks and loose material</u> down a slope, e.g. a cliff. It happens when the force of <u>gravity</u> acting on a slope is <u>greater than</u> the force <u>supporting</u> it.

2) Mass movements cause coasts to <u>retreat rapidly</u>.

3) They're <u>more likely</u> to happen when the material is <u>full of water</u> — it acts as a <u>lubricant</u>, and makes the material <u>heavier</u>.

4) There are <u>THREE</u> types of mass movement.

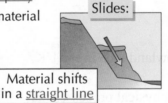

Material shifts in a <u>straight line</u>

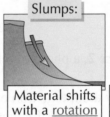

Slides:

Slumps:

Material shifts with a <u>rotation</u>

Rockfalls:

Material <u>breaks up</u> and <u>falls</u> down slope

Waves **Wear Away** the Coast Using **Three Processes** of **Erosion**

1) <u>Hydraulic power</u> — waves crash against rock and <u>compress</u> the <u>air</u> in the cracks. This puts <u>pressure</u> on the rock. <u>Repeated compression</u> widens the cracks and makes bits of rock <u>break off</u>.

2) <u>Abrasion</u> — eroded particles in the water <u>scrape</u> and <u>rub</u> against rock, <u>removing small pieces</u>.

3) <u>Attrition</u> — eroded particles in the water <u>smash into each other</u> and break into <u>smaller fragments</u>. Their <u>edges</u> also get <u>rounded off</u> as they rub together.

REVISION TIP

Practise sketching the three types of mass movement

This page is packed full of information, but it's just about how the coast is worn away and rocks are broken down into smaller pieces. Make sure you can sketch the diagrams without looking at the page.

Coastal Landforms Caused by Erosion

Erosion by waves forms many coastal landforms over long periods of time.

Coastlines can be Concordant or Discordant

1) The geological structure of a coastline influences the formation of erosional landforms.

2) Hard rocks like limestone and chalk are more resistant, so it takes longer for them to be eroded and weathered by physical processes.

3) Softer rocks like clay and sandstone are less resistant, which means they are eroded more quickly.

4) Joints and faults are cracks and weaknesses in the rock. Rocks with lots of joints and faults erode faster.

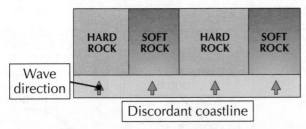

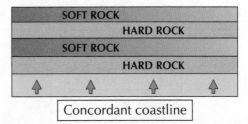

5) Some coastlines are made up of alternating bands of hard and soft rock that are at right angles to the coast — these are called discordant coastlines.

6) On a concordant coastline, the alternating bands of hard and soft rock are parallel to the coast.

7) Erosional landforms like bays and headlands are more common on discordant coastlines because the bands of rock are being eroded at different rates.

8) Concordant coastlines are eroded at the same rate along the coast. This means there are fewer erosional landforms.

The UK's Climate has an Impact on Coastal Erosion and Retreat

1) Temperature in the UK varies with the seasons. Temperatures are coldest in winter, warm through spring, hottest in summer, then cool through autumn.

2) Differences in temperature have an impact on processes along the coast, e.g. mild temperatures increase the rate of salt weathering (see previous page) because water evaporates more quickly.

3) Storms are very frequent in many parts of the UK, especially in winter. The strong winds create high energy, destructive waves which increase erosion of the cliffs. Intense rainfall can cause cliffs to become saturated — this makes mass movement (see previous page) more likely.

4) The prevailing (most common) winds in the UK are mostly warm south westerlies which bring storms from the Atlantic Ocean. The UK's south coast is exposed to these winds.

5) Cold northerly winds are also common, especially on the east coast of the UK.

Destructive Waves Wear Away the Coast

1) The waves that carry out erosional processes are called destructive waves.

2) Destructive waves are high, steep, and have a high frequency (10-14 waves per minute).

3) Their backwash (the movement of the water back down the beach) is more powerful than their swash (the movement of the water up the beach). This means material is removed from the coast.

4) Storms increase the erosional power of destructive waves, which can lead to increased rates of coastal retreat.

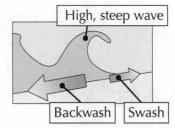

Learn the two different types of coastline

Remember — discordant coastlines tend to have a greater number of erosional landforms than concordant coastlines. This is because the bands of rock that make up a discordant coastline are being eroded at different rates.

Coastal Landforms Caused by Erosion

Those <u>destructive waves</u> from the previous page can form quite a few different coastal landforms.

Waves **Erode Cliffs** to Form **Wave-cut Platforms**

1) Waves cause <u>most erosion</u> at the <u>foot</u> of a cliff (see diagrams below).
2) This forms a <u>wave-cut notch</u>, which is enlarged as <u>erosion</u> continues.
3) The rock above the notch becomes <u>unstable</u> and eventually <u>collapses</u>.
4) The <u>collapsed material</u> is washed away and a <u>new</u> wave-cut notch starts to form.
5) <u>Repeated collapsing</u> results in the <u>cliff retreating</u>.
6) A <u>wave-cut platform</u> is the platform that's <u>left behind</u> as the <u>cliff retreats</u>.

> Hard rock cliffs tend to be more vertical, and soft rock cliffs tend to be more sloping.

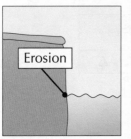
Erosion

Unstable rock | Wave-cut notch

Collapsed material

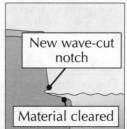
New wave-cut notch | Material cleared

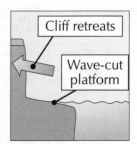
Cliff retreats | Wave-cut platform

Headlands and **Bays** Form Along **Discordant Coastlines**

1) <u>Soft</u> rocks or rocks with <u>lots of joints</u> have <u>low resistance</u> to erosion. <u>Hard</u> rocks with a <u>solid structure</u> have a <u>high resistance</u> to erosion.
2) <u>Headlands</u> and <u>bays</u> form where there are <u>alternating bands</u> of <u>resistant</u> and <u>less resistant</u> rock along a coast.
3) The <u>less resistant</u> rock (e.g. clay) is eroded <u>quickly</u> and this forms a <u>bay</u> — bays have a <u>gentle slope</u>.
4) The <u>resistant</u> rock (e.g. chalk) is eroded more <u>slowly</u> and it's left <u>jutting out</u>, forming a <u>headland</u> — headlands have <u>steep sides</u>.

⬜ = Less resistant rock
⬛ = Resistant rock
➤ = Erosion

Headland | Bay

Headlands are **Eroded** to form **Caves**, **Arches** and **Stacks**

1) Headlands are usually made of <u>resistant rocks</u> that have <u>weaknesses</u> like <u>cracks</u>.
2) <u>Waves</u> crash into the headlands and <u>enlarge</u> the cracks — mainly by <u>hydraulic power</u> and <u>abrasion</u>.
3) <u>Repeated erosion</u> and <u>enlargement</u> of the cracks causes a <u>cave</u> to form.
4) Continued erosion <u>deepens</u> the cave until it <u>breaks through</u> the headland — forming an <u>arch</u>, e.g. Durdle Door in Dorset.
5) Erosion continues to wear away the rock <u>supporting</u> the arch, until it eventually <u>collapses</u>.
6) This forms a <u>stack</u> — an <u>isolated rock</u> that's <u>separate</u> from the headland, e.g. Old Harry in Dorset.

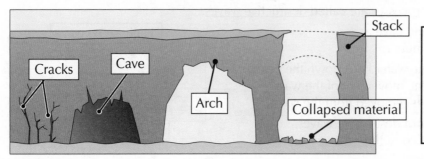
Cracks | Cave | Arch | Stack | Collapsed material

Arch | Durdle Door, Dorset

Caves are eroded to arches, which are eroded to stacks

This page might seem quite complicated to begin with, so take your time to learn how each landform is created. You could be asked about any landform in the exam, so make sure you learn this page off by heart.

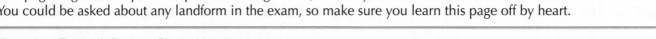

Coastal Landforms Caused by Deposition

The <u>material</u> that's been <u>eroded</u> is <u>moved around</u> the coast and <u>deposited</u> by waves.

Transportation is the Movement of Material

Material is transported <u>along coasts</u> by a process called <u>longshore drift</u>:

1) <u>Waves</u> follow the <u>direction</u> of the <u>prevailing wind</u>.

2) They usually hit the coast at an <u>oblique angle</u> (any angle that <u>isn't a right angle</u>).

3) The <u>swash</u> carries material <u>up the beach</u>, in the <u>same direction as the waves</u>.

4) The <u>backwash</u> then carries material <u>down the beach</u> at <u>right angles</u>, back towards the sea.

5) Over time, material <u>zigzags</u> along the coast.

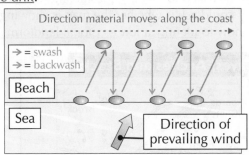

Constructive Waves Deposit Material

1) Deposition is when <u>material</u> being <u>carried</u> by the seawater is <u>dropped on the coast</u>. It occurs when water carrying sediment <u>slows down</u> so that it isn't moving <u>fast enough</u> to carry so much sediment.

2) Waves that <u>deposit more material</u> than they <u>erode</u> are called <u>constructive waves</u>.

3) Constructive waves are <u>low</u>, <u>long</u>, and have a <u>low frequency</u> (6-8 waves per minute).

4) The <u>swash</u> is <u>powerful</u> and it <u>carries material up the coast</u>.

5) The backwash is <u>weaker</u> and it <u>doesn't</u> take a lot of material <u>back down the coast</u>.

6) Constructive waves <u>deposit</u> material such as <u>sand</u> and <u>shingle</u> (gravel) along the coast to form <u>beaches</u>.

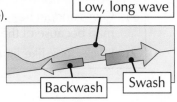

Deposited Sediment forms Spits and Bars

Spits

1) Spits form at <u>sharp bends</u> in the coastline, e.g. at a <u>river mouth</u>.

2) <u>Longshore drift</u> transports sand and shingle <u>past</u> the bend and <u>deposits</u> it in the sea.

3) Strong winds and waves can <u>curve</u> the end of the spit (forming a <u>recurved end</u>).

4) The <u>sheltered area</u> behind the spit is <u>protected from waves</u> — lots of material <u>accumulates</u> in this area, which means <u>plants</u> can grow there.

5) <u>Over time</u>, the sheltered area can become a <u>mud flat</u> or a <u>salt marsh</u>.

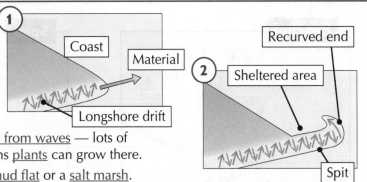

Bars

1) A bar is formed when a spit <u>joins two headlands together</u>.

2) The bar <u>cuts off</u> the bay between the headlands <u>from the sea</u>.

3) This means a <u>lagoon</u> can form <u>behind</u> the bar.

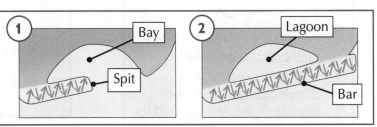

EXAM TIP

Bars are just spits that join two headlands together

If you're asked to explain coastal processes in the exam, you might find drawing a diagram helps. It doesn't have to be a work of art — just make sure you add labels to it so it's clear what it's showing.

Identifying Coastal Landforms

<u>Map skills</u> could well come in very useful in your exam so it's worth <u>practising</u> them now.

Identifying **Landforms Caused by Erosion**

You might be asked to <u>identify coastal landforms</u> on a <u>map</u> in the exam. The simplest thing they could ask is whether the map is showing <u>erosional</u> or <u>depositional landforms</u>, so here's how to <u>identify</u> a few <u>erosional landforms</u> to get you started:

 Have a look at pages 167-168 for more on reading maps.

Caves, Arches and Stacks

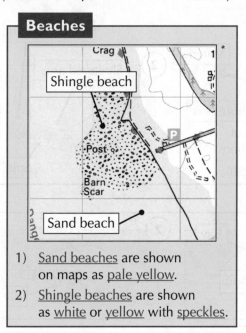

1) <u>Caves</u> and <u>arches</u> <u>can't be seen</u> on a map because of the rock <u>above them</u>.
2) <u>Stacks</u> look like <u>little blobs</u> in the sea.

Cliffs and Wave-cut Platforms

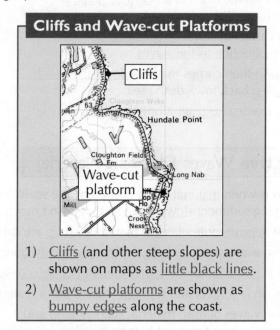

1) <u>Cliffs</u> (and other steep slopes) are shown on maps as <u>little black lines</u>.
2) <u>Wave-cut platforms</u> are shown as <u>bumpy edges</u> along the coast.

Identifying **Landforms Caused by Deposition**

<u>Identifying depositional landforms</u> is easy once you know that <u>beaches</u> are shown in <u>yellow</u> on maps. Here's how to <u>identify</u> a couple of <u>depositional landforms</u>:

Beaches

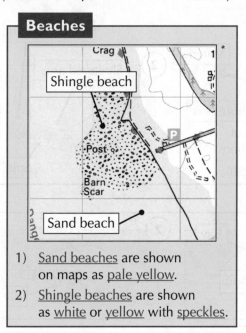

1) <u>Sand beaches</u> are shown on maps as <u>pale yellow</u>.
2) <u>Shingle beaches</u> are shown as <u>white</u> or <u>yellow</u> with <u>speckles</u>.

Spits

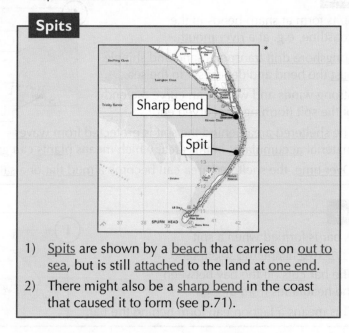

1) <u>Spits</u> are shown by a <u>beach</u> that carries on <u>out to sea</u>, but is still <u>attached</u> to the land at <u>one end</u>.
2) There might also be a <u>sharp bend</u> in the coast that caused it to form (see p.71).

Make sure you can identify each landform on a map

There are some easy marks up for grabs with map questions, so learn this page. Practise looking for landforms on any maps you can get hold of. Don't forget though — caves and arches can't be seen.

Human Activity at the Coast

The way <u>humans use</u> the coast can have an <u>effect</u> on the <u>landscape</u> and, you've guessed it, it's not always <u>positive</u>...

Human Activities have Direct and Indirect Effects on the Coast

1) <u>Direct effects</u> on the coastline are the <u>immediate result</u> of <u>human activities</u>. For example, building <u>coastal defences</u> will <u>prevent erosion</u>.

2) <u>Indirect effects</u> happen as a result of the <u>direct effects</u>. For example, building coastal defences will prevent erosion in <u>one place</u>, but it can increase erosion <u>further along the coast</u>.

Agriculture

1) Agricultural land has a <u>low economic value</u> which means it's often left <u>unprotected</u>. This has a direct effect on coastal landscapes because the sea can <u>erode</u> the cliffs and shape the land.

2) <u>Changing</u> the way <u>farmland</u> is used can affect the <u>stability</u> of cliffs.
   - <u>Vegetation</u> helps to bind the soil together and <u>stabilise</u> clifftops. <u>Clearing</u> vegetation from grazing land to make room for crops can <u>expose</u> the <u>soil</u> and underlying rock, leaving it vulnerable to <u>weathering</u> by wind and rain.

3) Land, e.g. <u>marshland</u>, is sometimes <u>reclaimed</u> and <u>drained</u> for agricultural use. Draining marshland directly affects the coast because it <u>reduces</u> the natural <u>flood barrier</u> that marshland provides.

Development

1) Coastal areas are popular places to <u>live</u> and <u>work</u>, so they often have lots of <u>development</u>, e.g. hotels and <u>infrastructure</u> (roads, rail, power lines etc.).

2) Coasts with lots of <u>settlement</u> may have more <u>coastal defences</u> than other areas because people want to <u>protect</u> their <u>homes</u> and <u>businesses</u>. This has a <u>positive</u> direct effect on the coastline because the land is <u>better protected</u> against erosion.

3) However, an <u>indirect effect</u> of development is the <u>change</u> in the <u>transportation</u> and <u>deposition</u> of material along the coast. Building on coastal lowlands can <u>restrict sediment</u> supply to <u>beaches</u>, making them narrower. Narrow beaches <u>don't protect</u> the coast as well, which means the land is more <u>vulnerable</u> to erosion.

Industry

1) Coastal <u>quarries</u> expose large areas of rock, making them more <u>vulnerable</u> to chemical <u>weathering</u> and <u>erosion</u>.

2) <u>Gravel</u> has been extracted from some <u>beaches</u> for use in the <u>construction industry</u>, e.g. for making concrete. This has <u>removed</u> material from the coast and <u>increased</u> the <u>risk</u> of <u>erosion</u> because there's <u>less</u> material to protect cliffs.

3) <u>Industrial growth</u> at <u>ports</u> has led to increased pressure to build on <u>salt marshes</u>. These areas provide <u>flat land</u> and <u>sheltered water</u>, which are ideal for <u>ports</u> and <u>industry</u>, but are also <u>natural flood barriers</u>. Building on them leaves the land <u>more vulnerable</u> to <u>erosion</u>.

Coastal Management

1) <u>Coastal management</u> is about <u>protecting coastal landscapes</u> from the <u>impacts</u> of <u>erosion</u>.

2) Some <u>management strategies</u> (see p.76) alter <u>sediment movement</u>, which <u>reduces</u> the amount of <u>protective</u> beach material further along the coast — this <u>increases erosion</u>.

3) <u>Coastal defences</u> can also <u>reduce erosion</u>. This has a direct effect on the coast because it <u>prevents</u> the landscape from <u>changing</u>, i.e. <u>retreating</u>.

Learn how human activity has an impact on the coast

It might not seem obvious how human activity affects the coast, but pretty much everything we do does. Read over this page until you're clear how each activity affects the rate of weathering and erosion and the impact this has.

Coastal Landscape

The <u>Holderness coast</u> in East Yorkshire has one of the <u>highest rates of coastal erosion</u> in Europe.

The **Holderness Coast** is on the **East Coast** of **England**

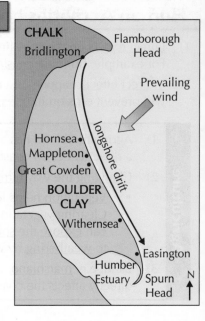

1) The Holderness coastline is <u>61 km long</u> — it stretches from <u>Flamborough Head</u> (a headland) to <u>Spurn Head</u> (a spit).

2) <u>Erosion</u> is causing the cliffs to <u>collapse</u>. About <u>1.8 m of land</u> is <u>lost</u> to the sea <u>every year</u> — in some places, e.g. <u>Great Cowden</u>, the rate of erosion has been <u>over 10 m per year</u> in recent years.

3) The cliffs are mostly made of <u>boulder clay</u> which is <u>easily eroded</u>. It's likely to <u>slump</u> when it's <u>wet</u>, causing the cliffs to collapse.

4) <u>Beaches</u> along the Holderness coast are <u>narrow</u>, which means they <u>don't</u> provide enough <u>protection</u> for the cliffs from the sea's <u>erosional power</u>.

5) Holderness faces the <u>prevailing wind direction</u>, which brings waves from the <u>north east</u> all the way from the <u>Norwegian Sea</u>. Waves <u>increase in power</u> over this <u>long distance</u>, so the coast is battered by <u>highly erosive waves</u>.

6) Eroded material is moved <u>south along</u> the coast by <u>longshore drift</u> instead of staying in the place it came from, <u>exposing</u> a <u>new</u> area of cliff to erosion and causing the <u>coastline</u> to <u>retreat</u>.

Parts of **Holderness** are **Protected** by **Coastal Defences**

1) <u>Over 11 km</u> of the Holderness coastline is protected by <u>hard engineering strategies</u> (see p.76) because:
   - There are <u>towns</u> and <u>villages</u> like Hornsea (population: over 8000), Withernsea (population: over 6000) and Mappleton where <u>people live</u>.
   - There is important <u>infrastructure</u> like the <u>B1242 road</u> which links many of the towns and businesses along the coast.
   - The <u>gas terminal</u> at <u>Easington</u> supplies <u>25%</u> of the UK's gas and is <u>right on the edge</u> of the <u>cliff</u>.

2) <u>Coastal defences</u> called <u>groynes</u> have been built at Mappleton.

3) There are also groynes and a sea wall at <u>Hornsea</u> and at <u>Withernsea</u>.

The **Defences** have **Caused Problems Further Along the Coast**

1) <u>Groynes</u> protect <u>local areas</u> but cause <u>narrow beaches</u> to form <u>further down</u> the Holderness coast. This increases erosion down the coast, e.g. <u>Great Cowden</u> (south of <u>Mappleton</u>) has lots of <u>farms</u> and <u>caravan parks</u> that are now <u>at risk</u> of <u>falling into the sea</u>.

2) The material produced from the erosion of Holderness is <u>normally transported south</u> into the <u>Humber Estuary</u> and <u>down</u> the <u>Lincolnshire coast</u>. Reducing the amount of material that's eroded and transported south <u>increases</u> the <u>risk</u> of <u>flooding</u> in the Humber Estuary, because there's <u>less material</u> to slow the floodwater down.

3) The rate of <u>coastal retreat</u> along the <u>Lincolnshire coast</u> has increased because <u>less new material</u> is being added.

4) <u>Spurn Head</u> is <u>at risk</u> of <u>being eroded away</u> because <u>less material</u> is being <u>added to it</u>.

5) <u>Bays</u> are forming <u>between</u> the <u>protected areas</u>, and the protected areas are becoming <u>headlands</u> which are being eroded <u>more heavily</u>. This means <u>maintaining the defences</u> in the protected areas is becoming <u>more expensive</u>.

Some of the coastal defences are moving the problems elsewhere

You don't have to learn this particular example if you've studied a different one in class — just make sure you know the ins and outs of how physical and human processes are affecting a specific coastal location. Located examples are a really good way of impressing the examiner and securing some extra marks.

Coastal Flooding

Coastal areas are increasingly at risk from flooding by the sea. This can cause a lot of problems for the environment and the people living there.

Climate Change is Increasing the Risk of Coastal Flooding

Rising sea levels and an increased frequency of storms are making coastal flooding more likely.

Rising Sea Levels

1) Rising sea levels (see p.7) pose a threat to low-lying and coastal areas.

2) An increase in sea levels could cause higher tides that would flood coastal areas more frequently.

3) Higher tides could also remove larger amounts of material from beaches. This could lead to increased erosion of cliffs because there's less material to protect them from the sea.

4) Rising sea levels could expose more of the coastline to erosion — beaches could become narrower as the sea will be able to move further inland.

Storm Frequency

1) Climate change is causing storms to become more frequent.

2) Storms give the sea more erosional power — areas of hard rock will be more vulnerable to erosion and areas of soft rock will erode more quickly.

3) The sea will also have more energy to transport material. High-energy waves can move more material for greater distances, which could lead to some areas being starved of material. This leaves these areas vulnerable to erosion and to flooding.

4) Storm surges (see p.12) could become more frequent and sea level rise could cause surges to reach areas further inland.

There are Threats to People and the Environment

Threats to People

1) Low-lying coastal areas could be permanently flooded or flood so often that they become impossible to inhabit.

2) Coastal industries may be shut down because of damage to equipment and buildings, e.g. fishing boats can be destroyed.

3) There's a risk of damage to infrastructure like roads and rail networks. For example, railway lines in Dawlish, Devon run parallel to the sea and are badly affected by flooding. Storms in 2014 damaged flood defences and parts of the track.

4) There's a booming tourist industry in coastal areas. Flooding and erosion can put people off visiting. Fewer tourists means businesses that rely on tourism may close, leading to a loss of livelihoods.

Threats to the Environment

1) Ecosystems will be affected because seawater has a high salt content. Increased salt levels due to coastal flooding can damage or kill organisms in an ecosystem. It can also affect agricultural land by reducing soil fertility.

2) The force of floodwater can uproot trees and plants, and standing floodwater drowns some trees and plants.

3) Some conservation areas are threatened by coastal erosion. For example, there are lagoons on the Holderness coast that are protected. The lagoons are separated from the sea by a bar. If this is eroded it will connect the lagoons to the sea and they would be destroyed.

Coastal areas are increasingly threatened by flooding

Coastal flooding can be very disruptive for local residents, and climate change is probably going to increase the frequency and impacts of floods. Make sure you learn the impacts of flooding on people and the environment.

Coastal Management

The <u>aim</u> of coastal management is to <u>protect</u> people and the environment from the <u>impacts</u> of erosion and flooding.

Coastal Defences Include Hard and Soft Engineering

Hard Engineering
<u>Man-made structures</u> built to <u>control the flow</u> of the sea and <u>reduce flooding</u> and <u>erosion</u>.

Soft Engineering
Schemes set up using <u>knowledge</u> of the sea and its <u>processes</u> to <u>reduce the effects of flooding</u> and <u>erosion</u>.

	Defence	What it is	Benefits	Costs
Hard Engineering	**Sea Wall**	A <u>wall</u> made out of a <u>hard material</u> like <u>concrete</u> that <u>reflects waves</u> back to sea.	It <u>prevents erosion</u> of the coast. It also acts as a <u>barrier</u> to <u>prevent flooding</u>.	It creates a <u>strong backwash</u>, which <u>erodes under</u> the wall. Sea walls are <u>very expensive</u> to <u>build</u> and to <u>maintain</u>.
	Groynes ← longshore drift	Wooden or stone <u>fences</u> that are built at <u>right angles</u> to the coast. They <u>trap material</u> transported by <u>longshore drift</u>.	They create <u>wider beaches</u> which <u>slow</u> the <u>waves</u>. This gives greater <u>protection</u> from <u>flooding</u> and <u>erosion</u>. They're a fairly <u>cheap</u> defence.	They <u>starve beaches</u> further down the coast of sand, making them <u>narrower</u>. Narrower beaches <u>don't protect</u> the coast as well, leading to <u>greater erosion</u> and <u>floods</u>.
Soft Engineering	**Beach Replenishment**	Sand and shingle from <u>elsewhere</u> (e.g. from the <u>seabed</u>) or from <u>lower down</u> the beach are <u>added</u> to the <u>upper part</u> of beaches.	It creates <u>wider beaches</u> which slow the waves. This gives greater <u>protection</u> from <u>flooding</u> and <u>erosion</u>.	Taking <u>material</u> from the <u>seabed</u> can <u>kill</u> organisms like <u>sponges</u> and <u>corals</u>. It's a <u>very expensive</u> defence. It has to be <u>repeated</u>.
	Slope Stabilisation	Slopes are <u>reinforced</u> by inserting <u>concrete nails</u> into the ground and covering the slope with <u>metal netting</u>.	It prevents <u>mass movement</u> by increasing the <u>strength</u> of the slope.	Slope stabilisation is <u>very expensive</u> and sometimes <u>very difficult</u> to <u>install</u>.
	Strategic Realignment	<u>Removing</u> an <u>existing defence</u> and allowing the land behind it to <u>flood</u>.	<u>Over time</u> the land will become <u>marshland</u>, creating <u>new habitats</u>. <u>Flooding</u> and erosion are <u>reduced</u> behind the marshland.	People may <u>disagree</u> over what land is <u>allowed to flood</u>, e.g. flooding farmland would affect the <u>livelihood</u> of farmers.

1) Another option is to <u>do nothing</u> — no new coastal defences are built and <u>erosion</u> and <u>flooding</u> are dealt with <u>as they happen</u>.

2) It <u>doesn't cost anything</u> to let the coast retreat <u>naturally</u>, but <u>infrastructure</u> (e.g. for <u>tourism</u>) may be <u>lost</u>.

3) <u>People</u> might also be forced to <u>move away</u> from the area because of the <u>risk of erosion</u> and <u>flooding</u>.

Management Strategies need to be Sustainable

1) In order to <u>protect</u> the coast and <u>avoid conflict</u>, management strategies need to be <u>sustainable</u>. This means making sure <u>erosion</u> and <u>flooding</u> are <u>controlled</u> without causing <u>more problems</u> elsewhere (e.g. erosion <u>further down</u> the coast) or affecting the <u>people</u> who <u>live</u> and <u>work</u> at the coast (e.g. <u>farmers</u> and <u>business owners</u>). Strategies also need to be <u>cheap</u> to avoid conflicts about the <u>spending</u> of <u>public money</u>.

2) <u>Integrated Coastal Zone Management</u> (<u>ICZM</u>) is an approach that aims to <u>protect</u> the coast while taking <u>everyone's interests</u> into account — this makes it <u>easier</u> to find <u>solutions</u> that people can <u>all agree on</u>.

3) It's also a <u>long-term</u> approach so it can be <u>adapted</u> to any <u>future needs</u> and <u>changes</u> along the coastline. This makes it a <u>sustainable</u> approach to managing the coast.

You might be asked to identify management strategies from a photo
Don't just learn the names of the different engineering strategies — make sure you know exactly what they look like, how they work and a couple of benefits and disadvantages of each one.

Worked Exam Questions

Have a read of these worked answers — they'll give you an idea of what you could write in the exam.

1   Study **Figures 1** and **2**. **Figure 1** shows a map of the Holderness coastline in the east of England. **Figure 2** shows a photograph of a cliff at Aldbrough.

Figure 1

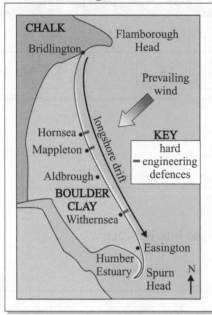

Figure 2

a)   Using **Figure 1**, identify **two** ways the location of the coastline may be leading to high rates of erosion.

1: The coastline faces the prevailing wind direction.

2: Waves from the north east have a long distance to increase in power.

[2]

b)   Explain how the location of the hard engineering defences might be changing the shape of the coastline.

They will protect local areas but increase erosion further down the coast. This could lead to the

formation of bays between the protected areas, with the protected areas remaining as headlands.

[2]

c)   Using **Figures 1** and **2**, suggest how the interaction of physical and human processes is influencing erosion at Aldbrough.

Hard engineering defences at Hornsea and Mappleton may be restricting the sediment supply to

the beach shown in Figure 2. A narrower beach means the cliffs at Aldbrough are less protected

from erosion. The cliffs at Aldbrough are made of boulder clay, which is a soft rock. Boulder clay is

likely to slump when wet, increasing the rate of erosion.

[4]

[Total 8 marks]

Exam Questions

1   Study **Figure 1**, which shows the frequencies of storms and floods between 2006 and 2015 in a coastal area of the UK.

Figure 1

Year	2006	2007	2008	2009	2010	2011	2012	2013	2014	2015
Number of storms	0	1	3	3	4	3	5	5	6	7
Number of floods	0	0	1	2	3	2	4	4	5	5

a)   Calculate the mean number of floods per year.

....

....
[1]

b)   Identify **one** way that the data could be presented to show the link between the number of storms and the number of floods.

....
[1]

c)   Explain how storms can increase the frequency of coastal flooding.

....

....

....

....

....
[4]

d)   Suggest **one** threat to people from increased frequency of coastal flooding.

....

....

....
[2]

e)   Describe **one** way that coastal flooding has a negative impact on the environment.

....

....

....
[2]

[Total 10 marks]

Revision Summary

That's the first half of Topic 4 done with. Here are some questions for you to have a go at before moving on.
*   Try these questions and tick off each one when you get it right.
*   When you've done all the questions under a heading and are completely happy with it, tick it off.

Rocks and the UK Physical Landscape (p.61-63) ☑

1) a)   How are igneous rocks formed? ☑
    b)   What are sedimentary rocks formed from? ☑
    c)   Describe how metamorphic rocks are formed. ☑
2) Give two ways in which tectonic activity has shaped the UK landscape. ☑
3) Outline the characteristics of slate and schist. ☑
4) Explain how the UK landscape has been shaped by glacial periods. ☑

Landscape Processes (p.64-65) ☑

5) Give three physical processes that alter the landscape. ☑
6) a)   Give an example of a lowland landscape. ☑
    b)   Outline how physical processes have created this landscape. ☑
7) How does forestry change the landscape? ☑
8) How does settlement alter the landscape? ☑

Coastal Processes and Landforms (p.68-72) ☑

9)   How does salt weathering break up rock? ☑
10) What are the three types of erosion caused by waves? Explain how they work. ☑
11) What is the difference between a discordant and a concordant coastline? ☑
12) What are the characteristics of destructive waves? ☑
13) Describe how erosion can turn a crack in a cliff into a cave. ☑
14) How does longshore drift transport sediment along a coast? ☑
15) What are the characteristics of constructive waves? ☑
16) Where do spits form? ☑
17) What do stacks look like on a map? ☑
18) How are cliffs shown on a map? ☑
19) On maps, what do speckles on top of yellow shading tell you? ☑

Human Activity and Coastal Management (p.73-76) ☑

20) Explain how agriculture can have a direct effect on the coast. ☑
21) How does development affect the coast? ☑
22) Give one effect of coastal management on the coastline. ☑
23) Describe one human process that is causing change on a named coastal landscape. ☑
24) Why does sea level rise increase the risk of coastal flooding? ☑
25) What is the difference between hard and soft engineering? Give an example of each. ☑
26) What are the disadvantages of using groynes for coastal management? ☑
27) What is strategic realignment? ☑
28) How are coastal management strategies being made more sustainable? ☑

River Landscapes

The shape of a river valley and a river's gradient change as the river flows downhill.

A River's **Long Profile** and **Cross Profile Vary** Over its Course

1) The path of a river as it flows downhill is called its course.
2) Rivers have an upper course (closest to the source of the river), a middle course and a lower course (closest to the mouth of the river).
3) Rivers form channels and valleys as they flow downhill.
4) They erode the landscape — wear it down, then transport the material to somewhere else where it's deposited.
5) The shape of the valley and channel changes along the river depending on whether erosion or deposition is having the most impact (is the dominant process).
6) The long profile of a river shows you how the gradient (steepness) changes over the different courses.
7) The cross profile shows you what a cross-section of the river looks like.

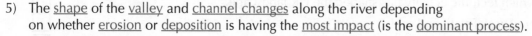

Valley

Channel

Water

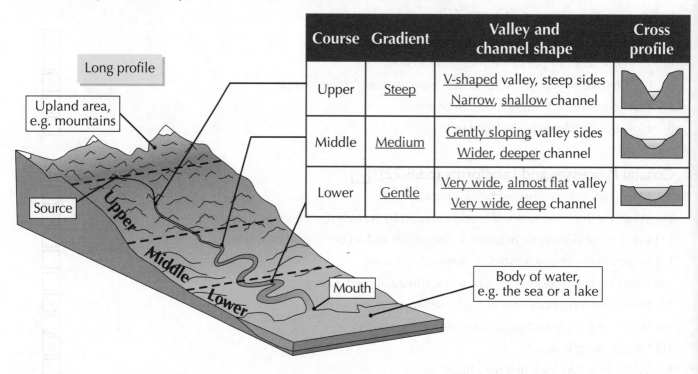

Course	Gradient	Valley and channel shape	Cross profile
Upper	Steep	V-shaped valley, steep sides \ Narrow, shallow channel	
Middle	Medium	Gently sloping valley sides \ Wider, deeper channel	
Lower	Gentle	Very wide, almost flat valley \ Very wide, deep channel	

Long profile

Upland area, e.g. mountains

Source

Upper

Middle

Lower

Mouth

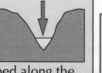

Body of water, e.g. the sea or a lake

Vertical and Lateral Erosion Change the Cross Profile of a River

Erosion can be vertical or lateral — both types happen at the same time, but one is usually dominant over the other at different points along the river:

There's more on the processes of erosion on the next page.

Vertical erosion

This deepens the river valley (and channel), making it V-shaped. It's dominant in the upper course of the river. High turbulence causes the rough, angular particles to be scraped along the river bed, causing intense downwards erosion.

Lateral erosion

This widens the river valley (and channel) during the formation of meanders (see page 84). It's dominant in the middle and lower courses.

REVISION TIP

Long profile = gradient, cross profile = a cross-section of the river

Try sketching the cross profile diagrams and describing the shape of the valley and channel, just to check you've got it all memorised. Make sure you learn where vertical and lateral erosion are more dominant.

River Landscapes

You can see many of the <u>landforms</u> of <u>erosion</u> and <u>deposition</u> typical to river landscapes along the <u>River Eden</u>.

The **River Eden's Landscape Changes** Along its **Course**

Eden basin

1) The River Eden is in <u>north-west England</u>, between the mountains of the <u>Lake District</u> and the <u>Pennines</u>. It's <u>145 km long</u> from source to mouth.

2) The River Eden's <u>source</u> is in the Pennine hills in south Cumbria. It flows north-west through <u>Appleby-in-Westmorland</u> and <u>Carlisle</u>. Its mouth is in the <u>Solway Firth</u> at the Scottish border.

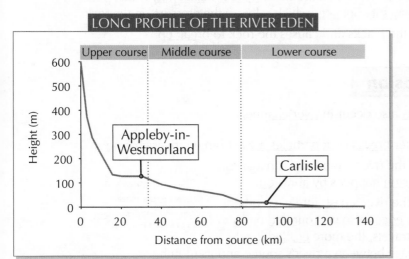
LONG PROFILE OF THE RIVER EDEN
Upper course | Middle course | Lower course
Appleby-in-Westmorland
Carlisle

UPPER COURSE

- The <u>source</u> of the Eden is about <u>600 m</u> above sea level in an area of <u>hard</u>, <u>resistant rock</u>.
- The valley is <u>steep-sided</u> due to <u>vertical erosion</u> and the channel has a <u>steep gradient</u>.
- The <u>river channel</u> is <u>narrow</u> and <u>shallow</u> — this means the <u>discharge</u> (see p. 90) is <u>low</u>. The <u>velocity</u> (speed) is <u>low</u> due to <u>friction</u> from the <u>rough channel sides</u> and <u>bed</u>.
- The river carries <u>large, angular stones</u>.

River Eden at Appleby

MIDDLE COURSE

- The <u>middle parts</u> of the <u>Eden basin</u> are made from <u>sandstone</u>, a <u>soft</u>, <u>less-resistant rock</u> which is <u>easily eroded</u> by the river. This means that the <u>river valley</u> becomes <u>wider</u> because of <u>lateral</u> (sideways) <u>erosion</u>.

A meander at Salkeld

- The valley sides become <u>gentle slopes</u> and the <u>gradient</u> of the channel is <u>less steep</u>.
- The river channel also becomes <u>wider</u> and <u>deeper</u>. Discharge <u>increases</u> as more <u>streams</u> join the main river.
- The river's <u>sediment load</u> is made up of <u>smaller</u> and <u>more rounded</u> rocks than it was in the <u>upper course</u> as erosion continues (see next page).

LOWER COURSE

- In the lower course, the <u>valley</u> is <u>very wide</u> and <u>flat</u>.

- By the time the Eden reaches <u>Carlisle</u>, it's only <u>a few metres</u> above sea level.
- The river has a <u>high velocity</u> (it's <u>flowing fast</u>) because there's <u>very little friction</u> from the channel's <u>smooth sides</u>. It also has a <u>very large discharge</u> because two other rivers (the Caldew and the Petteril) join the Eden in Carlisle.
- The <u>river channel</u> is <u>very wide</u> and <u>deep</u> — in the centre of Carlisle, the Eden is more than <u>50 m</u> wide. <u>Material</u> carried by the river is <u>fine</u> and <u>well-rounded</u> — most of it is carried by <u>suspension</u> or <u>solution</u> (see next page).

River Eden at Carlisle

The River Eden is affected by geological changes along its course

Most of the features along the River Eden are caused by changing geology along the basin of the river. Make sure you understand how different rock types are affected by erosion and deposition along a river's course.

River Processes

As rivers flow, they <u>erode</u> material, <u>transport</u> it and then <u>deposit</u> it further <u>downstream</u>.

Weathering Helps Shape River Valleys

Weathering <u>breaks down rocks</u> on the valley sides.
<u>Freeze-thaw weathering</u> is a type of <u>mechanical weathering</u> (see p. 68):

Chemical and biological weathering also affect river valleys.

1) <u>Freeze-thaw weathering</u> happens when the temperature alternates <u>above</u> and <u>below</u> 0 °C (the <u>freezing point</u> of water).

2) Water <u>gets into</u> rock that has <u>cracks</u>, e.g. granite. When the water <u>freezes</u> it <u>expands</u>, which puts <u>pressure</u> on the rock. When the water <u>thaws</u> it <u>contracts</u>, which <u>releases</u> the pressure on the rock.

3) <u>Repeated freezing</u> and <u>thawing</u> widens the cracks and causes the rock to <u>break up</u>.

There are Four Processes of Erosion

The <u>processes of erosion</u> that occur along <u>coasts</u> also occur in <u>river channels</u>:

1) <u>Hydraulic action</u> — the <u>force</u> of the water <u>breaks rock particles away</u> from the <u>river channel</u>.

2) <u>Abrasion</u> — eroded <u>rocks</u> picked up by the river <u>scrape</u> and <u>rub</u> against the <u>channel</u>, wearing it away. <u>Most erosion</u> happens by <u>abrasion</u>.

The faster a river's flowing, the more erosion happens.

3) <u>Attrition</u> — eroded <u>rocks</u> picked up by the river <u>smash into each other</u> and break into <u>smaller fragments</u>. Their <u>edges</u> also get <u>rounded off</u> as they rub together. The <u>further</u> material travels, the more <u>eroded</u> it gets — attrition causes <u>particle size</u> to <u>decrease</u> between a river's <u>source</u> and its <u>mouth</u>.

4) <u>Solution</u> — river water <u>dissolves</u> some types of rock, e.g. <u>chalk</u> and <u>limestone</u>.

Transportation is the Movement of Eroded Material

The <u>material</u> a river has <u>eroded</u> is <u>transported downstream</u>.
There are <u>four processes</u> of transportation:

Traction
<u>Large</u> particles like boulders are <u>pushed</u> along the <u>river bed</u> by the <u>force of the water</u>.

Suspension
<u>Small</u> particles like silt and clay are <u>carried along</u> by the water.

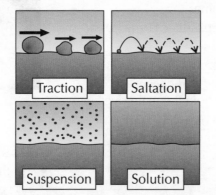

Saltation
<u>Pebble-sized</u> particles are <u>bounced along</u> the <u>river bed</u> by the <u>force of the water</u>.

Solution
<u>Soluble materials dissolve</u> in the water and are <u>carried along</u>.

Deposition is When a River Drops Eroded Material

Deposition is when a river <u>drops</u> the <u>eroded material</u> it's <u>transporting</u>.

It happens when a river <u>slows down</u> (<u>loses velocity</u>).

There are a <u>few reasons</u> why rivers slow down and deposit material:

1) The <u>volume</u> of <u>water</u> in the river <u>falls</u>.

2) The <u>amount</u> of <u>eroded material</u> in the water <u>increases</u>.

3) The water is <u>shallower</u>, e.g. on the <u>inside of a bend</u>.

4) The river <u>reaches</u> its <u>mouth</u>.

Learn the four processes of erosion and the four processes of transportation

There are lots of very similar names to remember here — try not to confuse saltation, solution and suspension. And yes, solution is both a process of erosion and transportation. Get them fixed in your head before moving on.

River Landforms — Erosion

The <u>processes</u> of erosion on the previous page <u>change the landscape</u> and create <u>distinctive landforms</u>. Now's your chance to find out all about them, starting with <u>waterfalls</u>...

Waterfalls and Gorges are Found in the Upper Course of a River

1) <u>Waterfalls</u> form where a river flows over an area of <u>hard rock</u> followed by an area of <u>softer rock</u>.

2) The <u>softer rock</u> is <u>eroded</u> (by <u>hydraulic action</u> and <u>abrasion</u> — see previous page) <u>more</u> than the <u>hard rock</u>, creating a 'step' in the river.

3) As water goes over the step it <u>erodes more and more</u> of the softer rock.

4) A <u>steep drop</u> is eventually created, which is called a <u>waterfall</u>.

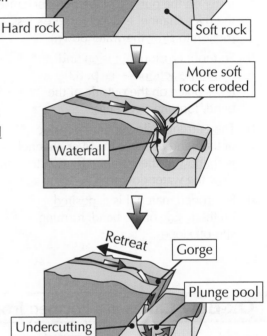

Step

Hard rock

Soft rock

More soft rock eroded

Waterfall

5) The <u>hard rock</u> is eventually <u>undercut</u> by erosion. It becomes <u>unsupported</u> and <u>collapses</u>.

6) The collapsed rocks are <u>swirled around</u> at the foot of the waterfall where they <u>erode</u> the softer rock by <u>abrasion</u>. This creates a deep <u>plunge pool</u>.

7) Over time, <u>more undercutting</u> causes <u>more collapses</u>. The waterfall will <u>retreat</u> (move back up the channel), leaving behind a steep-sided <u>gorge</u>.

Retreat

Gorge

Plunge pool

Undercutting

Some Rivers Wind around Interlocking Spurs

1) In the <u>upper course</u> of a river most of the <u>erosion</u> is <u>vertically downwards</u>. This creates <u>steep-sided</u>, <u>V-shaped valleys</u>.

2) The rivers <u>aren't powerful enough</u> to <u>erode laterally</u> (sideways) — they have to <u>wind around</u> the <u>high hillsides</u> that stick out into their paths on either side.

3) The <u>hillsides that interlock</u> with each other (like a zip if you were looking from above) as the river winds around them are called <u>interlocking spurs</u>.

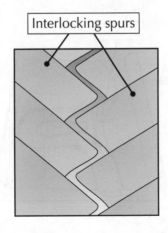

Interlocking spurs

Interlocking spurs along a river in Shropshire

Waterfalls, gorges and interlocking spurs are landforms resulting from erosion

Step over the hard rock and plunge into the pool — that's how I remember how waterfalls are formed. Geography examiners love river landforms (they're a bit weird like that) so make sure you learn how they form.

River Landforms — Erosion and Deposition

When a river's <u>eroding</u> and <u>depositing</u> material, <u>meanders</u> and <u>ox-bow lakes</u> can form.

Meanders are Formed by **Erosion** and **Deposition**

Rivers develop <u>large bends</u> called <u>meanders</u> in their <u>middle</u> and <u>lower courses</u>, in areas where there are both <u>shallow</u> and <u>deep</u> sections in the channel:

1) The <u>current</u> (the flow of the water) is <u>faster</u> on the <u>outside</u> of the bend because the river channel is <u>deeper</u> (there's <u>less friction</u> to <u>slow</u> the water down).

2) So more <u>erosion</u> (<u>abrasion</u> and <u>hydraulic action</u> — see p. 82) takes place on the <u>outside</u> of the bend, forming <u>river cliffs</u>.

3) The <u>current</u> is <u>slower</u> on the <u>inside</u> of the bend because the river channel is <u>shallower</u> (there's <u>more friction</u> to <u>slow</u> the water down).

4) So eroded material is <u>deposited</u> on the <u>inside</u> of the bend, forming <u>slip-off slopes</u>.

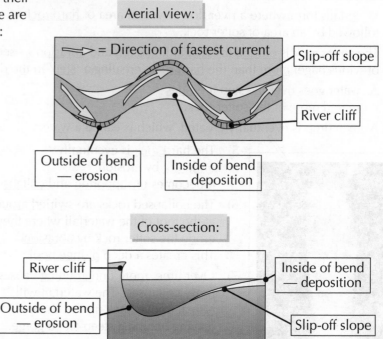

Ox-Bow Lakes are Formed from **Meanders**

Meanders get <u>larger</u> over time — they can eventually turn into an <u>ox-bow lake</u>:

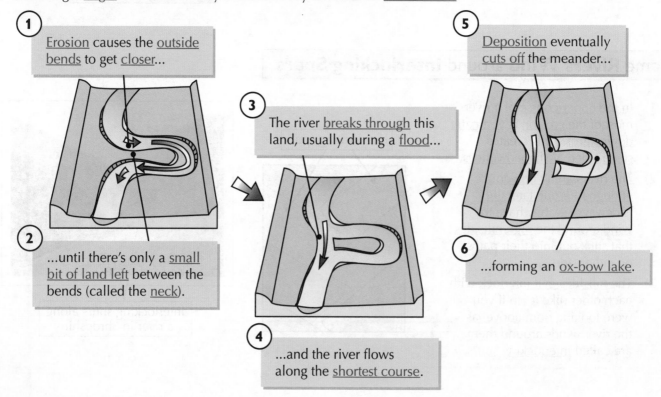

1) <u>Erosion</u> causes the <u>outside bends</u> to get <u>closer</u>...

2) ...until there's only a <u>small bit of land left</u> between the bends (called the <u>neck</u>).

3) The river <u>breaks through</u> this land, usually during a <u>flood</u>...

4) ...and the river flows along the <u>shortest course</u>.

5) <u>Deposition</u> eventually <u>cuts off</u> the meander...

6) ...forming an <u>ox-bow lake</u>.

The features of meanders are formed by erosion and deposition

In the exam, don't be afraid to draw diagrams of river landforms — examiners love a good diagram and they can help make your answer clear. Don't spend forever making them look pretty though...

River Landforms — Deposition

When rivers <u>flow fast</u>, they <u>erode</u> the landscape. As they <u>slow down</u>, they make <u>landforms</u> through <u>deposition</u>.

Flood Plains are Flat Areas of Land that Flood

1) The <u>flood plain</u> is the <u>wide valley floor</u> on either side of a river which occasionally <u>gets flooded</u>.
2) When a river <u>floods</u> onto the flood plain, the water <u>slows down</u> and <u>deposits</u> the <u>eroded material</u> that it's <u>transporting</u>. This <u>builds up</u> the flood plain (makes it <u>higher</u>).
3) <u>Meanders migrate</u> (move) <u>across</u> the flood plain, making it <u>wider</u>.
4) Meanders also migrate <u>downstream</u>, <u>flattening</u> out the valley floor.
5) The <u>deposition</u> that happens on the <u>slip-off slopes</u> of meanders also <u>builds up</u> the flood plain.

Flood plain

All these landforms are found in the lower course of a river.

Levees are Natural Embankments

1) Levees are <u>natural embankments</u> (raised bits) along the <u>edges</u> of a <u>river channel</u>.
2) During a flood, <u>eroded material</u> is <u>deposited</u> over the whole flood plain.
3) The <u>heaviest material</u> is <u>deposited closest</u> to the river channel, because it gets <u>dropped first</u> when the river <u>slows down</u>.
4) <u>Over time</u>, the <u>deposited material builds up</u>, creating <u>levees</u> along the edges of the channel.

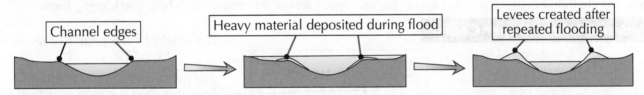

Channel edges | Heavy material deposited during flood | Levees created after repeated flooding

Deltas are Low-Lying Areas Where a River Meets the Sea or a Lake

1) Rivers are forced to <u>slow down</u> when they <u>meet the sea</u> or a <u>lake</u>. This causes them to <u>deposit</u> the <u>material</u> that they're carrying.
2) If the <u>sea doesn't wash away</u> the material it <u>builds up</u> and the <u>channel gets blocked</u>. This forces the channel to <u>split up</u> into lots of <u>smaller rivers</u> called <u>distributaries</u>.
3) Eventually the material <u>builds up so much</u> that <u>low-lying areas of land</u> called <u>deltas</u> are <u>formed</u>.

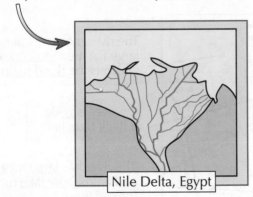

Nile Delta, Egypt

Ebro Delta, Spain

Deposition is common in the lower course of a river

As the river slows down in its lower course, material is dropped. This leads to the formation of different landforms. Make sure you know the characteristics of these landforms and you can describe the processes of their formation.

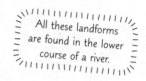

Identifying River Landforms

You can know all the facts about <u>rivers</u>, but if you don't know what their <u>features</u> look like on <u>maps</u> then some of the exam questions could get a wee bit tricky. Here's something I prepared earlier...

Contour Lines Tell you the Direction a River Flows

<u>Contour lines</u> are the <u>orange lines</u> drawn all over maps. They tell you about the <u>height</u> of the land (in metres) by the numbers marked on them, and the <u>steepness</u> of the land by how <u>close together</u> they are (the <u>closer</u> they are, the <u>steeper</u> the slope).

It sounds obvious, but rivers <u>can't</u> flow uphill. Unless gravity's gone screwy, a river flows <u>from higher</u> contour lines <u>to lower</u> ones. Have a look at this map of Cawfell Beck:

> ⑴ The <u>height values</u> get <u>smaller</u> towards the <u>west</u> (left), so west is <u>downhill</u>.

> Take a peek at pages 167-168 for more on reading maps.

> ⑵ Cawfell Beck is flowing from <u>east</u> to <u>west</u> (right to left).

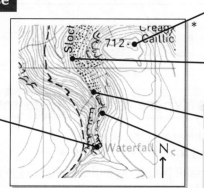

> ⑶ A <u>V-shape</u> is formed where the contour lines <u>cross</u> the river. The V-shape is <u>pointing uphill</u> to where the river came from.

Maps contain Evidence for River Landforms

Exam questions might ask you to look at a <u>map</u> and give the <u>evidence</u> for a <u>landform</u>. Remember, different landforms are found in the <u>upper</u> and <u>lower course</u> — you can use this evidence to help you <u>identify</u> them.

Evidence for the Upper Course

> <u>Waterfalls</u> are often marked on maps. The <u>symbol for a cliff</u> (black, blocky lines) and <u>close contour lines</u> can also be evidence of waterfalls.

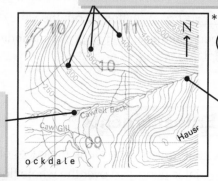

> The nearby land is <u>high</u> (712 m).

> The river <u>crosses lots</u> of <u>contour lines</u> in a <u>short distance</u>, which means it's <u>steep</u>.

> The river is <u>narrow</u> (a <u>thin</u> blue line).

> The <u>contour lines</u> are very <u>close together</u> and the valley floor is narrow. This means the river is in a <u>steep-sided V-shaped</u> valley.

Evidence for the Lower Course

> The nearby land is <u>low</u> (less than 15 m).

> The river doesn't <u>cross any contour lines</u> so it's <u>very gently sloping</u>.

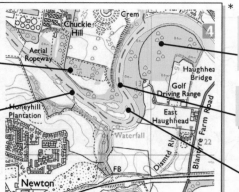

> The river meanders across a large flat area (<u>no contours</u>), which is the <u>flood plain</u>.

> The river is <u>wide</u> (a <u>thick</u> blue line).

> The river has <u>large meanders</u> and an <u>ox-bow lake</u> may be formed here.

EXAM TIP — **Pay close attention to contour lines, height values and symbols**
Map questions can be a goldmine of easy marks in the exam — all you have to do is say what you see. Make sure you know how to use a map to identify all the river landforms covered on this page.

Worked Exam Questions

Time to put your knowledge to the test... We've made life easier for you by giving you the answers to the first page of practice exam questions. Read over them to get an idea of what your exam answers should be like.

1 Study **Figure 1**, a cross profile of a river.

Figure 1

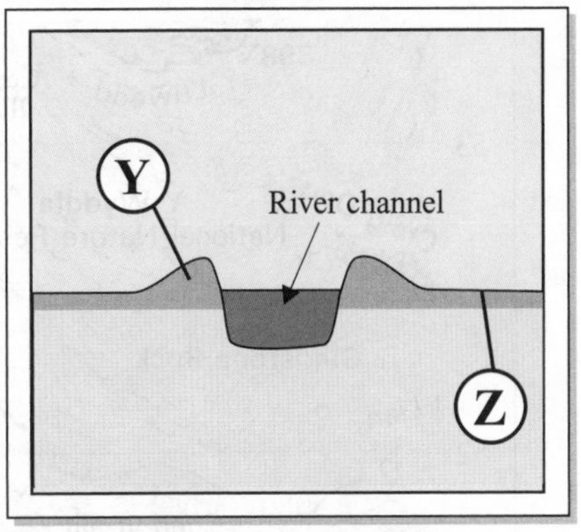

a) Identify the feature labelled Y on **Figure 1**.

    A   Levee   ⬤

    B   Estuary   ◯

    C   Flood plain   ◯

    D   Gorge   ◯

                                      [1]

b) Explain how the landform labelled Y in **Figure 1** is formed.

    During a flood, eroded material is deposited over the whole flood plain. The heaviest material

    is deposited closest to the river channel, because it gets dropped first when the river slows down.

    Over time, the deposited material builds up, creating levees along the edges of the channel.

                                          [3]

c) Explain how the landform labelled Z in **Figure 1** builds up over time.

    When the river floods onto the flood plain, the water slows down and deposits the eroded

    material that it's transporting, so if the river floods repeatedly, the flood plain builds up.

                                          [2]

                                 [Total 6 marks]

2 **Figure 2** shows a photograph of a delta in Inversanda Bay, Scotland.

Figure 2

Explain the processes involved in the formation of the landform shown in **Figure 2**.

    The river is forced to slow down as it reaches the coast, causing it to deposit the material it was

    carrying. This material builds up, forcing the channel to split up into smaller rivers (distributaries).

    The material builds up so much that it forms a low-lying area of land.

                                          [Total 4 marks]

Exam Questions

1 Study **Figure 1**, which is an Ordnance Survey® map showing part of Snowdonia, Wales.

Figure 1

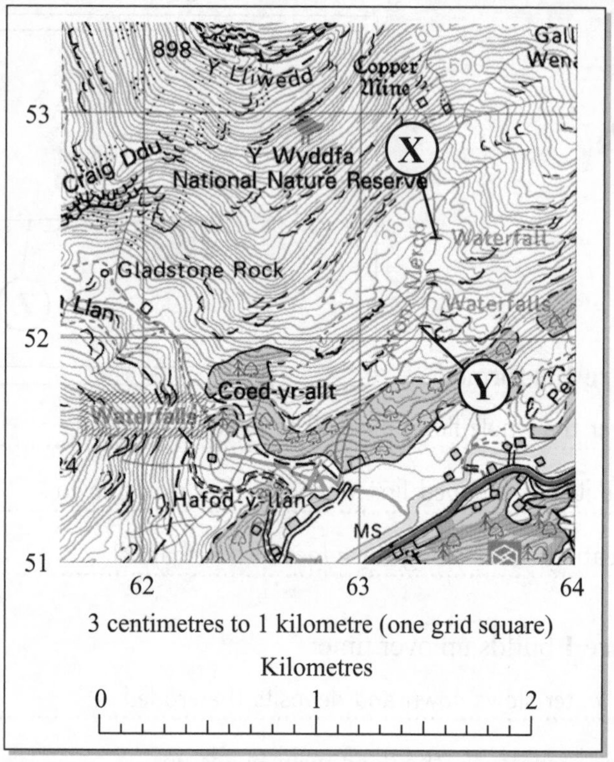

3 centimetres to 1 kilometre (one grid square)

Kilometres
0   1   2

* a) A waterfall is found at point X on **Figure 1**. Give the six figure grid reference for the waterfall.

....

[1]

b) There is another waterfall at point Y. State the distance between the two waterfalls.

.... km

[1]

c) Which waterfall, X or Y, is located on a steeper section of the river's course?

....

[1]

d) Suggest why waterfalls have formed along this stretch of the Afon Merch.

....

....

....

[2]

[Total 5 marks]

2 Study **Figure 2**, which shows another river landform that is likely to be found in the upper course of a river.

Explain the formation of this landform.

Figure 2

....

....

....

....

....

....

[Total 4 marks]

River Landscapes and Sediment Load

River landscapes are affected by quite a few different things, such as climate, geology and slope processes.

River Landscapes and Sediment Load are Influenced by Physical Factors

Climate, geology and slope processes all help to shape river landscapes and affect the sediment load (the material carried by a river):

Climate

1) Rivers in wetter climates have a higher discharge (see next page) because there's more water entering the river channel.

2) Higher discharge increases the rate of erosion — if a river has a higher volume of water, it has more power to erode the river banks and bed. This adds material to the river's load.

3) It also shapes the landscape, forming V-shaped valleys in the river's upper course (through vertical erosion) and a wide, flat flood plain in the lower course (through lateral erosion).

4) Transportation also increases when there's a higher discharge because the river has more energy to carry material.

5) Weathering increases the river's sediment load and can affect the shape of the landscape, e.g. freeze-thaw weathering makes rockfalls more likely (see p. 82).

Geology

1) Rivers flowing through areas of hard rock have a slower rate of erosion because hard rocks are more resistant. This means the river will have a lower sediment load.

2) Areas with softer rocks will experience more erosion — this adds more material to the river's sediment load.

3) Landscapes with more resistant rocks tend to have steeper valley sides. Landscapes with less resistant rocks have gentle sloping valley sides.

4) Waterfalls form where there is a layer of hard rock on top of softer rock.

5) Interlocking spurs (see p. 83) form where softer rock is eroded first, leaving areas of harder rock sticking out.

Slope Processes

1) Vertical erosion by rivers makes valley sides steeper, increasing the movement of material down the slopes.

2) Mass movement, e.g. slumping (see p. 68), can add large amounts of material to the river's load. Mass movements are more likely during colder weather (freeze-thaw weathering loosens material) and during periods of intense rainfall (the saturated ground becomes heavier and less stable).

Soil creep creates mini terraces on gentle slopes called 'terracettes'.

3) Soil creep is when soil particles move down a slope because of gravity. It's caused by the expansion and contraction of the soil. Water adds weight to the soil and makes it expand — this causes it to move down the slope. When the soil dries out, it contracts. Soil creep can add lots of fine material to the river's load.

Sediment load is the material transported by rivers and streams

More often than not, it's a combination of climate, geology and slope processes that shape river landscapes and influence sediment load — make sure you understand the effects of each of these three factors.

River Discharge

We've not really talked much about the actual water in a river. Well, all that's about to change.

Hydrographs Show the Change in River Discharge

1) River discharge is simply the volume of water that flows in a river per second. It's measured in cumecs — cubic metres per second (m^3/s).

2) Storm hydrographs show the changes in river discharge around the time of a storm:

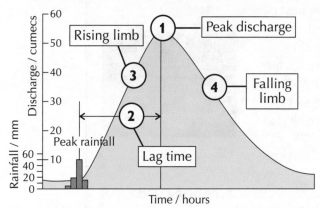

① **Peak discharge:** The highest discharge in the period of time you're looking at.

② **Lag time:** The delay between peak rainfall and peak discharge.

③ **Rising limb:** The increase in river discharge as rainwater flows into the river.

④ **Falling limb:** The decrease in river discharge as the river returns to its normal level.

3) Lag time happens because most rainwater doesn't land directly in the river channel — there's a delay as rainwater gets to the channel. It gets there by flowing quickly overland (called surface runoff, or just runoff), or by soaking into the ground (called infiltration) and flowing slowly underground.

Storm Hydrographs are Affected by Different Factors

1) If more water flows as runoff the lag time will be reduced. This means discharge will increase and the hydrograph will be steeper because more water gets to the river in a shorter space of time.

2) There are physical and human factors that affect lag time, discharge and the shape of the hydrograph:

GEOLOGY — water can't infiltrate into impermeable rocks, so there's more runoff.

SOIL TYPE — more impermeable soils (e.g. clays) can't absorb as much water as sandy soils, which increases runoff. Shallower soils also become saturated more quickly than deeper soils.

SLOPE — the steeper the slope, the less infiltration and the higher the runoff.

DRAINAGE BASIN TYPE — circular drainage basins have a shorter lag time and higher discharge than narrow basins because water reaches the main river channel at the same time. In a narrower basin, water from the far end of the basin takes a long time to reach the main channel.

ANTECEDENT CONDITIONS — previously wet or very cold weather can increase runoff because water can't infiltrate saturated or frozen soil.

'Antecedent' is just a fancy word for 'previous'.

URBANISATION — water can't infiltrate into impermeable surfaces (e.g. tarmac or concrete), so there's more runoff. Gutters and drains quickly take runoff to rivers, which rapidly increases discharge.

DEFORESTATION — trees take up water from the ground and store it, which reduces runoff. Cutting down trees increases runoff and causes more water to enter the river channel, which increases discharge.

You get lag time because rainwater doesn't fall directly into the river channel

Hydrographs are a good way of showing the changes in river discharge when there is a storm or lots of rainfall. There are lots of factors that affect peak discharge and lag time, which can increase the risk of flooding.

River Flooding

Flooding happens when the <u>level</u> of a river gets <u>so high</u> that it <u>spills over its banks</u> onto the <u>flood plain</u>.

The **River Eden** is **Prone** to **Flooding**

1) The <u>River Eden</u> (see p. 81) runs through <u>North Cumbria</u>.

2) <u>Flooding</u> in the Eden basin is <u>common</u> and some areas, e.g. <u>Carlisle</u>, are <u>very prone</u> to flooding.

3) A <u>combination</u> of <u>physical factors</u> and <u>human activities</u> increase the risk of flooding in this area:

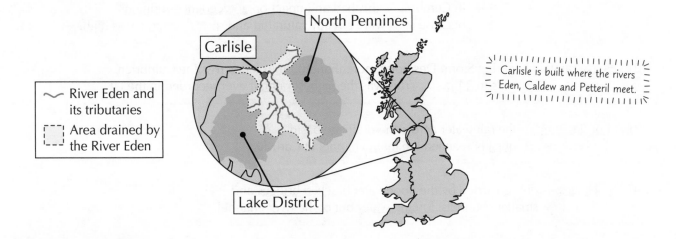

Carlisle is built where the rivers Eden, Caldew and Petteril meet.

Physical Factors

1) Cumbria is on the <u>west coast</u> of the UK, facing the prevailing <u>south-westerly</u> winds — the <u>climate</u> is <u>mild and wet</u>.

2) It's one of the <u>wettest</u> parts of the UK, often experiencing periods of <u>intense rainfall</u>. Many of the UK's <u>highest rainfall records</u> have been recorded in Cumbria.

3) The Eden basin is bordered by the <u>Lake District</u> to the west and the <u>North Pennines</u> to the east. Both these areas are made up of <u>hard</u>, <u>impermeable rocks</u>. This means water <u>can't soak</u> into the ground and <u>runs off</u> into the <u>river channel</u>.

4) <u>Snowfall</u> is <u>common</u> on higher ground during the <u>winter months</u>. Snow melt can add <u>lots of water</u> to the river channel in a <u>short space of time</u>.

Human Activities

1) Carlisle is a <u>large built-up area</u> and there has been lots of <u>development</u> on the Eden's <u>flood plain</u>. This has affected the flood plain's ability to <u>absorb</u> and <u>store floodwater</u>. The lack of <u>soil</u> or <u>vegetation</u> means there's <u>little infiltration</u> of rainfall, which leads to <u>high surface runoff</u>.

2) <u>Natural woodland</u> and <u>heathland</u> have been <u>cleared</u> from many upland areas in the Eden basin. This <u>increases</u> surface <u>runoff</u> when it rains, and means that <u>more water</u> ends up in the river channel <u>more quickly</u>.

3) Parts of the Eden valley have been <u>drained</u> to make them <u>more suitable</u> for <u>farming</u>. <u>Drainage ditches</u> mean water flows rapidly to the <u>river channel</u>.

Physical factors and human activity contribute to increased risk of flooding

You might have studied somewhere else in class — just make sure you've got your head around how physical and human processes are interacting to cause flooding on a named river and you'll be home and dry.

River Flooding

You saw on the previous page why the Eden basin is prone to flooding, so now it's time to look at one major flooding event that occurred there in 2015. Then it's on to why the UK is becoming more and more at risk of serious floods.

Several Factors Contributed to Flooding in the Eden Basin in 2015

The interaction of physical and human factors led to flooding in the Eden basin (including severe flooding in Carlisle) on 5th and 6th December 2015.

1) Antecedent conditions — November 2015 was the second wettest November ever recorded in Cumbria — this had an impact on antecedent conditions because soils were already saturated and river discharge was high.

2) Heavy rainfall — during Storm Desmond more than 300 mm fell across the Cumbrian hills in 24 hours. This was the highest rainfall ever recorded in the UK.

3) Short lag time — the rainwater across the drainage basin quickly reached the main channel at Carlisle.

4) Blockages — debris carried by the floodwater blocked bridges and smaller channels, forcing water out of the river channel.

5) Insufficient drainage — runoff from impermeable surfaces in Carlisle ran quickly into drainage systems. These couldn't cope with the volume of water and overflowed, making the flooding worse.

The Risk of Flooding is Increasing in the UK

Flood risk is increasing in the UK because of two main factors:

Increased Frequency of Storms

1) The frequency of storms in the UK is increasing — this could be a consequence of global climate change (see page 7).

2) It is also thought that storms are becoming more extreme — more intense rainfall is increasing the scale of flood events.

3) More periods of wet weather mean that the ground is saturated, making flooding more likely.

Land Use Change

1) As the UK's population grows, there's more pressure to expand urban areas. This leads to an increase in impermeable surfaces (e.g. concrete), which cause rapid surface runoff.

2) Removing vegetation and permeable surfaces means that water that would have been stored in the soil or plants and trees now flows quickly downstream.

3) Lots of development, e.g. house building, is taking place on flood plains. These areas are naturally prone to flooding and this increases the risk to developed areas.

4) More people living on flood plains mean that there are more people at risk of flooding if flood defences fail.

Make sure you know why the risk of flooding in the UK is increasing

Getting your head around those two main reasons for the increased risk of flooding in the UK will help you remember why the Eden basin flooded. A period of intense wet weather and the presence of a lot of impermeable surfaces made Carlisle vulnerable to flooding, and these factors are becoming more common all around the country.

More on River Flooding

The increasing risk of <u>river flooding</u> in the UK means that a greater number of <u>people</u> are going to be <u>affected</u> by flooding in some way. But flooding not only causes problems for people — it can <u>damage</u> the <u>environment</u> too.

Flooding **Threatens People...**

The <u>threats</u> that <u>flooding</u> cause to <u>people</u> include:

1) People can be <u>killed</u> or injured by <u>floodwater</u>.

2) <u>Roads</u>, <u>bridges</u> and <u>rail lines</u> can be damaged or destroyed.

3) <u>Floodwater</u> is often <u>contaminated</u> with <u>sewage</u>, which can lead to a lack of <u>clean drinking water</u>.

4) <u>Possessions</u> can be <u>damaged</u> or washed away.

5) People can be made <u>homeless</u> as their properties are <u>inundated</u> or <u>damaged</u>.

6) <u>Businesses</u> may be forced to <u>shut down</u> because of <u>flood damage</u> and disrupted <u>power supplies</u>. This leads to a <u>loss of livelihoods</u>.

2015 floods in Carlisle

...and the **Environment**

The <u>threats</u> that <u>flooding</u> cause to the <u>environment</u> include:

1) Floodwater <u>contaminated</u> with <u>sewage</u> and <u>rubbish</u> can <u>pollute</u> rivers, damaging <u>wildlife habitats</u>.

2) <u>Farmland</u> can be <u>ruined</u> by <u>silt</u> and <u>sediment</u> deposited <u>after a flood</u>.

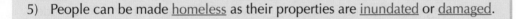

3) River banks are <u>eroded</u>, causing <u>huge changes</u> to the <u>river landscape</u>, e.g. <u>widening</u> of the <u>river channel</u> and increased <u>deposition</u> downstream.

4) The <u>force</u> of floodwater can <u>uproot</u> trees and plants, and <u>standing</u> floodwater may cause those that survive the initial wave of water to <u>die</u>.

Farmland ruined by flooding

REVISION TIP

Some impacts of flooding can last for a long time after the event

The impacts of river flooding and coastal flooding (p.75) are very similar — make sure you don't get them mixed up. To help get this page into your memory, grab a pen and paper, cover up the page and see if you can write out all the ways that flooding can threaten people and the environment.

River Management

Floods can be <u>devastating</u>, but there are a number of different <u>strategies</u> to stop them or lessen the blow.

Engineering can Reduce the Risk of Flooding or its Effects

There are <u>two</u> types of strategy to <u>deal with flooding</u>:

1) <u>Hard engineering</u> — <u>man-made structures</u> built to <u>control the flow</u> of rivers and <u>reduce flooding</u>.
2) <u>Soft engineering</u> — schemes set up using <u>knowledge</u> of a <u>river</u> and its <u>processes</u> to <u>reduce the effects of flooding</u>.

Different <u>hard engineering</u> strategies have different <u>costs</u> and <u>benefits</u>:

1) **FLOOD WALLS** — flood walls are <u>artificial barriers</u> built along river banks. They're designed to increase the <u>height</u> of the <u>river banks</u>, allowing the river channel to <u>hold more water</u>. However, flood walls are <u>very expensive</u> and they can be <u>unsightly</u> and <u>block the view</u> of the river.

2) **EMBANKMENTS** — embankments are <u>high banks</u> that are built <u>along</u> or near the <u>river banks</u>. They stop the river <u>flowing</u> into built-up areas during a <u>flood</u>, protecting <u>buildings</u> and <u>infrastructure</u> on the flood plain. They can be made from <u>earth</u> or other <u>natural materials</u>, making them <u>less unsightly</u> than flood walls. They're quite <u>expensive</u> to build and there's a risk of <u>severe flooding</u> if the water rises <u>above</u> the level of the embankments or if they <u>break</u>.

3) **FLOOD BARRIERS (FLOODGATES)** — floodgates, e.g. the <u>Thames Barrier</u>, are built on <u>river estuaries</u> to stop flooding from <u>storm surges</u> (see p. 12) or <u>very high tides</u>. They can be <u>shut</u> when there's a <u>surge forecast</u> to prevent flooding and they protect a <u>large area</u> of land, e.g. central London. Floodgates are <u>very expensive</u> to build and need to be <u>maintained regularly</u>.

4) **FLOOD BARRIERS (DEMOUNTABLE)** — demountable flood barriers provide <u>temporary</u> protection against flooding. The barriers are <u>only put up</u> when there's a <u>flood forecast</u> so there's always a risk they might not be put up <u>in time</u>. Demountable flood barriers are quite <u>expensive</u> to build, but they <u>don't spoil</u> the look of attractive locations.

<u>Soft engineering</u> strategies also have <u>costs</u> and <u>benefits</u>:

1) **FLOOD PLAIN RETENTION** — this strategy involves <u>maintaining</u> the river's <u>flood plain</u>, i.e. by <u>not building</u> on it. It helps <u>slow</u> floodwaters down and maintain the flood plain's <u>ability</u> to <u>store water</u>. <u>No money</u> has to be spent on building flood defences, but it <u>restricts development</u> and <u>can't</u> be used in <u>urban areas</u>.

2) **RIVER RESTORATION** — this involves making the river <u>more natural</u>, e.g. by removing man-made levees, so that the flood plain can <u>flood naturally</u>. There's <u>less risk</u> of flooding <u>downstream</u> because <u>discharge</u> is <u>reduced</u>. The river is left in its <u>natural state</u>, so there's very <u>little maintenance</u> required. However, river restoration can increase <u>local flood risk</u>, especially if <u>nothing</u> is done to prevent <u>major flooding</u>.

Hard engineering and soft engineering are both used to deal with flooding

Would you look at that — it's the end of rivers. It looks like there's a lot of stuff to learn here, but it's not difficult at all. Make sure you have at least a couple of costs and benefits for each strategy stashed away in your brain.

Worked Exam Questions

Now you've got through the last few pages of the topic, time to do some exam questions to see what you can remember. But first take a look at this worked exam question to see how you should be answering questions.

1   Study **Figure 1**, which shows storm hydrographs for two rivers.

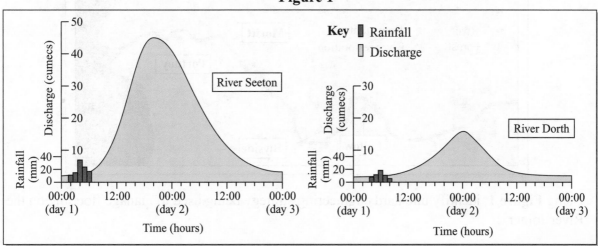

a)   At what time was the River Seeton at peak discharge?

20:00 on day 1

[1]

b)   Peak rainfall around the River Dorth was at 06:00 on day 1. What was the lag time?

18 hours

[1]

c)   Explain which river is more likely to flood.

The River Seeton is more likely to flood because it has a higher peak discharge, meaning that there is more water in the channel.

[2]

d)   The land around the River Seeton has been paved and built on. Suggest how land use in the catchment of the River Seeton might affect the shape of the hydrograph in **Figure 1**.

Built-up areas contain lots of impermeable surfaces and drains. Impermeable surfaces increase runoff and drains quickly take runoff to rivers, so the hydrograph will have a higher peak discharge and a shorter lag time.

[2]

e)   Explain how the shape of a drainage basin can affect the shape of a storm hydrograph.

Circular drainage basins have a shorter lag time and higher peak discharge than narrow basins because water from the whole of the basin reaches the main river channel at the same time.

[2]

[Total 8 marks]

Exam Questions

1 Study **Figure 1**, which shows some of the engineering strategies used to combat flooding along the River Joiner.

Figure 1

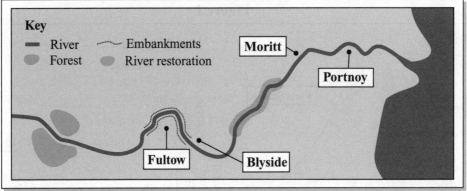

a) Using **Figure 1**, identify **one** hard engineering strategy being used to manage flooding on the River Joiner.

....
[1]

b) Explain how river restoration, as shown in **Figure 1**, may reduce the risk of flooding in Moritt.

....

....

....
[2]

c) Give **one** advantage of using embankments instead of flood walls to protect the town of Fultow.

....
[1]

d) Explain how the embankments used at Fultow could cause problems at Blyside.

....

....

....
[2]

e) Explain why there may be objections to using flood plain retention to manage flood risk at Portnoy.

....

....
[2]

[Total 8 marks]

Revision Summary

That's it for Topic 4. Now it's time to see how much information your brain has soaked up.
- Try these questions and tick off each one when you get it right.
- When you've done all the questions under a heading and are completely happy with it, tick it off.

River Landscapes and Processes (p.80-82) ☑
1) What does a river's long profile show?
2) Describe the cross profile of a river's lower course.
3) What is the difference between vertical and lateral erosion?
4) Compare the sediment size and shape in a river's upper and lower courses.
5) How does a river's discharge change along its course?
6) Describe the process of freeze-thaw weathering.
7) What's the difference between abrasion and attrition?
8) Name two processes of transportation.
9) When does deposition occur?

River Landforms (p.83-86) ☑
10) What are interlocking spurs?
11) a) Where is the current fastest on a meander?
    b) What feature of a meander is formed where the flow is fastest?
12) Name the landform created when a meander is cut off by deposition.
13) What is a flood plain?
14) Outline the main features of a delta.
15) What do the contour lines on a map show?
16) Give two pieces of map evidence for a waterfall.
17) Give two pieces of map evidence for a river's lower course.

River Landscapes, Sediment Load and Discharge (p.89-90) ☑
18) Explain how climate influences sediment load.
19) Give two ways geology influences river landscapes.
20) What is soil creep?
21) What is river discharge?
22) What is lag time?
23) Describe one physical factor and one human factor that alter storm hydrographs.

River Flooding and Management (p.91-94) ☑
24) Outline two physical factors that increase the risk of flooding on a named river.
25) What human activities are causing flooding on a river you have studied?
26) Outline two ways in which land use change is increasing the risk of flooding.
27) a) Give two threats of flooding to people.
    b) Give two threats of flooding to the environment.
28) Define hard engineering.
29) Define soft engineering.
30) Describe the costs of using flood walls to reduce the risk of flooding.
31) Describe the benefits of river restoration.

Topic 5 — The UK's Evolving Human Landscape

UK Human Landscape

This topic is all about why <u>places</u> and <u>people</u> in the UK are <u>changing</u>. In order to understand the stuff in this topic, it's important to have a firm grasp about how <u>people</u> are <u>spread</u> across the country. Read on to find out more...

Population Density is Highest in Urban Cores

Urban cores are the central parts of urban areas.

The <u>population distribution</u> in the UK is very <u>uneven</u>.

- Population density is <u>highest</u> in <u>cities</u>, e.g. London, Glasgow, Birmingham.
- It's also high in areas <u>around</u> major cities, or where <u>major cities</u> have developed into <u>conurbations</u> — towns that have merged to form <u>continuous urban areas</u>, e.g. Merseyside includes Liverpool, Knowsley and St Helens.

- <u>Upland areas</u> such as northern Scotland and central Wales are mostly <u>rural</u>. Rural areas are <u>sparsely</u> populated.
- Other <u>rural areas</u> include the south west and north of England and Northern Ireland.

Population density is a measure of the number of people per unit area, e.g. 300 people per km².

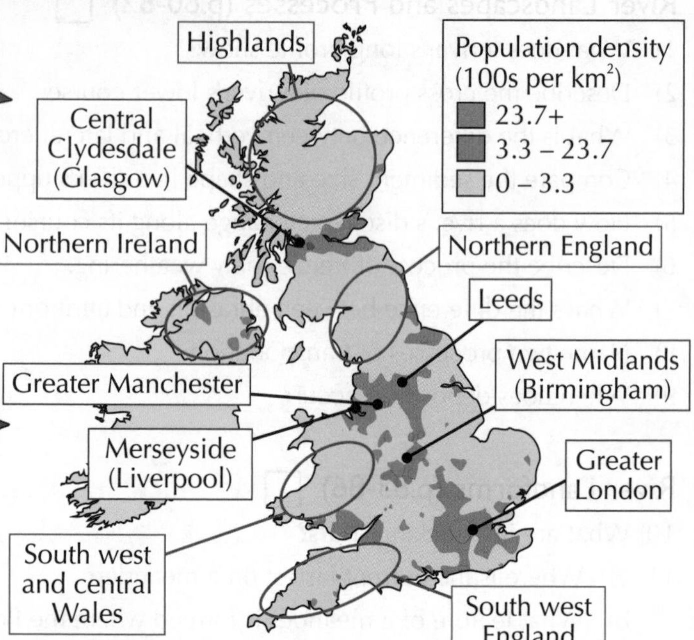

Map labels: Highlands, Central Clydesdale (Glasgow), Northern Ireland, Greater Manchester, Merseyside (Liverpool), South west and central Wales, Northern England, Leeds, West Midlands (Birmingham), Greater London, South west England

Population density (100s per km²)
- 23.7+
- 3.3 – 23.7
- 0 – 3.3

Urban Cores Have More Economic Activity

The <u>amount</u> and <u>type</u> of <u>economic activity</u> is different in <u>urban</u> and <u>rural</u> areas:

Urban Cores

1) Urban core areas have a higher concentration of <u>economic activity</u> — <u>60%</u> of jobs in cities are found there.
2) The main <u>employment opportunities</u> are in the <u>tertiary</u> sector (e.g. retail and finance) and in <u>manufacturing</u> (e.g. electronics and food and drink).
3) Lots of people live in <u>cities</u> because there are <u>more jobs available</u> there, which are often <u>better paid</u>.

Rural Areas

1) Rural areas usually have <u>fewer job opportunities</u>.
2) There is more <u>primary industry</u> — e.g. <u>farming</u>, <u>forestry</u>, <u>fishing</u> and <u>quarrying</u>.
3) Some areas also have a <u>seasonal tourism industry</u>, e.g. cafés and hotels in the <u>Lake District National Park</u> in northern England.
4) Some rural settlements that are near <u>urban areas</u> have become <u>commuter settlements</u> — people <u>live</u> there and <u>travel</u> into <u>urban</u> areas for <u>work</u>.

See page 49 for more on the types of economic sector.

Urban Cores Have a Younger Population

1) The <u>age structure</u> of <u>urban</u> and <u>rural</u> areas is different.
2) There is a <u>higher proportion</u> of <u>younger</u> people in <u>big cities</u>, such as London, Bristol and Manchester — people often live in cities to be closer to their <u>jobs</u>, so a higher proportion of the population is of <u>working age</u>.
3) There is a higher proportion of <u>older</u> people in <u>rural</u> areas, e.g. <u>Northern Ireland</u> and <u>Scotland</u>. <u>Older</u> people <u>move out</u> of <u>cities</u> to retire to a more peaceful environment and <u>younger</u> people <u>leave rural areas</u> to work in cities.

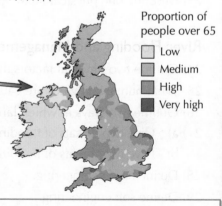

Proportion of people over 65
- Low
- Medium
- High
- Very high

Urban areas and rural areas normally have very different population densities

There, that wasn't so bad. It may seem pretty obvious stuff but the ideas on this page form the basis of everything that's coming up. So, head down and stick at it until you know the key differences between urban and rural areas.

UK Human Landscape

Not all areas of the UK are perfect — there are some <u>problems</u>. And where there are problems, we need <u>solutions</u>.

Some **Rural Areas** of th**e UK** Have High Levels of **Poverty**

Some rural areas of the UK are <u>struggling</u> to <u>grow economically</u>. These include:

1) <u>Isolated</u> rural areas on the <u>periphery</u> (edge) of the UK (e.g. north Wales, north west Scotland), which are relatively <u>inaccessible</u>. There are <u>few employment opportunities</u> because they are difficult to farm and have few natural resources. <u>Young people</u> have to <u>leave</u> to find jobs elsewhere — <u>depopulation</u> leads to <u>loss of services</u> (e.g. shops, doctors' surgeries) because they can no longer be supported.

2) Rural areas around the <u>former industrial areas</u>, e.g. north east England and parts of the Midlands, where the loss of <u>manufacturing industry</u> has caused <u>high unemployment</u> and new jobs haven't been created.

UK and EU Government Policies Aim to Reduce Differences in Wealth

There are lots of <u>strategies</u> to <u>reduce</u> the differences in <u>wealth</u> between <u>thriving urban cores</u> (see previous page) and rural areas with <u>high levels of poverty</u>. These happen at a range of <u>scales</u> and may involve <u>county councils</u>, the <u>national government</u> and the <u>European Union</u> (<u>EU</u>).

Creating Enterprise Zones

1) The UK government has created <u>55 Enterprise Zones</u> across England, Scotland and Wales.

2) These offer companies a range of benefits for locating in enterprise zones, including: <u>reduced taxes</u>, <u>simpler planning rules</u>, and <u>improved infrastructure</u> (e.g. superfast broadband).

3) These measures can be used to <u>encourage</u> companies to <u>locate</u> in areas of <u>high unemployment</u>, bringing <u>jobs</u> and <u>income</u> which could help <u>poorer rural</u> areas to develop.

4) For example, the new <u>Dorset Green</u> Enterprise Zone already has two <u>high tech engineering companies</u> and hopes to attract <u>55</u> more <u>businesses</u>, creating <u>2000 new jobs</u> in the region.

Transport Infrastructure

1) The <u>UK government</u> plans to link London, Birmingham, Leeds and Manchester with a new <u>high speed rail line</u>, HS2. This will increase <u>capacity</u> and allow <u>faster journeys</u> into major cities — promoting <u>industry</u> and <u>jobs</u> in poorer rural areas in the north of England.

2) On a local scale, Lancashire county council has built a <u>new road</u> to link the <u>port</u> of Heysham in Lancashire to the <u>M6</u>. This will encourage <u>businesses</u> to <u>invest</u> by <u>reducing travel times</u> and <u>easing congestion</u>, creating more <u>job opportunities</u> for people in the <u>surrounding rural areas</u>.

Regional Development

1) The EU has used the <u>European Regional Development Fund</u> (<u>ERDF</u>) to promote <u>growth</u> in poorer rural areas by investing in <u>small high-tech businesses</u>, providing <u>training</u> to improve local people's <u>skills</u> and funding infrastructure, e.g. high speed broadband to attract businesses. For example, the EU funded <u>superfast broadband</u> in Cornwall. This attracts <u>digital businesses</u>, such as Gravitas, and links regeneration projects and new research and development centres in the region. This is <u>creating</u> skilled <u>jobs</u> in the area, attracting young <u>graduates</u> and <u>boosting</u> the local <u>economy</u>.

2) The <u>Common Agricultural Policy</u> (<u>CAP</u>) is an EU initiative to make sure <u>EU farmers</u> can earn a <u>living</u> from farming. It includes <u>training</u> for farmers and <u>assistance</u> for young farmers starting up as well as <u>subsidies</u> for <u>rural diversification</u> projects (see p. 111).

3) The UK <u>left</u> the EU in <u>2020</u>, which means <u>future</u> regional development plans are <u>uncertain</u>.

Learn the strategies of reducing poverty in rural areas

Make sure you're comfortable with all of the UK government and EU policies covered on this page. Jot down the three headings in the boxes above, and then underneath each one write down everything you can remember about that type of policy. Then have a look back at the page to see how you did.

Migration

The UK's population is changing because people are constantly moving about — they do have their reasons though.

Migration Influences the Age Structure and Distribution of People in the UK

1) Roughly half the UK's population growth is driven by natural increase (more births than deaths), and about half by migration.

2) Between 1970 and 1982 more people left the UK than moved to the UK. There has been a constant flow of British people leaving the UK since 1970 — mostly to Australia, the USA, France and Spain.

3) Overall, since 1983 more people have moved to the UK than have left and net migration has generally been increasing — net migration has more than doubled in the last 10 years.

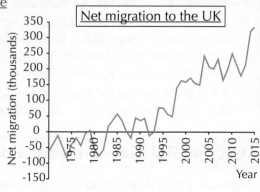

4) National and international migration affect the distribution and age structure of the population:

Distribution

1) Young national migrants and most international migrants move to major cities — this is where most jobs are and where universities are located. The most popular destinations for international migrants are London and the West Midlands.

2) There has been lots of counter-urbanisation (see p.50) as wealthy people move out of cities to seek a better quality of life in rural areas — the London region has the highest number of people leaving.

3) Many older people move to coastal areas in the east and south west of England when they retire.

Age Structure

1) The large number of young migrants (20-29) increases the population in this age group.

2) Migration also affects the age structure of the UK by increasing the birth rate, because many migrants are of child-bearing age. Immigrants make up about 13% of the UK population, but account for about 27% of babies born.

UK Immigration Policy has Increased Diversity

1) After the second world war, the UK encouraged immigration from Commonwealth countries, e.g. the Caribbean, India and Pakistan, to fill skills shortages in the UK workforce.

2) Later, entry was restricted but work permits for migrants with desirable skills, e.g. IT, were made available — many highly skilled Indians and Pakistanis still come to the UK.

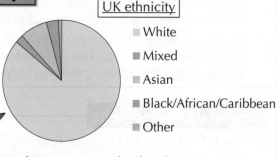

3) This has meant that the UK has a high proportion of people of Caribbean and Asian ethnicity — nearly 10%. This is much higher in some regions, e.g. 28.3% of the population of Leicester are of Indian heritage.

4) Since 1995 the EU has allowed free movement of people within member countries to find work — this increased the number of people migrating to the UK from Europe, e.g. from Germany.

5) In 2004 eight new countries joined the EU. Many moved from these countries, e.g. Poland, to find work in the UK. This was mainly in low-skilled jobs, e.g. catering and agriculture.

The UK left the EU in 2020 — this may affect immigration.

6) Between 2001 and 2011, the proportion of non-British white people increased more than any ethnic group — Polish people are now one of the largest non-UK born groups.

7) International immigration has increased cultural diversity — immigrants introduce languages, food, arts, festivals and fashion from their own culture, giving the UK a rich mix.

National and international migration affect UK society

It's not just migration from outside the country that affects the distribution and age structure of people in the UK — migration within the country has an impact too. Make sure you're fully clued-up on both types of migration.

The UK Economy

You might have worked out that while it's going pretty well in some <u>cities</u>, other places are having a tougher time. Well, that's largely down to how the <u>UK economy</u> has <u>changed</u> over time...

Primary and Secondary Industries have Declined

1) Since 1960 jobs in <u>primary</u> industries have <u>decreased</u>. Farming has become more <u>mechanised</u> so fewer people are needed. The <u>mining</u> industry also declined due to <u>competition</u> from abroad and <u>cheaper alternative fuels</u>.

2) Jobs in <u>secondary</u> industries have also <u>decreased</u> — people employed in <u>manufacturing</u> fell from <u>36%</u> of the workforce in 1961 to just <u>9%</u> in 2011. This was partly a result of <u>global shift</u> (see p.50).

3) Employment in the <u>service</u> sector (e.g. retail, banking, healthcare and education) has <u>increased</u>. <u>Retail</u> is the UK's <u>largest</u> sector employing <u>2.9 million people</u> — people have more <u>disposable</u> income to spend. <u>Finance</u> is also an important part of the <u>economy</u> — the <u>City of London</u> is home to many <u>global financial institutions</u>.

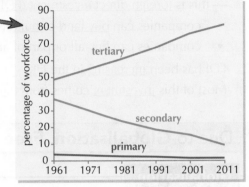

4) <u>Quaternary</u> industries, e.g. <u>IT</u> and <u>research and development</u> (R&D) are <u>increasing</u>, making use of the UK's skilled university graduates. In 2013, nearly <u>£30 billion</u> was spent on <u>R&D</u> in the UK.

Secondary Industry has Declined in Burnley

1) <u>Burnley</u> is a town in Lancashire, about 20 miles north of <u>Manchester</u>.

2) In the <u>early 20th century</u> Burnley had a <u>thriving economy</u> based on <u>textiles</u> — it was one of the world's leading <u>cotton weaving</u> towns.

3) From <u>1914</u>, the textiles industry in the UK began to <u>collapse</u> — partly due to cheap <u>imports</u>. The last cotton mill <u>closed</u> in the <u>1980s</u>.

4) Other <u>primary</u> and <u>secondary</u> industries also <u>struggled</u>. Several major factories <u>closed</u> in the <u>1990s</u> and early 2000s with the <u>loss</u> of <u>hundreds of jobs</u>.

Derelict street due to poverty and depopulation

5) Burnley has <u>struggled to recover</u> economically. The <u>employment</u> rate is only about 65% and <u>wages</u> are <u>well below</u> the UK average — low-skilled service sector jobs <u>don't pay well</u>. There is <u>very little</u> population <u>growth</u> — with few jobs on offer, people are more likely to <u>leave</u> than to move there.

6) The <u>manufacturing skills</u> existing in the area and the <u>low costs</u> of operating there have begun to attract <u>aerospace</u> engineering firms — meaning the area is still largely <u>dependent</u> on <u>manufacturing</u> industries for employment.

Tertiary and Quaternary Sectors are Growing in South Wales

1) For much of the <u>18th</u> and <u>19th centuries</u>, the economy of South Wales was based on <u>coal mining</u> and <u>ironmaking</u>. In the <u>20th century</u>, coal mining and iron working in South Wales <u>declined</u> due to <u>overseas competition</u>. <u>Unemployment</u> levels were <u>high</u>, and many people lived in <u>poverty</u>.

New buildings in Swansea

2) In <u>1992</u>, the <u>different parts</u> of the region started to <u>work together</u> more to achieve economic growth. They aimed to <u>improve transport networks</u>, <u>attract businesses</u>, <u>increase skills</u> and <u>draw visitors</u> to the area.

3) <u>Costs</u> are <u>lower</u> than London and the south east, making it <u>easier</u> to start up <u>new businesses</u>. <u>Universities</u> (in Swansea and Cardiff) supply a <u>skilled labour force</u>.

4) This has helped to <u>attract private investors</u> in <u>high tech</u> industries — South Wales is now home to lots of new <u>digital</u> and <u>media</u> companies and is a <u>thriving economic region</u>.

5) As <u>wealth</u> increases, people have more money to spend on <u>services</u>, creating <u>more jobs</u> in these industries.

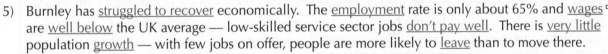

There are four types of industry — primary, secondary, tertiary and quaternary

The decline of secondary industry had a massive impact on the UK economy and has loads of knock-on effects. Go over this page until you've nailed it — it'll really help with the massive case study coming up on p.105.

UK Links with the Wider World

It's not just people that move to the UK — businesses do too. And more and more of them have been coming.

FDI has Increased in the UK...

1) A company based in one country can invest money in a different country
   — this is foreign direct investment (FDI). FDI can take two forms:
   - companies can buy land or buildings and locate their factory or office there.
   - companies can buy all or part of an already existing business.

2) FDI has been increasing in the UK — it rose from £726 billion in 2010 to £1 065 billion in 2014.

3) Most of this investment comes from transnational corporations (TNCs — see p.37).

...Due to Globalisation, Free Trade Policies and Privatisation

Globalisation

Globalisation is the process of countries becoming more integrated (see p.37). It has increased FDI because:

1) Transport and communications links have improved, making it easier for companies to operate in the UK.

2) London has developed as a global financial centre — many foreign banks, e.g. the German Deutsche Bank, have located there because of the business culture and networking opportunities.

Privatisation

Services that were previously run by the UK government have been offered to private firms. This has increased FDI because foreign firms can buy them or merge them with their existing businesses.

For example, many UK electricity boards are now owned by foreign companies — Scottish Power is owned by the Spanish energy company, Iberdrola.

Free Trade Policies

1) Free trade policies reduce import and export restrictions, making it easier for countries to trade.

2) The EU promotes free trade between member countries. While the UK was in the EU, companies could move goods and services freely between the UK and their home country. This increased FDI from the EU.

3) Since leaving the EU in 2020, the UK has been negotiating new free trade agreements — this may attract investors and increase FDI from non-EU countries.

The UK Economy is Increasingly Affected by TNCs

On the plus side...

1) Jobs are created, e.g. the US firm Grand Heritage Hotel Group is investing in a new resort in Derbyshire creating 1000 jobs.

2) Large scale projects can be built that the UK government can't afford to pay for, e.g. £15 billion has been invested in UK infrastructure, such as offshore wind turbines, sub-sea power cables etc.

3) TNCs often lead the way in developing new products, technology and business practices which can be used by other firms to increase productivity.

But there are also downsides...

1) It can lead to over-reliance on TNCs — if there's a problem elsewhere in the world, the UK's economy is affected, e.g. the world economic recession led to redundancies at the Nissan factory in Sunderland in 2009.

2) There are big effects if TNCs choose to relocate or change suppliers, e.g. many UK farmers are dependent on just one or two large TNCs who buy their produce.

3) Local businesses struggle to compete against TNCs, e.g. in some towns the arrival of the coffee chain Starbucks has forced independent coffee shops to close down.

The UK has seen more and more foreign direct investment

Economics can be tricky at first, but don't worry. Take your time to get your head around this stuff before moving on.

Worked Exam Questions

You know the routine by now — work carefully through these examples and make sure you understand them. Then it's on to the real test of doing some exam questions yourself.

1 Study **Figure 1**, a table showing the number of new foreign direct investments (FDI) in the UK each year from 2011 to 2016.

Figure 1

Year	2011/12	2012/13	2013/14	2014/15	2015/16
Number of new FDI	752	777	820	1058	1130

a) Using **Figure 1**, calculate the percentage increase in new investments between 2014/15 and 2015/16.

(1130 – 1058) ÷ 1058 = 0.068

0.068 x 100 = 6.8%

[2]

b) Explain how globalisation has increased FDI in the UK.

Transport and communications links have improved. This makes it easier for companies to operate in the UK. London has developed as a global financial centre. Many foreign financial companies have chosen to locate offices there because of the business culture and networking opportunities.

[4]

c) Name **one** factor, other than globalisation, that has contributed to the increase in FDI in the UK.

Free trade policies / privatisation

[1]

[Total 7 marks]

2 Study **Figure 2**, a graph showing change in the percentage of people employed in different sectors in the UK between 2001 and 2014.

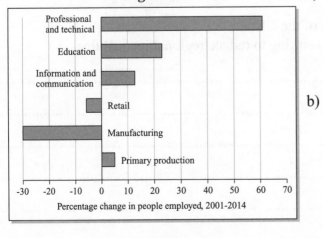

Figure 2

Percentage change in people employed, 2001-2014

a) Using **Figure 2**, state the percentage by which the number of people employed in education increased.

23%

[1]

b) Give **one** reason why professional and technical employment has increased.

Declining primary and secondary industry have led to a greater proportion of employment in tertiary and quaternary industry.

[1]

[Total 2 marks]

Exam Questions

1 Study **Figure 1**, a map showing the population density of the UK.

Figure 1

a) Describe the pattern of population density in the UK.

....

....

....

....

....

[2]

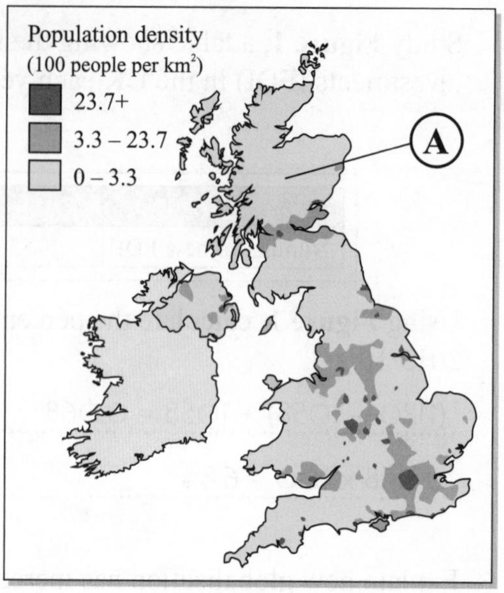

b) **Figure 2** is a map of the UK showing the distribution of people over the age of 65. Explain the relationship between population density and the distribution of people over 65 in the UK.

....

....

....

....

....

....

....

....

....

[4]

Figure 2

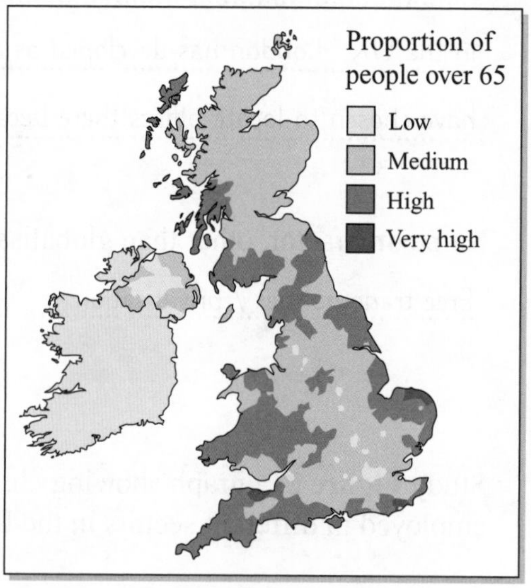

c) There are inequalities between some regions of the UK. Describe **two** ways that the UK government is trying to reduce regional inequalities.

1:..

....

....

2:..

....

....

[4]

[Total 10 marks]

Dynamic UK Cities

London is a classic example of how changes in a city provide both <u>opportunities</u> and <u>challenges</u>.

London is a **Global City** in **South East England**

1) London is sited on the <u>flat floodplain</u> of the <u>River Thames</u> where it meets the sea.

2) It is the UK's <u>capital city</u> and is an essential part of the UK's economy. <u>Over 20%</u> of the UK's <u>income</u> comes from London.

3) It is the centre of the UK's <u>transport</u> system. It was a major <u>port</u> until 1981 and still has <u>shipping links</u>. There are two major <u>international airports</u> (Heathrow and Gatwick) plus three <u>smaller</u> ones, e.g. London City Airport. There is easy <u>access</u> to <u>mainland Europe</u> via the Channel Tunnel.

4) It has a major <u>influence</u> on its <u>surrounding area</u>. Companies are attracted to the region by the <u>proximity</u> to London, which <u>increases jobs</u> and <u>wealth</u>. The <u>South East</u> and <u>East of England</u> are the two biggest <u>regional economies</u> in the UK outside London.

5) London's important <u>globally</u> too — it's a <u>world city</u> and, along with New York, one of the two most important <u>financial centres</u> in the world. There are more <u>foreign banks</u> in London than <u>anywhere else</u>.

You Need to Know the **City's Structure**

<u>Land use</u> and <u>building age varies</u> across the city (see p. 51).

Area (example)	Main Land Use	Description
CBD (Central Business District) — <u>City of London</u>	Commercial	Mix of <u>new high-rise office blocks</u> and <u>historical</u> buildings. Land is <u>expensive</u> so building <u>density</u> is <u>high</u>. There are a <u>few small parks</u>.
Inner city — <u>Newham</u>	Low-class residential	<u>High-density</u>, <u>old</u> terraced housing, <u>1960s-70s high-rise flats</u> and <u>modern apartment</u> buildings. <u>Poor</u> environmental quality, some <u>green space</u>.
Inner city — <u>Chelsea</u>	High-class residential	<u>80%</u> houses built <u>before 1919</u>. Land is <u>expensive</u> so building <u>density</u> is <u>high</u>. Lots of <u>large terraced houses</u>, some converted into <u>flats</u>. High quality <u>green space</u> — most houses have <u>gardens</u>.
Suburbs — <u>Surbiton, Kingston upon Thames</u>	Middle-class residential	Good quality <u>20th century semi-detached</u> housing, along with <u>shops</u> and <u>restaurants</u>. Most houses have <u>gardens</u> and there are <u>large</u> areas of good quality <u>green space</u>.
Rural-urban fringe — <u>Crockenhill, Sevenoaks</u>	High-class residential	<u>Large</u>, <u>detached</u> and <u>semi-detached</u> houses with <u>gardens</u> — the area is surrounded by <u>countryside</u>.
Rural-urban fringe — <u>Thurrock</u>	Industrial, commercial	Industry includes <u>oil refineries</u>, <u>manufacturing</u> and a <u>container port</u>. Lakeside <u>retail</u> park opened in <u>1990</u>.

The different areas of London have their own unique characteristics

Make sure you know the main features of each area of the city (the CBD, inner city, suburbs and rural-urban fringe) — it'll really help with the rest of this case study. For example, knowing how the land use changes between different parts of the city will help you to understand the inequalities between the different areas of London (see p.107).

Dynamic UK Cities

London is a very <u>popular</u> place to <u>live</u>. People from all over the world (including the UK) <u>move</u> to London to <u>study</u> and <u>work</u>. The migration of people to London has a big <u>impact</u> on different areas of the city.

Migration is Causing Parts of London to **Grow**

1) The <u>population</u> of London is now over <u>8.5 million people</u> and it's <u>growing</u> due to:
   - <u>International migration</u> — <u>net</u> migration to London in 2014 was <u>100 thousand people</u>.
   - <u>National migration</u> — within the UK, <u>young</u> adults move <u>to</u> the city for <u>work</u> or to <u>study</u>.
   - <u>Internal population growth</u> — the <u>young population</u> means there are <u>more births</u> than <u>deaths</u> in the city.

2) <u>Inner city</u> London has the <u>highest rate</u> of people moving <u>in</u> and <u>out</u> including both the <u>wealthiest</u> and <u>poorest</u> people. <u>Highly skilled</u> people move to the <u>inner city</u> to work in <u>high-paid jobs</u> (e.g. in banking) along with <u>low-paid migrants</u> looking for jobs in the <u>service sector</u> (e.g. cleaning and catering).

3) Migrants who have been in London for <u>longer</u> tend to move out to the <u>suburbs</u> as they become more <u>settled</u>. About 50% of the population of the outer London boroughs of <u>Harrow</u> and <u>Hounslow</u> are <u>foreign-born</u>.

Migration Influences the **Character** of Different Parts of the City

Age Structure

There is now a <u>high percentage</u> of people aged <u>25-34</u> in <u>inner city</u> London and a <u>lower proportion</u> of people <u>over 65</u>. Most <u>immigrants</u> are of <u>working age</u>.

Ethnicity

Ethnic diversity is <u>higher</u> in <u>inner city areas</u>, e.g. <u>52%</u> of people are foreign born in <u>Newham</u> compared to <u>29%</u> in <u>Kingston upon Thames</u>, but it's increasing rapidly in some suburbs, e.g. Bexley.

Population

Population <u>growth rates</u> are <u>increasing</u> in inner city areas because of <u>high immigration rates</u> and because many migrants are of <u>child-bearing age</u> (so birth rates are <u>higher</u>).

Services

In <u>inner city</u> areas where immigration rates are <u>high</u>, there is an increasing <u>demand</u> for <u>services</u> such as <u>education</u> and <u>health care</u> (e.g. for school places and maternity care). However, these areas are often amongst the <u>poorest</u> parts of the city, so it's <u>difficult</u> to provide what's needed.

Competition for school places is very high in parts of London.

Housing

Immigration may add to <u>overcrowding</u> in some areas. Poorer immigrants often live in <u>older terraces</u> and 1960s-70s <u>council tower blocks</u> in the <u>inner city</u>, which are more <u>affordable</u>.

Culture

London is very <u>culturally diverse</u>, with more than <u>200 languages</u> spoken. Many immigrants choose to settle near people with the <u>same ethnic background</u>, giving the area a <u>distinct ethnic character</u>, e.g. <u>Chinatown</u>. Lots of <u>food</u>, <u>music</u> and <u>goods</u> from that culture can be found there.

London is constantly growing and diversifying

This may seem like loads of information, but it's all pretty straightforward really. To help you remember it all, jot down a list of the impacts that migration has had on London (or the city you've studied in class).

Dynamic UK Cities

Not all areas of a city are equal — some are more <u>wealthy</u> than others. This causes an <u>inequality</u> in the services and job opportunities between different areas. You can measure this inequality using the <u>Index of Multiple Deprivation</u>.

There is **Lots** of **Inequality** in London

Most deprived

Least deprived

1) The <u>Index of Multiple Deprivation</u> (IMD) combines data on employment, health, education, crime, housing, services and the environment to give an overall figure for the <u>quality of life</u> in an area. <u>Deprived</u> areas have a <u>low</u> quality of life.

2) This map shows how the IMD varies across London. Deprivation is <u>highest</u> in the <u>inner city</u> and in parts of <u>north</u> London. <u>East</u> London is generally <u>more deprived</u> than <u>west</u> London.

3) <u>Poorer</u> people are <u>limited</u> in where they can <u>live</u>:
   - they can only afford <u>poor quality housing</u>, often in the <u>inner city</u>.
   - they may need to live <u>close</u> to <u>work</u> if they don't have a <u>car</u> or can't afford <u>public transport</u>.

   This can make it <u>difficult</u> for them to <u>leave</u> deprived areas — they become trapped in a cycle of poverty.

There are Different **Causes** of **Inequality**

<u>Deprivation</u> affects people's <u>access</u> to <u>jobs</u> and <u>services</u>, widening the <u>gap</u> between the rich and poor:

Services

<u>Rapid population growth</u> and <u>high turnover</u> of people puts <u>pressure</u> on services, e.g. health and education. Funding services is also harder in <u>deprived areas</u>, where councils get <u>less money</u> from <u>taxes</u> and <u>businesses</u>.

Health

<u>Unhealthy lifestyles</u>, e.g. drinking, smoking and poor diets, are more common in <u>deprived areas</u> — <u>life expectancy</u> is about <u>5 years lower</u> in <u>poorer</u> areas of the city than in wealthier areas. Health care is free on the NHS but services are often <u>overwhelmed</u> and poorer people <u>can't afford private</u> health care.

Employment

There are <u>fewer manufacturing jobs</u> in the inner city — <u>new industries</u> locate on the <u>outskirts</u>, so it's <u>harder</u> for people to find <u>suitable work</u>. Average <u>income</u> in Kensington and Chelsea is more than <u>£130 000</u>, but it's less than <u>£35 000</u> in Newham. More than <u>25%</u> of London's population are living in <u>poverty</u>, due to <u>unemployment</u> or <u>low wages</u>.

Education

The <u>best</u> state schools, e.g. Holland Park, are very <u>over-subscribed</u> and difficult to get into. <u>Wealthy parents</u> are able to send their children to <u>fee-paying</u> schools, but many children from <u>poorer families</u> end up in under-performing <u>state</u> schools. This can lead to a cycle of poverty, e.g. where a <u>lack of education</u> leads to a <u>limited</u> range of <u>job opportunities</u>, and <u>lower incomes</u>.

The level of inequality in London is higher than the UK average

It can be very difficult for people living in deprived areas to break out of the cycle of poverty. Even when more investment comes into a deprived area, and it becomes more developed (e.g. it becomes gentrified — see next page), this can simply lead to the area becoming too expensive for existing residents to remain living in.

Dynamic UK Cities

London has seen both <u>decline</u> and <u>growth</u>. It's a bit like a seesaw really — some areas are <u>going down</u> while others are on the <u>way up</u>. Decline may be <u>depressing</u>, but things have been done to <u>help</u>...

Parts of the **Inner City** and **CBD** Have **Declined**

<u>De-industrialisation</u> (see p.50) and <u>depopulation</u> led to <u>decline</u> in the <u>central</u> areas of London.

1) The <u>decline</u> of the <u>docks</u> and <u>manufacturing</u> industries in London's <u>East End</u> led to mass <u>unemployment</u> — 20% of jobs were lost between 1966 and 1976 in the dockland areas.

2) <u>De-industrialisation</u> and <u>unemployment</u> in the second half of the 20th century led to many families <u>moving away</u> from the area. Further <u>depopulation</u> of the inner city was caused by <u>suburbanisation</u>, the building of <u>satellite towns</u>, e.g. Milton Keynes, and <u>slum clearance</u> (old terraces were demolished and replaced with high-rise flats, e.g. the Aylesbury estate, Southwark).

3) As people moved away, many buildings were left <u>derelict</u>. There was also a <u>decrease</u> in local <u>services</u>, e.g. shops, schools and health care facilities, as there weren't enough <u>people</u> or <u>money</u> to continue them.

4) <u>De-centralisation</u> (when shops and businesses <u>move out</u> of the CBD) caused further <u>decline</u>. Many shops struggled to pay the <u>high rents</u> in the city centre and moved to <u>less central</u> locations, e.g. Lewisham. New <u>high-tech</u> industries located in <u>business parks</u>, e.g. North London Business Park, on the <u>edge</u> of London where land is <u>cheaper</u> and there are better <u>transport links</u> and easier <u>access</u>.

5) The growth of <u>e-commerce</u> (online shopping) has recently put further <u>pressure</u> on <u>high street shops</u>. Some firms have <u>moved</u> to distribution centres on the <u>edge</u> of the city where they can distribute goods to online shoppers more easily. Others have been forced to <u>close down</u>.

Parts of the **Rural-Urban Fringe** and **Inner City** have seen **Economic Growth**

Financial and business services and TNC investment

- The <u>growth</u> of <u>finance</u> and <u>business</u> services is <u>revitalising</u> the <u>CBD</u>. The City of London has emerged as a global centre for <u>banking</u>, <u>insurance</u> and <u>law</u> companies, which benefit from being <u>close</u> to each other.

- Many <u>TNCs</u> locate their <u>sales</u> and <u>marketing</u> departments and <u>headquarters</u> in London because of its <u>importance</u> as a <u>financial centre</u>. TNCs based in London include HSBC, Shell, GlaxoSmithKline and Virgin Atlantic Airways. These in turn attract <u>further investment</u> as they help to cement London's <u>identity</u> as a <u>global</u> city.

Gentrification and studentification

- Some areas, e.g. Islington, have been <u>gentrified</u> — <u>wealthier</u> people move in to <u>run down areas</u> and <u>regenerate</u> them by <u>improving</u> their houses. New <u>businesses</u> are springing up in gentrified areas to cater for the wealthier newcomers.

- Other areas, e.g. Camden, have been <u>studentified</u> — a high student population has led to <u>thriving services</u> and <u>entertainment venues</u>, generating <u>new jobs</u> and <u>wealth</u> for the area.

Urban sprawl

- Most <u>growth</u> has taken place in the <u>rural-urban fringe</u>. Large <u>shopping centres</u>, e.g. Bluewater, have been built on the <u>edge</u> of the city where land is <u>cheaper</u> and there is <u>less congestion</u> and <u>more parking space</u>.

- <u>Industrial</u> areas, e.g. Crossways Business Park by the QEII bridge, have also been developed on the <u>outskirts</u> of London.

- The availability of <u>jobs</u> has <u>attracted</u> many people to <u>live</u> there.

Leisure and culture

- London hosted the <u>Olympic games</u> in 2012, with most <u>investment</u> taking place in London's <u>East End</u>. This was one of London's <u>most deprived</u> areas but the area now has <u>new transport links</u> and the <u>athletes' village</u> has been developed into a modern <u>housing estate</u>. The sports stadiums are <u>open</u> for <u>community use</u> as well as <u>world sporting events</u>. New <u>jobs</u> have been <u>created</u> and lots of people are <u>moving to</u> the area.

Dynamic UK Cities

London Docklands was Regenerated and Rebranded

1) Rebranding is about improving a place's image so that people will want to go there. It usually involves regeneration — making actual improvements to an area, e.g. new buildings and services. It also involves using marketing to improve the reputation of a place.

2) The London Docklands area was regenerated and rebranded in 1980s-90s as a centre for finance and business, with new office space in Canary Wharf as well as shopping centres and housing developments.

Positive Impacts	Negative Impacts
• Transport links were improved — the new Docklands Light Railway and Jubilee Line extension carry thousands of passengers every day. • The environment has been improved and quality green space created, e.g. the Thames Barrier Park. • Businesses have been attracted back, creating jobs — Canary Wharf is now home to many media organisations and global banks, e.g. Barclays. • The population has increased and people have more money to spend in local shops and cafés, so many businesses have thrived.	• Many local people had to leave. 36% of the local population were unskilled workers and most lived in council housing, so couldn't afford the new houses and weren't suited to the new jobs. • Some traditional businesses, e.g. pubs, and old community centres closed, and were replaced with services for the wealthier newcomers, e.g. expensive restaurants and artisan bakeries. • Existing communities were broken up — people moved to new towns and estates on the edge of London, e.g. Chigwell in Essex.

Strategies are Needed to Make Urban Living More Sustainable

Sustainable strategies are about improving things for people today without negatively affecting future generations. They need to consider the environment, the economy and people's social well-being.

Big cities need so many resources that it's unlikely they'd ever be truly sustainable. But things can be done to make a city (and the way people live there) more sustainable.

1) **Employment** — increasing employment opportunities reduces poverty and improves economic sustainability. The London Living Wage encourages businesses to pay a fair wage that takes into account the high cost of living in London. Skills programmes, e.g. En-route to Sustainable Employment, mean that people can progress to higher paid jobs.

2) **Recycling** — more recycling means fewer resources are used, e.g. metal cans can be melted down and used to make more cans. Waste recycling schemes include the collection of household recycling boxes and recycling facilities for larger items, e.g. fridges. However, only 33% of rubbish in London is recycled — the lowest level in the whole of England.

3) **Green spaces** — green spaces have environmental benefits and make sure cities remain places where people want to live and work. London is 40% public green space with lots of parks in the city centre, e.g. Hyde Park, and larger open areas on the outskirts, e.g. Hampstead Heath.

4) **Transport** — noise and air pollution can be reduced, for example:
   • congestion charging discourages drivers from entering the city centre at peak times.
   • self-service bicycles and bike lanes make it easier and safer for people to cycle instead of drive.
   • electric buses and zero-emission taxis are helping to reduce emissions from public transport.

5) **Housing** — the BedZED development is a large-scale sustainable community in south London. The houses have thick insulation, solar heating systems and water-saving appliances, all of which help to reduce energy consumption and conserve resources. The houses are built from locally-sourced materials, giving them a smaller carbon footprint, and many properties on the development have subsidised rents (making them more affordable).

Make sure you know the difference between regeneration and rebranding

You also need to know about decline and growth in your chosen city as well as how life there can be improved.

Dynamic UK Cities

Neighbouring <u>urban</u> and <u>rural</u> areas are <u>influences</u> on each other. <u>London</u> and its <u>surrounding area</u> are no exception.

London and its Surrounding **Rural Areas** are **Interdependent**

<u>London</u> is <u>connected</u> to the <u>rural areas</u> around it — they <u>rely</u> on each other for <u>goods</u> and <u>services</u>.

Labour

1) Many people <u>commute</u> into London from the surrounding <u>rural areas</u> to <u>work</u>, e.g. around <u>40%</u> of people in <u>Sevenoaks District</u> (north west Kent) work in London.

2) <u>Students</u> and <u>young professionals</u> move <u>into</u> London — they often want to live <u>close</u> to their <u>work</u> in areas with <u>good entertainment facilities</u>, e.g. <u>Camden</u> has lots of pubs, clubs and restaurants.

Goods

1) London <u>relies</u> on the surrounding rural areas for <u>food</u> — many <u>farmers</u> sell their produce to <u>supermarkets</u> and <u>wholesalers</u> who transport it into the city.

2) Many <u>rural people</u> travel into <u>London</u> to do some of their <u>shopping</u> — there is a greater selection of <u>high street</u> and <u>luxury</u> shops, e.g. Harrods.

Services

1) London has excellent <u>hospitals</u> and <u>private schools</u> as well as <u>specialist services</u>, e.g. Great Ormond Street children's hospital — people travel from the <u>surrounding rural areas</u> to use them.

2) Many <u>Londoners</u> travel into the countryside for <u>leisure activities</u>, e.g. to play golf, walk in country parks, go horse riding etc.

The <u>interdependence</u> of urban and rural areas has <u>costs</u> and <u>benefits</u>:

Benefits	Costs
• Some <u>businesses</u> in rural areas (e.g. pubs with restaurants) have seen an increase in <u>business</u> as <u>newer residents</u> have <u>higher disposable incomes</u>. • Some <u>farmers</u> have <u>made money</u> from <u>selling land</u> or <u>buildings</u> or <u>diversifying</u> their business (see next page). • Some <u>existing houses</u> have been <u>improved</u>, e.g. traditional Kentish oast houses have been <u>renovated</u> and turned into <u>houses</u>. • There is <u>less pressure</u> on <u>housing</u> in <u>London</u>.	• Some villages, e.g. Ivy Hatch, may become <u>commuter settlements</u> — where people <u>live</u> in rural areas but <u>work</u> in London. This leaves villages <u>empty</u> during the day, so some shops and services may <u>close</u> because of <u>reduced demand</u> (see next page). • <u>New housing estates</u> have been built on open <u>countryside</u>, e.g. at Dunton Green, which has affected <u>wildlife habitats</u>. • Lots of <u>commuters drive</u> to Sevenoaks to catch the <u>train</u> into London — the <u>additional traffic</u> is increasing <u>air pollution</u> and <u>congestion</u> and causing <u>parking</u> issues.

Interdependence is Causing **Changes** to **Rural** Areas

1) <u>Sevenoaks District</u> is a largely <u>rural</u> area to the <u>south east</u> of London. Lots of people are moving there from London for a better <u>quality of life</u> (<u>counter-urbanisation</u> — see page 50). This puts pressure on housing, pushing up prices — <u>house prices</u> have <u>risen</u> by over <u>250%</u> since 1995 due to the <u>high demand</u>.

Kentish oast house

2) The <u>population</u> of Sevenoaks District is <u>changing</u>. Lots of people <u>retire</u> there because it is a <u>peaceful</u>, <u>pleasant environment</u>. At the same time, <u>younger people</u> are leaving, and many <u>move into London</u> for work. Sevenoaks District has a much <u>higher</u> than average proportion of people aged <u>over 50</u>, and a much <u>lower</u> than average proportion of people in their <u>twenties</u>.

3) London has a huge population of people with <u>more leisure time</u> and <u>higher incomes</u> than in the past. This creates demand for <u>leisure</u> and <u>recreation services</u>, e.g. tea rooms, golf courses and riding schools in the surrounding rural areas.

Interdependence has both good points and bad points

You might be asked to talk about the advantages and disadvantages of the interdependence of rural and urban areas in the exam. It can be really helpful to jot down all the pros and cons you can think of before you launch into the answer. This way, you can plan your answer so that it has a logical structure, and you're less likely to miss out a key piece of information. You might even feel a bit less stressed, too.

Dynamic UK Cities

Rural areas have got their fair share of problems, but they also have some economic opportunities.

There are Lots of Challenges for Rural Areas Around London

Quality of life can be measured using the Index of Multiple Deprivation (IMD — see page 107). Rural areas usually have lower IMD scores (higher quality of life) because people are generally wealthier and more people are retired (so aren't looking for work). However, there are challenges in some areas:

Employment

1) Employment deprivation is concentrated in a few small pockets, e.g. Swanley and Merstham.

2) Increased use of technology in agriculture and increasing farm sizes has decreased the number of workers needed in rural areas, e.g. Kent now has fewer agricultural workers and manufacturing has declined by more than 30% since 1998. Finding alternative employment can be a challenge.

Housing

Sevenoaks District is among the 30% most deprived areas for housing affordability. House prices in the Sevenoaks area are much higher than the UK average. This creates a challenge in providing affordable housing for young people, whose incomes are often lower.

Health Care and Education

1) Ageing populations require more health care and special facilities, e.g. nursing homes.

2) Some GP surgeries in smaller communities are threatened by closure. West Kingsdown surgery nearly closed in 2016.

3) Schools in some villages are closing due to declining numbers of pupils, e.g. there is now no secondary school in Edenbridge.

4) This creates challenges:
   - Many elderly people in rural areas don't own a car so they can struggle to get to shops and health care facilities.
   - Young people may have to travel long distances to get to school and for leisure activities.

Rural Diversification Creates Economic Opportunities

1) Many farmers struggle to earn enough to live on — prices for their goods are forced down by supermarkets and cheaper imports.

2) Some farmers are finding alternative ways of making money, either by farm-based activities or by starting a new business. This is known as rural diversification. Rural diversification includes:

	Example	Environmental impacts
Farm shops	Stanhill Farm in Wilmington, Kent has opened a farm shop selling produce from the farm and the local area.	Land can continue to be farmed. More varieties of crop are grown using more environmentally-friendly methods than monoculture (growing large areas of one crop for supermarkets).
Accommodation	Tanner Farm Park in Kent has turned some land into a large touring caravan and camping park.	Large caravan parks can be unsightly. There is more pressure on the natural environment from the large numbers of visitors — through increased use of water and energy and the amount of waste generated.
Leisure activities	The Hop Farm in Kent has an animal petting area, children's rides and places to eat.	Land is built on to create car parks, visitor facilities etc. Traffic increases in the area, leading to air pollution.

3) Tourism can also create new economic opportunities in rural areas. For example, Leeds Castle (in Kent) is a historic building that has developed various attractions (e.g. a maze and golf course) and events to encourage more people to visit. However, this can mean that new tourist facilities are built on greenfield land and lead to an increase in traffic congestion.

Rural areas have plenty of challenges and opportunities

Make sure you're familiar with the challenges facing rural areas of the UK, as well as the opportunities caused by rural diversification. Try drawing a colourful mind map to help you learn them all.

Worked Exam Questions

And here are the worked exam questions for this section. Remember, these answers are just suggestions — there are other correct answers — but they should give you an idea of the kinds of things to write.

1   Study **Figure 1**, which shows an area of Byrnshire in 1950 and 2016.

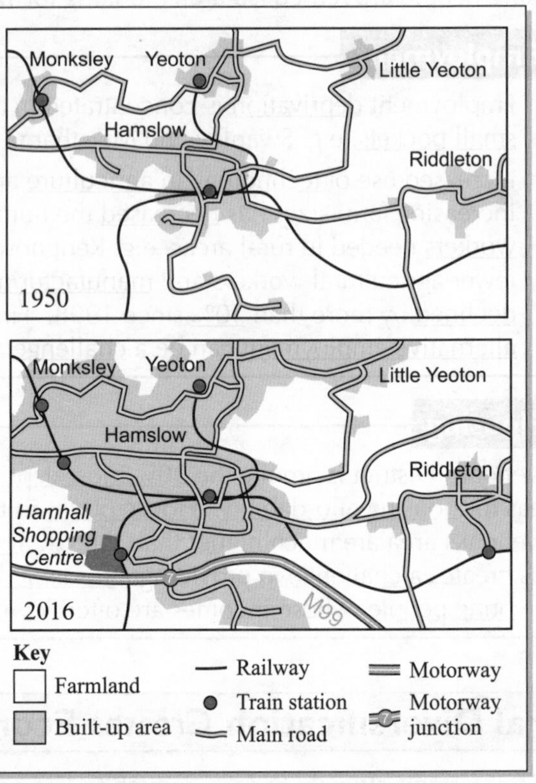

a)   State **two** ways that cities and the rural areas around them depend on each other.

1: People commute into cities from the surrounding rural areas.

2: Cities rely on farms in the surrounding rural areas for food.

[2]

Figure 1

b)   Using **Figure 1**, describe **one** environmental cost of the changes to the rural area around Hamslow between 1950 and 2016.

A motorway has been built , which will have increased noise and air pollution.

[2]

c)   Suggest **one** social challenge that Riddleton might face due to its links with the city of Hamslow.

Riddleton might have an ageing population because of older people moving there from Hamslow to retire and younger people moving into Hamslow for employment.

[2]

[Total 6 marks]

2   Study **Figure 2**, a graph showing the migration of males into and out of London in 2013 across a range of age groups.

a)   Using **Figure 2**, which age group experienced a net increase in population due to migration?

A   0-10 years   ⬭

B   11-20 years   ⬭

C   21-30 years   ⬤

D   31-40 years   ⬭

[1]

Figure 2

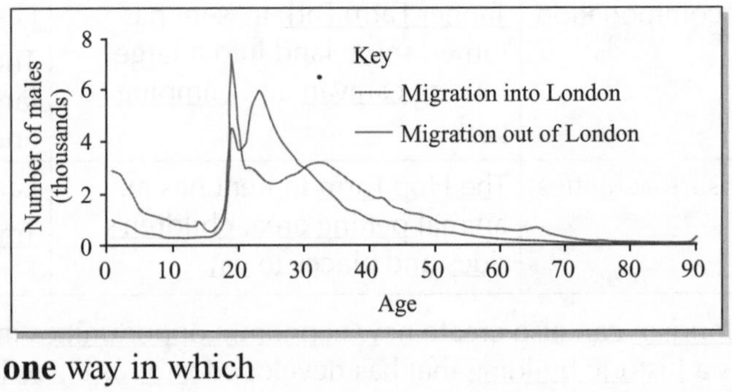

b)   For a UK city that you have studied, describe **one** way in which migration into the city has affected its character.

In London, immigrants often choose to settle near people with the same ethnic background as them, so certain parts of the city are associated with certain ethnic backgrounds, e.g. Chinatown.

[2]

[Total 3 marks]

Exam Questions

1   Study **Figure 1**, a map of central Newcastle, a regenerated city centre.

a) Give **two** pieces of evidence from **Figure 1** that indicate that the area shown is the CBD.

1:...

....

....

2:...

....

....
[2]

Figure 1

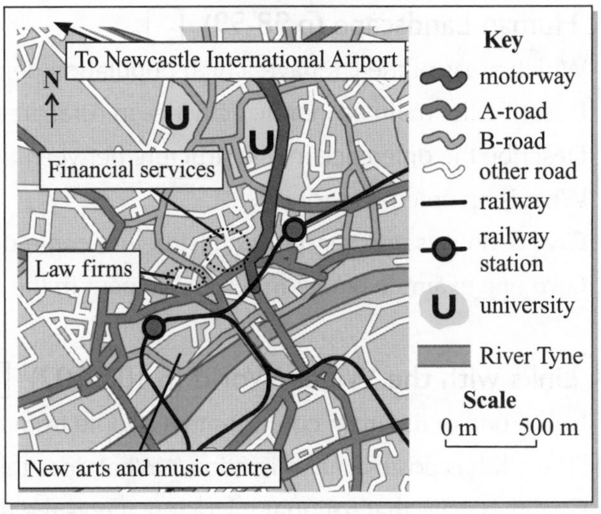

To Newcastle International Airport

Financial services

Law firms

New arts and music centre

Key
motorway
A-road
B-road
other road
railway
railway station
university
River Tyne

Scale
0 m   500 m

b) Regeneration is often involved in the 'rebranding' of a city. What is meant by this term?

....

....
[1]

c) Give **two** possible sources of economic growth in central Newcastle.

1:...

2:...
[2]

d) For a UK city you have studied, explain why some areas of the city have declined.

....

....

....

....

....
[4]

e) For a named city in the UK, explain **two** strategies that have been used to make the city more sustainable.

1:...

....

2:...

....
[4]

[Total 13 marks]

Revision Summary

You've reached the end of <u>Topic 5</u>. Just one more page of questions standing between you and a cuppa.

- Try these questions and <u>tick off each one</u> when you <u>get it right</u>.
- When you've done <u>all the questions</u> under a heading and are <u>completely happy</u> with it, tick it off.

UK Human Landscape (p.98-99) ☑

1) Which areas of the UK have a high population density?
2) Describe the main economic activities in rural areas.
3) Describe the difference in age structure between urban cores and rural areas.
4) What is an enterprise zone?
5) Give two ways that transport infrastructure can reduce differences in wealth in urban and rural areas.
6) Give one example of regional development in the UK.

UK Links with the Wider World (p.100-102) ☑

7) Name one of the main countries that people from the UK emigrate to.
8) 'The UK has positive net migration.' What does this mean?
9) Give two ways that national migration affects the distribution of population in the UK.
10) Give two examples of UK immigration policy.
11) How has the proportion of people employed in secondary industries in the UK changed since 1960?
12) Describe two other changes to the employment structure of the UK over the last 50 years.
13) Outline the differences in economic structure in two contrasting regions of the UK.
14) What is foreign direct investment (FDI)?

Dynamic UK Cities — Case Study (p.105-111) ☑

For a major city in the UK that you have studied:

15) How is the city connected to the country it is located in?
16) Describe the land use in the inner city.
17) Describe the variations in environmental quality in the city.
18) How has migration affected the ethnicity in different parts of the city?
19) Give one reason why there is inequality in health.
20) Give two parts of the city that have experienced economic growth.
21) What is gentrification?
22) Give two positive and two negative effects that rebranding has had on people.
23) Give three examples of interdependence between the city and the surrounding rural areas.
24) Give two benefits that interdependence has.
25) Explain why a rural area has experienced pressure on housing due to its links with the city.
26) Give two examples of rural diversification.
27) Give two environmental impacts from tourism projects in rural areas.

Fieldwork

For your Geography GCSE you need to complete <u>two</u> bits of <u>fieldwork</u>, and you'll be asked about them in the exam.

You have to Write About **Two Fieldwork Investigations** in the Exam

1) Fieldwork is <u>assessed</u> in the third part (<u>Part C</u>) of <u>Paper 2</u>. There's no <u>coursework</u>, but in the exam you need to be able to <u>write about</u> fieldwork that you have done.

2) You need to have done at least one <u>physical</u> and one <u>human</u> fieldwork investigation. The <u>physical</u> one will be on <u>either</u> 'Coastal Change and Conflict' <u>or</u> 'River Processes and Pressures'. The <u>human</u> one will be on <u>either</u> 'Dynamic Urban Areas' <u>or</u> 'Changing Rural Areas'. You'll be asked about <u>both</u> your physical and human fieldwork investigation in the exam.

Your teacher will tell you which topics you're doing.

3) The fieldwork part of the exam has <u>two</u> types of questions:
   - You'll have to answer questions about <u>your investigation</u> — you might be asked about your <u>question</u> or <u>hypothesis</u>, <u>methods</u>, what <u>data</u> you <u>collected</u> and <u>why</u>, how you <u>presented</u> and <u>analysed</u> it, how you could <u>extend your research</u> and so on.
   - You'll also be asked about fieldwork techniques in <u>unfamiliar</u> situations. You might have to answer questions about <u>techniques</u> for <u>collecting data</u>, how to <u>present data</u> you've been given or how <u>useful</u> the <u>different techniques</u> are.

For **Each** of your **Investigations**, You'll **Need to Know**...

1 Why You Chose Your Question

You may need to explain <u>why</u> the question or hypothesis you chose is <u>suitable</u> for a <u>geographical investigation</u>.

If you study <u>different sites</u> in the <u>study area</u>, make sure you know <u>why</u> they were <u>suitable</u> for the study. This could include that they gave a <u>good overall representation</u> of the study area or that they could be <u>compared</u> (if your investigation was a <u>comparison</u>).

2 How and Why You Collected Data

You may need to <u>describe</u> and <u>justify</u> what data <u>you collected</u>. This includes whether it was <u>primary data</u> (data that you collected <u>yourself</u>) or <u>secondary</u> data (data that <u>someone else</u> collected and you <u>used</u>), <u>why</u> you collected or used it, <u>how</u> you <u>measured</u> it and <u>how</u> you <u>recorded</u> it.

3 How You Processed and Presented Your Data

The way you <u>presented</u> your data, and <u>why</u> you <u>chose</u> that option, could come up. You may need to <u>describe what you did</u>, <u>explain</u> why it was <u>appropriate</u>, and discuss <u>how</u> you <u>adapted</u> your presentation method for <u>your data</u>. You might also be asked for a <u>different way</u> you <u>could</u> have presented your data.

There's more on analysing, concluding and evaluating on pages 117-118.

4 What Your Data Showed

You'll need to know:
- A <u>description</u> of your data.
- How you <u>analysed</u> your data.
- An <u>explanation</u> of your data.

This might include <u>links</u> between your <u>data sets</u>, the <u>statistical techniques</u> you used, and any <u>anomalies</u> (odd results) in the data that you spotted.

There's more on statistical techniques on pages 174-175.

5 The Conclusions You Reached

This means you may need to <u>explain how</u> your data provides <u>evidence</u> to <u>answer</u> the <u>question</u> or <u>support</u> the <u>hypothesis</u> you set at the <u>beginning</u>.

6 What Went Well, What Could Have Gone Better

You might be asked to <u>evaluate</u> your fieldwork:
- Were there <u>problems</u> in your <u>data collection methods</u>?
- Were there <u>limitations</u> in your <u>data</u>?
- What <u>other data</u> would it have been <u>useful</u> to have?
- How <u>reliable</u> are your <u>conclusions</u>?

Plan your fieldwork before you start...

...but don't worry if it doesn't quite go to plan. It's more important that you can write about it and say why things went wrong. It does help if you at least attempt to make it work though — so have another read through the page.

Completing Fieldwork

The <u>fun</u> part of fieldwork is <u>going out</u> and <u>doing it</u> — but before you grab your <u>anorak</u> and rush out the door, there are a couple of <u>important things</u> you need to <u>keep in mind</u>...

You **Need** to **Know How** You're Going to **Collect** Your **Data**

1) There are <u>rules</u> set by the <u>exam board</u> about the <u>type</u> of <u>data</u> that you have to <u>collect</u> in your <u>fieldwork</u>.

2) You might need to use <u>specialist techniques</u> to collect your data. For example, you may need to measure the <u>gradient</u> of a <u>beach</u> using a <u>clinometer</u> or <u>pantometer</u>, or the <u>velocity</u> of a river by timing <u>how long</u> it takes for a <u>float</u> to <u>travel</u> between two points.

3) To get the <u>best results</u>, you'll need to know <u>how</u> to <u>carry out</u> these techniques <u>accurately</u> and <u>consistently</u>. In the exam, you could get asked to <u>explain why</u> you <u>chose</u> the method you used.

There are **Different Types** of **Data** that You Can **Collect**

1) There are <u>two</u> types of data that you can use in your investigations — <u>primary</u> and <u>secondary</u> (see p.115).

2) Sometimes, you'll need to use <u>sampling techniques</u> when you're collecting <u>primary</u> data:

- <u>Random sampling</u> is where samples are chosen at <u>random</u>, e.g. picking pebbles on a beach.
- <u>Systematic sampling</u> is where samples are chosen at <u>regular intervals</u> — this is useful in places where what you want to investigate <u>changes frequently</u>, e.g. the number of pedestrians in an area.
- <u>Stratified sampling</u> is where you choose samples from <u>different groups</u> to get a <u>good overall representation</u>. This type of sampling is useful if you need to collect people's <u>perceptions</u>, e.g. of pollution in their area, and need to ask people of <u>different ages</u>.

3) The data you collect can be <u>quantitative</u> or <u>qualitative</u>:

- <u>Quantitative data</u> is <u>numerical data</u>, e.g. the <u>number</u> of <u>pedestrians</u> in an urban area. It's based on things you can <u>measure</u>.
- <u>Qualitative data</u> is based on information that <u>can't</u> be measured, e.g. <u>opinions</u>. For your fieldwork investigations, it's <u>likely</u> that you'll need to collect data on people's <u>views</u>, e.g. what <u>residents</u> think about <u>quality of life</u> in their area.

4) You need to use at least <u>two</u> secondary data sources for <u>each</u> of your <u>investigations</u>. <u>One</u> of these <u>must</u> be a source from a list <u>decided</u> by the <u>exam board</u>. You can choose any <u>other</u> sources you want to use <u>yourself</u>. The source that you <u>have</u> to use <u>depends</u> on which <u>investigation</u> you're carrying out:

- GEOLOGY MAPS — for <u>Coastal Changes and Conflicts</u>
- FLOOD RISK MAPS — for <u>River Processes and Pressures</u>
- CENSUS DATA — for <u>Dynamic Urban Areas</u> and <u>Changing Rural Areas</u>

You Need to **Think About Health** and **Safety**

1) You'll need to think about <u>safety</u> when choosing the sites you're going to study.

2) You need to know how to carry out a <u>risk assessment</u> for the <u>sites</u> you choose to study:

- Identify the <u>specific risks</u> at the site,
- Give them a <u>risk rating</u> up to <u>10</u> (where 10 is the <u>most severe</u> risk),
- Write down how they can be <u>managed</u>.

E.g.

Risk Identified	Risk Rating	How can it be managed?
Risk of accidents whilst surveying traffic passing through junction.	7	Wear a fluorescent vest and choose a safe place to stand away from the traffic flow.

You'll need to decide which sampling technique is the most suitable

When you've considered everything on this page, you're ready to go and collect your data. But there's more to fieldwork than gathering data — once you've collected it all, you need to decide what it shows...

Analysing and Concluding

Analysing your data and drawing conclusions from it can be pretty tricky — here's a summary of what you need to do. There's some more help with analysing data on pages 169-175.

You need to **Describe** and **Explain** what the **Data Shows**

When you analyse and interpret data, you need to:

Describe

1) Describe what the data shows — you need to describe any patterns and correlations (see page 171) and look for any anomalies.
2) Make sure you use specific points from the data and reference what graph, table etc. you're talking about.
3) You might also need to make comparisons between different sets of data.
4) Statistical techniques (see pages 174-175) help make the data more manageable, so it's easier to spot patterns and make comparisons.

Explain

1) Explain what the data shows — you need to explain why there are patterns and why different data sets are linked together.
2) Use your geographical knowledge to help you explain the results and remember to use geographical terms.

Here's an example:

> 38% of people who visited Cliffthorpe Valley in 2016 visited the tarn — 40 000 people (see Diagram 1). The tarn area may attract visitors due to its beauty and services such as a free car park, café and tourist information centre (see Leaflet 1). However, the largest amount of litter was found at the valley head (see Graph 1), which was the fourth most popular attraction (9.5% of visitors). There are fewer bins at the valley head, and more people tend to picnic there (see Table 1), which could be why there's more litter.

Conclusions are a **Summary** of the **Results**

A conclusion is a summary of what you found out in relation to the original question. It should include:

> Be careful when drawing conclusions. Some results show a link or correlation, but that doesn't mean that one thing causes the other.

1) A summary of what your results show.
2) An answer for the question you are investigating, and an explanation for why that is the answer.
3) An explanation of how your conclusion fits into the wider geographical world — think about how your conclusion and results could be used by other people or in further investigations.

You'll have to analyse the data you've collected

For the exam, you'll need to be able to write about how you analysed your data and your conclusion, so have some points ready before you hit the exam. You might also be asked to analyse some data that you're given and draw conclusions from it — the more practice you get now, the easier that'll be.

Evaluating

Evaluating data is all about working out how <u>accurate</u> it is, and whether it lets you <u>answer</u> your research question. You also need to think about how your investigation could be <u>improved</u> if you were to do it again.

Evaluations Identify Problems in the Investigation

Evaluation is all about <u>self assessment</u> — looking back at how <u>good or bad</u> your study (or the data you are given in the exam) was. You need to be able to:

1) Identify any <u>problems</u> with the <u>methods</u> used and suggest how they could be <u>improved</u>. Think about things like the <u>size</u> of the <u>data sets</u>, if any <u>bias</u> (unfairness) slipped in and if <u>other methods</u> would have been <u>more appropriate</u> or <u>more effective</u>.

2) Describe how <u>accurate</u> the results are and <u>link</u> this to the methods used — say whether any <u>errors</u> in the methods affected the results.

3) Comment on the <u>validity</u> of your <u>conclusion</u>. You need to talk about how <u>problems</u> with the methods and the <u>accuracy</u> of the results affect the <u>validity</u> of the conclusion. Problems with methods lead to <u>less</u> reliable and accurate results, which affects the validity of the conclusion.

Accurate

<u>Accurate</u> results are <u>as near</u> as possible to the <u>true answer</u> — they have <u>few errors</u>.

Reliable

<u>Reliable</u> means that data can be <u>reproduced</u>.

Valid

<u>Valid</u> means that the data <u>answers</u> the <u>original question</u> and is <u>reliable</u>.

For example:

I <u>concluded</u> that the river <u>flowed faster</u> further <u>downstream</u>. However, one <u>problem</u> with my data collection method was that it was <u>difficult</u> to put the float in at <u>exactly</u> the <u>same point</u> each time. This <u>reduced</u> the <u>accuracy</u> of my measurements. To make my investigation <u>more accurate</u>, I could have placed a tape measure across the river to <u>mark the exact point</u> of entry. Another <u>problem</u> was that I only took <u>two readings</u> at each site and I only used <u>one upstream site</u> and <u>one downstream site</u>. To make my data <u>more reliable</u> I could have taken <u>more readings</u> at each site, and used a larger <u>number of sites</u> both upstream and downstream. These <u>improvements</u> would have produced a more <u>valid</u> conclusion.

Be critical of your results — if you think some are unreliable, then say so

You can do some preparation for this bit as you're going along. While you're collecting your data, think about whether your results would be different if you'd chosen a different day or time, or if you were in a different location. Explain how they'd be different, and why. And don't forget to discuss the validity of your conclusions.

Worked Exam Questions

Remember, in the exam you'll be asked to write about someone else's fieldwork, like in the worked exam questions on this page, as well as about your own fieldwork, which you can practise on the next page.

1 A group of students is investigating how and why the quality of life varies within the city of Suninsky. One of their data sources is the 2010 Index of Multiple Deprivation (IMD). The IMD for each ward in Suninsky is presented in **Figure 1**.

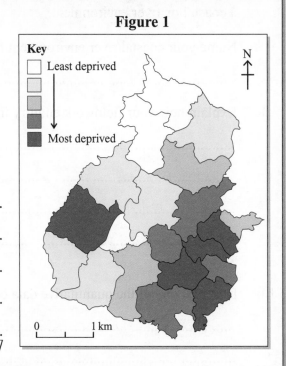

Figure 1

Key
- Least deprived
- Most deprived

N

0   1 km

a) Explain how suitable it is for the students to use data from the 2010 Index of Multiple Deprivation in their investigation.

The IMD is available for every neighbourhood in the

UK, and calculated in the same way, so it can be used

to compare wards with one another. However, the

data is from 2010, so might not represent current

deprivation levels in Suninsky.

[4]

b) Explain **one** limitation of using a choropleth map to show deprivation in **Figure 1**.

The choropleth map uses one colour for each entire ward, which means it looks like levels of deprivation

change at ward boundaries suddenly rather than gradually.

[2]

[Total 6 marks]

2 Some students investigated how quality of life varies in the rural area surrounding their school. They carried out environmental quality surveys at several sites by scoring various factors on a bipolar scale. The bipolar analysis table they used for data collection is shown in **Figure 2**.

Figure 2

Low quality	Environmental quality score							High quality
	-3	-2	-1	0	+1	+2	+3	
Very noisy								No noise pollution
Heavily littered								No litter
Obvious vandalism								No evidence of vandalism
Roads and pavements poorly maintained								Roads and pavements well maintained

Suggest **one** possible limitation of using this data collection method.

Different people will use different standards to judge a place, so if different students use this data to

assess areas, the results might not be directly comparable.

[Total 2 marks]

Exam Questions

1   You have carried out fieldwork in **either** a coastal **or** river environment.

You might not have completed your fieldwork yet — don't start this question until your enquiry is finished.

Name your coastal/river environment fieldwork location.

....

a)   Explain how your fieldwork enquiry improved your understanding of an area of geography.

....

....

....

....

[3]

b)   Describe **one** of the quantitative data collection techniques that you used.

....

....

....

[2]

c)   Explain how **one** of your primary data collection techniques was appropriate to the task.

....

....

....

....

[3]

d)   Describe **two** strengths of **one** of the data presentation techniques that you used.

Data presentation technique:...

1:...

....

....

2:...

....

....

[4]

[Total 12 marks]

Global Ecosystems

There are loads of different <u>ecosystems</u> in the world. Time for a whistle-stop tour...

You Need to Know the **Global Distribution** of **Major Biomes**

1) <u>Biomes</u> are large-scale, <u>global ecosystems</u> with distinctive vegetation.

2) An <u>ecosystem</u> includes all the <u>living</u> and <u>non-living</u> things in an area.

3) The <u>climate</u> in an area determines what <u>type of biome</u> forms.
So different parts of the world have <u>different biomes</u> because they have <u>different climates</u>:

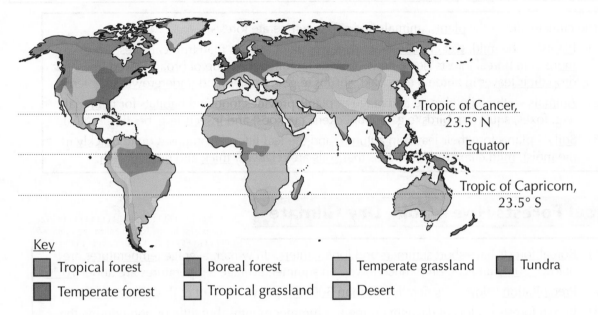

Tropic of Cancer, 23.5° N

Equator

Tropic of Capricorn, 23.5° S

<u>Key</u>

◼ Tropical forest   ◼ Boreal forest   ◼ Temperate grassland   ◼ Tundra

◼ Temperate forest   ◻ Tropical grassland   ◻ Desert

Tropical Forests Have a **Hot, Wet Climate**

See pages 133-136 for more on tropical forests.

Climate

1) The climate is <u>the same all year</u> round — there are <u>no definite seasons</u>.

2) It's <u>hot</u> (the temperature is generally between <u>20-28 °C</u> and only varies by a few degrees over the year). This is because near the <u>equator</u> the <u>Sun</u> is <u>overhead</u> all year round.

3) Because tropical forests are found near the <u>equator</u>, <u>day length</u> is the same (about <u>12 hours</u>) <u>all year</u> round. This means the forests get plenty of <u>sunshine</u> all year.

4) <u>Rainfall</u> is very <u>high</u>, around 2000 mm per year. It <u>rains every day</u>, usually in the <u>afternoon</u>.

Characteristics

The climate affects the <u>plants</u>, <u>animals</u> and <u>soil</u> in tropical forests:

Evergreen plants don't drop their leaves in a particular season.

1) <u>Plants</u> — most trees are <u>evergreen</u> to take advantage of the <u>continual growing season</u>. Plants grow <u>quickly</u> and are <u>adapted</u> to take in <u>maximum light</u>.

2) <u>Animals</u> — the <u>dense</u> vegetation provides lots of <u>food</u> and different <u>habitats</u>, so there are lots of <u>different species</u> of animal, for example <u>gorillas</u>, <u>jaguars</u>, <u>anacondas</u>, <u>tree frogs</u> and <u>sloths</u>. There are loads of species of <u>insects</u> and <u>birds</u>.

3) <u>Soil</u> — plants <u>grow quickly</u> and shed leaves all year round. These <u>decompose</u> quickly, so there's a constant supply of <u>nutrients</u> in the <u>soil</u>, and these nutrients are <u>cycled quickly</u>.

EXAM TIP

The distribution of biomes is determined by the climate

In the exam, you could be asked to identify biomes on a map, so make sure you know the map above. Don't be put off by the detail — the biomes are concentrated in distinct regions across the globe.

Global Ecosystems

Now that you know about <u>tropical forests</u>, it's time to look at two <u>other</u> types of <u>forest</u>, before moving onto <u>deserts</u>.

Temperate Forests Have a **Mild, Wet Climate**

Climate

1) Temperate forests have <u>four</u> distinct <u>seasons</u>. The <u>summers</u> are <u>warm</u> and the <u>winters</u> are <u>cool</u>.
2) <u>Rainfall</u> is very <u>high</u> (up to 1500 mm per year) and there's <u>rain all year</u> round.
3) Days are <u>shorter</u> in winter and <u>longer</u> in summer — the <u>hours</u> of <u>sunshine vary</u> through the year.

Characteristics

The climate affects the <u>plants</u>, <u>animals</u> and <u>soil</u> in temperate forests:

1) <u>Plants</u> — the <u>mild</u>, <u>wet climate</u> supports <u>fewer</u> plant species than tropical forests, but <u>more</u> than boreal forests (see below). Forests are often made up of <u>broad-leaved trees</u> that <u>drop their leaves</u> in autumn (e.g. oak), <u>shrubs</u> (e.g. brambles) and <u>undergrowth</u> (e.g. ferns).
2) <u>Animals</u> — the <u>mild</u> climate and range of <u>plants</u> provides <u>food</u> and <u>habitats</u> for <u>mammals</u> (e.g. foxes, squirrels), <u>birds</u> (e.g. woodpeckers, cuckoos) and <u>insects</u> (e.g. beetles, moths).
3) <u>Soil</u> — plants lose their leaves in <u>autumn</u>, and the leaf litter decomposes quite <u>quickly</u> in the <u>moist</u>, <u>mild</u> climate. This means that <u>soils</u> are relatively <u>thick</u> and <u>nutrient-rich</u>.

Boreal Forests Have a **Cold, Dry Climate**

> The boreal biome is also called the taiga.

Climate

1) <u>Boreal forests</u> have <u>short summers</u> and <u>long winters</u>. In winter, average <u>temperatures</u> are below <u>−20 °C</u> and can drop much lower. In summer, average temperatures are about <u>10 °C</u>.
2) <u>Precipitation</u> is <u>low</u> — generally <u>less than 500 mm</u> per year. A lot of this falls as <u>snow</u>.
3) Boreal forests get lots of <u>daylight</u> during the <u>summer</u> months, but little or none during the <u>winter</u>. Skies tend to be <u>clear</u>, so during daylight hours there's plenty of <u>sunshine</u>.

> See pages 142-143 for more about the characteristics of the taiga.

Characteristics

The climate affects the <u>plants</u>, <u>animals</u> and <u>soil</u> in boreal forests:

1) <u>Plants</u> — most trees are <u>evergreen</u>, so they can grow whenever there's <u>enough light</u>. <u>Coniferous trees</u> such as <u>pine</u> and <u>fir</u> are common, as are low-growing <u>mosses</u> and <u>lichen</u>.
2) <u>Animals</u> — there are relatively <u>few</u> animal species in boreal forests compared to e.g. tropical forests, because there is <u>less food</u> available and animals need to be <u>adapted</u> to the cold climate to survive. Animals that do live there include <u>black bears</u>, <u>wolves</u>, <u>elk</u> and <u>eagles</u>.
3) <u>Soil</u> — the <u>cool</u>, <u>dry climate</u> means that needles from the trees <u>decompose slowly</u>, so soils are quite <u>thin</u>, <u>nutrient-poor</u> and <u>acidic</u>. In some areas the ground is <u>frozen</u> for most of the year.

Deserts Have **Low Rainfall**

> Not every desert is hot — some are mild (e.g. the Atacama desert) and some are cold (e.g. the Gobi desert).

Climate

1) Rainfall is very low — <u>less than 250 mm</u> per year. It might only rain <u>once</u> every two or three years.
2) <u>Hot</u> desert <u>temperatures</u> range from very <u>hot</u> in the <u>day</u> (e.g. 45 °C) to <u>cold</u> at <u>night</u> (below 0 °C).
3) Hot deserts get more <u>daylight</u> during the <u>summer</u> than the <u>winter</u>. Because there is little <u>cloud cover</u>, they get lots of hours of <u>sunshine</u> every day.

Characteristics

The climate affects the <u>plants</u>, <u>animals</u> and <u>soil</u> in deserts:

1) <u>Plants</u> — plant growth is <u>sparse</u> due to <u>lack of rainfall</u>. A few plants do grow, e.g. <u>cacti</u>, <u>thornbushes</u>.
2) <u>Animals</u> — relatively <u>few</u> animal species live in hot deserts — those that do are <u>adapted</u> to cope with the harsh climate. Animals that live there include <u>lizards</u>, <u>snakes</u>, <u>insects</u> and <u>scorpions</u>.
3) <u>Soil</u> — the <u>sparse</u> vegetation means that there is <u>little leaf litter</u>, and the <u>dry</u> climate means that organic matter is <u>slow</u> to <u>decompose</u>. As a result, soils are mostly <u>thin</u> and <u>nutrient-poor</u>.

Global Ecosystems

Now for the last few biomes you need to know about — <u>tundra</u>, and both <u>temperate</u> and <u>tropical grasslands</u>...

Tundra Has a **Cold, Dry Climate**

Climate

1) <u>Temperatures</u> are low — around <u>5-10 °C</u> during the summer and lower than <u>−30 °C</u> in the winter.

2) <u>Precipitation</u> is also very low — <u>less than 250 mm</u> per year. Most of this falls as <u>snow</u>.

3) Tundra is found at <u>high latitudes</u>, so it gets <u>near-continuous daylight</u> in the <u>summer</u> and little or <u>no daylight</u> in the <u>winter</u>. There is more <u>cloud cover</u> in the <u>summer</u>.

Characteristics

The climate affects the <u>plants</u>, <u>animals</u> and <u>soil</u> in tundra regions:

1) <u>Plants</u> — the <u>cold</u> climate and <u>lack of light</u> in winter make it hard for plants to grow, and there are hardly any <u>trees</u>. Vegetation includes <u>mosses</u>, <u>grasses</u> and <u>low shrubs</u>.

2) <u>Animals</u> — the <u>cold</u> climate and lack of vegetation means that relatively <u>few</u> animal species live in the tundra. Those that do include <u>Arctic hares</u>, <u>Arctic foxes</u>, <u>mosquitoes</u> and lots of <u>birds</u>. Some animals <u>migrate south</u> for the winter.

3) <u>Soil</u> — the <u>sparse</u> vegetation produces <u>little leaf litter</u>, and the <u>cold</u>, <u>dry</u> climate means that organic matter <u>decomposes slowly</u>, so soil is <u>thin</u> and <u>nutrient-poor</u>. There is a layer of <u>permafrost</u> (permanently frozen ground) below the soil surface, which can <u>stop</u> water from <u>draining</u> away.

There are **Two Types** of **Grassland**

Climate

1) <u>Tropical</u> grasslands have quite <u>low rainfall</u> (800-900 mm per year) and <u>distinct wet and dry seasons</u>. Temperatures are <u>highest</u> (around 35 °C) just <u>before</u> the wet season and <u>lowest</u> (about 15 °C) just <u>after</u> it. They are found around the <u>equator</u>, so they get <u>lots of sunshine</u> all year round.

2) <u>Temperate</u> grasslands have <u>hot summers</u> (up to 40 °C) and <u>cold winters</u> (down to −40 °C). They receive <u>250-500 mm</u> precipitation each year, mostly in the <u>late spring</u> and <u>early summer</u>. Because they're <u>further</u> from the <u>equator</u>, the amount of <u>light</u> they receive <u>varies</u> through the year.

Characteristics

Rainfall is <u>too low</u> to support many <u>trees</u> in <u>tropical</u> or <u>temperate</u> grasslands, which affects <u>animals</u> and <u>soil</u>:

1) <u>Tropical</u> grasslands consist mostly of <u>grass</u>, <u>scrub</u> and <u>small plants</u>, with a few <u>scattered trees</u>, e.g. acacia. They are home to lots of <u>insects</u>, including <u>grasshoppers</u>, <u>beetles</u> and <u>termites</u>. Larger animals include <u>lions</u>, <u>elephants</u>, <u>giraffes</u>, <u>zebras</u> and <u>antelope</u>. Grass <u>dies back</u> during the <u>dry</u> season, forming a <u>thin</u>, <u>nutrient-rich soil</u>, but nutrients are <u>washed out</u> of the soil during the wet season.

2) <u>Temperate</u> grasslands are also dominated by <u>grasses</u> and <u>small plants</u>, and have very <u>few trees</u>. They are home to <u>fewer</u> animal species than tropical grasslands — mammals include <u>bison</u> and <u>wild horses</u>, and rodents such as <u>mole rats</u>. <u>High temperatures</u> in summer mean that decomposition is <u>fast</u>, so soils are relatively <u>thick</u> and <u>nutrient-rich</u>.

REVISION TIP

Make sure you know the temperatures and rain patterns of each biome

By reading through pages 121-123, you've got through all of the biomes you need to know for your exam. Before moving on, try shutting the book and testing yourself on each biome — see if you can jot down the type of climate, animals, plants and soils found in each one, then see how much you remembered.

Global Ecosystems

You saw on p.121 <u>where</u> different <u>biomes</u> occur in the world — this is mainly determined by the <u>climate</u>. However, within these general regions, different kinds of <u>species</u> live in <u>different areas</u>.

Biome **Distribution** is Affected by **Local Factors**

<u>Climate</u> (i.e. <u>temperature</u>, <u>rainfall</u> and <u>sunshine hours</u>) is the main factor influencing <u>biome distribution</u>, but there are other factors that alter distribution at a <u>smaller scale</u>:

Altitude

Altitude is the height above sea level.

- <u>Higher</u> altitudes are <u>colder</u>, so <u>fewer</u> plants grow there, which also <u>limits</u> the number of animal species.
- This means there's not much <u>organic matter</u>, so soils are <u>thin</u> or <u>non-existent</u>.

Rock type

- Some rock types are easily <u>weathered</u> (see p.63) to form soils, and different rock types contain different <u>minerals</u>. This affects how <u>nutrient-rich</u> the soil is.
- Some rocks are also <u>permeable</u> (water <u>can</u> flow through them) and others are <u>impermeable</u> (they <u>don't</u> let water through).

Soil type

- More <u>nutrient-rich</u> soils can support <u>more</u> plants.
- The <u>acidity</u> and <u>drainage</u> of soils also <u>varies</u>, affecting the <u>plants</u> that can <u>grow</u>.
- E.g. <u>peat soils</u> are very <u>acidic</u>, so only acid-tolerant plants such as conifers can grow, and <u>clay soils</u> are <u>sticky</u>, so <u>water can't</u> flow through very <u>easily</u>.

Drainage

- If drainage is <u>poor</u>, soil gets <u>waterlogged</u> and only plants <u>adapted</u> to wet conditions can grow there.
- Very wet areas may be home to <u>aquatic species</u> of plants and animals.

The **Biotic** and **Abiotic** Components of Biomes **Interact**

1) The <u>biotic</u> components are the <u>living</u> parts of a biome — e.g. <u>plants</u> (<u>flora</u>) and <u>animals</u> (<u>fauna</u>).
2) The <u>abiotic</u> components are the <u>non-living</u> parts — e.g. <u>soil</u>, <u>water</u>, <u>rock</u>, <u>atmosphere</u>.
3) The different components <u>interact</u> with each other, for example:

1) <u>Water</u> availability affects the <u>plants</u> that can grow — e.g. if the soil is very <u>dry</u>, only <u>desert</u> plants such as cacti will be able to survive. Plants <u>take in</u> water from the soil and <u>release</u> it into the <u>atmosphere</u>, providing moisture for further <u>rainfall</u>.

2) The <u>type</u> and <u>density</u> of vegetation that grows affects the type of <u>soil</u> that forms, and the type of <u>soil</u> that forms affects the type of <u>vegetation</u> that can grow — e.g. dense vegetation cover and lots of leaf fall means that lots of <u>nutrients</u> will be added to the soil, which can then support <u>more</u> plant growth.

3) Some organisms cause <u>biological weathering</u>. This is when <u>rocks</u> in the ground are <u>broken up</u> into smaller pieces by <u>living</u> things, e.g. <u>tree roots</u> breaking rocks up as they grow.

The rock type, soil type and drainage in an area can be inter-linked

Remember, the term 'biome' doesn't just cover the biotic (living) components of an area — biomes are also made up of abiotic components. Make sure you can describe a few of the ways in which they interact with each other.

Humans and the Biosphere

Resources are just all the things we use — and it turns out we get pretty much all of them from the biosphere.

The Biosphere Provides Lots of Resources

1) The biosphere includes all parts of the Earth that are occupied by living organisms — it's the plants, animals, bacteria and fungi as well as the soil and water that they live in.

2) Living organisms provide loads of goods that people need to survive. These are used by indigenous people (people who are native to an area) and others who live locally. For example:

FOOD — Many indigenous people get all of their food directly from plants and animals. Some forage for food, picking wild fruit, vegetables and nuts, hunting and trapping animals and catching fish. Others grow food for their own use, e.g. growing cereals, fruit and vegetables and raising livestock.

MEDICINE — Lots of plants have medicinal properties and are used to cure illnesses and keep people healthy. Plant species in tropical forests have been used to create over 7000 drugs, e.g. quinine from the cinchona tree is used to treat malaria.

BUILDING MATERIALS — Trees and other plants are often used as building materials, e.g. pine from taiga forests (see p.144) is used to make furniture and to build houses. Sap from trees can be used as glue or to make buildings waterproof, reeds and straw can be used for roofs and plant fibres can be used to make rope.

FUEL — Indigenous people rely on plants and animals for fuel for cooking and keeping warm. Wood, moss, dried grass and dried animal dung is burnt as fuel. Some indigenous people in areas with little vegetation (like the tundra), use animal fat, e.g. blubber from seals, as fuel for oil lamps.

Humans Exploit the Biosphere

The biosphere is also exploited by companies for commercial gain (to make a profit). Increasing demand and improving technology is increasing the scale of commercial exploitation. For example:

Energy
Demand for energy is increasing as the world population increases and people have more electronic devices, e.g. laptops and phones (see p.127-128). Large areas of forest are cut down to clear land for the growing of crops that can be used to make biofuels, or to make way for coal mines or power stations. Some areas of tropical forest have been flooded by the building of hydroelectric dams. Drilling for oil and gas in the tundra is damaging the biosphere because pipelines are melting the permafrost.

Water
Demand for water is also increasing because of increases in global population — people use water for washing, irrigating farmland etc. Water resources, e.g. lakes, rivers and aquifers (underground water stores), can be over-exploited — this is happening in arid areas like the Sahara desert. This can cause damage to the biosphere, as plants and animals no longer have enough water to survive.

Minerals
Minerals such as gold and iron are used in building, scientific instruments, electrical appliances and lots of other things — and demand for them is increasing. Minerals are often extracted by mining. Mines in tropical forests are responsible for lots of deforestation and toxic chemicals are washed into streams and rivers, killing wildlife. Open pit mining removes large areas of the land surface (see p.144).

Commercial exploitation of the biosphere is increasing

Indigenous people use resources in a sustainable way, so they aren't being used more quickly than they're replaced. Commercial exploitation is a different story — resources are being used unsustainably to make profit.

Role of the Biosphere

The <u>biosphere</u> is basically the <u>world's life support</u> and has several <u>really important</u> jobs to do.

The Biosphere Helps to **Regulate** the **Gases** in the **Atmosphere**...

1) The biosphere helps to <u>control</u> the proportion of different <u>gases</u> in the atmosphere:

- <u>Plants</u> take in <u>carbon dioxide</u> (CO_2) and give out <u>oxygen</u> during <u>photosynthesis</u>.
- <u>Animals</u> take in <u>oxygen</u> from the air and give out <u>carbon dioxide</u> when they breathe.

2) Maintaining the <u>balance</u> of gases in the atmosphere is <u>important</u> because:

- Most <u>living organisms</u> need <u>oxygen</u> to survive.
- <u>Increased</u> levels of CO_2 lead to <u>global warming</u> (see p.6).
- <u>Increased</u> levels of CO_2 can also make the <u>oceans acidic</u>, <u>affecting</u> the <u>organisms</u> that live there.
- <u>Some CO_2</u> is needed to keep the Earth <u>warm enough</u> to support life.

Forests are essential in maintaining the balance of gases because they take in huge amounts of CO_2 and release huge amounts of oxygen.

... to Keep **Soil Healthy**...

The biosphere is important for maintaining <u>soil nutrients</u> and <u>structure</u>:

- <u>Plant roots</u> and <u>animals</u> (e.g. earthworms) spread nutrients through the soil — this helps to maintain <u>soil structure</u> and <u>fertility</u>, which allows plants to <u>grow</u>.
- The <u>roots</u> of vegetation also <u>hold</u> the soil together — without this, the soil can be <u>eroded</u> by wind and rain.
- Vegetation <u>intercepts</u> (catches) rainfall before it reaches the ground. This helps to prevent <u>leaching</u> — where <u>nutrients</u> in the soil are <u>washed downwards</u> out of reach of <u>plants</u>.

The nutrient cycle is the way that nutrients move through an ecosystem. For more on nutrient cycles, see p.135.

Plants absorb nutrients from the soil and use them to grow.

Animals eat plants, taking in the nutrients they contain.

Plants drop their leaves.

Animals and plants die and decompose, returning nutrients to the soil.

... and to **Regulate** the **Water Cycle**

1) The <u>water cycle</u> (or <u>hydrological cycle</u> if you're feeling fancy) is the movement of water between the <u>land</u>, bodies of <u>water</u> (e.g. lakes, rivers, the sea) and the <u>atmosphere</u>. It looks a bit like this.

2) The biosphere is an important <u>control</u> on the water cycle:

- Water is <u>taken up</u> by plants, so <u>less</u> reaches rivers. This helps to prevent <u>flooding</u> (see p.90) and <u>soil erosion</u>.
- Plants also help to <u>regulate</u> the <u>global water cycle</u> by <u>storing</u> water and releasing it into the atmosphere <u>slowly</u>. Large areas of <u>forest</u>, e.g. the Amazon rainforest, can reduce the <u>risk</u> of <u>drought</u> and <u>flooding</u> in areas a long way away.

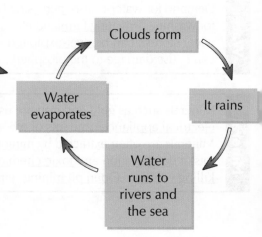

Clouds form

It rains

Water runs to rivers and the sea

Water evaporates

The biosphere is important in sustaining life on Earth

So, the biosphere is pretty important for keeping the Earth ticking over comfortably, as it turns out. Make sure you understand all the ways that the biosphere regulates the Earth's systems, then head on over to the next page.

Demand for Resources

There are an awful lot of <u>people</u> on our planet, and they all need <u>food</u>, <u>water</u> and <u>energy</u>. No one's quite sure how the human population will <u>change</u> in the future, and how that'll affect the <u>availability</u> of the things we need.

Population Growth is Increasing Demand for Resources

1) The world's population is <u>increasing</u>. <u>More people</u> require <u>more resources</u> (e.g. food, water and energy), so demand <u>increases</u>.

2) The world's population is <u>predicted</u> to continue to <u>rise</u>:

- <u>Population projections</u> are <u>predictions</u> of <u>how many people</u> there will be in the world in the <u>future</u>.

- We know <u>past</u> and <u>present</u> values of population pretty <u>accurately</u>, but it's <u>more difficult</u> to predict <u>future</u> global population — it gets <u>harder</u> the <u>further forward</u> in time you go.

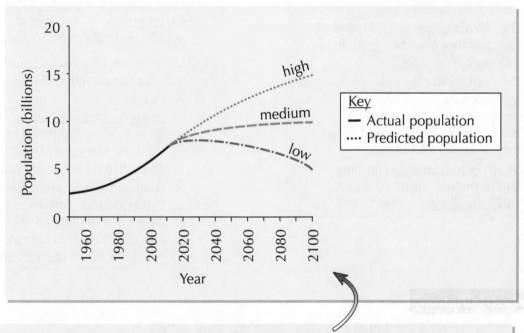

- The <u>UN</u> has made three <u>predictions</u> about <u>population growth</u> up to the <u>end of this century</u>. The <u>highest</u> prediction shows the <u>world's total population</u> reaching <u>14 billion people</u>.

There's a Link Between the Demands for Different Resources

Increased demand for <u>one resource</u> can also increase demand for <u>another</u>, for example:

- <u>More people</u> means that <u>more food</u> needs to be grown, which increases demand for <u>water</u>.
- As demand for <u>water</u> increases, it may need to be <u>transported</u> from areas where there's plenty to areas where there's not enough — this takes lots of <u>energy</u>.

Population growth is a major factor in the increase in demand for resources

This is pretty straightforward — as there are more and more people on the planet, there is a higher demand for resources, just as you'd expect. Just make sure you understand that there are different projections for the world's human population size, and how a high demand for one resource can lead to a high demand for another.

Demand for Resources

You've seen on the previous page that <u>population growth</u> is increasing the global <u>demand</u> for resources. However, that's not the <u>only</u> factor involved — there a few <u>other reasons</u> people are using more food, water and energy.

Other Factors Also **Increase Demand** for Resources

1) Increasing <u>wealth</u>, <u>urbanisation</u> and <u>industrialisation</u> are increasing the demand for resources.

2) In <u>emerging</u> countries, e.g. China and Brazil, there has been <u>rapid industrialisation</u> and <u>urbanisation</u> and people are getting <u>wealthier</u> (see pages 47-48).

3) Over the next few decades most <u>economic</u> growth is expected to take place in <u>Africa</u>.

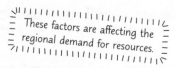
These factors are affecting the regional demand for resources.

1 Increasing Wealth

1) <u>Economic development</u> means that people are getting <u>wealthier</u> (more <u>affluent</u>).

2) Wealthier people have <u>more disposable income</u>, which affects their <u>resource consumption</u>:

- They have <u>more money</u> to spend on <u>food</u> and they often buy <u>more</u> than they <u>need</u>.

- They can afford <u>cars</u>, <u>fridges</u>, <u>televisions</u> etc., all of which use <u>energy</u>. Manufacturing these goods and producing energy to run them also uses a lot of <u>water</u>.

- More people can <u>afford</u> flushing toilets, showers, dishwashers etc. This <u>increases water use</u>.

2 Urbanisation

1) <u>Urbanisation</u> is the <u>growth</u> in the <u>proportion</u> of a country's population living in urban areas.

2) Urbanisation tends to <u>increase resource consumption</u> because:

- Cities tend to be more <u>resource-intensive</u> than rural areas — street lights and neon signs use <u>energy</u>, and fountains and urban parks require <u>water</u>.

- Food and water have to be <u>transported</u> long distances to meet the increased demand in cities, and <u>waste</u> needs to be <u>removed</u> — this increases <u>energy use</u>.

3 Industrialisation

1) Industrialisation is the <u>shift</u> in a country's main economic activity from <u>primary production</u> (e.g. farming) to <u>secondary production</u> (e.g. manufacturing goods).

2) <u>Manufacturing goods</u> such as cars, chemicals and electrical appliances uses a lot of <u>energy</u> — e.g. to run machines or heat components so they can be shaped. Manufacturing also uses a lot of <u>water</u> — e.g. for cooling and washing components. As countries become more <u>industrialised</u>, their demand for energy and water <u>increases</u>.

3) Industrialisation is <u>increasing</u> the <u>production</u> of <u>processed</u> goods, e.g. foods such as margarine. This <u>increases</u> the <u>demand</u> for ingredients such as <u>palm oil</u>, which are often grown on huge <u>plantations</u>.

EXAM TIP

People in richer countries consume more food, water and energy

In the exam, you might be asked why the demand for resources in a country might be increasing. The most obvious answer is that the population is growing, but don't forget about these other factors. And remember to be specific — saying the demand for resources increases as a country gets wealthier is correct, but you might get more marks if you say why, e.g. because more people can afford cars etc.

Demand for Resources

For all the reasons you've seen on the last two pages, the <u>demand</u> for <u>food</u>, <u>water</u> and <u>energy</u> is <u>increasing</u>, which raises the question of whether <u>supply</u> can <u>keep up</u> with demand. There are some <u>different ideas</u> on this...

Malthus and Boserup Had Different Theories About Resource Supply

Malthus and Boserup both came up with theories about how <u>population growth</u> and <u>resource availability</u> are <u>related</u>:

Malthus's Theory

- <u>Thomas Malthus</u> was an 18th-century economist. He thought that <u>population</u> was increasing <u>faster</u> than <u>supply of resources</u>, so eventually there would be <u>too many people</u> for the <u>resources</u> available.

- He believed that, when this happened, people would be killed by catastrophes such as <u>famine</u>, <u>illness</u> and <u>war</u>, and the population would <u>return</u> to a level that could be <u>supported</u> by the resources available.

- The point where the <u>lines cross</u> on the graph is the point of <u>catastrophe</u> — population starts to <u>decrease</u> after this, until it is <u>low enough</u> that there are enough resources to <u>support</u> it again.

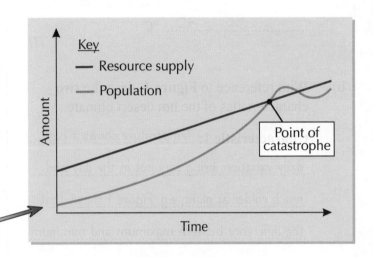

Boserup's Theory

- <u>Ester Boserup</u> was a 20th-century economist. Her theory was that <u>however big</u> the world's population grew, people would always produce <u>sufficient resources</u> to meet their needs.

- She thought that, if <u>resource supplies</u> became <u>limited</u>, people would come up with <u>new ways</u> to <u>increase production</u> (e.g. by making technological advances) in order to <u>avoid hardship</u>.

- The graph shows that, as population <u>increases</u> to be <u>equal</u> with resource supply, resource supply <u>increases</u> so there are always <u>enough resources</u> available for the population.

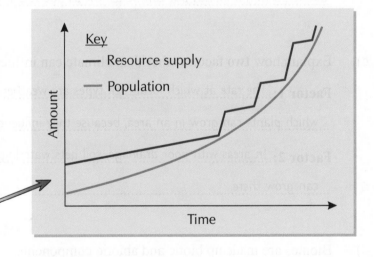

Neither theory has been proved completely <u>right</u> or completely <u>wrong</u>. There have been <u>famines</u> in some areas, but on a <u>global scale</u>, food production has <u>so far kept up</u> with population growth.

Boserup thought that the population will keep on growing

A handy way to make sure you get these theories the right way round is to remember that in the graph for <u>Boserup's</u> theory, <u>both</u> lines keep going <u>up</u>. In Malthus's theory, the population size falls after the point of catastrophe, when there aren't enough resources to sustain further population growth.

Worked Exam Questions

Here's a typical exam question with the answers filled in to help. They won't be there on the real exam though, so you'd better learn how to answer them yourself...

1   Study **Figure 1**, which shows climate data for a hot desert.

a)   Using **Figure 1**, identify the average maximum temperature for December.

........................40.... °C

[1]

Figure 1

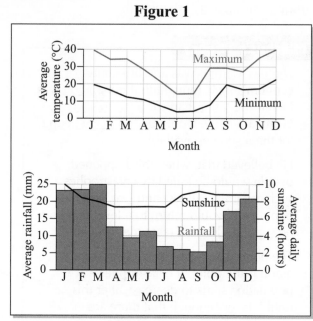

b)   With reference to **Figure 1**, describe **two** characteristics of the hot desert climate.

Characteristic 1: Temperature shows a high daily variation, being very hot in the day and much colder at night, e.g. Figure 1 shows that the difference between maximum and minimum temperature in January is about 20 °C.

Characteristic 2: There is very little rainfall, e.g. Figure 1 shows that the average rainfall peaks at about 25 mm a month but can be as low as about 5 mm a month.

[4]

c)   Explain how **two** factors other than climate can influence the local distribution of biomes.

Factor 1: The rate at which local rock types are weathered, and the minerals they contain, will affect which plants can grow in an area, because they influence the quantity and quality of the soil.

Factor 2: In areas with poor drainage, soil gets waterlogged so only plants adapted to wet conditions can grow there.

[4]

d)   Biomes are made up biotic and abiotic components.
Describe **two** ways that biotic components interact with abiotic components in an ecosystem.

1: Water availability affects the type of plants that can grow. Plants release the water they take in back into the atmosphere, providing moisture for further rainfall.

2: The type and density of vegetation that grows affects the type of the soil that forms, and the type of soil that forms affects the type of vegetation that can grow.

[4]

[Total 13 marks]

Exam Questions

1 There are differing theories about the relationship between population growth and resource availability.

a) Which **one** of the following is not a feature Malthus's theory about population and resources?

A Population will increase faster than the supply of resources. ◯

B Population will fall after a 'point of catastrophe'. ◯

C Technological advances mean that access to resources will increase. ◯

D Resource supply dictates population numbers. ◯

[1]

b) **Figure 1** is a graph representing Boserup's theory. Describe what it shows.

....

....

....

....

....

[2]

[Total 3 marks]

Figure 1

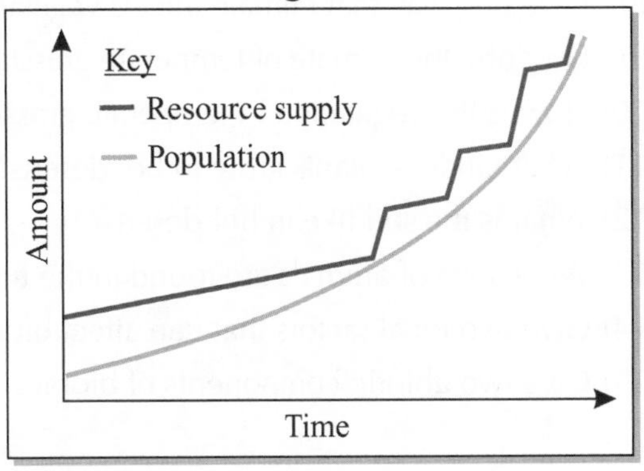

2 Study **Figure 2**, which shows temperature and rainfall data for an area of forest.

a) Which month has the highest average temperature?

....

[1]

b) Identify the type of forest biome that is likely to have developed in the climate shown in **Figure 2**.

....

[1]

c) Describe the vegetation found in this type of forest.

....

....

....

....

....

[2]

[Total 4 marks]

Figure 2

Month	Average temperature / °C	Average rainfall / mm
January	2	64
February	5	42
March	6	33
April	12	42
May	19	45
June	19	48
July	21	69
August	19	62
September	12	45
October	10	55
November	4	65
December	2	52

Revision Summary

That's just about it for <u>Topic 7</u> — so now's an excellent moment to <u>test</u> your <u>knowledge</u> with some questions.
- Try these questions and <u>tick off each one</u> when you <u>get it right</u>.
- When you've done <u>all the questions</u> under a heading and are <u>completely happy</u> with it, tick it off.

Global Ecosystems (p.121-124) ☑

1) What is a biome?
2) Why do different parts of the world have different biomes?
3) Where are temperate forests found?
4) Give one biome that is mostly found between the Tropics of Cancer and Capricorn.
5) True or false: tropical forests have a distinct summer and winter.
6) Describe the climate of tropical forests.
7) Describe the soil in the temperate forest biome.
8) Give one way that climate affects vegetation in boreal forests.
9) Describe the climate of temperate grasslands.
10) How is the vegetation in temperate grasslands different from that in tropical grasslands?
11) What kinds of plants grow in hot deserts?
12) What is the soil like in hot deserts?
13) What sorts of animals are found in the tundra biome?
14) Give two local factors that can affect biome distribution.
15) Give two abiotic components of biomes.

Human Use of the Biosphere (p.125) ☑

16) What does 'indigenous' mean?
17) a) Give one way that indigenous people rely on the biosphere for food.
    b) Give one way that indigenous people rely on the biosphere for fuel.
    c) Name two other resources that indigenous people get from the biosphere.
18) What is meant by the phrase 'commercial exploitation of the biosphere'?
19) Give two examples of how the biosphere is exploited for water.

Role of the Biosphere (p.126) ☑

20) How does the biosphere regulate the composition of the atmosphere?
21) Give one reason why maintaining the balance of gases in the atmosphere is important.
22) Describe one way in which the biosphere helps to keep soil healthy.
23) a) Sketch the water cycle.
    b) How does the biosphere affect the water cycle?

Demand for Resources (p.127-129) ☑

24) True or false: global population is fairly steady.
25) How does global population change affect the demand for resources?
26) What impact does urbanisation have on the demand for resources?
27) Name two other factors that can affect resource demand.
28) a) What did Malthus believe would happen to resource supply as population increased?
    b) What did Boserup believe would happen to resource supply as population increased?

Tropical Rainforests

It's time to venture deep into the heart of the rainforest and find out some of its special features.
First up, how all the different parts of the ecosystem are connected.

Rainforests are Interdependent Ecosystems

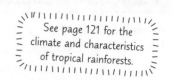

See page 121 for the climate and characteristics of tropical rainforests.

The biotic (living) components of rainforests (plants, animals and people)
and the abiotic (non-living) components (climate, soils, water) are closely related
— if one of them changes, the others are affected. For example:

1) The warm and wet climate means that plants grow quickly. The dense leaf cover protects the forest floor
   from wind and heavy rainfall, while root systems hold the soil together — this stops it being eroded.

2) The lack of wind near the forest floor means that many plants there have to rely on bees, butterflies,
   or other animals for pollination. Symbiotic relationships between plants and animals (where they
   each depend on the other for survival) are very common in tropical rainforests. For example:

   > Agouti (a rodent) are one of the only animals who can crack open the hard seed pod of the Brazil nut
   > to eat the nut inside. Sometimes, the agouti bury the nuts — these can sprout into new seedlings.
   > If the agouti became extinct, the Brazil nut trees would decline and so could all the other animals who
   > live in or feed on the Brazil nut trees. People who sell Brazil nuts to make a living may also be affected.

3) There are lots of epiphytes (plants that grow on other plants) in rainforests. They get access to light
   by growing high up on other plants, but they don't have access to the nutrients in the soil — they are
   dependent on rainfall to provide water and nutrients.

4) Changes to the rainforest ecosystem can have knock-on effects on the whole ecosystem.
   For example, deforestation reduces the amount of CO_2 being absorbed from the atmosphere,
   which adds to the greenhouse effect and changes the climate (see p.6).

Plants in the Rainforest are Stratified

Tropical rainforests have a layered structure — they are stratified. This affects how much sunlight can
reach the different levels of vegetation. Plants are adapted to the conditions found in each layer.

The emergents are the tallest trees, which poke
out of the main canopy layer. They have straight
trunks and only have branches and leaves at the
top where they can get light. They also have big
roots called buttress roots to support their trunks.

The main canopy is a continuous layer
of trees. Like emergents, they only have
leaves at the top. The dense layer of
leaves shades the rest of the forest.

The undercanopy is
made up of younger
trees that have yet to
reach their full height.
They can only survive
where there are breaks
in the canopy to let a
little bit of light through.

EMERGENTS — 40 m

MAIN CANOPY — 30 m

UNDERCANOPY — 20 m

SHRUB LAYER — 10 m

The shrub layer is
nearest the ground
where it's quite
dark. Shrubs have
large, broad leaves
to absorb as much
of the available
light as they can.

Rainforests are hot and wet with dense vegetation

You might be given a picture of a tropical rainforest in the exam and asked to identify features of it. See
if you can make out the different layers of vegetation in it, and the characteristics that are typical of each.

Tropical Rainforests

You may be wondering how <u>plants</u> and <u>animals</u> are able to <u>survive</u> in this <u>hot</u>, <u>steamy</u> environment...

Plants are Adapted to the Hot, Wet Climate

As well as having a <u>stratified structure</u>, plants in tropical rainforests have many <u>other adaptations</u> to the climate, for example:

1) Plants have <u>thick</u>, <u>waxy leaves</u> with <u>pointed tips</u>. The pointed tips (called <u>drip-tips</u>) channel the water to a point so it <u>runs off</u> — that way the <u>weight</u> of the water doesn't <u>damage</u> the plant, and there's no standing water for <u>fungi</u> and <u>bacteria</u> to grow in. The waxy coating of the leaves also helps <u>repel</u> the rain.

2) Many trees have <u>smooth</u>, <u>thin bark</u> as there is no need to <u>protect</u> the trunk from cold temperatures. The smooth surface also allows water to <u>run off easily</u>.

3) <u>Climbing plants</u>, such as lianas, use the <u>tree trunks</u> to <u>climb</u> up to the sunlight.

4) Plants <u>drop</u> their <u>leaves</u> gradually throughout the year, meaning they can go on growing <u>all year round</u>.

Animals have Also Adapted to the Physical Conditions

<u>Animals</u> are <u>adapted</u> in different ways so that they can <u>find food</u> and <u>escape predators</u>:

1) Many animals spend their <u>entire lives</u> high up in the <u>canopy</u>. They have <u>strong limbs</u> so that they can spend all day <u>climbing</u> and <u>leaping</u> from tree to tree, e.g. howler monkeys.

2) Some animals have <u>flaps of skin</u> that enable them to <u>glide</u> between trees, e.g. flying squirrels. Others have <u>suction cups</u> for <u>climbing</u>, e.g. red-eyed tree frogs.

3) Some animals are <u>camouflaged</u>, e.g. leaf-tailed geckos look like leaves so they can <u>hide</u> from <u>predators</u>.

4) Many animals are <u>nocturnal</u> (active at <u>night</u>), e.g. sloths. They <u>sleep</u> through the day and <u>feed</u> at night when it's <u>cooler</u> — this helps them to <u>save energy</u>.

5) Some animals are adapted to the <u>low light levels</u> on the rainforest floor, e.g. anteaters have a sharp sense of <u>smell</u> and <u>hearing</u>, so they can <u>detect predators</u> without seeing them.

6) Many rainforests animals can <u>swim</u>, e.g. jaguars. This allows them to cross <u>river channels</u>.

Adaptations help animals and plants to thrive in the hot, wet conditions

If you're asked to explain different ways plants or animals are adapted to the conditions in tropical rainforests, first think about what those conditions are — then it'll be easier to remember how life has adapted to them.

Tropical Rainforests

Nutrients are stored in various places in the rainforest ecosystem and move between them in the nutrient cycle. The warm, moist conditions of the rainforest affect how quickly nutrients move through the ecosystem.

Most of the Nutrients in Tropical Rainforests are Stored in Biomass

1) Nutrients are stored in three ways in the ecosystem:
   - living organisms (biomass),
   - dead organic material, e.g. fallen leaves (litter),
   - the soil.

2) The nutrient cycle is the way that nutrients move through an ecosystem.

3) In the cycle, nutrients are transferred between these three stores.

4) The store and transfer of nutrients in different ecosystems can be shown as flow diagrams. The size of the circles and arrows is proportional to the amount of nutrients.

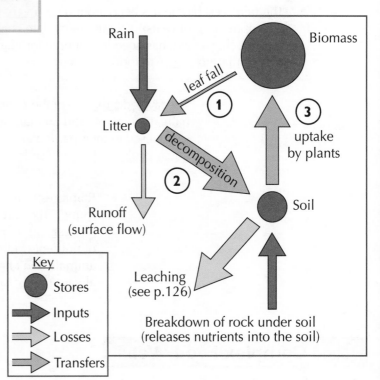

Nutrients are Cycled Quickly in Tropical Rainforests

In tropical rainforests most nutrients are stored as biomass and the transfer of nutrients is very rapid. This is because:

1) Trees are evergreen, so dead leaves and other material fall all year round.

2) The warm, moist climate means that fungi and bacteria decompose the dead organic matter quickly. The nutrients released are soluble (they dissolve in water) and are soaked up by the soil.

3) Dense vegetation and rapid plant growth mean that nutrients are rapidly taken up by plants' roots.

Take the time to understand how nutrients are cycled in rainforests

Make sure you understand that nutrient cycle diagram. Try copying it out a few times. Remember, the sizes of the circles and arrows are important — they indicate relative amounts of nutrients being stored or transferred.

Tropical Rainforests

All the parts in ecosystems are linked together, and one of the ways we can show this is using food webs. Biodiversity is high in tropical rainforests, which means the food webs are complex.

Rainforests Have **Very High Biodiversity**...

1) Biodiversity is the variety of organisms living in a particular area — both plants and animals.

2) Rainforests have extremely high biodiversity — they contain around 50% of the world's plant, animal and insect species, and may contain around half of all life on Earth. This is because:

> • The rainforest biome has been around for a very long time (10s of millions of years) without the climate changing very much, so there has been lots of time for plants and animals to evolve to form new species.

> • The layered structure of the rainforest provides lots of different habitats — plants and animals adapt to become highly specialised to their particular environment and food source (their 'ecological niche') so lots of different species develop.

> • Rainforests are stable environments — it's hot and wet all year round. They are also very productive (the plants grow quickly and all year round, producing lots of biomass) because of the high rate of nutrient cycling (see previous page). This means that plants and animals don't have to cope with changing conditions and there is always plenty to eat — so they are able to specialise (see above).

...and **Complex Food Webs**

1) Food chains show what's eaten by what in an ecosystem.

2) They always start with a producer, e.g. a plant. Producers make their own food using energy from the Sun.

> Consumers are organisms that eat other organisms. 'Primary' means 'first', so primary consumers are the first consumers in a food chain. Secondary consumers are second and tertiary consumers are third.

3) Producers are eaten by primary consumers, e.g. bats and insects. Primary consumers are then eaten by secondary consumers, e.g. snakes, and secondary consumers are eaten by tertiary consumers, e.g. crocodiles and jaguars.

4) All these organisms eventually die and get broken down by decomposers.

5) Ecosystems usually contain many different species — which means lots of different possible food chains. Food webs show how all the food chains overlap.

> Food webs in tropical rainforests are very complex:
> • there are so many different species that there are loads and loads of links — e.g. jaguars also eat deer, sloths, tapir, monkeys and so on.
> • some animals can be both primary and secondary consumers, e.g. bats eat the fruit of banana trees, but they also eat mice, which have in turn eaten grass.

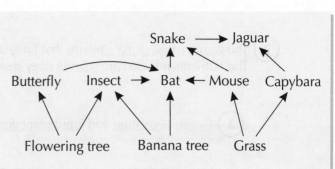

Food webs show multiple interlinked food chains

Food webs are useful for showing how parts of an ecosystem are linked together. Just remember that the arrows go from what's being eaten to what's doing the eating — producer to primary consumer to secondary consumer...

Threats to Tropical Rainforests

Removal of trees from forests is called deforestation. It's happening on a huge scale in many tropical rainforests.

Deforestation is a Direct Threat to Tropical Rainforests

There are lots of reasons why areas of tropical rainforest are destroyed:

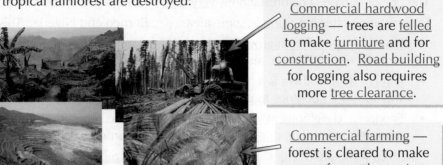

Local demand for fuel wood — local people chop down trees to use as fuel for cooking or to burn to make charcoal.

Commercial hardwood logging — trees are felled to make furniture and for construction. Road building for logging also requires more tree clearance.

Mineral resources — minerals (e.g. gold, copper and iron ore) are often found in tropical rainforests. Explosives are sometimes used to clear earth or deep pits are dug to reach the deposits.

Commercial farming — forest is cleared to make space for cattle grazing, or for huge palm oil or soya plantations.

Subsistence farming — forest is cleared so farmers can grow food for themselves and their families.

Electricity (HEP) — many tropical rainforests have large rivers. Building dams to generate hydroelectric power (HEP) floods large areas of forest behind the dams.

Demand for biofuels — biofuels are fuels made from plants. Growing the crops needed to make biofuels takes up large amounts of land — trees have to be cut down to make space for them.

Deforestation has environmental impacts:

1) With no trees to hold the soil together, heavy rain washes it away (soil erosion). This can lead to landslides and flooding.

2) Without a tree canopy to intercept (catch) rainfall and tree roots to absorb it, more water reaches the soil. This reduces soil fertility as nutrients in the soil are washed away, out of reach of plants.

3) Trees remove CO_2 from the atmosphere. Also, burning vegetation to clear forest produces CO_2. So deforestation means more CO_2 in the atmosphere, which adds to the greenhouse effect.

Climate Change is an Indirect Threat to Tropical Rainforests

Tropical rainforests also face indirect threats — things that don't involve deliberately chopping down trees but still lead to damage to the ecosystem. One of the main indirect threats is climate change (see pages 6-7):

- Climate change can severely impact tropical rainforests. In some areas temperature is increasing and rainfall is decreasing, which leads to drought.
- Droughts lead to ecosystem stress — plants and animals living in tropical rainforests are adapted to moist conditions, so many species die in dry weather. Frequent or long periods of drought could lead to extinction of some species.
- Drought can also lead to forest fires, which can destroy large areas of forest.

Deforestation has major environmental impacts

A bit of a serious page this one, but an important one nonetheless — you should know the main causes of deforestation like the back of your hand. And remember, tropical rainforests are threatened by climate change too.

Tropical Rainforests — Conservation

Some countries are managing to <u>turn off</u> the chainsaws and are even <u>joining together</u> to protect the world's rainforests.

The **Rate** of Deforestation **Varies Globally**

1) The <u>rate</u> of rainforest deforestation is <u>very high</u> — roughly 130 000 km² per year.

2) Deforestation rates are <u>rising</u> in some areas, e.g. Borneo and Nigeria. This is largely a result of:
   - <u>Poverty</u> — <u>population growth</u> and <u>poverty</u> mean there are many <u>more</u> small-scale <u>subsistence</u> farmers, e.g. in Borneo, and <u>greater</u> use of <u>fuel wood</u> (as other fuels are expensive), e.g. in Nigeria.
   - <u>Foreign debt</u> — there is a huge <u>market</u> for goods from tropical rainforests, so it's an easy way for <u>poor countries</u> to make money to <u>pay back</u> the <u>debt</u> they owe to richer countries.
   - <u>Economic development</u> — <u>road</u> and <u>rail</u> projects to promote development <u>open up</u> areas of the rainforest to <u>logging</u>, <u>mining</u> and <u>farming</u>, e.g. Borneo has huge palm plantations for biofuels.

3) However, some areas, e.g. Costa Rica and Brazil, are <u>reducing</u> deforestation rates as a result of:
   - <u>Government policies</u> — e.g. the Costa Rican government has invested in <u>ecotourism</u> (see next page) and pays landowners to <u>reforest</u> areas. Now, forest cover is <u>increasing</u>.
   - <u>International condemnation</u> — puts pressure on companies by <u>naming</u> and <u>shaming</u> those that are <u>involved</u> in deforestation. Many companies have <u>pledged zero-deforestation</u> as a result.
   - <u>Monitoring systems</u> — e.g. Global Forest Watch (GFW) provides <u>satellite data</u> to <u>track forest loss</u>. This means authorities can act more <u>quickly</u> to <u>stop illegal logging</u> etc.

REDD and **CITES** are **Global Actions** to **Protect** Tropical Rainforests

1) The threats to tropical rainforests involve the <u>whole world</u> — the <u>goods</u> from rainforests are <u>traded internationally</u> and all countries contribute to <u>climate change</u>.

2) This means that <u>global actions</u> are needed to try to <u>protect</u> rainforest <u>plants</u> and <u>animals</u>. For example:

	REDD	CITES
Overview	<u>REDD</u> (Reduced Emissions from Deforestation and forest Degradation) is a scheme that aims to <u>reward</u> forest owners in poorer countries for <u>keeping forests</u> instead of cutting them down.	<u>CITES</u> (Convention on International Trade in Endangered Species of Wild Fauna and Flora) is an agreement to tightly control <u>trade</u> in <u>wild animals</u> and <u>plants</u>.
Advantages	• Deals with the <u>cause</u> of <u>climate change</u> as well as <u>direct impacts</u> of <u>deforestation</u>. • The forest is <u>protected</u> so remains a <u>habitat</u> for species — <u>biodiversity</u> is not lost. • <u>Everyone</u> benefits from reducing emissions and it's a relatively <u>cheap</u> option for doing so.	• The issue is tackled at a <u>global</u> level — the trade of <u>endangered species</u> is controlled <u>worldwide</u>. • Encourages <u>sharing of information</u> about the wildlife trade between countries, which raises <u>awareness</u> of <u>threats</u> to biodiversity. • Helps different <u>sectors</u> work <u>together</u>.
Disadvantages	• Deforestation may <u>continue</u> in <u>another area</u>. • Aspects of REDD are <u>not clear</u>, meaning that it may be possible to <u>cut down</u> rainforests, but still <u>receive</u> the <u>rewards</u> if they are <u>replaced</u> with <u>other types</u> of forest, e.g. with <u>palm oil plantations</u>, which are <u>low</u> in <u>biodiversity</u>. • <u>Preventing</u> activities, e.g. <u>agriculture</u> and <u>mining</u>, may affect <u>local communities</u> who <u>depend</u> on the <u>income</u> from them.	• Although <u>individual species</u> are protected from <u>poaching</u>, it doesn't protect their <u>habitat</u> — they could still go extinct, e.g. due to the impacts of <u>climate change</u>. • Some rules are <u>unclear</u>, e.g. on the trade of ivory. • <u>Not all</u> countries are <u>members</u> — some countries even <u>promote</u> the trade of materials from <u>endangered species</u>.

Some areas are experiencing higher rates of deforestation than others

Many countries are experiencing deforestation, but only some are trying to stop it. Make sure you know about some strategies being used to reduce deforestation, and their advantages and disadvantages, before moving on.

Tropical Rainforests — Conservation

When it comes to <u>conservation</u> you <u>don't</u> have to go <u>global</u> — a <u>little</u> can go a long way, or so they say...

Achieving Sustainable Forest Management is a Challenge

1) <u>Sustainable forest management</u> is when a forest is used in a way that <u>prevents</u> long-term damage, whilst allowing <u>people</u> to <u>benefit</u> from the <u>resources</u> it provides in the <u>present</u> and in the <u>future</u>.

2) Techniques include <u>selective logging</u> (where only <u>certain</u> trees are <u>removed</u>, rather than <u>large areas</u> being <u>cleared</u>) and <u>replanting</u> (where the trees that have been <u>removed</u> are <u>replaced</u>).

3) There are lots of <u>challenges</u> involved in <u>successful</u> sustainable forest management:

Economic

1) The <u>economic benefits</u> of sustainable management are only seen in the <u>long-term</u> — this affects <u>poorer</u> countries who need income <u>immediately</u>.

2) Sustainable forestry is usually <u>more expensive</u>, so it can be <u>difficult</u> to persuade <u>private companies</u> to adopt <u>sustainable</u> methods.

3) Many sustainable forestry schemes are <u>funded</u> by <u>government departments</u> and <u>NGOs</u> (see p.39). If the <u>priorities</u> of these organisations <u>change</u>, <u>funding</u> could <u>stop</u> quite quickly.

Environmental

1) If trees are <u>replanted</u>, the new forest may not resemble the <u>natural</u> forest — the <u>trees</u> are <u>replaced</u> but the entire <u>ecosystem</u> may <u>not</u> be <u>restored</u>.

2) Trees that are <u>replanted</u> for <u>logging</u> in the future can be very <u>slow growing</u> — companies may <u>chop down</u> more <u>natural forest</u> whilst they are waiting for the <u>new</u> trees to <u>mature</u>.

3) Even <u>selective logging</u> can <u>damage</u> lots of trees in the process of <u>removing</u> the <u>target trees</u>.

Social

1) Sustainable forest management generally provides <u>fewer jobs</u> for <u>local people</u> than conventional forestry, so many locals <u>won't</u> see the <u>benefits</u>. Some may turn to illegal logging, which is <u>difficult</u> to police.

2) If the <u>population</u> of a forest area <u>increases</u>, the <u>demand</u> for <u>wood</u> and <u>land</u> from the forest <u>increases</u>. Sustainable forestry is <u>unlikely</u> to provide enough resources to match the <u>increasing demand</u>.

Alternative Livelihoods Might be a Better Long-Term Option

The best way to <u>protect</u> tropical rainforests may be to encourage <u>alternative</u> ways of making a <u>living</u> from the rainforest that <u>don't</u> involve <u>large-scale deforestation</u>. For example:

Ecotourism

1) Ecotourism is <u>tourism</u> that <u>minimises damage</u> to the <u>environment</u> and <u>benefits</u> the <u>local people</u>.

2) Only a <u>small number</u> of visitors are allowed into an area at a time. <u>Environmental impacts</u> are minimised, e.g. by making sure <u>waste</u> and <u>litter</u> are <u>disposed</u> of <u>properly</u> to prevent land and water <u>contamination</u>.

3) Ecotourism provides a source of <u>income</u> for <u>local people</u>, e.g. they act as <u>guides</u> and <u>provide accommodation</u> and <u>transport</u>. It can also raise <u>awareness</u> of <u>conservation issues</u> and bring in more <u>money</u> for rainforest conservation.

4) If <u>local people</u> are employed in tourism, they don't have to <u>log</u> or <u>farm</u> to <u>make money</u>, meaning fewer trees are <u>cut down</u>. If a country's economy <u>relies</u> on <u>ecotourism</u>, there's an <u>incentive</u> to conserve the environment.

Sustainable Farming

Sustainable farming techniques <u>protect</u> the <u>soil</u> so that the land <u>remains productive</u> — there is no need to <u>clear new land</u> every few years. They include:

- <u>Agro-forestry</u> — <u>trees</u> and <u>crops</u> are planted at the <u>same time</u>, so that the tree roots <u>bind</u> the <u>soil</u> and the <u>leaves</u> protect it from <u>heavy rain</u>.

- <u>Green manure</u> — plants which <u>add nutrients</u> to the soil as they grow are planted to maintain <u>soil fertility</u>.

- <u>Crop rotation</u> — crops are <u>moved</u> between different fields each year with one <u>left empty</u>, so the soil has time to <u>recover</u>.

There are many barriers to achieving sustainable forest management

This may seem like a lot of information, but you don't need every detail — just make sure you understand the main challenges involved in sustainable forest management, and how ecotourism and sustainable farming can help.

Worked Exam Questions

With the answers written in, it's very easy to skim these worked examples and think you've understood. But that's not going to help you, so take the time to make sure you've really understood everything here.

---

1 Study **Figure 1**, a diagram showing layers of vegetation in a tropical rainforest.

a) Using **Figure 1**, state the physical conditions in the layers labelled A and B.

A: There is lots of light and it is exposed to wind and heavy rainfall.

B: It is quite dark and sheltered.

[2]

Figure 1

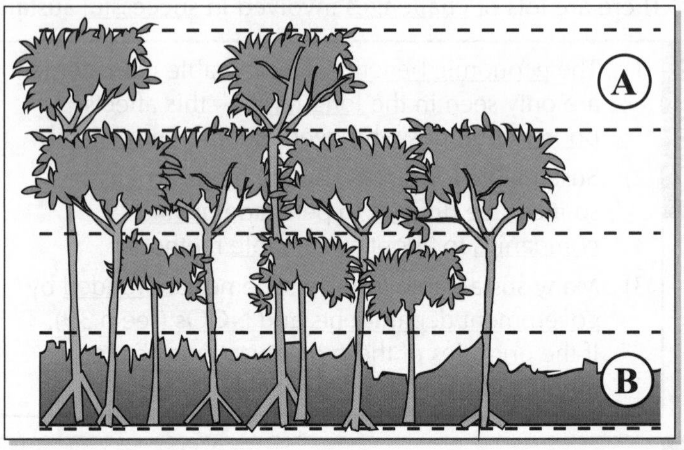

b) Explain **two** ways that trees in the layer labelled A are adapted to their environment.

1: The trees are very tall so that they can break through the canopy layer to reach the sunlight.

2: The trees have big buttress roots to support their trunks.

[4]

c) Suggest how the soil and plants in tropical rainforests are dependent on one another.

The nutrient-rich soil means that plants can grow quickly and vegetation is dense. Plants lose leaves all year round, returning nutrients to the soil, so the soil remains fertile.

[2]

[Total 8 marks]

---

2 Deforestation is rapidly reducing the size of the world's tropical rainforests.

a) Describe **one** global action that could help to reduce the rate of deforestation.

CITES (Convention on International Trade in Endangered Species of Wild Flora and Fauna) is an agreement to tightly control trade in wild animals and plants.

[2]

b) Identify **one** advantage and **one** disadvantage of your chosen global action.

1: Advantage: It raises awareness of threats to biodiversity through education.

2: Disadvantage: Individual species are protected from poaching, but it doesn't protect their habitat.

[2]

[Total 4 marks]

Exam Questions

1 Study **Figure 1**, a diagram showing how nutrients are cycled in a tropical rainforest.

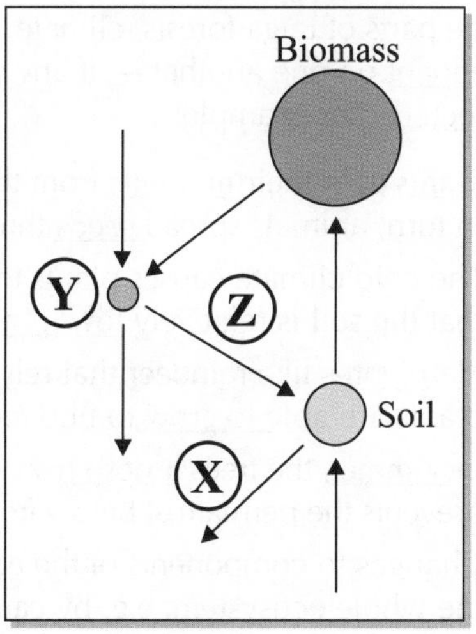

a) Which of the following is the process occurring at the arrow labelled X?

    A   Leaching   ◯

    B   Precipitation   ◯

    C   Surface runoff   ◯

    D   Rock weathering   ◯

    [1]

Figure 1

Biomass

Y   Z

Soil

X

b) Name the nutrient store labelled Y.

....
[1]

c) State the form in which most nutrients in tropical rainforests are stored.

....
[1]

d) Describe how nutrients are transferred along the arrow labelled Z.

....

....

....
[2]

[Total 5 marks]

2 Ecotourism is one method used in the conservation of tropical rainforests.

a) State what is meant by 'ecotourism'.

....

....
[1]

b) Explain the benefits of using ecotourism to promote conservation of tropical rainforests.

....

....

....

....

....

....
[4]

[Total 5 marks]

Taiga Forests

Taiga forests are <u>found</u> just <u>south</u> of the <u>tundra zone</u> in Russia, Scandinavia and Canada, where it is <u>warm</u> and <u>wet</u> enough for trees to grow. It's still <u>pretty cold</u> and <u>dry</u> though, so animals and plants have had to <u>adapt</u>.

Taiga Forests are **Interdependent** Ecosystems

<u>All</u> the parts of taiga forests (climate, soils, water, plants, animals and people) are <u>dependent</u> on one another — if any one of them <u>changes</u>, <u>everything</u> else is <u>affected</u>. For example:

> Taiga (boreal) forests are part of the boreal biome — the climate is cool, dry and highly seasonal (see page 122).

1) <u>Plants</u> gain their <u>nutrients</u> from the <u>soil</u>, and <u>provide</u> nutrients to the animals that eat them. In turn, animals spread <u>seeds</u> through their <u>dung</u>, helping the plants to <u>reproduce</u>.

2) The cold climate causes plants to <u>grow slowly</u> and also to <u>decompose</u> very slowly. This means that the soil is relatively <u>low in nutrients</u> — further <u>reducing</u> the ability of plants to <u>grow</u>.

3) <u>Herbivores</u> like reindeer that rely on plants like <u>mosses</u> to survive must migrate to areas where plants are <u>able to grow</u> to find food. <u>Carnivores</u> like wolves have to <u>follow</u> the <u>herbivores</u>.

> Permafrost is permanently frozen ground.

4) In <u>summer</u>, the trees <u>absorb heat</u> from the sun and shade the ground below — this prevents the permafrost below from <u>thawing</u>. The permafrost provides <u>water</u> for plants.

5) Changes to components of the ecosystem, such as <u>chopping down trees</u>, can have <u>knock-on effects</u> on the <u>whole ecosystem</u>, e.g. by causing permafrost to <u>melt</u>. Melting permafrost can <u>flood land</u>, preventing plants from growing. It also <u>releases</u> trapped <u>greenhouse gases</u> — leading to increased <u>global warming</u>, and changes to the <u>climate</u> of cold environments, threatening <u>plants</u> and <u>animals</u>.

Plants and **Animals** are **Adapted** to the **Cool**, **Dry Climate**

1) Taiga forests have a much <u>simpler structure</u> than tropical rainforests (see p.133) — lots of <u>tall trees</u> growing quite <u>close together</u> and not much else.

2) There aren't many plants on the <u>forest floor</u> because the <u>soils</u> are <u>poor</u> and very <u>little light</u> gets through the <u>dense canopy</u>. Plants that do survive include <u>mosses</u> and <u>lichens</u>.

3) Most of the trees are <u>conifers</u>, which are <u>adapted</u> to the cold, dry climate:

> * They are <u>evergreen</u> (they don't drop their leaves in a particular season), so they can make best use of the <u>available light</u>.
> * They have <u>needles</u> instead of flat leaves — this reduces <u>water loss</u> from strong, cold winds because it reduces the <u>surface area</u>.
> * They are <u>cone-shaped</u> — this means that <u>heavy winter snowfall</u> can <u>slide</u> straight off the <u>branches</u> without <u>breaking them</u>. The branches are also quite <u>bendy</u> so they're less likely to snap.

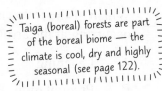

4) <u>Animals</u> in the taiga forest need to find ways to <u>survive</u> the <u>long</u>, <u>cold winters</u>. They also need to be able to find <u>enough food</u> and <u>escape</u> from <u>predators</u>.

> * Many of the <u>larger mammals</u>, e.g. caribou, are <u>migratory</u> — they move <u>long distances</u> through the forest in order to <u>find food</u>.
> * Many animals are <u>well-insulated</u> against the winter cold, e.g. wolves have <u>thick fur</u>, and birds, e.g. ptarmigan, have <u>thick layers</u> of <u>downy feathers</u>.
> * Some animals <u>hibernate</u> to conserve energy and survive the <u>winter</u>, e.g. brown bears and marmots.
> * Some animals, e.g. snowshoe hares, have <u>white coats</u> in the <u>winter</u>, so they are <u>camouflaged</u> against the winter <u>snow</u> — this helps them <u>hide</u> from predators. Camouflage also helps predators to <u>sneak up</u> on prey <u>undetected</u>.

Caribou

REVISION TIP

Most trees are cone-shaped conifers with needles instead of leaves

To help you remember the adaptations of animals in the taiga, think about how you would cope with the cold — put on a coat (thick fur) or stay indoors (hibernate). Go over this page until you've got it all.

Taiga Forests

The cold climate of the taiga forest leads to <u>slow nutrient cycling</u> and <u>lack of biodiversity</u>.

Slow Nutrient Cycling Leads to Slow Plant Growth

Look back at page 135 to compare nutrient cycling in taiga forests to tropical rainforests.

1) In taiga forests, <u>few nutrients</u> are added through <u>precipitation</u> or <u>weathering</u>. Quite a lot of the nutrients that are added are <u>lost</u> through <u>runoff</u> and <u>leaching</u>.

2) <u>Most</u> of the nutrients are <u>stored</u> in dead organic material (<u>litter</u>), e.g. the layer of <u>fallen needles</u> on the forest floor.

3) The <u>cold</u>, <u>dry climate</u> means that nutrient cycling is much <u>slower</u> in taiga forests than in tropical rainforests.

1) Trees are <u>evergreen</u>, so drop their needles <u>all year round</u>.

2) Despite the constant leaf fall, <u>low temperatures</u> mean that it takes a <u>long time</u> for the litter to be <u>broken down</u> (<u>decomposed</u>) and added to the <u>soil</u> — conditions are <u>too harsh</u> for many <u>decomposers</u>. This means the soil <u>isn't very fertile</u>.

3) The <u>cold climate</u> also means that <u>plants grow slowly</u> — the <u>rate</u> of <u>transfer</u> of nutrients from soil to plants is <u>low</u>.

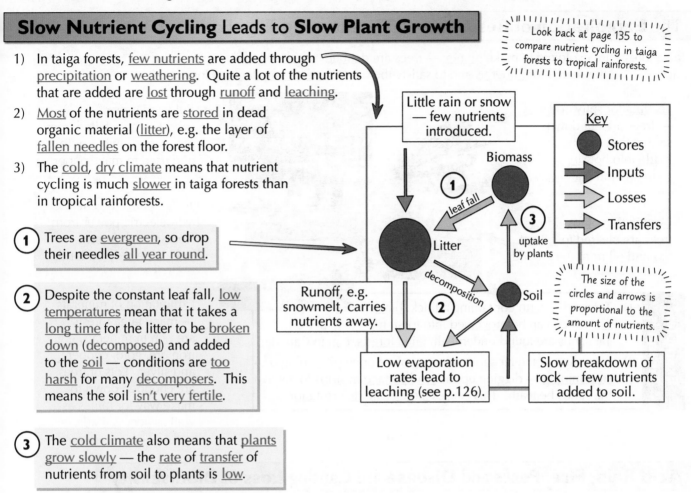

Little rain or snow — few nutrients introduced.

Biomass

1 leaf fall

3 uptake by plants

Litter

decomposition

2

Soil

Key
- Stores
- Inputs
- Losses
- Transfers

The size of the circles and arrows is proportional to the amount of nutrients.

Runoff, e.g. snowmelt, carries nutrients away.

Low evaporation rates lead to leaching (see p.126).

Slow breakdown of rock — few nutrients added to soil.

Taiga Forests have Low Biodiversity

Taiga forests have much <u>lower</u> biodiversity than tropical rainforests — many areas of forest contain a <u>single type</u> of tree, e.g. spruce, fir or pine. This is because:

1) The <u>land</u> was much colder and covered by <u>ice</u> until around 15 000 years ago. Species have had relatively <u>little time</u> to <u>adapt</u> to the current climate.

2) The <u>simple structure</u> means there aren't many different <u>habitats</u> — there are <u>fewer ecological niches</u> (see page 136) for organisms to fill, so <u>fewer</u> varieties of <u>species</u>.

3) Taiga forests are much <u>less productive</u> than tropical rainforests (plants grow <u>slowly</u>, so there's less biomass) and <u>nutrients</u> take a long time to be <u>returned</u> to the <u>soil</u> because it's so <u>cold</u>. The <u>growing season</u> is also <u>very short</u> — just a few months in the summer. This means there's <u>not much food</u> available, so there is a constant <u>struggle</u> for <u>survival</u>.

4) Some groups of animals are <u>under-represented</u> — there aren't many <u>amphibians</u> or <u>reptiles</u> because they <u>can't cope</u> with the <u>cold</u> climate (e.g. reptiles can't regulate their own body temperature and depend on the <u>sun</u> to stay warm).

Nutrient cycling is much slower in taiga forests than in tropical rainforests

Taiga forests are less productive than rainforests — they have slower plant growth and lower biodiversity. Re-read the page and see if you can explain why the biggest store of nutrients in taiga forests is in the leaf litter.

Threats to Taiga Forests

Taiga forests are facing <u>deforestation</u> as well as a whole host of <u>indirect threats</u>.

The **Exploitation** of **Resources** is **Threatening** Taiga Forests

Taiga forests are <u>exploited</u> to make <u>money</u> — trees are <u>deliberately chopped down</u> for <u>wood</u> and <u>paper</u>, in the search for <u>minerals</u> and to satisfy the world's <u>increasing demand</u> for <u>energy</u>.

<u>Logging for softwood</u> — trees are cut down so that they can be made into <u>housing</u>, <u>furniture</u> and <u>matches</u>.

<u>Pulp and paper</u> <u>production</u> — felled trees are <u>mashed</u> into a <u>pulp</u> and used to make <u>paper</u>.

<u>Exploitation of fossil fuels</u> — trees are cleared to <u>extract</u> <u>gas</u> and <u>oil</u> from the ground.

<u>HEP</u> — <u>dams</u> to generate hydroelectric power from rivers in taiga forests <u>flood large areas</u> of land.

Example: Tar sands

1) Tar sand is <u>earth</u> containing a thick, <u>black</u> <u>oil</u>, which can be <u>processed</u> into <u>fossil fuels</u> (e.g. petrol). Tar sands are found underneath <u>taiga forests</u>, e.g. in Canada.

2) Extraction of the tar sands often involves <u>open pit mining</u> or <u>strip mining</u> — digging up the <u>land surface</u> in <u>strips</u> to get to the sands beneath. This causes <u>large-scale deforestation</u>.

<u>Exploitation of minerals</u> — many taiga forests are <u>rich</u> in <u>minerals</u>, e.g. iron ore, gold, copper and silver. Lots of trees are chopped down to make way for <u>mines</u> as well as <u>access roads</u>.

Acid Rain, Fire, Pests and **Disease** are Causing **Loss** of **Biodiversity**

Acid Precipitation

1) <u>Burning fossil fuels</u> releases gases, such as sulfur dioxide and nitrogen oxides. These dissolve in <u>water</u> in the atmosphere to form <u>acids</u>. When it <u>rains</u> or <u>snows</u>, the acids are <u>deposited</u> on plants and soils.

2) <u>Acid rain</u> damages plants' <u>leaves</u> and makes it <u>harder</u> for them to cope with the <u>cold</u>. It can also make the soils too <u>acidic</u> to support <u>growth</u> and <u>kills</u> organisms in <u>lakes</u> and <u>streams</u>.

Pests & Diseases

1) <u>Pests</u> and <u>diseases</u> cause <u>damage</u> to <u>organisms</u>.

2) Many pests and diseases are <u>specific</u> to <u>one</u> <u>species</u>, e.g. Spruce Bark Beetles attack spruce trees. As there is often a <u>single tree species</u> in a particular area in taiga forests, it's <u>easy</u> for the pests and diseases to <u>spread</u> and <u>multiply</u> — they can do <u>a lot</u> of <u>damage</u>.

3) It is thought that <u>warming</u> caused by <u>climate</u> <u>change</u> is making it <u>easier</u> for pests and disease-causing pathogens to <u>survive</u> — <u>new pests</u> and <u>diseases</u> are arriving and the <u>frequency</u> of attack is <u>increasing</u>.

Forest Fires

1) <u>Wildfires</u> are a natural part of the <u>ecosystem</u> — they allow <u>new growth</u> and <u>regenerate</u> the forest.

2) However, it's thought that <u>climate change</u> is leading to <u>warmer</u>, <u>drier</u> conditions in taiga forests. This is increasing the <u>frequency</u> of fires and making the fire season <u>longer</u>.

3) Forest fires can destroy <u>huge numbers</u> of trees and may change the <u>distribution</u> of <u>species</u> as some species are better at recolonising burnt areas. They may also <u>break</u> forests up into <u>smaller</u> <u>sections</u>, which makes it hard for <u>migratory animals</u> that need a <u>lot of space</u> to find <u>enough food</u>.

The taiga forest is under threat from lots of different factors

Human exploitation is leading to deforestation. On top of this, acid rain, fire, pests and disease are all putting extra pressure on the ecosystem. Make sure you can explain how these pressures are leading to biodiversity loss.

Taiga Forests — Conservation

Taiga forests are under threat but it's not all bad news — here are some ways they can be conserved...

Conservation Methods Include Protected Areas and Sustainable Forestry

1) Taiga forests cover a huge area — a lot of them are inaccessible and very remote.
   However, human activity is expanding into these wilderness areas, particularly in Canada and Russia.

2) The forests can be conserved by setting up protected areas or by controlling the way that they are used.

Method	Overview	Strengths	Challenges
Creating a Wilderness Area	An area that is undisturbed by human activity that is managed with the aim of protecting the landscape.	Has the highest level of protection — most human activity is banned. The area is kept as pristine (untouched by humans) as possible. Usually covers a very large area so large-scale processes can still take place, e.g. animal migrations.	The large, remote areas are hard to police. There is economic pressure on governments from logging, mining and energy companies who want to use the resources. There is pressure from companies and tourists to build roads to allow greater access.
Creating a National Park	An area that is mostly in its natural state that is managed to protect biodiversity and promote recreation.	May be established to protect particular species, e.g. wood bison. Often cover a large area. Unsustainable human activity such as logging and mining is not permitted. There is good access for tourists and recreational users.	National parks must take into account the needs of indigenous communities, who may use the land for hunting etc. Tourism may be required to pay for the conservation, but access roads, infrastructure and pollution from tourists can harm the ecosystem.
Sustainable Forestry	Ways of harvesting the timber from the forest without damaging it in the long-term.	Limits can be placed on the number of trees felled or the size of clear-cut areas to allow the forest to regenerate. Companies may be required to regenerate the area after logging. Selective logging means some trees remain to become part of the new forest.	Some countries struggle to enforce the restrictions, e.g. Russia — lots of illegal logging takes place. There may be a lack of clear management or information about the ecosystem. Different groups may not agree with the rules and restrictions, e.g. indigenous people, loggers, government, environmentalists.

There are Conflicting Views on Managing Taiga Forests

Some people think that taiga forests should be protected. Other people think that the forest and its natural resources should be exploited. You need to know the reasons for each view point.

Protection

1) Taiga forests store lots of carbon — deforestation will release some of this as CO_2, which causes global warming.

2) Some species are only found in taiga forests. Because they are adapted to the conditions, the destruction of the habitat could lead to their extinction.

3) Many indigenous people, e.g. the Sami people of Scandinavia, depend on the forest for their traditional way of life.

Exploitation

1) The demand for resources is increasing — people need the wood, fuel and minerals that the forests provide.

2) Forest industries, e.g. logging and mining, provide a lot of jobs (e.g. forestry and logging employ 25 thousand people in Canada).

3) The exploitation of the forest generates a lot of wealth for the countries involved (e.g. the forestry industry in Sweden is worth nearly US $15 billion each year).

The future of taiga forests is uncertain

There's no agreement on how to manage the taiga forests — exploiting them provides more resources, jobs and wealth, but there are also many benefits to protecting the forests. You should be able to make the case for both sides.

Worked Exam Questions

Make sure you pay attention to this page — it will show you how to answer exam questions to get the highest marks. When you've read it through, have a go at the questions on the next page on your own.

1 Study **Figure 1**, a diagram showing the interdependence between biotic and abiotic factors in taiga forests.

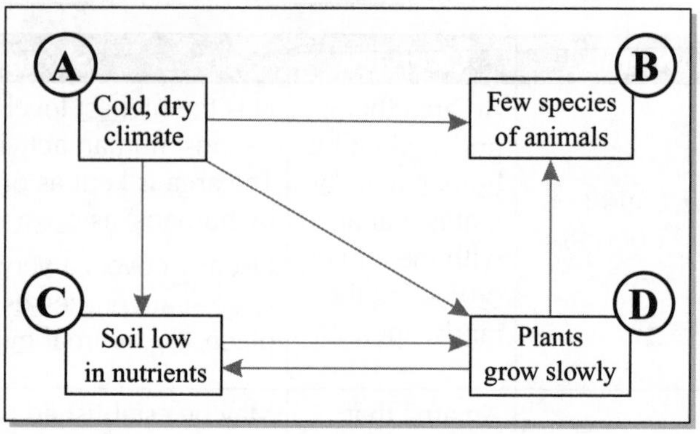

a) Identify which of the following statements is true.

Figure 1

- **A** A and C are abiotic factors. ●
- **B** B and C are abiotic factors. ○
- **C** C and D are biotic factors. ○
- **D** A and D are biotic factors. ○

[1]

b) Using **Figure 1** and your own knowledge, describe how the climate can affect the soil fertility in a cold environment.

Low temperatures mean that it takes a long time for the litter to be broken down (decomposed).

This means the soil is relatively low in nutrients.

[2]

[Total 3 marks]

2 One major threat to taiga forests is the exploitation of the fossil fuels found underneath them.

a) Explain the direct threat to the taiga forest caused by the exploitation of fossil fuels.

Mining methods, e.g. open pit mining, involve digging up the land surface, so large areas of forest are

chopped down to get to the fuels underneath.

[2]

b) State **two** other ways that humans exploit the resources available in taiga forests, which cause a direct threat to the forests.

1: Using the trees for paper production.

2: Building dams to generate hydroelectric power (HEP).

[2]

c) Explain how burning fossil fuels can threaten the taiga forest ecosystem.

Burning fossil fuels releases gases such as sulfur dioxide and nitrogen oxides. These dissolve in water

in the atmosphere to form acids, which are deposited on plants and soils when it rains or snows.

Acid rain damages the plants' leaves and makes it harder for them to cope with the cold. It can also

make the soils too acidic to support growth.

[4]

[Total 8 marks]

Exam Questions

1 Study **Figure 1**, a photograph of an area of taiga forest in a national park.

Figure 1

a) What is a 'national park'?

....

....

....
[1]

b) Explain the benefits of creating a national park.

....

....

....

....
[4]

c) State **two** challenges that may be encountered in managing taiga forests.

1:...

....

2:...

....
[2]

d) Explain how sustainable forestry could help protect the taiga forest.

....

....

....
[2]

e) State **two** reasons why people may object to setting aside protected areas in taiga forests.

1:...

....

2:...

....
[2]

[Total 11 marks]

Revision Summary

And that does it for <u>Topic 8</u> — but before you go, check how much of it you <u>really know</u>.

- Try these questions and <u>tick off each one</u> when you <u>get it right</u>.
- When you've done <u>all the questions</u> under a heading and are <u>completely happy</u> with it, tick it off.

Tropical Rainforests (p.133-136) ☑

1) Give one example of interdependence in the tropical rainforest ecosystem. ☑
2) What are stratified layers? ☑
3) Name the four stratified layers in a tropical rainforest. ☑
4) Why do some trees in the rainforest have buttress roots. ☑
5) What are 'drip tips'? ☑
6) Name the three nutrient stores in the tropical rainforest ecosystem. ☑
7) Why are nutrients cycled quickly in tropical rainforests? ☑
8) Why does the layered structure of tropical rainforests increase biodiversity there? ☑

Tropical Rainforests — Threats and Conservation (p.137-139) ☑

9) True or false: chopping down trees is an indirect threat to rainforests. ☑
10) Give three reasons why rainforests are being destroyed. ☑
11) Give two environmental impacts of chopping down tropical rainforests. ☑
12) Give two reasons why the rate of deforestation of tropical rainforests is decreasing in some areas. ☑
13) What is the purpose of REDD? ☑
14) Give one advantage of using REDD as a method of conservation. ☑
15) What is CITES? ☑
16) Give one disadvantage of using CITES as a method of conservation. ☑
17) What is sustainable forest management? ☑
18) Suggest three challenges to the success of sustainable forest management schemes. ☑
19) How does sustainable farming help protect tropical rainforests? ☑

Taiga Forests (p.142-143) ☑

20) True or false: taiga forests have a more complex structure than tropical rainforests. ☑
21) Why do trees in taiga forests have needles rather than leaves? ☑
22) Why are trees in taiga forests cone-shaped? ☑
23) How does the cold, dry climate affect the rate of nutrient cycling in taiga forests? ☑

Taiga Forests — Threats and Conservation (p.144-145) ☑

24) How does the generation of hydroelectric power (HEP) threaten taiga forests? ☑
25) Name two other human activities that are threatening taiga forests. ☑
26) What is acid rain? ☑
27) How do forest fires threaten the biodiversity of taiga forests? ☑
28) What is a wilderness area? ☑
29) Give two benefits of protecting taiga forests by creating wilderness areas. ☑
30) Give two challenges of protecting taiga forests by creating national parks. ☑
31) Why do some people want to protect taiga forests? ☑
32) Give one reason why some people want to exploit taiga forests. ☑

Energy Resources

Energy is a pretty important resource — it's needed for lighting and heating homes, cooking, producing goods and so on. There are quite a few different ways we can generate energy.

Energy Sources can be Split into Three Categories

1) Energy sources can be renewable, non-renewable or recyclable.

2) An energy source is renewable if it can be replenished on a very short timescale. They're also known as flow resources because the planet has an endless supply of each one.

3) Wind energy, solar energy and hydroelectric power (HEP) are all renewable resources.

Renewable

WIND ENERGY — Turbines use the energy of the wind to generate electricity, either on land or out at sea. Turbines are often built in large windfarms.

SOLAR ENERGY — Energy from the Sun is used to heat water and solar cookers or to generate electricity using photovoltaic cells.

HYDROELECTRIC POWER (HEP) — HEP uses the energy of falling water. Water is trapped by a dam and allowed to fall through tunnels, where the pressure of the falling water turns turbines to generate electricity.

4) Non-renewable energy sources can't be replenished quickly — they take millions of years to form. This means that they can run out.

5) They're also known as stock resources as the planet has a limited supply (stock) of each one.

6) Fossil fuels (coal, oil and natural gas) are non-renewable resources.

Non-Renewable

FOSSIL FUELS — Fossil fuels formed millions of years ago from the remains of dead organisms. They can be extracted from the ground and seabed. As technology develops, it has become possible to extract resources that were previously too difficult or costly to use, e.g. by fracking (see page 153).

7) Recyclable energy sources are those made from waste products or whose waste products can be used to generate more energy.

8) Nuclear energy and biofuels are recyclable sources of energy because they have usable waste products.

Recyclable

NUCLEAR ENERGY — This uses uranium atoms — when they split lots of heat is produced, which is used to boil water. The steam turns a turbine, generating electricity. New breeder reactors can generate more fuel during the splitting process, making nuclear energy more like a renewable energy source. Radioactive waste can also be processed so it can be used to generate more energy.

BIOMASS — Biomass (wood, plants or animal waste) can be burnt to release energy or used to produce biofuels. It's easy to produce biomass because living organisms grow quickly. Sometimes, biomass is already available as a waste product from other processes, e.g. farming. Sometimes the waste products from the production of biofuels can also be used as a fuel. For example, sugar cane is fermented to produce ethanol, a biofuel often used in transport. The leftover cane is then burnt to produce more energy, e.g. for heating.

Learn which energy sources are renewable, non-renewable and recyclable

The idea of 'flow' and 'stock' resources might seem confusing, but it's actually really simple. We have a constant flow of renewables, but a limited stock of fossil fuels. Recyclables are a bit trickier to get your head around — nuclear energy and biomass aren't renewable, but they produce waste that is useful for energy production.

Impacts of Energy Production

Producing energy can cause <u>all sorts of problems</u> — particularly for the <u>environment</u>.

Mining and Drilling have Impacts on the Environment...

1) The <u>extraction</u> of fossil fuels, e.g. by <u>mining</u> and <u>drilling</u>, can damage the environment.

2) Mining has <u>several</u> environmental impacts:

- <u>Surface mining</u> strips away large areas of <u>soil</u>, <u>rock</u> and <u>vegetation</u> so that miners can reach the materials they want. This can <u>permanently scar</u> the landscape.
- Habitats are <u>destroyed</u> to make way for mines, e.g. through <u>clearing forests</u>, leading to <u>loss of biodiversity</u>.
- Clearing forests also affects the <u>water cycle</u> (see p.126) because there are <u>fewer</u> trees to <u>take up</u> water from the ground. This can lead to increased <u>soil erosion</u>.
- Mining processes can release <u>greenhouse gases</u>, e.g. <u>carbon dioxide</u> (CO_2) and <u>methane</u> (CH_4), into the atmosphere. These gases contribute to <u>global warming</u> (see p.6).

3) Extracting <u>oil</u> and <u>gas</u> involves <u>drilling</u> into <u>underground</u> reserves. It can be done <u>inland</u> (onshore) and <u>at sea</u> (offshore).

4) Drilling has negative <u>impacts</u> on the <u>environment</u>:

- Onshore drilling requires land to be <u>stripped</u> of vegetation to make space for the <u>drills</u> and <u>roads</u> to access the sites.
- <u>Oil spills</u> cause major damage to the environment — especially <u>out at sea</u>. The <u>Deepwater Horizon oil spill</u> in 2010 leaked around <u>4 million barrels of oil</u> into the <u>Gulf of Mexico</u>. Oil <u>coats</u> the <u>feathers</u> and <u>fur</u> of animals, which <u>reduces</u> their ability to <u>move freely</u> or <u>feed</u>.
- Extracting <u>natural gas</u> from underground reserves can cause methane to <u>leak</u> into the <u>atmosphere</u>, making the <u>greenhouse effect stronger</u> and contributing to <u>global warming</u>.

...and so do Some Forms of Renewable Energy

Although it has <u>fewer</u> impacts than non-renewable energy, generating <u>renewable energy</u> can still <u>affect</u> the environment:

Wind Energy

1) <u>Large numbers</u> of wind turbines are needed to produce significant amounts of electricity and they need to be set quite far apart. This means they take up <u>lots of space</u>.

2) Wind farms produce a <u>constant humming noise</u> — some people living close to wind farms have complained about this <u>noise pollution</u>.

3) The <u>spinning blades</u> on turbines can <u>kill</u> or <u>injure birds</u> and <u>bats</u>.

Solar Energy

1) Some <u>solar farms</u> use <u>ground</u> and <u>surface water</u> to <u>clean</u> their <u>solar panels</u>. This can lead to water shortages in arid areas, which <u>disrupts ecosystems</u>.

2) The <u>heat</u> reflected from <u>mirrors</u> in solar farms can <u>kill</u> wildlife, e.g. birds.

3) Solar panels built on the <u>ground</u> can <u>disturb</u> and <u>damage habitats</u>.

Hydroelectric Power (HEP)

1) HEP plants use <u>dams</u> to <u>trap</u> water for energy production — this creates a <u>reservoir</u>, which <u>floods</u> a large area of land.

2) The <u>river</u> on which the dam is built can be affected by <u>changes in water flow</u>, e.g. <u>sediment</u> is deposited in the reservoir instead of <u>further downstream</u>.

3) A <u>build-up</u> of sediment can <u>block sunlight</u>, causing <u>plants</u> and <u>algae</u> in the river to <u>die</u>.

Even renewable energy sources can damage the environment

If you get asked about the negative impacts of energy production, fossil fuels might be the first thing to spring to mind — don't forget you could also write about wind farms, solar farms, and HEP plants.

Access to Energy

With more than 7 billion people in the world, supplying everyone with energy isn't easy.

Access to Energy is Affected by Many Factors

1) Energy resources are unevenly distributed — some countries naturally have more resources than others.
   E.g. Russia has almost 25% of the world's natural gas reserves, whereas Algeria only has around 2%.

2) There are also other factors that have an impact on a country's access to energy:

   TECHNOLOGY — some countries are not able to exploit their energy resources as the technology
   required is unavailable or too expensive. For example, Niger has large uranium
   reserves but does not have the technology to develop nuclear power plants.
   Developed countries can exploit more renewable energy supplies, e.g. solar and
   wind power, but developing countries often have to rely more on fossil fuels.

   GEOLOGY — fossil fuels are found in sedimentary rocks, where impermeable rocks have trapped the oil
   and gas in the permeable rocks below. Countries located on plate boundaries (see p.20)
   may be able to access geothermal energy (using the earth's heat to generate power).

   ACCESSIBILITY — an area might have large energy resources but be unable to access them. For example,
   permafrost (permanently frozen ground) makes it very difficult to access fossil fuels.
   Some resources are also found in protected areas, e.g. Antarctica, and can't be exploited.

   CLIMATE — solar power requires large amounts of sunlight to generate energy.
   Countries with sunny climates, e.g. Spain, can use solar power more
   effectively than countries with duller climates, e.g. the UK.

   LANDSCAPE — wind turbines are most efficient in areas with a steady and reliable source of wind,
   e.g. on high ground or along the coast. Hydroelectric power usually requires lots
   of water to generate energy, and steep-sided valleys to use as reservoirs.

Global Energy Consumption is Unevenly Distributed

1) This map shows the energy consumption per person across the world in 2014.

2) There's a strong relationship between
   development and energy consumption:

   • Developed countries, e.g. Australia, Norway and USA, tend to
   consume lots of energy per person because they can afford to.
   Most people in these countries have access to electricity and
   heating, and use energy-intensive devices like cars.

   • Economic development is increasing wealth in emerging
   countries, e.g. China. People are buying more things that
   use energy, e.g. cars, fridges and televisions.

   • Developing countries, e.g. Chad and Mongolia, consume
   less energy per person as they are less able to afford it.
   Less energy is available and lifestyles are less dependent on high energy consumption.

Energy consumption per person (tonnes oil equivalent)
■ 6.0 and over ■ 3.0 – 4.5 ■ 0 – 1.5
■ 4.5 – 6.0 ■ 1.5 – 3.0

3) Some regions rely on traditional fuel sources. For example, in sub-Saharan Africa, energy networks are
   poorly connected, which means people have to rely on biomass such as wood for cooking and heating.
   There's very little development, so countries can't afford to exploit their own energy reserves or improve
   existing infrastructure.

4) Industrial activities require large amounts of energy, e.g. to power machinery or for transport:

   • Manufacturing industries in developed and emerging countries use huge amounts of energy.

   • Developing countries have more primary industry (e.g. agriculture), which uses very little energy.

Energy consumption increases as people get wealthier

You need to understand how access to energy will have an impact on people. It's pretty hard for a country
to develop if it's struggling to get the energy it needs — this is the situation in many developing countries.

Oil Supply and Demand

Oil is one of the world's <u>main energy sources</u>. It's <u>constantly</u> in demand, so it's <u>pretty vital</u> that you learn about it.

Oil Reserves and Oil Production are Unevenly Distributed

1) Oil <u>reserves</u> are the amount of <u>recoverable oil</u> — oil that can be <u>extracted</u> using <u>today's technology</u>.
   Oil <u>production</u> is the process of <u>extracting</u> and <u>refining</u> crude (<u>unrefined</u>) oil.

2) The world's major <u>oil reserves</u> are found in a <u>handful</u> of countries — most of these are in the <u>Middle East</u>.

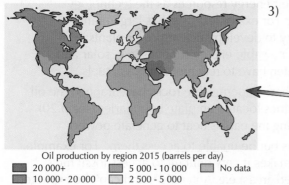

Oil production by region 2015 (barrels per day)
- 20 000+
- 10 000 - 20 000
- 5 000 - 10 000
- 2 500 - 5 000
- No data

3) Oil production doesn't just depend on a country's oil reserves — there are <u>several factors</u> that affect it:

- <u>Infrastructure</u> — in order to produce oil, a country needs the right <u>equipment</u> and <u>technology</u>. Russia, Saudi Arabia and the USA are the world's <u>biggest</u> oil producers.

- <u>Domestic demand</u> — Saudi Arabia relies on oil to meet its <u>own</u> energy needs.

- <u>Shrinking reserves</u> — oil production from <u>North Sea</u> reserves has been <u>declining</u> as reserves are <u>used up</u>.

4) <u>Global oil consumption</u> is <u>increasing</u> as countries develop. Between 2015 and 2016, the amount of oil consumed worldwide rose by <u>1.4 million barrels a day</u>.

- As <u>GDP per capita</u> (see p.29) increases, so does oil <u>consumption</u>. People in <u>wealthier</u> countries have more <u>energy-intensive goods</u>, e.g. cars. Around <u>65%</u> of all oil is used to <u>fuel vehicles</u>.

- <u>Rapid industrialisation</u> in <u>emerging economies</u>, e.g. China and India, also increases oil consumption. The combination of a <u>growing population</u>, a <u>boom</u> in industry and the <u>expansion of cities</u> leads to <u>higher consumption</u> of oil.

Oil Supply and Oil Prices are Affected by Different Factors

1) Oil <u>supply</u> and oil <u>prices</u> are <u>closely linked</u> and can <u>fluctuate</u> for a number of reasons.

2) Generally, periods of <u>oversupply</u> cause oil prices to <u>fall</u> and periods of <u>undersupply</u> cause prices to <u>increase</u>.

- <u>CONFLICTS</u> (e.g. those in the <u>Middle East</u> in the 1970s) can <u>disrupt</u> oil production, which leads to a <u>decrease</u> in oil <u>supply</u>. <u>Shortages</u> of oil cause <u>prices</u> to <u>increase</u>.

- <u>DIPLOMATIC RELATIONS</u> — oil prices may <u>increase</u> because of <u>tensions</u> between <u>oil-producing countries</u>. For example, relations between <u>Saudi Arabia</u> and <u>Iran</u> have led to <u>uncertainty</u> about oil production in the region.

- <u>RECESSIONS</u> (e.g. the <u>global financial crisis</u> in 2008) <u>lower</u> the <u>demand</u> for oil because <u>industrial activities</u> and <u>economic growth</u> slow down. This <u>causes</u> prices to <u>fall</u>.

- <u>ECONOMIC BOOMS</u> — oil prices <u>increase</u> during periods of <u>rapid economic growth</u> because of <u>increased consumption</u> and <u>demand</u>.

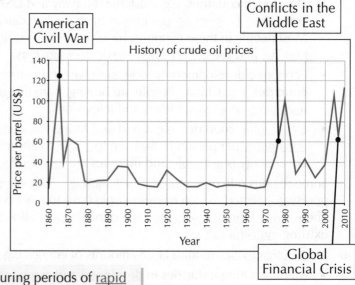

The Earth only has a limited supply of oil

We don't know when oil reserves will run out, but if we all keep consuming oil at the rate we are today, it won't be long before we need to look at exploiting new reserves. The next page describes how that's beginning to happen...

Increasing Energy Supply

If we're going to keep up with the world's energy needs, we'll need to start thinking about increasing our supplies.

Conventional Oil and Gas Reserves are being Exploited in Sensitive Areas

1) Despite the development of renewable energy, we still rely heavily on fossil fuels.

2) The pressure of meeting growing energy demands means new, ecologically-sensitive areas are being explored for conventional energy reserves, e.g. the Arctic circle and the Amazon rainforest.

Conventional energy reserves are easily exploited, e.g. through drilling. Extracting oil or gas from them is quick and cheap.

3) Exploiting new oil and gas reserves brings economic benefits:

- Countries with oil and gas reserves can save money by reducing energy imports, e.g. Peru is exploiting natural gas reserves in the Amazon rainforest that could save the country billions of dollars.
- These countries can also make money from exporting energy.
- Oil and gas companies bring investment and jobs to an area. For example, one oil company in Alaska has invested 4.5 million dollars into communities and employs over 1700 people.

4) However, these economic benefits come at a cost to the environment:

- In order to reach new reserves (e.g. in the Amazon), land may have to be cleared to make way for pipelines and roads. This can disrupt fragile ecosystems and cause a loss of biodiversity.
- Exploring offshore oil and gas reserves, e.g. in the Arctic Ocean, can have a big impact on marine life. Noise and vibrations from drills can confuse whales and other marine mammals that rely on sound to communicate, navigate and find food.
- Opening up isolated areas with roads and industry increases air pollution and can pollute soils and water.

Shale Gas and Tar Sands are Unconventional Gas and Oil Reserves

1) Unconventional energy reserves are exploited using more expensive methods, e.g. hydraulic fracking, that need specialist technology. Extraction takes a lot longer than from conventional reserves.

2) Shale gas is a form of natural gas that is trapped in shale rock underground. It's extracted by fracking:

- Liquid is pumped into the shale rock at high pressure.
- This causes the rock to crack (fracture), releasing the gas, which is collected as it comes out of the well.

Fracking negatively affects the environment:

- The chemicals used in fracking liquid as well as the shale gas itself can pollute groundwater and drinking water. This has become a big problem in some fracking areas in the USA, where people have been able to set fire to their tap water.
- Land has to be cleared to build drilling pads for fracking — this destroys animal habitats and disrupts ecosystems, e.g. mule deer populations have been affected in Wyoming.

3) Tar sands contain bitumen, which can be refined to produce oil. It's mainly extracted by mining:

- Surface mines collect tar sand and transport it to processing plants, which use water and chemicals to separate the bitumen from the sands.

Surface mining negatively affects the environment:

- Vast amounts of space are needed, which devastates habitats (see p.144). This can cause a reduction in the biodiversity of the area as organisms have less space to live and find food.
- Processing tar sands creates huge amounts of liquid waste full of harmful chemicals. These can pollute water supplies if they aren't managed properly.

Decisions about energy supply cause a lot of debate

Examiners love relevant geography topics, so it's a good idea to take a look at the latest articles about fracking and tar sand mining on a news website, to get a better understanding of the issues around them.

Sustainable Energy Use

There are lots of things that can help us use <u>less energy</u> and use it more <u>efficiently</u>.

The **Demand** for **Energy** can be **Reduced**

1) The demand for energy can be <u>reduced</u> by conserving energy and making energy use more efficient:
   - <u>Energy conservation</u> — conserving energy is about <u>changing our behaviour</u> as consumers.
     E.g. <u>driving less</u>, drying clothes on a <u>washing line</u> instead of in a <u>dryer</u>.
   - <u>Energy efficiency</u> — if something is energy-efficient, it does the <u>same job</u> but using <u>less energy</u>.
     E.g. a <u>low-energy lightbulb</u>.
2) Energy efficiency and conservation also make energy supplies <u>last longer</u> and <u>reduce carbon emissions</u>.
3) <u>Transport</u> and the <u>home</u> environment are two areas where the <u>demand</u> for energy can be effectively <u>reduced</u>:

Home

1) <u>Insulation</u> — by insulating <u>walls</u>, <u>roofs</u> and <u>floors</u>, less energy is required to <u>heat</u> homes.
2) <u>Modern boilers</u> — new boilers are more <u>efficient</u> than older models, so will use <u>less energy</u> in homes.
3) <u>Solar panels</u> can be fitted to the <u>roofs</u> of homes providing <u>renewable</u>, <u>low-carbon</u> energy.

Transport

1) <u>Hybrid</u> cars, vans and trains combine <u>diesel</u> and <u>electric</u> power to increase efficiency. They use <u>electricity</u> when possible, and <u>recharge</u> their <u>batteries</u> using <u>diesel</u> power.
2) <u>Regenerative braking</u> — road vehicles and trains can be fitted with devices to <u>store</u> the energy <u>lost under braking</u>, either to be used <u>later</u> or <u>returned</u> to the national grid.
3) <u>Engine manufacturers</u> are making <u>more efficient engines</u> in response to <u>laws</u> and <u>rising fuel costs</u>.
4) <u>Improving public transport</u> and <u>encouraging walking</u> or <u>cycling</u> reduces <u>demand</u> for energy used for <u>transport</u>.

Reducing the **Use** of **Fossil Fuels** has Lots of **Advantages**

There are <u>three main advantages</u> to reducing the use of fossil fuels:

1 Reducing carbon footprints

1) <u>Burning fossil fuels</u> releases <u>greenhouse gases</u> into the atmosphere, contributing to <u>global warming</u> (see p.6).
2) The greenhouse gas <u>emissions</u> are measured as people's <u>carbon footprints</u> (see p.157).
3) Carbon footprints include <u>direct emissions</u> (those produced from things that <u>use energy</u>) as well as <u>indirect emissions</u> (those produced making things that we <u>buy</u>).
4) By <u>reducing</u> their use of <u>energy</u> generated by using <u>fossil fuels</u>, people can <u>shrink</u> their carbon footprints.

2 Improving energy security

1) <u>Energy security</u> means having a <u>reliable</u>, <u>uninterrupted</u> and <u>affordable</u> supply of energy <u>available</u>.
2) Switching to <u>renewable</u> sources of energy will make sure energy is still <u>available</u> when the supply of fossil fuels <u>runs out</u>.

3 Diversifying the energy mix

1) Reducing <u>reliance</u> on finite <u>fossil fuels</u> and <u>increasing</u> the amount of energy generated by <u>alternative</u> methods will <u>diversify</u> the <u>energy mix</u>.
2) Having a <u>diverse</u> energy mix reduces a country's <u>reliance</u> on a <u>single</u> source of energy.
3) This <u>increases energy security</u> because countries are <u>less affected</u> by <u>shortages</u> of one energy source, reducing the <u>risk</u> of <u>energy deficits</u> — where the amount of energy produced isn't <u>enough</u> to meet a population's <u>needs</u>.
4) Using <u>renewable</u> energy sources instead of fossil fuels will also make <u>non-renewable</u> energy sources <u>last longer</u>.

Sustainable Energy Use

Alternatives to Fossil Fuels have Costs and Benefits

1) There are many <u>alternatives</u> to burning <u>fossil fuels</u>, including <u>renewable</u> and <u>recyclable sources</u> of <u>energy</u>.

2) These can help to <u>reduce carbon footprints</u>, <u>improve energy security</u> and <u>diversify the energy mix</u> (see previous page).

3) Each has <u>costs</u> and <u>benefits</u>:

See page 149 for how energy is generated from these fuels.

ENERGY SOURCE	COSTS	BENEFITS
BIOFUELS	• <u>Sources</u> of biomass have to be <u>managed sustainably</u> to make sure that they don't run out. • Growing crops for biofuels <u>reduces</u> the amount of <u>food crops</u> that can be grown and <u>lots</u> of <u>water</u> is needed. • Growing crops for biofuels is leading to <u>deforestation</u> in some areas (see p.137).	• Biofuels cause <u>less pollution</u> than fossil fuels when they're burned. • Some biofuels are made from <u>waste products</u> (see p.149), so they <u>reduce</u> the total amount of waste produced.
WIND ENERGY	• Wind is <u>unpredictable</u>, so the <u>amount</u> of electricity produced <u>varies</u>. • Wind turbines can cause <u>environmental issues</u> (see p.150). • It's <u>expensive</u> to <u>transport</u> the electricity produced from <u>offshore</u> wind farms to where it's needed.	• After the turbines have been made and transported to a suitable area, they don't release any <u>greenhouse gas emissions</u>. • It's a relatively <u>cheap</u> source of renewable energy.
SOLAR ENERGY	• <u>Sunny climates</u> are needed to produce <u>large amounts</u> of electricity, so it's <u>not</u> a <u>reliable</u> energy source in places where there's very <u>little sun</u>. • <u>Toxic</u> metals, e.g. mercury, are used in the <u>construction</u> of solar panels. • Solar panels can affect <u>habitats</u> and <u>ecosystems</u> (see p.150).	• Once the panels have been made and fitted, <u>no emissions</u> are produced. • Solar panels don't require much <u>maintenance</u> once they've been installed. • The technology is <u>widely available</u>.
HYDROELECTRIC POWER (HEP)	• Hydroelectric power plants are <u>expensive</u> to build and require <u>lots</u> of <u>water</u> and <u>land</u>. • <u>Methane</u> (a greenhouse gas) may be released from <u>rotting organic matter</u> in the <u>reservoirs</u> created behind the dams. • Hydroelectric power plants can cause other <u>environmental issues</u> (see p.150).	• <u>No emissions</u> are produced when hydroelectric power plants are used to generate electricity. • The <u>flow</u> of water through the turbines can be <u>controlled</u>, so the supply of energy is <u>reliable</u>.
HYDROGEN FUEL	• <u>Hydrogen</u> rarely exists <u>by itself</u> on Earth — energy is required to <u>extract</u> it, e.g. from <u>water</u>. The energy often comes from burning <u>fossil fuels</u>, releasing <u>greenhouse gases</u>. • The technology is <u>expensive</u> and <u>not widely available</u>, meaning that it is currently <u>unlikely</u> to be able to increase <u>energy security</u>. • <u>Storing</u> hydrogen is <u>dangerous</u> — it's <u>flammable</u>.	• Burning hydrogen doesn't release any <u>harmful emissions</u> — the only by-product is <u>water</u>. • Hydrogen is usually extracted from <u>water</u>, so it's <u>not limited</u> to particular areas.

Hydrogen fuel cells are currently only used on a small-scale but it is hoped they could be used to provide clean power for transport in the future.

Examiners love getting you to weigh up different options

The resource booklet in Paper 3 might have information on alternative energy options in a country. If you're asked to compare them, you may need to use both the information you're given and your own knowledge to get top marks, so learn the pros and cons of each alternative energy source now.

Energy Futures

The <u>future</u> of <u>global energy use</u> is uncertain. Some people think we need to make <u>significant changes</u> to make sure we have enough energy in the future, but others are quite happy to <u>carry on as usual</u>...

There are **Contrasting Views** about **Energy Futures**

1) There are two main <u>energy futures</u> to remember:

- **BUSINESS AS USUAL** — Everything <u>carries on as normal</u>. We go on getting most of our energy from <u>fossil fuels</u> and <u>don't</u> increase the use of <u>renewable energy sources</u>.

- **MOVE TO SUSTAINABILITY** — We <u>reduce</u> the amount of fossil fuels we use and increase our use of <u>renewable energy sources</u>.

2) <u>Different groups</u> have different <u>attitudes</u> towards energy futures:

1 Consumers

1) Consumers want <u>secure</u> energy supplies that won't be <u>disrupted</u> in the future.

2) When <u>fossil fuels</u> start to <u>run out</u>, <u>energy security</u> will decrease, increasing the risk of energy <u>shortages</u>.

3) Consumers also want <u>cheap</u> power — sustainable energy requires <u>investment</u>, which can <u>increase the price</u>.

4) Many consumers currently favour <u>business as usual</u>, as it provides a <u>cheap</u>, <u>secure</u> supply of energy. However, as supplies of fossil fuels <u>run out</u>, and <u>environmental awareness increases</u>, some consumers are beginning to favour a <u>move</u> to <u>sustainability</u> (see next page).

2 TNCs (Transnational Corporations)

1) Many TNCs, e.g. Shell, are involved in <u>extracting</u> and <u>refining</u> fossil fuels and <u>invest</u> a lot of money into the <u>energy sector</u>.

2) Controlling <u>oil reserves</u> gives TNCs lots of <u>power</u> and <u>wealth</u>, which means they may <u>lose</u> money if there is a shift towards using more <u>renewable</u> energy sources.

3) Sustainable energy needs <u>more investment</u> than fossil fuels, so these TNCs would have <u>higher costs</u> and potentially <u>lower gains</u> — this means they may <u>favour</u> the <u>business as usual</u> scenario.

4) TNCs <u>not</u> involved in the fossil fuel industry may also favour <u>business as usual</u> as <u>sustainable energy</u> is more <u>expensive</u> and would be likely to increase their <u>energy costs</u>.

3 Governments

1) Governments want to <u>secure</u> future energy supplies — fossil fuels are a <u>cheap</u> and <u>reliable</u> way of supplying energy in the <u>short-term</u>, but a more <u>sustainable</u> approach will be needed in the <u>long-term</u>.

2) In <u>developed countries</u>, governments are starting to come <u>under pressure</u> from some <u>consumers</u> to <u>protect the environment</u> — this means they want to start using more <u>sustainable energy</u>.

3) Fossil fuels have helped countries to <u>develop</u> and the <u>governments</u> of many <u>emerging</u> countries have <u>concerns</u> about whether sustainable energy sources will <u>continue</u> to help them <u>develop</u>.

4 Climate Scientists

1) <u>Climate scientists</u> study climate and how <u>human activities</u> are affecting it. The IPCC's <u>climate change scenarios</u> (see p.8) predict a temperature increase of up to 4 °C by the year 2100 under the <u>business as usual</u> scenario.

2) They want to reduce <u>reliance</u> on fossil fuels in order to lessen the <u>consequences</u> of climate change, e.g. <u>serious temperature increases</u> and <u>rising sea levels</u>.

5 Environmental Groups

1) <u>Environmental groups</u>, e.g. Greenpeace, want to <u>stop</u> people relying on fossil fuels for energy because their extraction and use <u>damages the environment</u>.

2) They want people to <u>reduce</u> their use of <u>fossil fuels</u> and <u>switch</u> to <u>renewable</u> energy sources in line with the <u>move to sustainability</u> scenario.

Energy Futures

Attitudes to Energy Futures are Changing

1) In <u>recent years</u>, many people have become <u>more aware</u> of the need to make energy use <u>sustainable</u> and <u>reduce</u> their <u>carbon footprint</u> (see below).

2) This is especially true in <u>developed countries</u>:

Rising Affluence

1) People with <u>more money</u> can afford to make a <u>choice</u> about <u>energy use</u>, e.g. buying <u>newer</u> cars that are more <u>fuel-efficient</u> or investing in <u>solar panels</u> for their <u>homes</u>.

2) <u>Governments</u> in <u>developed countries</u> have more money to invest in <u>public transport</u> and <u>renewable energy</u>.

Education

1) People in developed countries have <u>better access</u> to <u>education</u> through <u>school</u> and the <u>media</u> — this means they have a better <u>understanding</u> of the <u>consequences</u> of <u>unsustainable energy use</u> and <u>increasing emissions</u>.

2) People learn how to <u>reduce</u> their <u>carbon footprint</u>, which means there's more interest in using <u>cleaner energy sources</u> and <u>reducing energy consumption</u>.

Environmental Concerns

1) <u>Increased access</u> to <u>education</u> means people are more <u>worried</u> about <u>permanently damaging</u> the <u>environment</u> — they're <u>more likely</u> to try to <u>reduce</u> their <u>carbon footprint</u>.

2) Developed countries can afford to <u>invest</u> in <u>research</u> into the <u>environmental impacts</u> of different <u>energy sources</u> — this creates more <u>awareness</u> about <u>energy consumption</u> and how to reduce carbon footprints.

3) In <u>developing</u> countries, <u>economic development</u> can overshadow <u>environmental concerns</u>. As a country <u>develops</u>, the environment can become a <u>higher priority</u>.

Carbon and Ecological Footprints are Calculated Using Several Factors

1) A <u>carbon footprint</u> is a measure of the <u>amount</u> of <u>greenhouse gases</u> generated by the activities of an <u>individual</u> or <u>organisation</u>, or by a <u>product</u> over its lifetime.

2) An <u>ecological footprint</u> is a measure of how much <u>land</u> is needed to <u>support</u> an individual's lifestyle. It can also be used on a <u>larger scale</u> to calculate the impact of <u>cities</u>, <u>countries</u> or the <u>world population</u>.

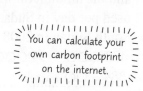

You can calculate your own carbon footprint on the internet.

3) Both are calculated from these key areas:

- <u>FOOD</u> — e.g. how much <u>meat</u> you eat (the process of meat production produces huge amounts of <u>greenhouse gases</u> and takes up <u>lots</u> of <u>land</u>), <u>food wastage</u> and whether you eat <u>locally produced food</u>.

- <u>HOME</u> — e.g. the <u>size</u> of your house and <u>how many people</u> live in it. It also looks at the type of <u>energy</u> you use to heat your home and whether your home has <u>energy-saving features</u>.

- <u>TRAVEL</u> — this is do to with <u>air travel</u>, <u>commuting</u> and what sort of <u>transport</u> you use.

- <u>LIFESTYLE</u> — this is to do with how much you spend on <u>clothes</u> and <u>electrical devices</u> in a <u>year</u> and how much <u>recycling</u> you do.

People are getting more interested in reducing their energy use

It's hard to tell what the future of energy is going to be like. People are now more aware of the need to use energy sustainably, but it's yet to be seen how far that'll go towards persuading governments and TNCs to make changes.

Worked Exam Questions

Exams can be pretty scary, but answering practice exam questions will help you to prepare.
Read this page to get an idea of how to answer them, then have a go at the lot on the next page yourself.

1   Study **Figure 1**, a map of Barmouth Bay, Wales.

a)   Which location, A-E, would be the
     best site for an onshore wind farm?
     Give **one** reason for your choice.

     Location:....C.......................................
     [1]

     Reason: C is exposed on all sides, so turbines

     will be powered by wind from all directions.
     [1]

b)   Suggest why location E is not suitable
     for a solar power plant.

     E would not be suitable for a solar plant

     because it is in a forest in a valley, where trees

     and the valley sides would block the sunlight.
     [2]

     [Total 4 marks]

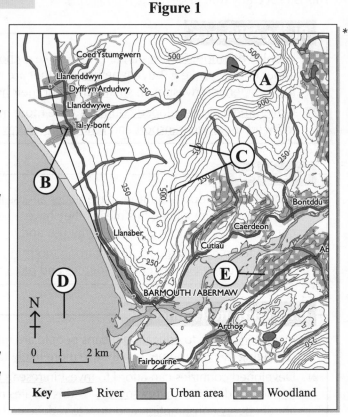

Figure 1

Key — River | Urban area | Woodland

2   Study **Figure 2**, a data table showing the amount of oil produced and
     amount of oil products used in Brazil and Sudan and South Sudan.

a)   Calculate the difference between
     the amount of oil produced
     and the amount of oil products
     used per day in Sudan and
     South Sudan in 2008.

     478 000 – 94 000 =
     384 000 barrels
     [1]

Figure 2

	Brazil		Sudan & South Sudan	
Year	Oil produced (1000 barrels per day)	Oil products used (1000 barrels per day)	Oil produced (1000 barrels per day)	Oil products used (1000 barrels per day)
2008	1812	2205	478	94
2009	1950	2481	483	125
2010	2055	2699	486	115
2011	2105	2777	453	111
2012	2061	2923	112	107
2013	2024	3033	247	107
2014	2255	3144	259	108

b)   State **one** possible reason for the
     decrease in oil production in
     Sudan and South Sudan in 2012.

     Conflict disrupting oil production.
     [1]

c)   Brazil has oil reserves of around 15 billion barrels. State what is meant by the term 'oil reserves'.

     Oil reserves are the amount of oil that can be extracted using today's technology.
     [1]

     [Total 3 marks]

*Contains OS data © Crown copyright and database right (2017)

Exam Questions

1 Study **Figure 1**, pie charts showing the proportion of UK energy from different sources in 1970 and 2014.

Figure 1

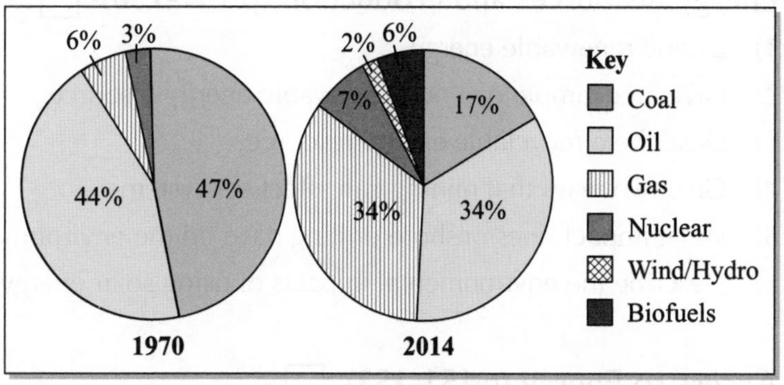

a) State which source of energy the UK most relied on in 1970.

....
[1]

b) State which energy source increased its share the most between 1970 and 2014.

....
[1]

1970

2014

Key
- Coal
- Oil
- Gas
- Nuclear
- Wind/Hydro
- Biofuels

1970: 6%, 3%, 44%, 47%

2014: 2%, 6%, 7%, 17%, 34%, 34%

c) Using **Figure 1**, describe the changes in energy sources in the UK between 1970 and 2014.

....

....

....

....
[3]

d) The changes in energy sources shown in **Figure 1** are similar in many developed countries. State **two** reasons why rising affluence can lead to more sustainable energy use.

1:...

2:...
[2]

e) Other than rising affluence, explain why sustainable energy use has been increasing in developed countries.

....

....

....

....

....
[4]

f) Explain why some governments of less developed countries are concerned about having to increase their use of renewable energy sources.

....

....

....
[2]

[Total 13 marks]

Revision Summary

Well, that's <u>Topic 9</u> out of the way — all that remains is to try these questions.
- Try these questions and <u>tick off each one</u> when you <u>get it right</u>.
- When you've done <u>all the questions</u> under a heading and are <u>completely happy</u> with it, tick it off.

Energy Resources and Production (p.149-150) ☑

1) Define renewable energy.
2) Give an example of a non-renewable energy resource.
3) Describe a recyclable energy resource.
4) Give two ways that mining can affect ecosystems.
5) What impact does onshore drilling have on the environment?
6) Describe the environmental impacts of using solar energy.

Access to Energy (p.151-153) ☑

7) Briefly describe three factors that affect access to energy.
8) Give one way that development affects energy consumption.
9) Briefly describe three factors that affect oil production.
10) Give two reasons why oil consumption is increasing.
11) a) How might diplomatic relations affect the supply of oil?
    b) What effect do recessions have on oil prices?
12) What is a conventional energy reserve?
13) a) Give two economic benefits of exploiting conventional energy reserves in isolated areas.
    b) Give two environmental costs of exploiting conventional energy reserves in isolated areas.
14) What are unconventional energy reserves?
15) How does fracking affect the environment?
16) Describe the environmental impacts of extracting energy from tar sands in ecologically sensitive areas.

Sustainable Energy Use (p.154-155) ☑

17) What is the difference between energy conservation and energy efficiency.
18) a) Explain how homes can be made more energy-efficient.
    b) Describe two ways that transport can be designed to better conserve energy.
19) How does reducing fossil fuel use reduce carbon footprints?
20) Give two benefits of using biofuels instead of fossil fuels.
21) Give two disadvantages of wind energy.
22) Give one disadvantage of replacing fossil fuels with hydroelectric power.
23) Describe the advantages of hydrogen fuel.

Energy Futures (p.156-157) ☑

24) a) What is the 'business as usual' scenario for future energy use?
    b) What is the 'move to sustainability' scenario for future energy use?
25) Why might transnational corporations (TNCs) favour the business as usual scenario?
26) Give one reason why environmental groups support the move to sustainability.
27) a) What does a person's carbon footprint measure?
    b) What does a person's ecological footprint measure?
28) Give two factors used to calculate carbon and ecological footprints.

Making Geographical Decisions

Knowing all the facts isn't quite enough to get you through your exams — you'll also have to use what you've learnt to come to a decision about a geographical dilemma.

You'll Have to Make a Decision About a Geographical Issue

Section D of Paper 3 asks you to make a decision about a geographical issue and justify your choice. You will be given three options to choose from and there will be 12 marks available for your answer — plus 4 marks for SPaG (spelling, punctuation and grammar).

1) The issue could be based anywhere in the world and could vary in scale from local to international.

2) It will relate to what you've learnt in Topics 7, 8 and 9 — e.g. how to manage an area of forest or increase energy supply in an area.

3) It will involve elements of physical and human geography.

4) You'll need to link in what you've learnt from the rest of the course and it might extend into new contexts that you haven't studied before.

You'll Be Given a Resource Booklet to Help You

1) In the exam, you'll get a resource booklet. It will contain loads of information about the issue.

2) The booklet could include several different types of information, such as:

- Maps
- Graphs
- Photographs

- Diagrams
- Statistics
- Newspaper articles

- Quotes from people involved

Make sure you can read all the common types of maps and graphs — see pages 163-173 for more on this.

3) You'll need to use all the information in the booklet to make your decision, but don't worry — you'll get to use the sources to answer questions in Sections A, B and C, which will help you to understand what they show.

Use All the Information to Form an Opinion About the Issue

1) You'll be asked to argue your point of view using the information, e.g. suggesting how an area could best be managed to meet the needs of everyone involved.

2) There's no single right or wrong answer — but you need to be able to justify your argument, so make sure you can use the data from the resource booklet to support it.

3) Whatever your view is, you need to give a balanced argument. Try to think of the potential impacts of the decision, both positive and negative, including:

- Economic impacts — e.g. will the decision bring more money to a country?
- Political impacts — e.g. are other countries likely to approve of the decision? If not, what effect might this have?
- Social impacts — e.g. will the decision improve quality of life for people in the area?
- Environmental impacts — e.g. is the decision likely to damage natural habitats?

You could also think about how any negative impacts could be reduced.

4) It's likely to be a complex issue with lots of different parties involved. So think about possible conflicts that your solution might cause between different groups of people, or between people and the environment, and how they could be resolved.

You'll need to justify your decision by giving reasons why you chose it

This might seem a bit daunting, but don't panic — just carefully read the information you're given and then try and relate it to what you've learnt on the rest of your course. Do that and you're well on the way to exam success.

Answering Questions

This section is filled with lots of techniques and skills that you need for your exams. It's no good learning the content of this book if you don't learn the skills you need to pass your exam too. First up, answering questions properly...

Make Sure you Read the Question Properly

It's dead easy to misread the question and spend five minutes writing about the wrong thing.
Four simple tips can help you avoid this:

1) Figure out if it's a case study question — if the question wording includes 'using named examples' or 'for a named country' you need to include a case study or examples you've learnt about.

2) Underline the command words in the question (the ones that tell you what to do):

Answers to questions with 'explain' in them often include the word 'because' (or 'due to').

When writing about differences, 'whereas' is a good word to use in your answers, e.g. 'Upland areas in the UK are often formed of igneous or metamorphic rocks, whereas lowland areas are often formed of sedimentary rocks.'

Command word	Means write about...
Describe	what it's like
Explain	why it's like that (i.e. give reasons)
Compare	the similarities AND differences
Suggest why	give reasons for
Assess	weigh up all factors
Evaluate	judge the success of something
Justify	give reasons

If a question asks you to describe a pattern (e.g. from a map or graph), make sure you identify the general pattern, then refer to any anomalies (things that don't fit the general pattern).
E.g. to answer 'describe the global distribution of volcanoes', first say that they're mostly on plate margins, then mention that a few aren't (e.g. in Hawaii).

3) Underline the key words (the ones that tell you what it's about), e.g. volcanoes, immigration, energy supply.

4) If the question says 'using Figure 2', make sure you've talked about what Figure 2 shows. Don't just wheel out all of your geographical knowledge and forget all about the photo you're supposed to be talking about. Re-read the question and your answer when you've finished, just to check.

Some Questions are Level Marked

Questions worth 8 marks or more with longer written answers are level marked, which means you need to do these things to get the top level and a high mark:

1) Read the question properly and figure out a structure for your answer before you start. Your answer needs to be well organised and structured, and written in a logical way.

2) If it's a case study question, include plenty of relevant details:

- This includes things like place names, dates, statistics, names of organisations or companies.
- Don't forget that they need to be relevant though — it's no good including the exact number of people killed in a flood when the question is about the causes of a flood.

3) Some questions have 4 extra marks available for spelling, punctuation and grammar. To get top marks you need to:

- Make sure your spelling, punctuation and grammar are consistently correct.
- Write in a way that makes it clear what you mean.
- Use a wide range of geographical terms (e.g. sustainable development) correctly.

Answers to level marked questions should be well structured

It may all seem a bit simple to you, but it's really important to understand what you're being asked to do. This can be tricky — sometimes the differences between the meanings of the command words are quite subtle.

Maps

Maps are a <u>staple</u> of most Geography exams, so make sure you know how to <u>read</u> them.

Latitude and Longitude are Used for Global Coordinates

1) The <u>position</u> of anywhere on Earth can be given using <u>coordinates</u> if you use <u>latitude</u> and <u>longitude</u>.

2) Lines of <u>latitude</u> run <u>horizontally</u> around the Earth.
They measure how far north or south from the <u>equator</u> something is.

3) Lines of <u>longitude</u> run <u>vertically</u> around the Earth. They measure how far east or west from the <u>Prime Meridian</u> (a line of longitude running through <u>Greenwich</u> in London) something is.

4) Latitude and longitude are measured in <u>degrees</u>.

5) For example, the <u>coordinates</u> of <u>London</u> are 51° N, 0° W. New York is at 40° N, 74° W.

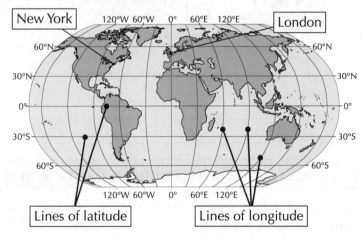

Describing Distributions on Maps — Describe the Pattern

1) In your exam you could get questions like, 'use the map to <u>describe</u> the <u>distribution</u> of volcanoes' and '<u>explain</u> the <u>distribution</u> of deforestation'.

2) Describe the <u>general pattern</u> and any <u>anomalies</u> (things that <u>don't fit</u> the general pattern).

3) Make <u>at least</u> as many <u>points</u> as there are <u>marks</u> and use <u>names</u> of places and <u>figures</u> if they're given.

4) If you're asked to give a <u>reason</u> or <u>explain</u>, you need to describe the <u>distribution first</u>.

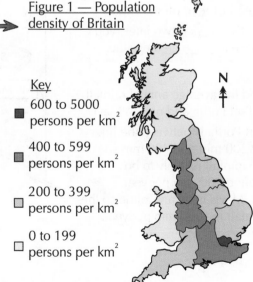

Figure 1 — Population density of Britain

Key

■ 600 to 5000 persons per km^2

■ 400 to 599 persons per km^2

□ 200 to 399 persons per km^2

□ 0 to 199 persons per km^2

Q: Use Figure 1 to explain the pattern of population density in Britain.

A: The <u>London area</u> has a <u>very high</u> population density (<u>600 to 5000</u> per km²). There are also areas of <u>high</u> population density (<u>400 to 599</u> per km²) in the <u>south east</u>, the <u>Midlands</u> and <u>north west</u> of England. These areas include <u>major cities</u> (e.g. Birmingham and Manchester). More people live in and around cities because there are <u>better services</u> and <u>more job opportunities</u> than in rural areas. <u>Scotland</u> and <u>Wales</u> have the <u>lowest</u> population densities in Britain (<u>less than 199</u> per km²)...

Remember, lines of l<u>a</u>titude go <u>a</u>cross...

...don't get them mixed up with lines of longitude, which are vertical. Make sure you're happy with what they are and how they're measured in degrees — you might need to refer to them when describing a map in the exam.

Maps

There's a bit more on how to <u>read</u> maps and <u>write answers</u> about them on this page.

Describing Locations on Maps — Include Details

1) In your exam you could get a question like, 'describe the location of cities in ...'.

2) When you're asked about the <u>location</u> of something say <u>where</u> it is, what it's <u>near</u> and use <u>compass points</u>.

3) If you're asked to give a <u>reason</u> or <u>explain</u>, you need to describe the <u>location first</u>.

Q: Use the maps to describe the location of the National Parks.

Spondovia

Key:
■ National Parks

Spondovia

Key: ■ *Mountains*
● *Cities*

A: The National Parks are found in the <u>south west</u> and <u>north east</u> of Spondovia. They are all located in <u>mountainous</u> areas. Three of the parks are located near to the city of <u>Strava</u>.

Isolines on Maps Link up Places with Something in Common

1) <u>Isolines</u> are lines on a map <u>linking</u> up all the places where something's the <u>same</u>, for example:
   • <u>Contour lines</u> are isolines linking up places at the same <u>altitude</u>.
   • Isolines on a <u>weather map</u> (called <u>isobars</u>) link together all the places where the <u>pressure's</u> the same.

2) Isolines can be used to link up lots of things, e.g. <u>average temperature</u>, <u>wind speed</u> or <u>rainfall</u>.

3) Isolines are normally <u>labelled</u> with their <u>value</u>. The <u>closer together</u> the <u>lines</u> are, the <u>steeper</u> the <u>gradient</u> (how quickly the thing is changing) <u>at that point</u>.

1 Reading Isoline Maps

1) <u>Find</u> the place you're interested in on the map and if it's on a line just <u>read</u> off the value.

2) If it's <u>between</u> two lines, you have to <u>estimate</u> the value.

Q: Find the average annual rainfall in Port Portia and on Mt. Mavis.

A: Port Portia is between the lines for 200 mm and 400 mm so the rainfall is likely to be around 300 mm per year. Mt. Mavis is on an isoline so the rainfall is 1000 mm per year.

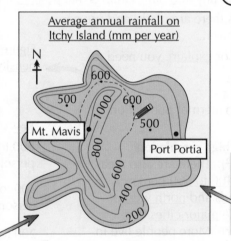

Average annual rainfall on Itchy Island (mm per year)

Mt. Mavis

Port Portia

2 Completing Isoline Maps

1) Drawing an isoline's like doing a <u>dot-to-dot</u> — you just join up all the dots with the <u>same numbers</u>.

2) Make sure you don't <u>cross</u> any <u>other isolines</u> though.

Q: Complete on the map the isoline showing an average rainfall of 600 mm per year.

A: See the red line on the map.

EXAM TIP

If a point is between two isolines, you can only estimate its value

Like in the example at the top of the page, you could be given two maps to use for one question in the exam — you'll have to link the information from the two maps together for your answer.

Maps

There are a lot of <u>different types</u> of map you might have to interpret in the exam — such as the ones below.

Dot Maps Show **Distribution** and **Quantity** Using **Identical Symbols**...

1) Dot maps use <u>identical dots</u> to show how something is <u>distributed</u> across an <u>area</u>.

2) Use the <u>key</u> to find out what <u>quantity</u> each dot represents.

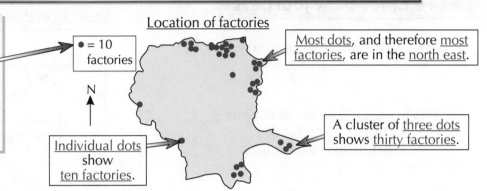

Location of factories

● = 10 factories

N

<u>Individual dots</u> show <u>ten factories</u>.

<u>Most dots</u>, and therefore <u>most factories</u>, are in the <u>north east</u>.

A cluster of <u>three dots</u> shows <u>thirty factories</u>.

...**Proportional Symbol Maps** use Symbols of **Different Sizes**

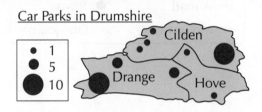

Car Parks in Drumshire

● 1
● 5
● 10

Cilden

Drange

Hove

1) <u>Proportional symbol maps</u> use symbols of different <u>sizes</u> to represent different <u>quantities</u>.

2) A <u>key</u> shows the <u>quantity</u> each <u>different sized</u> symbol represents. The <u>bigger</u> the symbol, the <u>larger</u> the amount.

3) The symbols might be <u>circles</u>, <u>squares</u>, <u>semi-circles</u> or <u>bars</u>, but a <u>larger symbol</u> always means a <u>larger amount</u>.

Q: Which area of Drumshire has the most car parks?

A: Drange, with 20.

Flow Lines show **Movement**

1) <u>Flow line maps</u> have <u>arrows</u> on, showing how things <u>move</u> (or are moved) from one place to another.

2) They can also be <u>proportional symbol maps</u> — the <u>width</u> of the arrows show the <u>quantity</u> of things that are <u>moving</u>.

Q: From which <u>area</u> do the <u>greatest</u> number of people entering the UK come from?

A: <u>USA</u>, as this arrow is the largest.

Q: The number of people entering the UK from the <u>Middle East</u> is <u>roughly half</u> the number of people entering from the <u>USA</u>. Draw an <u>arrow</u> on the map to <u>show</u> this.

A: Make sure your arrow is going in the <u>right direction</u> and its <u>size</u> is appropriate (i.e. <u>half the width</u> of the USA arrow).

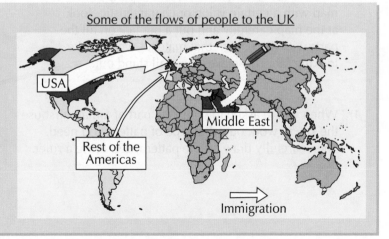

Some of the flows of people to the UK

USA

Middle East

Rest of the Americas

Immigration

Flow lines can be used to show movement of people or products

There are lots of ways that putting symbols onto maps can provide information. Turn over for more about flow lines.

Maps

You read about <u>flow lines</u> on the previous page — here you have a particular type of flow line called <u>desire lines</u>. Then there's just <u>one more</u> type of map to learn about, before it's time to move onto OS® maps on the next page.

Desire Lines show Journeys

1) <u>Desire line maps</u> are a type of flow line as they show <u>movement</u> too.

2) They're <u>straight lines</u> that show <u>journeys</u> <u>between</u> two <u>locations</u>, but they <u>don't follow roads</u> or <u>railway lines</u>.

3) <u>One line</u> represents <u>one journey</u>.

4) They're used to show <u>how far</u> all the people have <u>travelled</u> to get to a <u>place</u>, e.g. a shop or a town centre, and <u>where</u> they've <u>come from</u>.

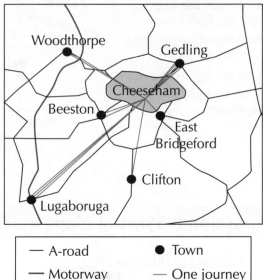

Desire Lines showing journeys to Cheeseham

— A-road   ● Town
— Motorway   — One journey

Choropleth Maps show How Something Varies Between Different Areas

1) <u>Choropleth maps</u> show how something varies between different areas using <u>colours</u> or <u>patterns</u>.

2) The maps in exams often use <u>cross-hatched lines</u> and <u>dot patterns</u>.

3) If you're asked to talk about all the parts of the map with a certain <u>value</u> or <u>characteristic</u>, look at the map carefully and put a <u>big tick</u> on all the parts with the <u>pattern</u> that <u>matches</u> what you're looking for. This makes them all <u>stand out</u>.

4) When you're asked to <u>complete</u> part of a map, first use the <u>key</u> to work out what type of <u>pattern</u> you need. Then <u>carefully</u> draw on the pattern, e.g. using a <u>ruler</u>.

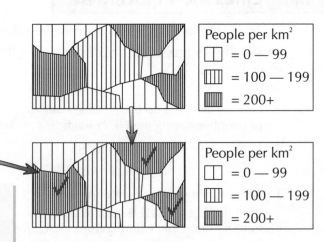

People per km² : = 0 — 99, = 100 — 199, = 200+

Make sure you study the key for any map

If you have to complete a map, check all the info on the map before you start drawing — that way you're less likely to muck it up. Make sure you do it in pencil too, so if you do make a mistake you can rub it out.

Ordnance Survey Maps

Next up, the dreaded <u>Ordnance Survey®</u> maps. Don't worry, they're easy once you know how to use them.

Learn These **Common Symbols**

Ordnance Survey (OS®) maps use lots of <u>symbols</u>. It's a good idea to learn some of the most <u>common ones</u> — like these: ⟹

▬ Motorway	– · – · County boundary	⁚⁚⁚⁚⁚ Footpaths
▬ Main (A) road	░░ National Park	⅍ Viewpoint
▬ Secondary (B) road	⸺ boundaries	*i* Tourist information centre
⊨ Bridge	☐ Building	**P** Parking
⸺ Railway	⬡ Bus station	+ ♦ ♦ Places of worship

You have to be able to Understand **Grid References**

You need to be able to use <u>four figure</u> and <u>six figure</u> grid references for your exam.

Q: Give the four figure and six figure grid reference for the place of worship.

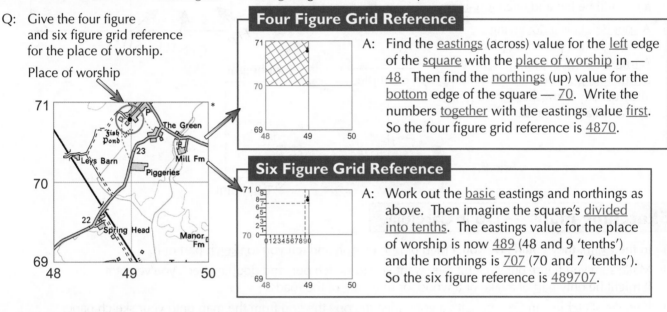

Four Figure Grid Reference

A: Find the <u>eastings</u> (across) value for the <u>left</u> edge of the <u>square</u> with the <u>place of worship</u> in — <u>48</u>. Then find the <u>northings</u> (up) value for the <u>bottom</u> edge of the square — <u>70</u>. Write the numbers <u>together</u> with the eastings value <u>first</u>. So the four figure grid reference is <u>4870</u>.

Six Figure Grid Reference

A: Work out the <u>basic</u> eastings and northings as above. Then imagine the square's <u>divided into tenths</u>. The eastings value for the place of worship is now <u>489</u> (48 and 9 'tenths') and the northings is <u>707</u> (70 and 7 'tenths'). So the six figure reference is <u>489707</u>.

You need to Know your **Compass Points**

You've got to know the compass — for giving <u>directions</u>, saying <u>which way</u> a <u>river's flowing</u>, or knowing what they mean if they say 'look at the river in the <u>NW</u> of the map' in the exam. Read it <u>out loud</u> to yourself, going <u>clockwise</u>.

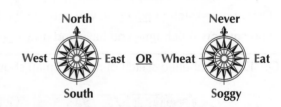

You Might have to **Work Out** the **Distance** Between **Two Places**

To work out the <u>distance</u> between <u>two places</u> on a <u>map</u>, use a <u>ruler</u> to measure the <u>distance</u> in <u>cm</u> then <u>compare</u> it to the scale to find the distance in <u>km</u>.

Q: What's the distance from the bridge (482703) to the church (489707)?

A: They're 2.2 cm apart on the map... ...which means they're 1.1 km apart in real life.

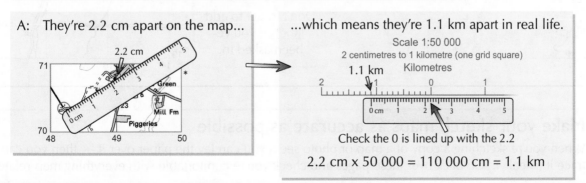

Scale 1:50 000
2 centimetres to 1 kilometre (one grid square)

Check the 0 is lined up with the 2.2

2.2 cm x 50 000 = 110 000 cm = 1.1 km

Ordnance Survey Maps

Almost done with <u>map skills</u> now. Just this final page on <u>contour lines</u> and <u>sketching</u> from OS® maps or photos left.

The **Relief** of an Area is Shown by **Contours** and **Spot Heights**

1) <u>Contour lines</u> are the <u>browny-orange lines</u> drawn on maps — they join points of <u>equal height</u> above sea level (<u>altitude</u>).

2) They tell you about the <u>relief</u> of the land, e.g. whether it's hilly, flat or steep.

3) They show the <u>height</u> of the land by the <u>numbers</u> marked on them. They also show the <u>steepness</u> of the land by how <u>close together</u> they are (the <u>closer</u> they are, the <u>steeper</u> the slope).

4) For example, if a map has <u>lots</u> of contour lines on it, it's probably <u>hilly</u> or <u>mountainous</u>. If there are only a <u>few</u> it'll be <u>flat</u> and often <u>low-lying</u>.

5) A <u>spot height</u> is a <u>dot</u> giving the height of a particular place. A <u>trigonometrical point</u> (trig point) is a <u>blue triangle</u> plus a height value. They usually show the <u>highest point</u> in that area (in metres).

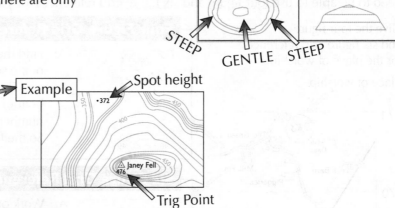

Sketching Maps — Do it Carefully

1) In the <u>exam</u>, they could give you a <u>map</u> or <u>photograph</u> and tell you to <u>sketch</u> part of it.

2) Make sure you figure out <u>what bit</u> they want you to sketch out, and <u>double check</u> you've <u>got it right</u>. It might be only <u>part</u> of a lake or a wood, or only <u>one</u> of the roads.

3) If you're <u>sketching</u> an OS® map, it's a good idea to <u>copy</u> the <u>grid</u> from the map onto your sketch paper — this helps you to copy the map <u>accurately</u>.

4) Draw your sketch <u>in pencil</u> so you can <u>rub it out</u> if it's <u>wrong</u>.

5) Look at how much <u>time</u> you have and <u>how many marks</u> it's worth to decide how much <u>detail</u> to add.

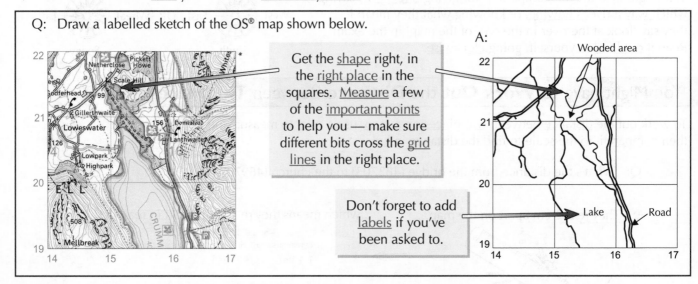

Q: Draw a labelled sketch of the OS® map shown below.

Get the <u>shape</u> right, in the <u>right place</u> in the squares. <u>Measure</u> a few of the <u>important points</u> to help you — make sure different bits cross the <u>grid lines</u> in the right place.

Don't forget to add <u>labels</u> if you've been asked to.

Make your sketch maps as accurate as possible

EXAM TIP

When you're sketching a copy of a map or photo see if you can lay the paper over it — then you can trace it (sneaky). Go back over these pages and check you're comfortable with everything map-related.

© Crown copyright 2018 OS 100034841

Charts and Graphs

Stand by for <u>charts</u> and <u>graphs</u>. Make sure you can <u>interpret</u> (read) and <u>construct</u> (draw) each of them...

Describing what **Graphs** Show — **Include Figures** from the Graph

When <u>describing</u> graphs make sure you mention:
1) The general pattern — when it's <u>going up</u> and <u>down</u>, and any <u>peaks</u> (highest bits) and <u>troughs</u> (lowest bits).
2) Any <u>anomalies</u> (odd results).
3) Specific <u>data points</u>.

Q: Use the graph to describe population change in Cheeseham.

A: The population halved between 1950 and 1960 from 40 thousand people to 20 thousand people. It then increased to 100 thousand by 1980, before falling slightly and staying steady at 90 thousand from 1990 to 2000.

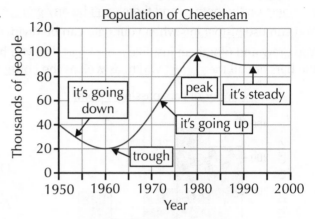

Bar Charts — Draw the Bars **Straight** and **Neat**

To read a bar chart

1) Read along the <u>bottom</u> to find the <u>bar</u> you want.
2) To find out the <u>value</u> of a bar in a <u>normal</u> bar chart — go from the <u>top</u> of the bar <u>across</u> to the <u>scale</u>, and <u>read off</u> the number.
3) To find out the <u>value</u> of <u>part</u> of the bar in a <u>divided</u> bar chart — find the <u>number at the top</u> of the part of the bar you're interested in, and <u>take away</u> the <u>number at the bottom</u> of it (see example below).

To complete a bar chart

1) First find the number you want on the <u>vertical scale</u>.
2) Then <u>trace</u> a line across to where the <u>top</u> of the bar will be with a <u>ruler</u>.
3) Draw in a bar of the <u>right size</u> using a <u>ruler</u>.

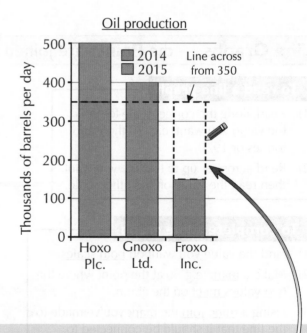

Q: How many barrels of oil did Hoxo Plc. produce per day in 2015?
A: 500 000 – 350 000 = <u>150 000 barrels</u> per day

Q: Complete the chart to show that Froxo Inc. produced 200 000 barrels of oil per day in 2015.
A: 150 thousand (2014) + 200 thousand = <u>350 000 barrels</u>. So draw the bar up to this point.

You're more likely to read a chart correctly if you use a ruler

Don't be put off by divided bar charts like the one above — they might look complicated, but they're really quite simple. Just make sure you don't read the value for the whole bar if you only need to know about one part of it.

Geographical Skills

Charts and Graphs

There are still four more pages of <u>charts and graphs</u> to get through, I'm afraid. Any of these could crop up in your <u>exam</u> or be a useful presentation method for your <u>fieldwork</u>, so it's a good idea to get used to all of them now.

Histograms are a Lot Like Bar Charts

1) <u>Histograms</u> are very <u>similar</u> to <u>bar charts</u>, but they have a <u>continuous scale</u> of <u>numbers</u> on the <u>bottom</u> and there <u>can't</u> be any <u>gaps between the bars</u>.

2) You can use <u>histograms</u> when your <u>data</u> can be divided into <u>intervals</u>, like <u>this</u>:

3) You <u>draw</u> and <u>plot</u> them just like a <u>bar chart</u>, but you have to make sure that the bars are all the <u>correct width</u>, as well as the <u>correct height</u>.

Time	Cars
0700-0800	334
0800-0900	387
0900-1000	209
1000-1100	121
1100-1200	?

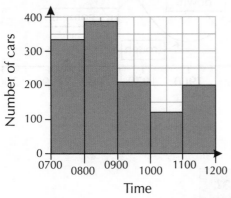

Number of cars passing a point

Q: How many cars were recorded between 1100 and 1200?

A: Trace a line from the top of the 1100-1200 bar and read the answer off — <u>200 cars</u>.

Line Graphs — the Points are Joined by Lines

To read a line graph

1) Read along the <u>correct scale</u> to find the <u>value</u> you want, e.g. 20 thousand tonnes or 1920.

2) Read <u>across</u> or <u>up</u> to the line you want, then read the value off the <u>other</u> scale.

To complete a line graph

1) Find the value you want on <u>both scales</u>.

2) Make a <u>mark</u> (e.g. ×) at the point where the <u>two values meet</u> on the graph.

3) Using a <u>ruler</u>, <u>join</u> the <u>mark</u> you've made to the <u>line</u> that it should be <u>connected to</u>.

Coal production

— New Wales Ltd.
— Old Wales Ltd.

Q: Complete the graph to show that Old Wales Ltd. produced 10 thousand tonnes of coal in 1930.

A: Find 1930 on the bottom scale, and 10 thousand tonnes on the vertical scale. Make a mark <u>where they meet</u>, then join it to the <u>blue</u> line <u>with a ruler</u>.

EXAM TIP

Lines, bars and crosses should be neat and legible

If you're asked to read a value off a graph, or add some data to it, remember to read the scale carefully — it's easy to assume that each division is worth one, but sadly that's not always the case.

Charts and Graphs

Now onto <u>scatter graphs</u> and <u>population pyramids</u>...

Scatter Graphs Show Relationships

<u>Scatter graphs</u> tell you how <u>closely related</u> two things are, e.g. altitude and air temperature. The fancy word for this is <u>correlation</u>. <u>Strong</u> correlation means the two things are <u>closely</u> related to each other. <u>Weak</u> correlation means they're <u>not very</u> closely related. The <u>line of best fit</u> is a line that goes roughly through the <u>middle</u> of the scatter of points and tells you about what <u>type</u> of correlation there is. Data can show <u>three</u> types of correlation:

1) <u>Positive</u> — as one thing <u>increases</u> the other <u>increases</u>.

2) <u>Negative</u> — as one thing <u>increases</u> the other <u>decreases</u>.

3) <u>None</u> — there's <u>no relationship</u> between the two things.

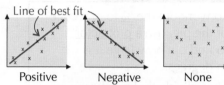

Positive   Negative   None

① Reading Scatter Graphs

1) If you're asked to <u>describe</u> the <u>relationship</u>, look at the <u>slope</u> of the graph, e.g. if the line's moving <u>upwards</u> to the <u>right</u> it's a <u>positive correlation</u>. You also need to look at how <u>close</u> the points are to the <u>line of best fit</u> — the <u>closer</u> they are the <u>stronger</u> the correlation.

2) If you're asked to <u>read off</u> a <u>specific point</u>, just follow the <u>rules</u> for a <u>line graph</u> (see previous page).

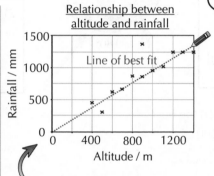

Relationship between altitude and rainfall

② Completing Scatter Graphs

1) You could be asked to <u>draw</u> a <u>line of best fit</u> — just draw it roughly through the <u>middle</u> of the scatter of points.

2) If you're asked to <u>add a point</u> — just follow the <u>rules</u> for adding a point to a <u>line graph</u> (see previous page).

Q: Describe the relationship shown by the scatter graph.

A: Altitude and rainfall show a strong, positive correlation — as altitude increases, so does the amount of rainfall.

- You can use your <u>line of best fit</u> to make <u>predictions</u> by <u>reading off values</u> from the graph.
- If you're confident your best fit line will <u>continue</u>, you can <u>extend</u> it <u>beyond</u> the data you have collected. This means you can make <u>predictions outside the range</u> of data you <u>collected</u>.

Population Pyramids Show the Structure of a Population

1) <u>Population pyramids</u> are a bit like <u>two bar charts</u> on their <u>sides</u>.

2) It's way of showing the <u>population</u> of a country by <u>age</u> and <u>gender</u>.

3) The <u>number of people</u> goes on the <u>horizontal axis</u>, and the <u>age groups</u> go on the <u>vertical axis</u>. The <u>left side</u> is the <u>male population</u> and the <u>right side</u> is the <u>female population</u>.

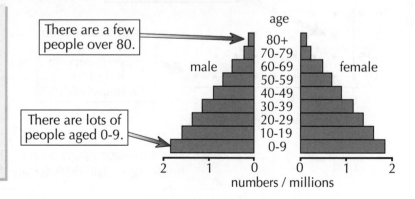

There are a few people over 80.

There are lots of people aged 0-9.

Population pyramids only have a wide base if a lot of the population is young

Scatter graphs might look similar to line graphs (see previous page), but there's a big difference — in a line graph, all the dots are joined up, whereas a scatter graph might have a line of best fit through the middle of the scatter of points.

Charts and Graphs

You've probably come across <u>pie charts</u> before, but they can be quite tricky to construct yourself.
<u>Dispersion diagrams</u> might sound less familiar — luckily, they're pretty simple to understand.

Pie Charts Show **Amounts** or **Percentages**

The important thing to remember with pie charts is that <u>the whole pie = 360°</u>.

1 Reading Pie Charts

1) To work out the <u>%</u> for a wedge of the pie, use a <u>protractor</u> to find out how large it is in <u>degrees</u>.

2) Then <u>divide</u> that number by <u>360</u> and <u>times</u> by <u>100</u>.

3) To find the <u>amount</u> a wedge of the pie is <u>worth</u>, work out your <u>percentage</u> then turn it into a <u>decimal</u>. Then times the <u>decimal</u> by the <u>total amount</u> of the pie.

Pie Chart of Transport Type

Bicycle
Bus
Car
0°
90°
126°
180°
198°
270°
324°

Q: Out of 100 people, how many used the bus?
A: 126 − 90 = 36°, so (36 ÷ 360) × 100 = 10%, so 0.1 × 100 = <u>10 people</u>.

2 Completing Pie Charts

1) To <u>draw</u> on a <u>new wedge</u> that you know the <u>%</u> for, turn the % into a <u>decimal</u> and <u>times</u> it by <u>360</u>. Then draw a wedge of that many <u>degrees</u>.

Q: Out of 100 people, 25% used a bicycle. Add this to the pie chart.
A: 25 ÷ 100 = 0.25, 0.25 × 360 = <u>90°</u>.

2) To add a <u>new wedge</u> that you know the <u>amount</u> for, <u>divide</u> your amount by the <u>total amount</u> of the pie and <u>times</u> the answer by <u>360</u>. Then <u>draw</u> on a wedge of that many <u>degrees</u>.

Q: Out of 100 people, 55 used a car. Add this to the pie chart.
A: 55 ÷ 100 = 0.55, 0.55 × 360 = <u>198°</u> (198° + 126° = <u>324°</u>).

Dispersion Diagrams Show the **Frequency** of Data

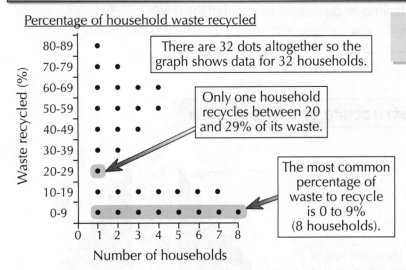

Percentage of household waste recycled

Waste recycled (%)
Number of households

There are 32 dots altogether so the graph shows data for 32 households.

Only one household recycles between 20 and 29% of its waste.

The most common percentage of waste to recycle is 0 to 9% (8 households).

1) Dispersion diagrams are a bit like a cross between a <u>tally chart</u> and a <u>bar chart</u>.

2) The <u>range</u> of <u>data that's measured</u> goes on one axis. <u>Frequency</u> goes on the other axis.

3) <u>Each dot</u> represents <u>one piece</u> of information — the <u>more dots</u> there are in a particular category, the <u>more frequently</u> that event has happened.

4) The dispersion diagram on the left shows the <u>percentage</u> of <u>household waste</u> that's <u>recycled</u> for <u>households</u> in a <u>particular village</u>.

You'll need a protractor to draw a pie chart

Make sure you remember to convert any percentages into degrees before you draw a wedge of a pie chart.

Charts and Graphs

You guessed it — there are <u>even more</u> charts and graphs to learn. These are the <u>last ones</u>, I <u>promise</u>.

Pictograms Use **Pictures** to Show **Quantities**

1) <u>Pictograms</u> use <u>symbols</u> instead of <u>numbers</u> to show frequency.

2) In a pictogram each <u>picture</u> or <u>symbol</u> represents a <u>certain number of items</u>.
   The <u>pictogram</u> below shows the <u>number of new houses</u> built in Bogdon from 2010-2015:

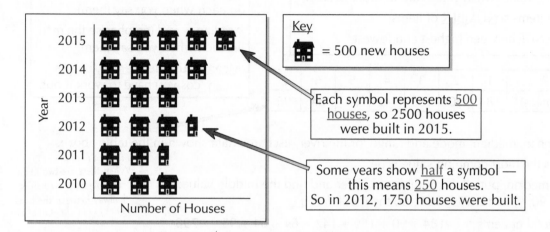

Key

🏠 = 500 new houses

Each symbol represents <u>500</u> <u>houses</u>, so 2500 houses were built in 2015.

Some years show <u>half</u> a symbol — this means <u>250</u> houses. So in 2012, 1750 houses were built.

Cross-Sections show the **Land** from **Sideways** on

1) <u>Cross-sections</u> show what the landscape looks like if it's <u>chopped</u> down the <u>middle</u> and <u>viewed</u> from the <u>side</u>.

2) In geography, they're useful for showing things like the <u>change</u> in the <u>height</u> of the land, the <u>shape</u> of a <u>river channel</u> or the <u>shape</u> of a <u>beach</u>.
   They're often presented in a <u>graph</u> with <u>height</u> and <u>distance</u> shown along the <u>x</u> and <u>y axes</u>.
   For example:

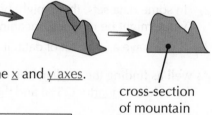

cross-section of mountain

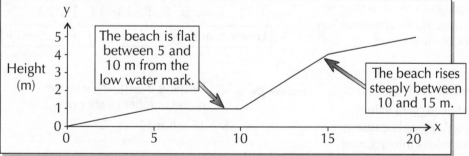

The beach is flat between 5 and 10 m from the low water mark.

The beach rises steeply between 10 and 15 m.

3) When you're <u>drawing</u> a cross-section graph, use the <u>y-axis</u> to plot the contour heights. <u>Join</u> all the points, then <u>label</u> the cross-section to show <u>features</u> of the landscape (e.g. valley sides, hilltops etc.) Don't forget to label both the <u>horizontal</u> and <u>vertical scales</u> (the x and y axes).

4) If you're <u>interpreting</u> a cross-section graph, make sure you look at both the <u>horizontal</u> and <u>vertical scales</u> carefully. Describe the <u>general trends</u>, e.g. the beach generally slopes upwards away from the sea, and then pick out the <u>key features</u>, e.g. where the land is <u>steepest</u> and where it is <u>flatter</u>.

You might have to interpret a cross-section in the exam

Cross-sections can be used show beach shape, like in the graph above, or the shape of a river valley — you might remember from p.80 that this will differ depending on whether it's the upper, middle or lower course of the river.

Statistics

You might be asked to do a bit of <u>maths</u> in the exam — it should all be <u>familiar</u> from <u>maths lessons</u>...

Learn the Definitions for **Mode, Median, Mean** and **Range**...

<u>Mode</u>, <u>median</u> and <u>mean</u> are measures of <u>average</u> and the <u>range</u> is how <u>spread out</u> the values are:

<u>MODE</u> = <u>MOST</u> common
<u>MEDIAN</u> = <u>MIDDLE</u> value (when values are in order of size)
<u>MEAN</u> = <u>TOTAL</u> of items ÷ <u>NUMBER</u> of items
<u>RANGE</u> = <u>DIFFERENCE</u> between highest and lowest

REMEMBER:
Mo<u>de</u> = <u>mo</u>st (emphasise the 'mo' in each when you say them)
Me<u>dian</u> = <u>mid</u> (emphasise the m*d in each when you say them)
<u>Mean</u> is just the <u>average</u>, but it's mean 'cos you have to work it out.

Sample	1	2	3	4	5	6	7
River discharge (cumecs)	184	90	159	142	64	64	95

Q: Calculate the mean, median, mode and range for the river discharge data shown in the table above.

A: • The mode is the most common value = <u>64</u>.
   • To find the median, put all the numbers in order and find the middle value:
     64, 64, 90, <u>95</u>, 142, 159, 184. So the median is <u>95</u>.

When there are two middle numbers, the median is halfway between the two.

   • Mean = $\dfrac{\text{total of items}}{\text{number of items}}$ = $\dfrac{184 + 90 + 159 + 142 + 64 + 64 + 95}{7}$ = $\dfrac{798}{7}$ = <u>114</u>

   • The range is the difference between highest and lowest value, i.e. 184 – 64 = <u>120</u>

1) Each of these methods has <u>weaknesses</u>. The <u>mean</u> and the <u>range</u> are affected by any <u>outliers</u> (values that are a lot <u>bigger</u> or <u>smaller</u> than most of the other values) — this reduces their <u>accuracy</u>.

2) In some data sets, there might be <u>more than one mode</u> — or each value might be <u>different</u>, meaning there <u>isn't</u> a mode.

3) If you have a <u>large</u> set of data, it takes <u>longer</u> to calculate the <u>median</u>.

As well as finding the <u>median</u> (the middle value in a list), you can also find the <u>upper</u> and <u>lower quartiles</u> — the values a <u>quarter</u> (25%) and <u>three-quarters</u> (75%) of the way through the <u>ordered data</u>.

Q: The number of shoppers in each shop in a village were counted. Find the median and the quartiles of the data set.

A: 2, 3, 6, 6, 7, 9, 13, 14, 17, 22, 22
   Lower quartile | Median | Upper quartile

1) The <u>interquartile range</u> is the <u>difference between</u> the <u>upper quartile</u> and the <u>lower quartile</u>.

2) It contains the middle <u>50%</u> of values — this is one of its <u>weaknesses</u> because it <u>doesn't</u> take <u>all</u> the values into account.

Q: Find the interquartile range of the number of shoppers.
A: 17 – 6 = <u>11</u>

You also Need to **Know** How to Find the **Modal Class**

If your data is <u>grouped</u> you might need to find the <u>modal class</u>. This is just the <u>group</u> with the <u>most values</u> in.

Q: Find the modal class of the population data shown in the table.
A: Modal class = <u>20-39 years</u>

Age	Number of people
0-19	21
20-39	37
40-59	27
60+	15

Remember, the modal class will be the group — not how many items are in that group.

EXAM TIP

Read the question carefully and check your answer

There are some easy marks up for grabs here as long as you calculate the right figure — don't miss out on them by working out the median rather than the mean, or typing the wrong number into your calculator.

Statistics

You're not quite done with <u>maths</u> — you might have to deal with <u>percentages</u> and <u>percentiles</u> in the exam.

You Need to be Able to **Calculate Percentages** and **Percentage Change...**

To give the amount X as a <u>percentage</u> of a sample Y, you need to <u>divide</u> X by Y and <u>multiply by 100</u>.

> Q: This year, 35 out of the 270 houses in Foxley were burgled.
> Calculate the percentage of houses burgled in Foxley.
>
> A: $35 \div 270 \times 100$
> $= \underline{13\%}$

Calculating <u>percentage change</u> lets you work out <u>how much</u> something has <u>increased</u> or <u>decreased</u>.
You use this <u>formula</u>:

> $$\text{Percentage change} = \frac{\text{final value} - \text{original value}}{\text{original value}} \times 100$$

> A <u>positive</u> value shows an <u>increase</u> and a <u>negative</u> value shows a <u>decrease</u>.

> Q: Last year in Foxley, only 24 houses were burgled. Calculate the percentage change in burglaries in Foxley.
> A: $\dfrac{35 - 24}{24} \times 100 = \underline{46\%}$ increase in the number of burglaries in Foxley.

Percentiles Tell You **Where** in Your **Data Set** a **Data Point** Lies

1) Percentiles are useful if you want to compare the value of <u>one data point</u> to the <u>rest</u> of your data.

2) To find a percentile, you <u>rank</u> your data from smallest to largest, then <u>divide</u> it into <u>one hundred equal chunks</u>. Each chunk is <u>one percentile</u>.

3) This means that each percentile represents <u>one percent</u> of the data, and so the <u>value of a percentile</u> tells you what <u>percentage</u> of the data has a value <u>lower than</u> the data points in that percentile.

> E.g. A stone is in the <u>90th percentile</u> for <u>weight</u> in its section of the river bed. This means that <u>90%</u> of the stones are <u>lighter</u> than it.

4) Percentiles can be used to give a more realistic idea of the <u>spread</u> of data than the <u>range</u> — by finding the range between the <u>10th</u> and <u>90th percentiles</u> in a data set (the middle 80% of the data), you can look at the spread of the data while ignoring any <u>outlying</u> results.

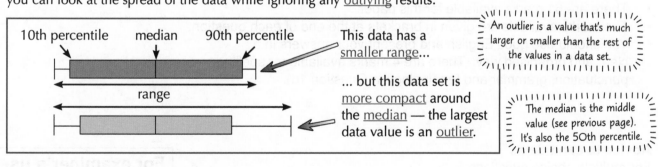

An outlier is a value that's much larger or smaller than the rest of the values in a data set.

This data has a <u>smaller range</u>...

... but this data set is <u>more compact</u> around the <u>median</u> — the largest data value is an <u>outlier</u>.

The median is the middle value (see previous page). It's also the 50th percentile.

5) Percentiles have a couple of <u>weaknesses</u>:

- Any <u>outliers</u> in the data set are given the <u>highest</u> or <u>lowest percentile</u>.
- If a lot of the data is <u>very close</u> to the mean, any <u>differences</u> are <u>exaggerated</u> by percentiles.

A data point's percentile tells you how much of the data set has a lower value

And there we have it — you've finished the last page of revision. When you're ready, have a go at tackling the mini set of exam practice papers that start on the next page. They'll help you get a feel of what the real exam will be like.

Practice Exams

Once you've been through all the questions in this book, you should feel pretty confident about the exams.
As final preparation, here is a mini set of **practice exams** to give you a taste of what the exams will be like.
Each of your real exam papers will be longer than these, but they will follow a very similar structure.

CGP Practice Exam Paper
GCSE Geography

GCSE Geography

Paper 1: Global Geographical Issues

In addition to this paper you should have:
• A calculator.

Centre name			
Centre number			
Candidate number			

Time allowed:
• 1 hour

Surname	
Other names	
Candidate signature	

Instructions to candidates
• Use black ink.
• Write your name and other details in the spaces provided above.
• Answer **all** questions in the spaces provided.
• In calculations, show your working out and clearly identify your answer.

Information for candidates
• There are 61 marks available for this paper.
• The marks available are given in brackets at the end of each question.
• You should use good English and present your answers in a
  clear and organised way. There are 4 marks available for spelling,
  punctuation, grammar and terminology in Question 1d).

Advice to candidates
For multiple choice questions:
• Clearly shade the oval next to your chosen answer. For example:
• If you wish to change your answer, put a cross through your original
  answer. For example:
• If you wish to change your answer to one that you have previously
  crossed out, draw a circle around the answer. For example:

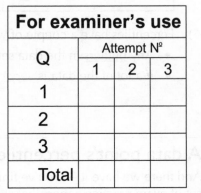

For examiner's use

Q	Attempt Nº		
	1	2	3
1			
2			
3			
Total			

Section A: Hazardous Earth
Answer **all** the questions in this section.

1 Study **Figure 1**, a map of the world showing bands of high and low pressure and surface winds.

Figure 1

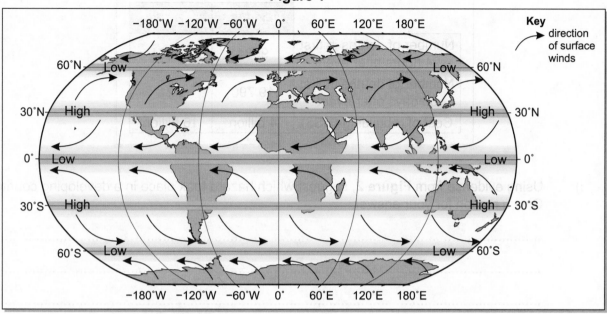

a) i) Which of the statements below best describes the movement of air at the equator?

A Air rises up. ⬭

B Air sinks down. ⬭

C Air moves up and down. ⬭

D Air is still and does not move. ⬭

[1]

ii) Which of the following descriptions matches the normal weather conditions at a high pressure belt?

A Low rainfall, often cloudy. ⬭

B High rainfall, often cloudy. ⬭

C Low rainfall, rarely cloudy. ⬭

D High rainfall, rarely cloudy. ⬭

[1]

iii) Identify the latitude which receives the most solar radiation.

....
[1]

iv) Explain how atmospheric circulation distributes heat energy from the equator to the poles.

....

....

....

....

....
[4]

Turn over ▶

b) **Figure 2** shows the effects of **two** tectonic hazards in different parts of the world.
One occurred in a developing country and one occurred in a developed country.

Figure 2

	Hazard A	Hazard B
Number of deaths in first 24 hours after event	9084	208
Number of deaths in first 30 days after event	19 790	221
Cost of rebuilding (US$)	4 billion	16 billion

i) Using evidence from **Figure 2**, suggest which hazard took place in a developing country.
Give a reason for your answer.

....

....

....
[2]

ii) Calculate the ratio of the cost of rebuilding after Hazard A to
the cost of rebuilding after Hazard B.

....
[1]

c) Scientists monitor gases and ground vibrations in tectonically active areas.
Explain how this helps them to predict tectonic hazards.

....

....

....
[2]

d) 'Preparation reduces the impact of tectonic hazards.' Assess this statement using
examples of hazards in countries of contrasting levels of development.

[8 + 4 SPaG]

[Total 24 marks]

Section B: Development Dynamics
Answer **all** the questions in this section.

2   Study **Figure 3**, which shows Rostow's modernisation theory
of the stages of economic development.

Figure 3

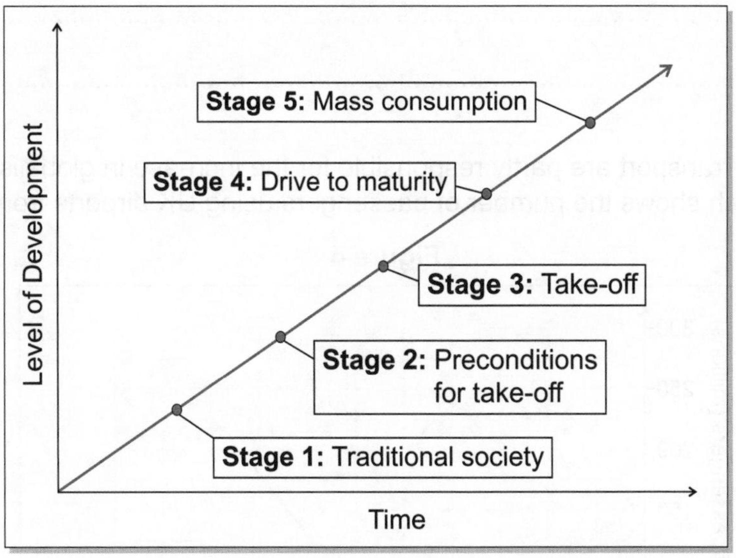

a)   i)   Which of the following features is a defining characteristic
of Stage 3 of Rostow's modernisation theory?

    A   Widespread use of technology.   ◯

    B   Subsistence farming.   ◯

    C   Manufacturing starts to develop.   ◯

    D   Large-scale industrialisation.   ◯

[1]

   ii)   Which statement best describes Stage 4 of Rostow's modernisation theory?

    A   Manufacturing industries begin to develop, along with the infrastructure
needed to support them.   ◯

    B   The population becomes increasingly wealthy, the use of technology
increases and standards of living rise.   ◯

    C   The economy is largely subsistence-based and there is very little
international trade.   ◯

    D   Goods are mass produced, and the wealthy population
means that levels of consumption are very high.   ◯

[1]

   iii) Frank's dependency theory suggests that neo-colonialism is holding development back in
some countries. What is meant by 'neo-colonialism'?

....

....

[1]

Turn over ▶

iv) Explain why neo-colonialism may hinder development according to Frank's dependency theory.

....

....

....

....

....

[4]

b) Improvements in air transport are partly responsible for the increase in globalisation. Study **Figure 4**, which shows the number of passengers using UK airports from 1960 to 2015.

Figure 4

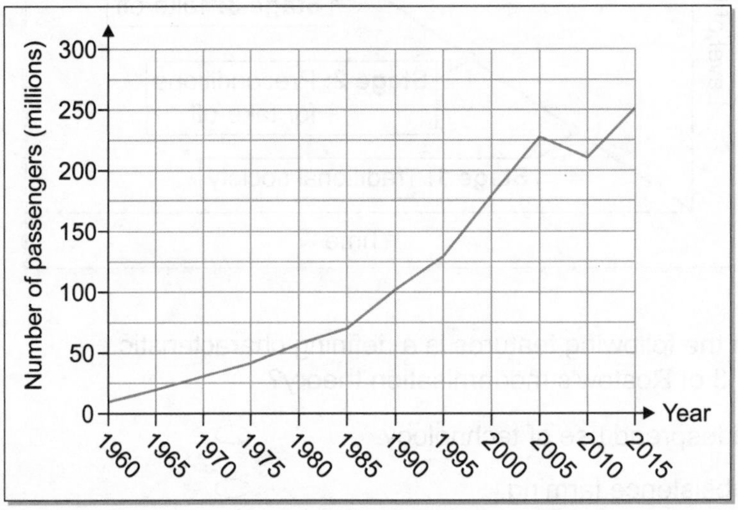

i) Using **Figure 4**, calculate the difference between the number of passengers using UK airports in 1960 and in 2000.

....

[1]

ii) Suggest how improvements in air travel have increased globalisation.

....

....

....

[2]

c) Some people think that globalisation is increasing global inequalities. Development strategies can help to reduce global inequalities. These strategies can be described as 'top-down' or 'bottom-up'. Which of the following statements best describes 'bottom-up' development strategies?

A Strategies where transnational corporations direct projects designed to increase development with little or no input from local communities. ◯

B Strategies which usually use high-tech equipment and machinery, often operated by skilled workers from developed countries. ◯

C Strategies funded by governments or companies to aid development with the aim of generating profit. ◯

D Strategies where local people and communities decide on ways to improve things for their own community. ◯

[1]

d)   Development strategies are often led by NGOs. What is an NGO?

....
[1]

e)   Large-scale infrastructure projects may be funded by inter-governmental organisations (IGOs) or transnational corporations (TNCs). Give **one** benefit for the recipient country of infrastructure projects funded by IGOs or TNCs.

....

....
[1]

f)   Explain the disadvantages of 'top-down' strategies for the recipient country.

....

....

....

....

....

....
[4]

[Total 17 marks]

Section C: Challenges of an Urbanising World
Answer **all** the questions in this section.

3   The populations of many megacities in developing and emerging countries are growing rapidly.

a)   i)   Which of the following statements is correct?

A   Megacities have a population of less than 10 000 people.   ◯

B   Megacities have a population of less than 1 million people.   ◯

C   Megacities have a population of more than 10 million people.   ◯

D   Megacities have a population of more than 100 million people.   ◯
[1]

ii)   State **two** locational factors that can influence the growth of a megacity.

1:...

2:...
[2]

Turn over ▶

iii) Explain why the population is growing rapidly in a megacity in an emerging or a developing country you have studied.

....

....

....

....

....

[4]

b) Study **Figure 5**, an extract from a website promoting the Can-Can Squatter Settlement Redevelopment Project, a bottom-up strategy being run in a megacity in an emerging country.

Figure 5

The Can-Can Squatter Settlement Redevelopment Project started in 2006 to help improve life for residents of this squatter settlement. The project involves self-help and local authority schemes including the installation of a sewage disposal system. The project also aims to improve quality of life by improving health care and education.

Year	Literacy rate	% people in work	% people with access to clean water	No. of people per doctor	Average life expectancy
1995	3%	27	33	2000	49
2005	3%	26	36	2000	49
2015	37%	69	73	500	57

i) By how much did life expectancy increase between 1995 and 2015?

....

[1]

ii) State **one** disadvantage of 'bottom-up strategies' being used in megacities.

....

....

[1]

iii) Use evidence from **Figure 5** to describe the success of the Can-Can project.

....

....

....

....

[2]

c) Study **Figure 6**, a diagram showing land use in a model megacity in an emerging country.

Figure 6

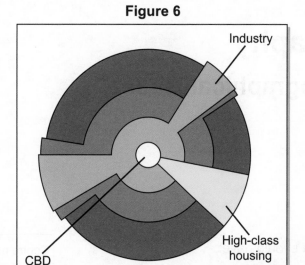

i) Label the diagram in **Figure 6** to show where the oldest buildings are likely to be found.

[1]

ii) Identify the part of a city where rapid growth is most likely to be taking place.

....

[1]

iii) Identify the part of a city where high density low-quality housing is most likely to be found.

....

[1]

iv) Suggest **one** reason for the location of industry in **Figure 6**.

....

....

....

[2]

d) Describe **two** ways that rapid population growth has led to a change in land use in a megacity in an emerging or developing country that you have studied.

1: ....

....

....

2: ....

....

....

[4]

[Total 20 marks]

END OF QUESTIONS

GCSE Geography
Paper 2: UK Geographical Issues

In addition to this paper you should have:
- A calculator.

Centre name				
Centre number				
Candidate number				

Time allowed:
- 1 hour

Surname
Other names
Candidate signature

Instructions to candidates
- Use black ink.
- Write your name and other details in the spaces provided above.
- Answer **all** questions in **Sections A** and **B**.
- In **Section C1** answer either **Question 8** or **Question 9**.
- Answer **all** the questions in **Section C2**.
- In calculations, show your working out and clearly identify your answer.

Information for candidates
- There are 63 marks available for this paper.
- The marks available are given in brackets at the end of each question.
- You should use good English and present your answers in a clear and organised way. There are 4 marks available for spelling, punctuation, grammar and terminology in Question 7.

Advice to candidates
For multiple choice questions:
- Clearly shade the oval next to your chosen answer. For example: ⬤
- If you wish to change your answer, put a cross through your original answer. For example: ⊗
- If you wish to change your answer to one that you have previously crossed out, draw a circle around the answer. For example: ⊗

		For examiner's use						
Q	Attempt Nº			**Q**	Attempt Nº		
	1	2	3		1	2	3
1				7			
2				8			
3				9			
4				10			
5				Total			
6							

Section A: The UK's Evolving Physical Landscape
Answer **all** the questions in this section.

1 Study **Figure 1**, which shows the distribution of different rock types in the UK.

a) Which **two** of the following statements are true of metamorphic rocks?

Figure 1

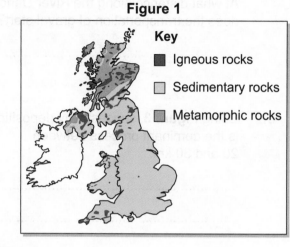

Key
■ Igneous rocks
□ Sedimentary rocks
▨ Metamorphic rocks

A   All metamorphic rocks are permeable.   ○

B   Carboniferous limestone is an example of a metamorphic rock.   ○

C   Metamorphic rocks are formed when other rocks are changed by heat and pressure.   ○

D   Metamorphic rocks are very soft and are easily weathered.   ○

E   Metamorphic rocks are harder and more compact than sedimentary rocks.   ○

[2]

b) Using **Figure 2**, describe the distribution of igneous rocks in the UK.

....

....

....

[2]

[Total 4 marks]

Coastal Change and Conflict

2 Study **Figure 2**, an Ordnance Survey® map of a coastal area in Devon.

Figure 2

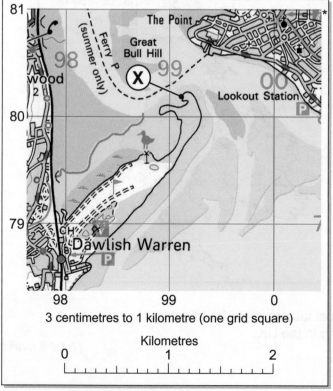

3 centimetres to 1 kilometre (one grid square)

Kilometres
0   1   2

*© Crown copyright 2018 OS 100034841

a) The end of the spit is marked X on **Figure 2**. Give the six figure grid reference for the end of the spit.

....

[1]

b) Explain how the spit shown in **Figure 2** was formed.

....

....

....

....

....

....

[2]

[Total 3 marks]

Turn over ▶

River Processes and Pressures

3 Study **Figure 3**, which shows how river velocity and particle size vary along the River Dance.

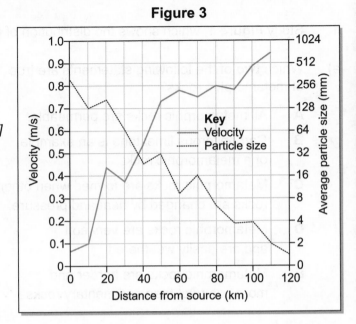

Figure 3

a) Small gravel particles are transported by velocities above 0.1 m per second.
At what distance along the River Dance does the transportation of gravel start?

....
[1]

b) Using **Figure 3**, suggest why deposition is the dominant process between 20 and 30 km.

....

....

....

....

....

[2]

[Total 3 marks]

Investigating a UK Geographical Issue

4 Study **Figure 4**, a map of the UK showing the location of major rivers and areas of possible flood risk, and **Figure 5**, showing population density in the UK.

Figure 4

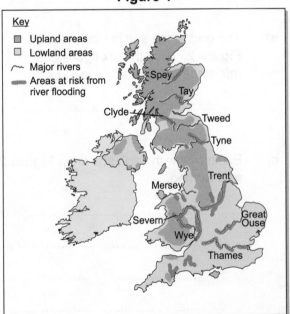

Figure 5

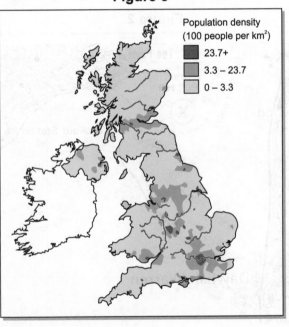

Assess the extent to which human and physical factors might be affecting the number of people at risk from river flooding in the UK.

[Total 8 marks]

Section B: The UK's Evolving Human Landscape
Answer **all** the questions in this section.

5 Study **Figure 6**, a table showing net international migration into the UK between 2001 and 2015.

Figure 6

	Net international migration
2001	153 200
2002	190 900
2003	194 200
2004	209 900
2005	336 000
2006	254 800
2007	304 900
2008	284 100
2009	220 100
2010	255 600
2011	270 500
2012	165 500
2013	188 500
2014	264 900
2015	341 400

a) Using **Figure 6**, calculate the range of the net international migration values.

....

[1]

b) Explain how international migration has altered the age structure of the UK.

....

....

....

....

....

....

....

[4]

c) State **two** trends in national migration in the UK.

1: ....

2: ....

[2]

[Total 7 marks]

Turn over ▶

Dynamic UK Cities

6 Migration can influence the character of a city.

a) Explain the patterns of migration for a named UK city.

....

....

....

....

....

[4]

b) For a UK city that you have studied, describe **two** ways in which migration into the city has affected its character.

1:..

....

....

2:..

....

....

[4]

[Total 8 marks]

Investigating a UK Geographical Issue

7 Analyse **Figure 7**, which shows the Index of Multiple Deprivation (IMD) ranking of different areas in the West Midlands. The IMD ranks every neighbourhood in England, with the most deprived having a rank of 1. The table also shows where these neighbourhoods rank in England for employment, health and housing and services deprivation.

Figure 7

Location	IMD Rank	Employment deprivation Rank	Health deprivation Rank	Housing and services deprivation Rank
Aston (inner city)	668	324	6747	235
Kings Heath (suburb)	7392	11 124	8712	16 684
Hampton-in-Arden (commuter village)	30 336	30 571	29 492	11 417
Diddlebury (rural village)	12 311	24 319	23 657	177

Assess the reasons for variation in IMD in cities and their surrounding areas.

[8 + 4 SPaG]

[Total 12 marks]

Section C1: Geographical Investigations: Fieldwork in a Physical Environment
Answer either **Question 8** or **Question 9** in this section.

Investigating Coastal Change and Conflict

8   You have carried out fieldwork in a coastal environment.

Name your coastal environment fieldwork location.

....

a)   Using an annotated diagram, explain the effectiveness of
one coastal management measure you studied.

[4]

A student wanted to investigate how the cross-profile of a beach is affected by
different coastal management strategies along the shore. **Figure 8** shows the
method she used to find the cross-profile of the beach. She measured the
profile at three points along the beach. The results are shown in **Figure 9**.

Figure 8

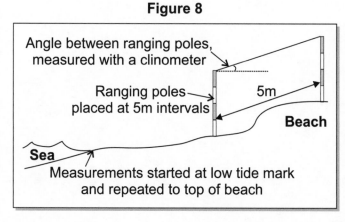

Figure 9

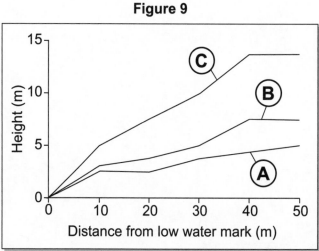

Turn over ▶

b)   Describe **two** possible sources of inaccuracy in the method used.

1: ....
....

2: ....
....

[2]

c)   Suggest how the student might have chosen the points along the beach at which to measure the cross-profiles.

....
....

[2]

[Total 8 marks]

Investigating River Processes and Pressures

9   You have carried out fieldwork in a river environment.

Name your river environment fieldwork location.

....

a)   Using an annotated diagram, explain **one** factor influencing the flood risk at the river you studied.

[4]

As part of a fieldwork enquiry into factors influencing flood risk, a student collected data on river velocity. He placed a float in the river and recorded the time taken for the float to travel 10 metres downstream. The results are shown in **Figure 10**.

Figure 10

b) State **one** appropriate item that could be used as the float. Give **one** reason for your answer.

Sample	Time (s)
1	315
2	255
3	278
4	310
5	947
6	302
7	279
8	297

Item:..

Reason: ....

....

....

[1]

c) Identify the sample in the data that is an anomaly.

....

[1]

d) Suggest **one** possible reason for the anomaly.

....

....

....

[2]

[Total 8 marks]

Section C2: Geographical Investigations: Fieldwork in a Human Environment
Answer **all** the questions in this section.

Investigating Dynamic Urban Areas or Changing Rural Areas

10 You have carried out fieldwork investigating variations in the quality of life in **either** an urban **or** a rural area.

Name your urban/rural environment fieldwork location.

....

a) Explain why you used **one** of the primary data collection techniques involved in your enquiry.

Primary data collection technique: ....

Explanation:...

....

....

[2]

b) Evaluate the suitability of the sites you chose for data collection.

[8]

[Total 10 marks]

END OF QUESTIONS

GCSE Geography

Paper 3: People and Environment Issues —
Making Geographical Decisions

In addition to this paper you should have:
*   A calculator.

Centre name				
Centre number				
Candidate number				

Time allowed:
*   52 minutes

Surname	
Other names	
Candidate signature	

Instructions to candidates
*   Use black ink.
*   Write your name and other details in the spaces provided above.
*   Answer **all** questions in the spaces provided.
*   In calculations, show your working out and clearly identify your answer.

Information for candidates
*   There are 37 marks available for this paper.
*   The marks available are given in brackets at the end of each question.
*   You should use good English and present your answers in a
    clear and organised way. There are 4 marks available for spelling,
    punctuation, grammar and terminology in Question 4.

Resource Booklet

The issue: tar sands production in the Canadian taiga forest

There are more than 300 million hectares of taiga forest in Canada, covering roughly 35% of the country. One of the biggest threats to the forest is the exploitation of the tar sand deposits in Alberta. Almost three quarters of Canada's indigenous communities live within the taiga forest and their traditional way of life is being threatened by mining activities. However, the tar sands have an important economic value to Canada and mining developments are expanding as more and more companies are investing in the area.

Figure 1: Map of taiga forests

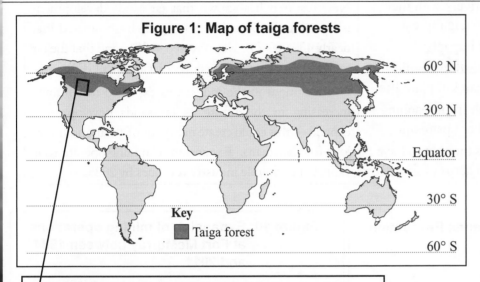

Key

Taiga forest

Figure 3: Trees found in a taiga forest

Figure 2: Tar Sand Deposits and Mining Area

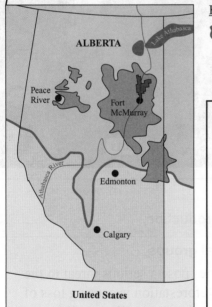

Key

Canadian taiga forest

Tar sand deposits

Surface mining area

Figure 4: Human Use of Taiga Forest

Trees are felled for house and furniture building and to make paper. Indigenous communities rely on the taiga forest for food, water and traditional medicines.

Figure 5: Oil Extraction

The tar sands are the world's third largest proven oil reserve and lie under the taiga forest. The sands contain bitumen, which can be refined to produce oil. Sand is collected in surface mines and is then taken to processing plants where the bitumen is extracted using a mixture of chemicals and water.

Figure 6: A snowshoe hare

Turn over ▶

Figure 7: Renewable Energy in Canada

Almost a fifth of Canada's primary energy is generated from renewable sources.

Hydroelectric Power (HEP)

Canada is a major world producer of HEP. There are over 600 hydroelectric dams in the country, many of which are on rivers with their source in or flowing through the taiga forest.

HEP has several environmental impacts:

- Changes in water flow can lead to a build-up of silt in reservoirs, which can kill plant life.
- Dams prevent migratory fish from reaching their breeding grounds further upstream.
- The creation of reservoirs is thought to have destroyed almost 13 million acres of forest.

Figure 8: Newspaper article

DAILY NEWS
SEPTEMBER 2014

TAR SANDS PLAY IMPORTANT ROLE IN CANADIAN ECONOMY

New research has shown that tar sands development is boosting the Canadian economy. It's estimated that nearly 480,000 jobs were created in 2012 and that the tar sands industry represented 5% of Canada's GDP.

Investment in the industry is expected to continue increasing in the future as tar sands developments expand — this could create hundreds of thousands more jobs for Canadians. Expansion of mining operations is expected to double industry revenues by 2025.

Figure 9: Growth in Tar Sands Production

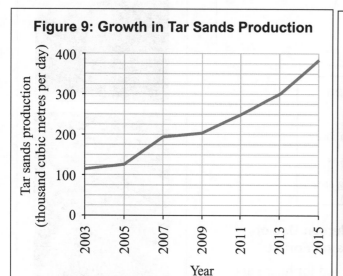

Figure 10: Expansion of mining operations at Fort McMurray between 1984 and 2011

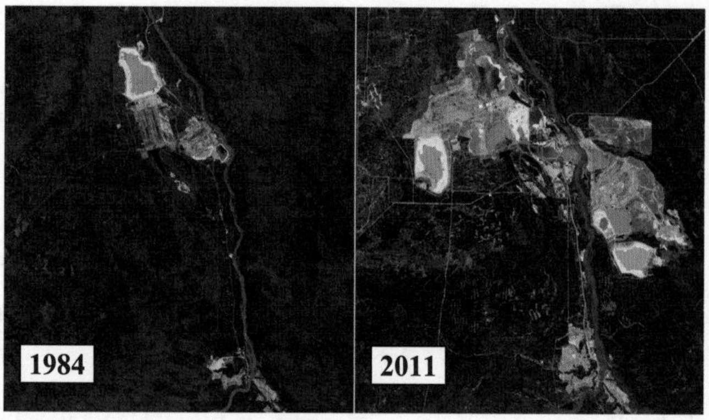

Figure 11: Attitudes towards tar sands production

Tar sands production company

"The extraction processes we use are carefully monitored to ensure we cause as little environmental damage as possible. We have a responsibility to protect the land for the future."

Environmental groups

"Tar sands mines pose a serious threat to the taiga forest. Deforestation is causing loss of habitat and the mines are polluting rivers and other water courses."

Government official

"The tar sands are an important sector of the economy and help to provide jobs for thousands of people. Without them, we'd lose lots of investment in goods and infrastructure."

Indigenous communities

"The toxic emissions from the mines are causing serious health problems in our communities. We rely on the forest for food and water, but it's being replaced by mines."

Section A: People and the Biosphere
Answer **all** questions in this section.

1   Study **Figure 1**, a map showing the distribution of taiga forests, part of the boreal biome.

a)   Using **Figure 1**, describe the global distribution of taiga forests.

....

....

....
[2]

b)   Tundra environments are found to the north of taiga forests.
Describe the climate in tundra environments.

....

....

....
[2]
[Total 4 marks]

Section B: Forests Under Threat
Answer **all** questions in this section.

2   Study **Figure 3**, photographs of trees found in taiga forests,
and **Figure 6**, a photograph of a snowshoe hare.

a)   Explain **two** ways in which the trees shown in **Figure 3** are adapted to their habitat.

1: ....

....

2: ....

....
[4]

b)   Explain **one** way in which the snowshoe hare shown in **Figure 6** is adapted to its habitat.

....

....
[2]

c)   Explain **two** other ways in which animals can be adapted to survive in the taiga forest ecosystem.

1: ....

....

2: ....

....
[4]

Turn over ▶

d)   Describe **one** example of interdependence between plants and animals in taiga forests.

....

....
                                                                                                            [2]
                                                                                              [Total 12 marks]

Section C: Consuming Energy Resources
Answer **all** questions in this section.

3   Many countries rely heavily on fossil fuels for their energy rather than having a diverse energy mix.

a)   Explain how diversifying the energy mix can improve energy security.

....

....

....

....
                                                                                                            [3]

b)   Study **Figure 9**, a graph showing the growth in tar sands production in Alberta, Canada.
     Calculate the percentage change in tar sands production between 2005 and 2013.

....
                                                                                                            [2]
                                                                                               [Total 5 marks]

Section D: Making a geographical decision

4   Study the **three** options below for how Canada should develop energy sources in the taiga forest.

     Option 1: Continue exploiting the tar sand deposits to create more job opportunities and
                    further economic growth in Canada.

     Option 2: Place restrictions on the development of tar sands, introduce measures to reduce
                    environmental damage and invest more money in sustainable energy sources.

     Option 3: Stop the development of tar sands and promote the production of
                    hydroelectric power in the taiga forest.

     Select the option that you think would be the best **long-term** decision for Canada.
     Justify your choice using evidence from the information provided in the Resource Booklet
     and your own knowledge.
                                                                                                    [12 + 4 SPaG]
                                                                                              [Total 16 marks]

END OF QUESTIONS

Topic 1 — Hazardous Earth

Page 10

1 a) Temperature has changed in cycles of approximately 100 000 years *[1 mark]*. The temperature difference ranges between -9 °C and +3 °C from the present day *[1 mark]*.

b) Ice sheets are made up of layers of ice, with one new layer formed each year *[1 mark]*. By analysing the gases trapped in the layers of ice, scientists can tell what the temperature was in each year *[1 mark]*.

c) E.g. changes in the Earth's orbit affect the amount of solar radiation/energy that the Earth receives *[1 mark]*. Periods of warming could have been caused by the Earth receiving more solar energy as it came closer to the Sun *[1 mark]*. / The Sun's output of energy changes in short cycles of about 11 years *[1 mark]*, so periods of cooling could have been caused by periods of reduced solar output *[1 mark]*.

You could also have written about material released from volcanic eruptions or thrown up by asteroid collisions reflecting the Sun's rays back out to space, meaning that less energy reached the Earth.

d) Any two from: e.g. diary entries *[1 mark]* often have details of harvest dates and the number of days of snow or rain *[1 mark]*. / Paintings *[1 mark]* provide a visual record of what the weather was like in the past *[1 mark]*. / Tree rings *[1 mark]* because their width shows how warm or cold the climate was at different times *[1 mark]*.

Page 18

1 a) A *[1 mark]*

b) Predicting where and when a tropical cyclone will hit gives people in Miami time to evacuate, so fewer people will be injured or killed *[1 mark]*. It also gives people time to protect their homes and businesses, e.g. by boarding up windows, so there will be less damage to property *[1 mark]*.

c) E.g. sea walls can be built along the coast *[1 mark]* to prevent damage from storm surges *[1 mark]*. Buildings could be put on stilts *[1 mark]* to reduce the damage caused by floodwater *[1 mark]*.

d) Any three from: e.g. buildings in developing countries are of poorer quality than in developed countries so are more easily damaged *[1 mark]*. / Healthcare in developing countries isn't as good as in developed countries, so developing countries may struggle to treat all the casualties *[1 mark]*. / Developing countries have less money for flood defences than developed countries because of poor infrastructure *[1 mark]*. / People in developing countries are less likely to have insurance to cover the cost of damage than those in developed countries *[1 mark]*.

e) This question is level marked.
How to grade your answer:
Level 0: There is no relevant information. *[0 marks]*
Level 1: There are a few points about the effectiveness of the preparation methods used. *[1-2 marks]*
Level 2: There is a clear evaluation of the effectiveness of the preparation methods used. *[3-5 marks]*
Level 3: There is a detailed evaluation of the effectiveness of the preparation methods used. *[6-8 marks]*

Your answer must refer to named examples.
Here are some points your answer may include:
- A brief description of the level of development in your chosen countries.
- The preparation methods that are used by each country, e.g. forecasting, evacuation and physical defences.
- An assessment of how successful these preparation methods are in reducing the impacts of tropical cyclones.
- You could refer to a specific tropical cyclone in your answer.
- E.g. you could refer to the USA and how it prepared for Hurricane Katrina. The USA had a sophisticated monitoring system in place, which effectively predicted that the hurricane was coming. This allowed time to evacuate 70-80% of New Orleans residents before it hit land, which reduced the number of casualties. The flood defences in New Orleans were not effective, as they failed and over 80% of the city was flooded.
- E.g. you could refer to Myanmar and how it prepared for Cyclone Nargis. The government was only warned 48 hours before Cyclone Nargis hit, and there were no emergency preparation plans. Warnings were issued on TV and radio, but this wasn't an effective strategy because many people in poor rural communities did not receive these. Mangrove forests protected the coast from flooding to some extent, but many had been chopped down in the decade before Nargis hit, reducing the effectiveness of this defence method.

Page 27

1 a) Tension builds up as one plate gets stuck as it moves down past the other into the mantle *[1 mark]*. The plates eventually jerk past each other *[1 mark]*, sending out shock waves *[1 mark]*.

b) D *[1 mark]*

Deep-focus earthquakes have a focus between 70 km and 700 km below the Earth's surface. They tend to do less damage than shallow-focus earthquakes because shock waves have to travel through more rock to reach the surface, so they lose power.

c) Shallow-focus earthquakes under the sea cause the seabed to move *[1 mark]*, which displaces large amounts of water, causing waves to spread out from the epicentre *[1 mark]*.

2 a) The lava that comes out of shield volcanoes is runny *[1 mark]*. This means the lava flows quickly down the sides and spreads over a wide area, forming a low, flat volcano *[1 mark]*.

b) Any three from: e.g. shield volcanoes are low and flat, whereas composite volcanoes are steep sided *[1 mark]*. / Composite volcanoes are made of layers of lava and ash, whereas shield volcanoes are made of layers of lava only *[1 mark]*. / Composite volcanoes erupt thick andesitic lava, whereas shield volcanoes erupt runny basaltic lava *[1 mark]*. / Composite volcanoes have explosive eruptions, whereas shield volcanoes are not very explosive *[1 mark]*.

Topic 2 — Development Dynamics

Page 36

1 a) Any one from: e.g. birth rates are often higher in less developed countries than in more developed countries *[1 mark]* because education about contraception is often limited in less developed countries *[1 mark]*. / Birth rates are often higher in less developed countries than in more developed countries *[1 mark]* because lower standards of health care in less developed countries mean that many infants die, so women have more children *[1 mark]*.

b) E.g. individual indicators can be misleading if they are used on their own because as a country develops, some aspects develop before others *[1 mark]*. HDI is calculated using several different indicators, so it is likely to give a much more accurate idea of how developed a country is *[1 mark]*.

c) E.g. the Corruption Perceptions Index (CPI) *[1 mark]* is a measure of the level of corruption in the public sector on a scale of 1-100 where a lower score indicates more corruption *[1 mark]*. Less developed countries generally have more corruption, so a lower CPI score *[1 mark]*.

d) Canada is the most developed country *[1 mark]*. Any two from: e.g. it has a higher GNI per capita than Malaysia or Angola, suggesting that its citizens are wealthy *[1 mark]*. / Canada has relatively low birth and infant mortality rates and a high life expectancy, suggesting that health care there is good *[1 mark]*. / It has a higher literacy rate than the other countries, suggesting that it has a successful education system *[1 mark]*.

Page 45

1 a) A *[1 mark]*
Rural areas in emerging countries often benefit less from economic development than urban areas. This means that access to health care, education and well-paid employment is usually worse in rural areas.

b) The growth in manufacturing and services associated with economic development is often concentrated in urban areas more than rural areas *[1 mark]*. This means that the GDP per capita increases more in urban areas because that's where new and better paid jobs are created *[1 mark]*.

c) E.g. the literacy rate is usually lower in areas of an emerging country where access to education is lower *[1 mark]*. Access to education is usually lower in more rural areas, which benefit less economically from development *[1 mark]*.

You could also write about children in rural areas having less access to education because they're more likely to need to work to make money for the family rather than go to school.

d) Your answer will vary depending on the country you have chosen. E.g. in India, the proportion of young people in the population is high but falling *[1 mark]*, because birth rates are high but beginning to fall due to growing wealth and better education *[1 mark]*. The proportion of people over 60 is increasing *[1 mark]*, because death rates are falling due to better health care and health education *[1 mark]*.

e) This question is level marked. There are 4 extra marks available for spelling, punctuation and grammar. How to grade your answer:

Level 0: There is no relevant information. *[0 marks]*

Level 1: There is a basic description of the positive or negative impacts of development on one or two groups of people. *[1-3 marks]*

Level 2: There is a clear explanation of the positive and negative impacts of development on several groups of people. There is an attempt to draw conclusions. *[4-6 marks]*

Level 3: There is a detailed and comprehensive discussion about the positive and negative impacts of development on different groups of people across the population. There is a clear conclusion, supported with evidence. *[7-8 marks]*

Make sure your spelling, punctuation and grammar is consistently correct, that your meaning is clear and that you use a range of geographical terms correctly *[0-4 marks]*.

Your answer must refer to a named example. Here are some points your answer may include:

• A number of positive and negative impacts of development on different groups of people in a named emerging country.

• Reasoned conclusions which evaluate the impact of development on different groups of the population.

- Your answer could refer to India, where young people have benefitted from better education, so have access to better jobs. However, they often have to move to urban areas to find work, and may have to do dangerous jobs. The elderly are living longer, and all groups have access to better health care. As a result, infant and maternal mortality rates have decreased in India. Gender equality has improved in some ways, e.g. literacy rates for women have increased, and women have better access to contraception and family planning advice. However, there has been a large increase in crimes against women in urban areas such as Delhi. Women may still find themselves being left to care for entire households in rural areas of India when men leave to find jobs in cities, which means they often have to balance their own job with housework.

Topic 3 — Challenges of an Urbanising World

Page 59

a) Any two from: e.g. Figure 1 shows children in school uniform — cities offer better access to services such as education compared to rural areas *[1 mark]*. / Figure 1 shows electricity and telephone cables connecting buildings — cities offer better access to resources such as electricity *[1 mark]*. / There are motorbikes parked outside the buildings in Figure 1, showing that people are reasonably wealthy — cities offer more jobs and better wages than rural areas *[1 mark]*.

The question tells you to use the figure, so make sure you comment on opportunities you can identify from the photo.

b) E.g. it is likely that there are lots of poor people moving to the cities who can't afford good quality housing *[1 mark]*, so they have to live in slums on undesirable land *[1 mark]*. The wealthy can afford better housing *[1 mark]*, so can live in high-class housing with good access to services *[1 mark]*.

You could also talk about inequalities in employment, services, traffic or health.

c) Your answer will depend on the megacity you have chosen. E.g. in Lagos, there are different development priorities between the wealthy, who want investment in high-class, modern office space *[1 mark]*, and the poor, who want investment in housing improvements and more services *[1 mark]*. There is also a problem with corruption, as wealthy people can bribe the police if they get caught breaking laws *[1 mark]*. This makes it hard for the government to introduce and enforce new laws, e.g. to regulate traffic *[1 mark]*.

d) This question is level marked. There are 4 extra marks available for spelling, punctuation and grammar.
How to grade your answer:
Level 0: There is no relevant information. *[0 marks]*
Level 1: There is a basic description of at least one strategy used to make a megacity more sustainable. *[1-3 marks]*
Level 2: There is a clear explanation of two or more strategies that have been used to make a megacity more sustainable, and an attempt to assess how effective they were. *[4-6 marks]*
Level 3: There is a detailed explanation of a range of strategies used to make a megacity more sustainable and a clear assessment of how effective they were. *[7-8 marks]*
Make sure your spelling, punctuation and grammar is consistently correct, that your meaning is clear and that you use a range of geographical terms correctly *[0-4 marks]*.
Your answer must refer to a named example.
Here are some points your answer may include:
- A brief description of your chosen megacity and the sustainability problems it faces.
- The pros and cons of bottom-up and top-down approaches.
- An assessment of examples of top-down strategies in your chosen megacity, such as attempts by governments and IGOs to improve water supply, waste disposal, air quality and traffic congestion.
- An assessment of examples of bottom-up strategies in your chosen megacity, such as attempts by communities and NGOs to improve health, education and city housing.
- A conclusion that summarises the effectiveness of the strategies used, e.g. in general, bottom-up strategies have been more effective than top-down strategies at improving sustainability.
- Your answer could refer to Lagos, Nigeria, where many strategies have been undertaken, with varying levels of effectiveness. E.g. the government banned the import of small electricity generators to reduce air pollution in an effort to make the city more environmentally sustainable. However, the strategy affected the poor much more than the rich, as they were less able to afford cleaner alternatives. Therefore this strategy was limited in its effectiveness.

Topic 4 — The UK's Evolving Physical Landscape

Page 67

1 a) B *[1 mark]*
 b) D *[1 mark]*
 c) E.g. ice eroded the landscape, carving out large U-shaped valleys *[1 mark]*. / As glaciers melted, they deposited thick layers of till/ unsorted material on the landscapes *[1 mark]*.
2 E.g. the meandering river may have eroded the valley laterally, widening the valley floor *[1 mark]*. The wet climate in the UK may have led to flooding *[1 mark]*. The overflowing river may have deposited silt on the valley floor, forming a flood plain *[1 mark]*.

Page 78

1 a) 2.6 *[1 mark]*
The mean is the total of the values divided by the number of values. The total is O + O + 1 + 2 + 3 + 2 + 4 + 4 + 5 + 5 = 26. There are 10 years, so the mean is 26 ÷ 10 = 2.6.
 b) Scatter graph *[1 mark]*
 c) E.g. storms give the sea more energy *[1 mark]*, which means waves transport material further *[1 mark]*. This can leave some areas starved of material *[1 mark]* so that they have less protection from flooding *[1 mark]*.
 d) Any one from: e.g. people may not be able to inhabit some low-lying coastal areas any more *[1 mark]* because they are permanently flooded or are flooded too often *[1 mark]*. / Coastal industries may be shut down *[1 mark]* because of damage to equipment and buildings *[1 mark]*. / Transport can be disrupted *[1 mark]* because of flood damage to roads and rail networks *[1 mark]*. / Flooding can damage tourism in coastal areas *[1 mark]* by putting people off visiting *[1 mark]*. / Agricultural land can be damaged by saltwater *[1 mark]* because it reduces soil fertility *[1 mark]*.
 e) Any one from: e.g. flooding with seawater increases salt levels in ecosystems *[1 mark]*, which can damage or kill organisms *[1 mark]*. / Floodwater can kill plants *[1 mark]* by uprooting or drowning them *[1 mark]*.

Page 88

1 a) 633524 *[1 mark]*
 b) 0.4 km *[1 mark]*
 c) Waterfall Y *[1 mark]*
Remember that the steeper the gradient, the closer together the contour lines will be.
 d) Waterfalls form where a river flows over an area of hard rock followed by an area of softer rock *[1 mark]*, so the Afon Merch must flow over rocks with alternating hardness *[1 mark]*.
2 In the upper course of a river most of the erosion is vertically downwards, creating steep-sided, V-shaped valleys *[1 mark]*. In the upper course, rivers aren't powerful enough to erode laterally (sideways) *[1 mark]*, so they wind around the high hillsides that stick out into their paths on either side *[1 mark]*. The hillsides interlock with each other as the river winds around them, forming interlocking spurs *[1 mark]*.

Page 96

1 a) Embankments *[1 mark]*
 b) The river is allowed to flood naturally where river restoration is in place *[1 mark]*, which reduces discharge downstream, making flooding less likely in Moritt *[1 mark]*.
 c) E.g. embankments are less unsightly than flood walls *[1 mark]*.
 d) E.g. the water is channelled past Fultow, instead of spilling over the banks and being stored on the flood plain *[1 mark]*, so a large amount of water can reach Blyside more quickly, increasing the risk of flooding there *[1 mark]*.
 e) E.g. it could restrict development *[1 mark]*, so further building in the parts of Portnoy situated on the flood plain would be prevented *[1 mark]*.

Topic 5 — The UK's Evolving Human Landscape

Page 104

1 a) The west and north of the UK generally have a low population density *[1 mark]*. Population density is highest in the south east and the midlands *[1 mark]*.
 b) E.g. the proportion of people over 65 is high in parts of the country with low population densities *[1 mark]*, because these are rural areas with fewer employment opportunities *[1 mark]*. People of working age tend to move away from rural areas into densely populated urban areas so they can live closer to where they work *[1 mark]*, whereas retired people often move to the countryside for a more peaceful environment *[1 mark]*
 c) E.g. the UK government provides benefits (e.g. reduced taxes) for companies that locate in Enterprise Zones *[1 mark]* to bring jobs and income into poorer rural areas where unemployment is high *[1 mark]*. It is planning to link major cities with a high speed rail line *[1 mark]*, which will promote jobs and industry in the north of England *[1 mark]*.

Page 113

1 a) Any two from: e.g. two railway stations *[1 mark]* / major roads *[1 mark]* / financial services *[1 mark]* / law firms *[1 mark]*
 b) Improving a place's image/reputation so that people will want to go there *[1 mark]*.
 c) Any two from: e.g. growth of finance/business services *[1 mark]* / investment in culture *[1 mark]* / studentification *[1 mark]* / investment by TNCs *[1 mark]*.
 d) Your answer will depend on the city you have chosen. E.g. in London, the East End experienced a decline because of de-industrialisation *[1 mark]*, which resulted in many workers in the docks and manufacturing industries becoming unemployed *[1 mark]*. This led to the depopulation of the area *[1 mark]*, which meant many local services closed and buildings were left derelict *[1 mark]*.

e) Your answer will depend on the city you have chosen. E.g. in London, there are self-service bicycles and bike lanes *[1 mark]*, which helps to reduce noise and air pollution from motor vehicles *[1 mark]*. The housing in the BedZED development in south London is designed to conserve energy, e.g. by using solar water heaters *[1 mark]*. This helps to reduce greenhouse gas emissions *[1 mark]*.

You might also have mentioned strategies to do with increasing green space, increasing employment opportunities or encouraging more recycling.

Topic 6 — Geographical Investigations

Page 120

1 a) Your answer should state your enquiry question and briefly outline the conclusions that you came to. Your conclusions should then be linked to an appropriate area of geography. E.g. I investigated whether groynes were an effective method for retaining the width of the beach *[1 mark]*. I found that they increased the beach width by up to 28% compared to an area of the beach without groynes *[1 mark]*. This helped me to understand beach processes and the effectiveness of some of the management options available *[1 mark]*.

b) The technique you describe should relate to physical geography data that you collected yourself, e.g. beach/ river profiles / sediment analysis / soil analysis etc. Your answer should give a description of what you did, e.g. sample frequency, method of measurement etc. E.g. I recorded beach profiles by following transect lines from the sea to the top of the beach *[1 mark]*. At consecutive points where the slope angle changed, I measured the distance between two ranging poles with a tape measure, and measured the angle between them using a clinometer *[1 mark]*.

c) Your explanation should include why you collected the data and how it helped you answer your original question. E.g. I analysed pebble size at different points along the river to find out how it changed due to attrition *[1 mark]*. I took a random sample of 10 pebbles at every site to make sure that the data collected was reliable *[1 mark]*. The data showed that pebble size decreased as the distance from the source of the river increased, so I was able to answer my original question *[1 mark]*.

d) Your data presentation technique may be a map, e.g. a land use map or a dot map; a particular type of chart or graph, e.g. a dispersion graph, pie chart or a scatter graph; or an annotated field sketch or photograph. The strengths could relate to how the variables are presented, the scales used, how the trends and patterns are presented, or how effective they are. E.g. **Data presentation technique:** pie charts **Strengths:** Any two from: e.g. pie charts clearly show the proportion of each class of data investigated *[1 mark]*, so using a pie chart for each place makes it easy to see the patterns between different places *[1 mark]*. / Pie charts allow a large amount of data to be summarised *[1 mark]*, so pie charts make the data easier to understand *[1 mark]*.

Topic 7 — People and the Biosphere

Page 131

1 a) C *[1 mark]*
It was Boserup, not Malthus, who said that people would make technological advances to increase resources if they became limited.

b) As population increases so that demand becomes equal with resource supply, resource supply increases *[1 mark]*, so there are always enough resources available for the population *[1 mark]*.

2 a) July *[1 mark]*

b) Temperate forest *[1 mark]*

c) Temperate forests have lots of broad-leaved trees (e.g. oak) *[1 mark]*. There are also lots of shrubs and undergrowth (e.g. brambles) *[1 mark]*.

Topic 8 — Forests Under Threat

Page 141

1 a) A *[1 mark]*

b) (Leaf) litter *[1 mark]*

c) Biomass *[1 mark]*

d) The dead organic litter is broken down by fungi and bacteria *[1 mark]*. The nutrients are soluble and soak into the soil *[1 mark]*.

2 a) Ecotourism is tourism that minimises damage to the environment and benefits the local people *[1 mark]*.

b) E.g. it provides a source of income for local people *[1 mark]*, meaning that they don't have to rely on logging or farming to make money, so fewer trees are cut down *[1 mark]*. It can also raise awareness of conservation issues *[1 mark]*, bringing in more money for rainforest conservation *[1 mark]*.

Page 147

1 a) A national park is an area that is managed to protect biodiversity and promote recreation *[1 mark]*.

b) E.g. it will protect species that are only found in taiga ecosystems *[1 mark]* by conserving their habitats *[1 mark]*. Protecting the forest will also help to reduce the amount of global warming *[1 mark]* because taiga forests store lots of carbon *[1 mark]*.

You could also mention that national parks take into account the needs of indigenous people who depend on the forest for their traditional way of life.

c) Any two from: e.g. there is economic pressure from logging, mining and energy companies, which want to use the resources *[1 mark]*. / Schemes designed to protect the forest must take into account the needs of indigenous communities, who may use the land for hunting *[1 mark]*. / Restrictions designed to protect the forest are difficult to police *[1 mark]*.

d) Sustainable forestry is using ways of harvesting the timber from a forest *[1 mark]* without damaging the forest in the long-term *[1 mark]*.

e) Any two from: e.g. people may no longer be able to get enough of the resources that the forest provides *[1 mark]*. / Jobs related to the forest would be lost if the industries were restricted or stopped *[1 mark]*. / Countries wouldn't be able to generate wealth from exploiting the forest *[1 mark]*.

Topic 9 — Consuming Energy Resources

Page 159

1 a) coal *[1 mark]*

b) gas *[1 mark]*

c) E.g. the proportion of energy from coal and oil decreased from 91% in 1970 to 51% in 2014 *[1 mark]*. The proportion of energy from gas increased hugely from 6% in 1970 to 34% in 2014 *[1 mark]*. Between 1970 and 2014, a variety of renewable sources of energy were introduced *[1 mark]*.

d) E.g. people with more money can afford to buy more efficient products and invest in sustainable energy for their homes *[1 mark]*. Governments in developed countries have more money to invest in public transport and renewable energy *[1 mark]*.

e) E.g. people in developed countries have better access to education through school and the media *[1 mark]*, meaning that they have a better understanding of the consequences of unsustainable energy use and increasing emissions *[1 mark]*. People learn about how to reduce their carbon footprint *[1 mark]*, so are more likely to use sustainable energy sources in order to reduce their impact on the environment *[1 mark]*.

f) E.g. renewable energy sources are more expensive than fossil fuels *[1 mark]*. This could affect the amount of money available for development *[1 mark]*.

Practice Exam Paper 1:
Global Geographical Issues

Pages 177-183

1 a) i) A *[1 mark]*

ii) C *[1 mark]*

iii) 0° (the equator) *[1 mark]*

iv) The Sun heats the Earth at the equator, causing air to warm up and rise *[1 mark]*. As the air rises it cools and moves away from the equator *[1 mark]*. The cool air sinks and some is drawn towards the poles as surface winds *[1 mark]*. This process is repeated, transferring heat from the equator to the poles *[1 mark]*.

b) i) E.g. Hazard A killed far more people in the first 24 hours than Hazard B *[1 mark]*, suggesting that people weren't prepared for it, which is more likely in a developing country *[1 mark]*. / It cost a lot less to rebuild after Hazard A than Hazard B *[1 mark]*, suggesting that the buildings and infrastructure were made from cheaper materials, which is more likely in a developing country *[1 mark]*.

ii) 1:4 *[1 mark]*

c) Gases are often released just before an earthquake/volcanic eruption and there may be small tremors *[1 mark]*. Monitoring these activities means that scientists can determine unusual levels that indicate an earthquake/volcanic eruption is about to happen *[1 mark]*.

d) This question is level marked. There are 4 extra marks available for spelling, punctuation and grammar.
How to grade your answer:

Level 0: There is no relevant information. *[0 marks]*

Level 1: There is a basic description of preparation methods for tectonic hazards in a developed and less developed country. *[1-3 marks]*

Level 2: There is a clear comparison of preparation methods for tectonic hazards in a developed and less developed country and an assessment of how effective they were. *[4-6 marks]*

Level 3: There is a detailed comparison of multiple preparation methods for tectonic hazards in a developed and less developed country and a detailed assessment of how they reduced the impacts of the hazards. *[7-8 marks]*

Make sure your spelling, punctuation and grammar is consistently correct, that your meaning is clear and that you use a range of geographical terms correctly *[0-4 marks]*.
Your answer must refer to named examples.
Here are some points your answer may include:

- A brief description of a hazard in a developing country and a developed country — when they happened, where they happened and what happened.

- A comparison of the preparation methods in the two countries, such as training for emergency services, laws about building design, education programmes, evacuation routes and stockpiling of emergency supplies, and how these affected the impact of the hazards.

- Answers may refer to Japan (earthquake in 2011) and Pakistan (Kashmir earthquake in 2005). In Japan, there was better preparation, e.g. advanced warning systems and education meant people knew they had to evacuate dangerous areas and get to high ground, no buildings in Tokyo collapsed because they were designed to withstand earthquakes, and 'bullet' trains were designed to stop automatically in the event of an earthquake so there were no deaths on the rail network. In Pakistan, the impact was more severe because there was less preparation, e.g. buildings were constructed from flimsy materials, e.g. wood and concrete, evacuations weren't planned because of poor communications, and there were no education programmes or early warning systems in place.

2 a) i) D *[1 mark]*
Stage 3 (Take-off) is characterised by rapid and intensive economic growth and a move towards large-scale industrialisation.

ii) B *[1 mark]*
Stage 4 (Drive to maturity) is when the economic wealth generated from the large-scale industrialisation in Stage 3 is spread throughout the population, so that people are generally wealthier and standards of living rise. People can also afford new technologies, so the use of technology becomes widespread.

iii) Neo-colonialism is when richer countries continue to control former colonies indirectly after they have gained independence *[1 mark]*.

iv) Richer, colonial countries continue to take advantage of the cheap raw materials and labour available in poorer countries *[1 mark]*. Poorer countries produce primary products to sell cheaply to richer countries *[1 mark]*. This means they need to import manufactured goods at higher cost from richer countries *[1 mark]*. This traps them in poverty and makes them dependent on the economy of richer countries *[1 mark]*.

b) i)   170 million passengers *[1 mark]*

Any answer between 160 and 180 million passengers would get you a mark.

ii) They have made it easier for people all over the world to communicate with each other face to face *[1 mark]*. They have also made it easier for companies to get supplies and distribute their products all over the world *[1 mark]*.

c)   D *[1 mark]*

d)   Non-governmental organisation *[1 mark]*. / A not-for-profit group that isn't linked to a government *[1 mark]*.

e)   E.g. large infrastructure projects funded by TNCs/IGOs can improve the country's economy by promoting industry *[1 mark]*.

f)   E.g. the projects are often very expensive *[1 mark]*, and there may be conditions for borrowing the money, e.g. paying back loans with interest or removing trade barriers *[1 mark]*. The projects are often high-tech and energy intensive *[1 mark]*. This means that the host country becomes dependent on technology and workers from richer countries *[1 mark]*.

a) i)   C *[1 mark]*

ii) Any two from: e.g. proximity to the sea *[1 mark]* / connectivity to other major cities *[1 mark]* / availability of natural resources *[1 mark]*

iii) Your answer will vary depending on the megacity you have chosen. E.g. Lagos in Nigeria has a rapidly growing population mostly because of rural-urban migration *[1 mark]*. People from bordering countries such as Chad and Niger are moving to Lagos to escape poverty and conflict in their own countries *[1 mark]*. National migrants are also arriving from northern Nigeria to escape ethnic and religious conflict and poverty *[1 mark]*. The rate of natural increase is high *[1 mark]*.

b) i)   8 years *[1 mark]*

ii) E.g. the projects are usually on a smaller scale than top-down projects so reach fewer people *[1 mark]*. / Funds may be limited, especially during economic recessions, when the strategy may be needed the most *[1 mark]*. / They can lack coordination because there may be several organisations with the same aims working separately *[1 mark]*.

iii) E.g. the literacy rate increased from 3% in 2005 to 37% in 2015. It had been steady at 3% since 1995 *[1 mark]*. The increase in literacy rate after the project began suggests that it has had some success in improving the quality of life for people in the squatter settlement *[1 mark]*.

You need to describe what changed using figures. Then say whether these changes mean the project has been a success. You could also have mentioned improvements in life expectancy, number of people per doctor, percentage of people with access to clean water or percentage of people in work.

c) i)

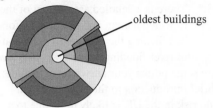

[1 mark]

ii) The rural-urban fringe / outskirts *[1 mark]*

iii) The inner city *[1 mark]*

iv) E.g. industry may have located along major roads or rivers *[1 mark]* so it is easier to transport goods into and out of the city *[1 mark]*.

d)   Your answer will depend on the megacity you have chosen. E.g. in Lagos, slums have developed within the city *[1 mark]*, in areas that were previously wasteland *[1 mark]*. / Land has been reclaimed from the lagoon in Lagos *[1 mark]* and high-class housing in gated communities has been built on it *[1 mark]*.

Practice Exam Paper 2: UK Geographical Issues

Pages 185-191

1 a)   C *[1 mark]*, E *[1 mark]*

b)   Igneous rocks are generally found in the north and west of the UK *[1 mark]*. They are mostly found in Scotland and Northern Ireland *[1 mark]*.

2 a)   991802 *[1 mark]*

b)   Longshore drift transported sand and shingle north east past a sharp bend in the coastline *[1 mark]* and deposited it in the sea, forming a spit *[1 mark]*.

3 a)   10 km *[1 mark]*

b)   Between 20 and 30 km the river's velocity drops *[1 mark]*. When rivers slow down they deposit the material they are carrying *[1 mark]*.

4 This question is level marked.
How to grade your answer:
Level 0: There is no relevant information. *[0 marks]*
Level 1: There is a basic assessment of the extent to which human and physical factors might be affecting the number of people at risk of river flooding in the UK. *[1-2 marks]*
Level 2: There is a clear assessment of the extent to which human and physical factors might be affecting the number of people at risk of river flooding in the UK. *[3-5 marks]*
Level 3: There is a detailed assessment of the extent to which human and physical factors might be affecting the number of people at risk of river flooding in the UK. *[6-8 marks]*

Here are some points your answer may include:
- A brief introduction to the issue, e.g. that flood risk in the UK is likely to be due to a combination of physical and human factors and that the number of people likely to be affected by river flooding varies across the UK.
- The patterns in the risk of flooding shown in Figure 4, e.g. that the areas at risk of flooding are concentrated along major rivers, e.g. the River Thames, the River Severn and the River Trent. There is also a flood risk in south west England and north Wales.
- The patterns in the number of people at risk shown in Figure 5, e.g. it is likely that higher numbers of people are at risk in the south east, along the Great Ouse in the towns north of London and along the River Trent in the Midlands because these areas are more densely populated. Population density tends to be lower in upland areas so there are fewer people at risk from flooding in these areas.
- The physical reasons for the variations, e.g. wetter weather is more likely in the north and west leading to more saturated ground; high runoff rates are more likely from upland areas leading to lots of water entering some rivers (e.g. the Severn and Wye) in a short time after a storm event; low lying, flat flood plains in the south and east of the UK meaning water spreads over a wide area if it overtops the river banks; possible flood risk in estuaries from tidal surges.
- The human reasons for the variations, e.g. there is a high density of people on the flood plains of the rivers Thames, Great Ouse and Trent; where there is a greater amount of built up land, water can't infiltrate which leads to more runoff; gutters and drains may take water quickly to rivers, rapidly increasing discharge and making flooding more likely.
- How the risk of flooding may be being reduced in some areas, e.g. through flood management strategies (flood walls, flood barriers, embankments, river restoration etc.) and afforestation.

- The effectiveness of flood management strategies, e.g. the risk of catastrophic flooding if hard engineering defences fail, managed flooding when using soft engineering strategies and the resulting need for effective land use planning and zoning.
- A brief conclusion that states how far human and physical factors are affecting the number of people at risk of river flooding in the UK, supported with evidence from the main body of your answer.

5 a) 188 200 *[1 mark]*
Work out the range by subtracting the lowest value from the highest value, which here is 341 400 − 153 200.

b) International migration has increased the number of young adults in the UK *[1 mark]*, because lots of people have moved to the UK for work *[1 mark]*. The number of children in the UK has increased *[1 mark]*, because many immigrants are of child-bearing age *[1 mark]*.

c) Any two from: e.g. young adults tend to move into cities *[1 mark]*. / Wealthy people tend to move into rural areas (counter-urbanisation) *[1 mark]*. / Older people tend to move to rural and coastal areas *[1 mark]*.

6 a) Your answer will depend on the city you have chosen. E.g. many of the national migrants to London are young people *[1 mark]* who are moving there for work or study *[1 mark]*. The inner city is the part of London attracting the most international migrants *[1 mark]*, especially low-paid migrants who move there to work in the service sector *[1 mark]*.

b) Your answer will depend on the city you have chosen. E.g. in London, immigrants often choose to settle near people with the same ethnic background as them *[1 mark]*, so certain parts of the city are associated with certain ethnic backgrounds, e.g. Chinatown *[1 mark]*. / The age structure of London is being altered by immigration *[1 mark]* because it is mainly young adults who are moving there *[1 mark]*.

7 This question is level marked. There are 4 extra marks available for spelling, punctuation and grammar.
How to grade your answer:
Level 0: There is no relevant information. *[0 marks]*
Level 1: There is a basic description of one or two reasons for the variations in IMD. *[1-2 marks]*
Level 2: There is a clear description of reasons for variations in IMD that makes some links between them and an attempt to provide evidence for the judgements made. *[3-5 marks]*
Level 3: There is a detailed description of reasons for variations in IMD that makes clear links between them. Judgements are well-supported with evidence. *[6-8 marks]*

Make sure your spelling, punctuation and grammar is consistently correct, that your meaning is clear and that you use a range of geographical terms correctly *[0-4 marks]*.

Here are some points your answer may include:

- A brief introduction explaining what the IMD is and the link between deprivation and quality of life.
- An overview of the trends in deprivation between the inner city and surrounding rural areas, e.g. deprivation is generally higher in the inner city, and neighbourhoods get less deprived further out from the city centre (the inner city area of Aston ranks 668 compared to the commuter village, Hampton-in-Arden, which ranks 30 336).
- Reasons why deprivation is generally high in the inner city, e.g. de-industrialisation has reduced access to jobs particularly in former industrial regions such as north east England and the Midlands, poorer people tend to live there because they can only afford low-quality housing and might have to live near to where they work if they can't afford transport.
- Reasons why some inner city areas have lower deprivation, e.g. if they have experienced regeneration, studentification or gentrification.
- Reasons why suburbs and commuter villages are generally less deprived than the inner city, e.g. de-centralisation has increased employment opportunities outside of the city, there are fewer planning regulations so houses can be bigger, people move out of the city when they are wealthy enough to afford better housing or when they retire.
- Any anomalies in the component scores, e.g. housing and services deprivation is higher in commuter villages than other forms of deprivation (Hampton-in-Arden ranks 11 417 for housing and services deprivation but 30 571 for employment deprivation), because house prices are high. This makes it hard to provide affordable housing for young people.
- Reasons why some rural areas are relatively deprived compared to many commuter villages (Diddlebury ranks 11 311 for IMD compared to Hampton-in-Arden, which ranks 30 336), e.g. lack of access to services such as schools, banks and shops due to closures resulting from reduced demand, de-population as young people move to urban areas to find work.
- A brief summary of your main argument supported by evidence from the body of your answer.

8 a) You should draw a clear and accurate diagram *[2 marks]* and use detailed labels to explain what it is showing *[2 marks]*.
E.g. the effectiveness of groynes:
Before groynes are installed:
Longshore drift slowly moves the sand further along the coast, reducing the width of the beach.

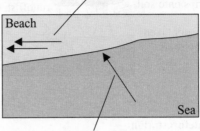

Direction of prevailing wind

After groynes are installed:
Groynes trap material transported by longshore drift.

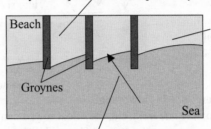

This creates a wider beach, which gives more protection from flooding and erosion.

Direction of prevailing wind

Groynes may starve beaches further down the coast of sand, making them narrower and less able to prevent erosion and flooding.

b) Any two from: e.g. the ranging poles may not have been held straight, affecting the angles recorded *[1 mark]*. / The ranging poles may sink into the sand, affecting the angles recorded *[1 mark]*. / It can be difficult to take accurate readings with a clinometer *[1 mark]*. / It might be difficult to identify the low water mark *[1 mark]*. / The tide will be going in or out during the data collection, changing the point where measuring starts unless all profiles are taken at the same time by different groups *[1 mark]*. / The 5 m interval could include a break of slope, so the results wouldn't show the true profile *[1 mark]*.

c) E.g. she might have selected a part of the beach with no management strategy in place, and two parts with different strategies *[1 mark]*, so that she could compare them to learn how different strategies affect the cross-profile of the beach *[1 mark]*. / She might have chosen points at regular intervals along the beach *[1 mark]*, to investigate how the cross-profile changes along the shore *[1 mark]*.

Her decision might also have been affected by accessibility and safety concerns.

9 a) You should draw a clear and accurate diagram
[2 marks] and use detailed labels to explain what it is
showing *[2 marks]*.
E.g. how deforestation influences flooding:

Before deforestation

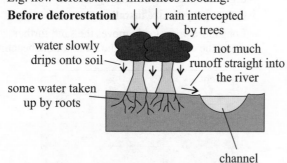

After deforestation

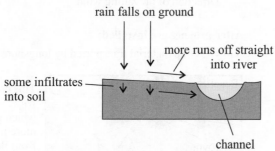

b) E.g. **Item:** dog biscuit/orange
Reason: any one from: e.g. they float so you can
take measurements from them *[1 mark]*. / They
don't have much surface area above the water, so
they are less likely to be affected by wind *[1 mark]*. /
They biodegrade so the investigation won't harm the
environment if the floats aren't caught *[1 mark]*.

c) Sample 5 *[1 mark]*

d) E.g. the float got caught on something, e.g. a rock as it
passed downstream *[1 mark]* so it took much longer for
the float to reach the end of the timed section *[1 mark]*.

10a) The technique you describe should relate to human
geography data that you collected yourself. You need
to explain why you used the technique, for example
how it helped you to answer your original question
and how it provided reliable and accurate data.
E.g. Technique: environmental survey.
Explanation: The survey enabled me to identify areas
that were experiencing environmental challenges so
that I could assess why quality of life varied within
the city *[1 mark]*. The score sheet I used in the survey
meant that the results were numerical, so the data
could be easily compared between sites *[1 mark]*.

b) This question is level marked.
How to grade your answer:

Level 0: There is no relevant information. *[0 marks]*
Level 1: There are a few points about the suitability
of the sites used. *[1-2 marks]*
Level 2: There is a clear evaluation of the suitability
of the sites used and the answer attempts
to come to a conclusion. *[3-5 marks]*
Level 3: There is a detailed evaluation of the
suitability of the sites used and the answer
comes to a clear conclusion. *[6-8 marks]*

Here are some points your answer may include:
- An outline of the sites used and the conclusions
that could be drawn from the data collected
there. Whether these sites gave a good overall
representation of the study area, in order to draw
conclusions that answered the original question.
- An outline of the limitations of the choice of
data collection sites, and how they may have
affected the validity of the conclusion.
- An overall conclusion about the choice of data
collection sites in answering the research question.

Practice Exam Paper 3: People and Environment Issues — Making Geographical Decisions

Pages 195-196

1 a) Taiga forests are found around 60° north of the
equator *[1 mark]*, in the northern parts of North
America and Asia, and north-east Europe *[1 mark]*.

b) Tundra environments are very cold with temperatures
usually less than 10 °C *[1 mark]*. Precipitation is
low — usually less than 250 mm per year *[1 mark]*.

2 a) Any two from: e.g. they are evergreen *[1 mark]*,
so they can make the best use of available light
[1 mark]. / They have needles instead of flat leaves
[1 mark], which have a smaller surface area, so
reduce water loss caused by strong, cold winds
[1 mark]. / They are cone-shaped *[1 mark]*, which
means that heavy winter snowfall can slide straight
off the branches without damaging them *[1 mark]*. /
Their branches are quite bendy *[1 mark]*, so are less
likely to snap under the weight of snow *[1 mark]*.

b) Any one from: e.g. it has a light-coloured coat in
the winter to camouflage it against the winter snow
[1 mark], helping it to hide from predators *[1 mark]*. /
It has thick fur *[1 mark]* to keep it insulated / to reduce
the amount of energy needed to keep it warm *[1 mark]*.

c) E.g. many larger mammals are migratory *[1 mark]*
which means that they move long distances
through to forest in order to find food *[1 mark]*.
/ Some animals hibernate *[1 mark]* to conserve
energy and survive the winter *[1 mark]*.

d) E.g. plants provide nutrients to the animals that eat
them *[1 mark]*. In turn, animals spread seeds through
their dung, helping the plants to reproduce *[1 mark]*.

3 a) E.g. having a diverse energy mix reduces a country's
reliance on a single source of energy *[1 mark]*.
This increases energy security because countries
are less affected by shortages of one energy source
[1 mark]. Diversifying to use renewable sources
of energy will make sure energy is still available
when the supply of fossil fuels runs out *[1 mark]*.

b) $\frac{300 - 125}{125} \times 100$ *[1 mark]*

= 140% *[1 mark]*

4 This question is level marked. There are 4 extra marks available for spelling, punctuation and grammar.
How to grade your answer:

Level 0: There is no relevant information. *[0 marks]*

Level 1: There is a basic view stated and a simple justification. *[1-4 marks]*

Level 2: There is a clear view stated and an adequate justification using at least one figure and other knowledge. *[5-8 marks]*

Level 3: There is a thorough evaluation of the effectiveness of each option and a clear justification. The answer draws on evidence from multiple figures. *[9-12 marks]*

Make sure your spelling, punctuation and grammar is consistently correct, that your meaning is clear and that you use a range of geographical terms correctly *[0-4 marks]*.

It doesn't matter which option you choose as long as you identify the pros and cons of all three options and then explain why your chosen option is the best one for Canada's long-term development. Here's how you could structure your answer:

- A brief introduction to the issue.
- Any advantages of the two options you have rejected.
- The disadvantages of the two options you have rejected.
- Any disadvantages of the option you have chosen.
- The advantages of the option you have chosen.
- A conclusion that states clearly which option you have chosen, supported with evidence from the main body of your answer.

Here are some points your answer may include:

Option 1
Pros: e.g. that tar sands are an important part of the economy, continued investment is necessary for continued economic growth and that jobs will be created for local communities.
Cons: e.g. that there will be damage to the taiga forest ecosystem and this will increase global warming, that it's likely that there will be an increase in pollution from mines, and loss of source of food, water and medicine sources for indigenous communities.

Option 2
Pros: e.g. that the expansion of tar sands mines can be sustainably managed to avoid environmental damage, that investing in renewable energy will diversify the energy mix and increase energy security, and that creating protected areas could conserve areas of forest for sustainable use by indigenous communities.
Cons: e.g. that expansion of tar sands mines will still create some pollution, that investment in renewable energy is expensive, that there may be fewer jobs created for local people and that renewable energy sources may also have negative environmental impacts on the taiga forest.

Option 3
Pros: e.g. that tar sands will eventually run out so renewable energy is a better long-term investment, that the health of local people would be protected, that there would be less pollution, and that HEP is already a part of Canada's energy mix, so the technology is already well-developed, which could make it easier to expand production.
Cons: e.g. the negative environmental effects of HEP such as the build up of silt and flooding of large areas of forest, possible objections from indigenous communities about the flooding of their land and changes to their supply of water, and potential limited growth of the Canadian economy without the investment of oil companies.

Remember, to get full marks you must support your answer with evidence from the figures. For example, if you chose Option 1, you might have made reference to the news article (Figure 8), which explains that revenues from the industry are likely to continue increasing in the future. You might also have chosen to use evidence about the attitudes to tar sands production (Figure 11) — particularly those of tar sands production companies or the government.

Acknowledgements

Estimated temperature variations for Central England (1000-2000) on page 5 based on Palaeogeography, Palaeoclimatol., Palaeoecol., 1 (1965) 13-37 , H. H. Lamb, The early medieval warm epoch and its sequel, p25, Copyright © 1965, with permission from Elsevier.

*Photograph on **p.7** (UK flooding) © Rose and Trev Clough/ **p.54** (Makoko slum) © Heinrich-Böll-Stiftung / **p.61** (Grampian Mountains) © Trevor Littlewood/ **p.61** (Cheshire Plain) © Peter Styles/ **p.61** (Snowdonia) © Bill Boaden/ **p.61** (The Weald) © Peter Jeffery/ **p.63** (Limestone Pavement) © Martyn Gorman/ **p.64** (Llyn Idwal) © Dudley Smith/ **p.64** (Dry Valley) © Colin Smith/ **p.67** (meandering River Wampool) © Simon Ledingham/ **p.70** (Old Harry) © Raymond Knapman/ **p.73** (tractor in field) © Roger Lombard/ **p.73** (coastal town) © Lewis Clarke/ **p.73** (quarry) © Mike Faherty/ **p.73** (industry) © David Dixon/ **p.73** (groyne) © N Chadwick/ **p.74** (rock groyne) © J Thomas/ **p.77** (cliff erosion) © Stephen McKay/ **p.81** (Hell Gill Force) © Roger Templeman/ **p.81** (Eden at Salkeld) © Greg Fitchett/ **p.81** (Eden floodplain) © Rose and Trev Clough/ **p.81** (Eden at Appleby) © Steve Daniels/ **p.83** and **p.88** (interlocking spurs) © Bob Bowyer/ **p.87** (Inversanda Bay) © Alan Reid/ **p.89** (River Kent) © Karl and Ali/ **p.93** (Flooding in Carlisle and flood aftermath) © Rose and Trev Clough/ **p.94** (flood wall in Edinburgh) © Robin Stott/ **p.94** (embankment) © Chris Denny/ **p.94** (Thames Barrier) © John M/ **p.94** (Demountable flood barrier) © Chris Whippet/ **p.94** (grasslands) © Richard Croft/ **p.108** (Central London) © Philip Halling/ **p.108** (Bluewater shopping centre) © Ken Brown/ **p.110** (Converted oast house) © Oast House Archive/ **p.118** (river fieldwork) © Robbie Livingstone.*

Licensed under the Creative Commons Attribution-Share Alike 2.0 Generic Licence. http://creativecommons.org/licenses/by-sa/2.0/

Graphs showing future temperature and sea level rise on page 8 based on Figure SPM.6 from Climate Change 2014: Synthesis Report. Contribution of Working Groups I, II and III to the Fifth Assessment Report of the Intergovernmental Panel on Climate Change [Core Writing Team, Pachauri, R.K. and Meyer, L. (eds.)]. IPCC, Geneva, Switzerland.

Graph of sea level rise on page 9 adapted from Climate Change 2001: The Scientific Basis. Contribution of Working Group I to the Third Assessment Report of the Intergovernmental Panel on Climate Change. Figure 5. Cambridge University Press.

Satellite image on page 12: Jeff Schmaltz, MODIS Rapid Response Team, NASA/GSFC.

HDI data on pages 30, 31, 36 and 40 from 2015 Human Development Report, United Nations Development Programme from hdr.undp. org. Licensed for re-use under the Creative Commons Attribution 3.0 IGO license (https://creativecommons.org/licenses/by/3.0/igo/).

Data used to compile table on page 30 (except HDI), create pyramids on pages 30 and 31, and produce a table on page 36 (except GNI per head and HDI values) from The World Factbook. Washington, DC: Central Intelligence Agency, 2017.

Data used to produce quintiles diagram on page 33 and graph of % urban population 1980-2015 on page 47 from The World Bank: World Development Indicators, licensed under the Creative Commons Attribution 4.0 International License (CC BY 4.0) https://creativecommons.org/licenses/by/4.0/legalcode

GNI per head data in table on page 36 from The World Bank: Indicators, licensed under the Creative Commons Attribution 4.0 International License (CC BY 4.0) https://creativecommons.org/licenses/by/4.0/legalcode

India GDP and GNI per capita on page 40: The World Bank: India: World Bank national accounts data, and OECD National Accounts data files, licensed under the Creative Commons Attribution 4.0 International License (CC BY 4.0) https://creativecommons.org/licenses/by/4.0/legalcode

India industrial sector data on page 40: The World Bank: Employment in agriculture and industry (% of total employment): International Labour Organization, Key Indicators of the Labour Market database, licensed under the Creative Commons Attribution 4.0 International License (CC BY 4.0) https://creativecommons.org/licenses/by/4.0/legalcode

Primary education data on page 41: UNESCO Institute for Statistics (UIS), http://uis.unesco.org

India development data on page 41: The World Bank: India: Life expectancy at birth, total (years)/ Fertility rate, total (births per woman): United Nations Population Division. World Population Prospects, licensed under the Creative Commons Attribution 4.0 International License (CC BY 4.0) https://creativecommons.org/licenses/by/4.0/legalcode

India urban population data on page 41: The World Bank: India: Urban population (% of total): United Nations, World Urbanization Prospects, licensed under the Creative Commons Attribution 4.0 International License (CC BY 4.0) https://creativecommons.org/licenses/by/4.0/legalcode

Urban Population & Literacy rate data for Bihar and Maharashtra on page 41 © Office of the Registrar General & Census Commissioner, India.

GDP per capita data for Bihar and Maharashtra on page 41 from statisticstimes.com.

HDI data for Bihar and Maharashtra on page 41 © Copyright 2016 United Nations Development Programme.

Female literacy rate on page 42 from The World Bank: India: Literacy rate, adult female (% of females ages 15 and above): United Nations Educational, Scientific, and Cultural Organization (UNESCO) Institute for Statistics. Licensed under the Creative Commons Attribution 4.0 International License (CC BY 4.0) https://creativecommons.org/licenses/by/4.0/legalcode

Projection of future urban population % and map of countries categorised by HDI on pages 47 and 58 © Copyright 2016 United Nations Development Programme.

Satellite images on pages 53 and 54: USGS/NASA Landsat.

Extent of Lagos by 1920, 1960, 1990 (overlays on satellite image on page 53) adapted from Planning, Anti-planning and the Infrastructure Crisis Facing Metropolitan Lagos, page 373, by Matthew Gandy and adapted from 'Piecemeal Urbanisation at the Peripheries of Lagos'. African Studies, 9 June 2014, 1–19, by Lindsay Sawyer 2014 https://doi.org/10.1080/00020184.2014.925207.

Acknowledgements

Birth and death rates in Nigeria on page 53: The World Bank: Nigeria: Death rate, crude (per 1,000 people). Licensed under the Creative Commons Attribution 4.0 International License (CC BY 4.0) https://creativecommons.org/licenses/by/4.0/legalcode

Topographic map of the United Kingdom on page 61 by Captain Blood, licensed under the Creative Commons Attribution-Share Alike 3.0 Unported license. https://creativecommons.org/licenses/by-sa/3.0/deed.en

Geological map of the UK on page 62 contains British Geological Survey materials ©NERC 2017.

Map extracts on pages 64, 65, 66, 72, 86, 88, 167, 168, 185 reproduced with permission by Ordnance Survey® © Crown copyright 2018 OS 100034841.

Photograph of the Ebro delta on page 85: © iStock.com/imv.

Data used to construct maps on pages 98 and 104 and graphs on page 100, ethnicity data on page 100, UK industrial data on page 101, data used to construct graph on page 101, FDI and infrastructure data on page 102, international migration figure on page 106, housing deprivation data on page 111, UK migration data on page 187: Office for National Statistics licensed under the Open Government Licence v.3.0. http://www.nationalarchives.gov.uk/doc/open-government-licence/version/3/

UK FDI data on p.103 source: Department for International Trade licensed under the Open Government Licence v.3.0. http://www.nationalarchives.gov.uk/doc/open-government-licence/version/3/

Graph on page 103 adapted from Welsh Government - Statistics © Crown Copyright 2015.

Satellite image of London on page 105 courtesy of NASA/GSFC/MITI/ERSDAC/JAROS, and U.S./Japan ASTER Science Team.

Ethnicity statistic on page 106 and IMD data on page 107, Docklands employment data, London recycling data on page 109, pie charts on page 159, UK airport data on page 180, map of population density of UK on page 186 and deprivation statistics on page 188 all contain public sector information licensed under the Open Government Licence v3.0. http://www.nationalarchives.gov.uk/doc/open-government-licence/version/3/

Outline map of London boroughs on page 107: Contains National Statistics data © Crown copyright and database right [2012] and Contains Ordnance Survey data © Crown copyright and database right [2012]. http://data.london.gov.uk/documents/Geography-licensing.pdf

Graph of London migration on page 112 adapted from data from the Office for National Statistics licensed under the Open Government Licence v.3.0. http://www.nationalarchives.gov.uk/doc/open-government-licence/version/3/

Map of central Newcastle on page 113 contains OS data © Crown copyright and database right 2017.

Population projection graph on page 127: from World Population to 2300, by Department of Economic and Social Affairs, Population Division, © 2004 United Nations. Reprinted with the permission of the United Nations.

Global Energy Consumption map on page 151 and graph showing history of crude oil price on page 152 © BP Statistical Review of World Energy 2016.

Data used to create map of global oil production on page 152 from OPEC Annual Statistical Bulletin 2016.

Oil consumption data on page 152 and data in table on page 158 source: U.S. Energy Information Administration (Jan 2017).

Data relating to oil industry investment and employment in Alaska on page 153 © BP in Alaska Statistical Review 2016.

Map on page 158 by David Maliphant. Contains OS data © Crown copyright and database right 2017.

Data used to construct the Population density of the UK map on page 163 and flow map of immigration on page 165 - Source Office for National Statistics © Crown Copyright used under the terms of the Open Government Licence.

Tar sands GDP data on page 194 from IHS CERA Special Report Oil Sands Economic Benefits Today and in the future © 2014 IHS.

Data used to construct graph of tar sands production on page 194 from National Energy Board, Canada Oil Sands Facts and Information.

Photograph on page 194: NASA Goddard Space Flight Center. Image credit goes to Rob Simmon and Jesse Allen, NASA's Earth Observatory.

Index

Index

Index